Motivation and Self-Regulated Learning

Theory, Research, and Applications

Motivation
and Self-Regulated
Learning | Theory, Research, and Applications

Edited by
Dale H. Schunk • Barry J. Zimmerman

Lawrence Erlbaum Associates
Taylor & Francis Group

New York London

Lawrence Erlbaum Associates
Taylor & Francis Group
270 Madison Avenue
New York, NY 10016

Lawrence Erlbaum Associates
Taylor & Francis Group
2 Park Square
Milton Park, Abingdon
Oxon OX14 4RN

Printed in the United States of America on acid-free paper
10 9 8 7 6 5 4 3 2

International Standard Book Number-13: 978-0-8058-5898-3 (Softcover) 978-0-8058-5897-6 (Hardcover)

Library of Congress Cataloging-in-Publication Data

Motivation and self-regulated learning : (re) theory, research, and applications / Dale
   H. Schunk, Barry J. Zimmerman, editors.
     p. cm.
   ISBN-13: 978-0-8058-5898-3 (alk. paper)
    1. Motivation in education. 2. Learning. 3. Academic achievement. I. Schunk, Dale
  H. II. Zimmerman, Barry J.

LB1065.M6692 2007
370.15'4--dc22   2007016803

Visit the Taylor & Francis Web site at
http://www.taylorandfrancis.com

Contents

Preface

Self-regulated learning (or *self-regulation*) refers to the process by which learners personally activate and sustain cognitions, affects, and behaviors that are systematically oriented toward the attainment of learning goals. Research on academic self-regulated learning began as an outgrowth of psychological investigations into self-control among adults and its development in children. Much early self-regulation research was conducted in therapeutic contexts, in which researchers taught participants to alter dysfunctional behaviors, such as aggression and addictions. Currently, researchers apply self-regulatory principles to academic studying and other forms of learning, such as social and motor skills.

Part of the impetus for studying academic self-regulated learning came from research showing that learners' skills and abilities did not fully explain student achievement, which suggested that factors such as self-regulation and motivation were important. Applying self-regulation to education also broadened its scope to actual learning beyond the historical emphasis on performance of previously learned actions. Self-regulated learning is seen as a mechanism to help explain achievement differences among students and as a means to improve achievement.

Most early self-regulation research in education focused on cognitive strategies and behaviors, such as monitoring, organizing, rehearsing, managing time, and establishing a productive work environment. In the last several years, however, researchers have increasingly addressed the roles of motivational processes such as goals, attributions, self-efficacy, outcome expectations, self-concept, self-esteem, social comparisons, emotions, values, and self-evaluations.

PURPOSE AND FOCUS OF THIS BOOK

This book addresses this recent emphasis by focusing on the role of motivational processes in self-regulated learning. Its primary objectives are to (a) provide theoretical and empirical evidence demonstrating the role of motivation in self-regulated learning, and (b) discuss detailed applications of principles of motivation and self-regulation in educational contexts. To accomplish these objectives, we invited as chapter authors nationally known researchers who have conducted self-regulation research that included motivational variables. To ensure some uniformity of presentation across chapters, we asked authors to address the following elements in their chapters: description of the motivational variables, theoretical rationale for their importance, research evidence to support their role in self-regulation, and suggestions for ways to incorporate motivational variables into learning contexts to foster self-regulatory skill development and achievement outcomes.

In addition to its use as a resource for educational researchers and practitioners, this book is designed for use by graduate students—many of whom will be educational professionals (for example, teachers, administrators)—and by advanced undergraduates who have a minimal background in education and psychology. This book is appropriate for any course that addresses self-regulation in some depth, such as introductory courses in learning, development, educational psychology, and instructional design, as well as specialty courses in learning, human development, motivation, cognition, and instruction.

ORGANIZATION

The introductory chapter (chapter 1) by Zimmerman and Schunk provides an overview of the various ways that motivational processes are involved in students' efforts to initiate and regulate their cognitions, affects, and behaviors. This chapter also raises key issues and offers a framework for studying the role of motivation in self-regulation.

The ensuing chapters reflect the diversity of self-regulation research addressing motivational variables. Chapter 2 by Dweck and Master explores the role of theories of intelligence and how they can affect goal orientations and motivation for self-regulated learning.

Fryer and Elliot (chapter 3) address the differences between mastery-performance goals and approach-avoidance goals and how different combinations (for example, mastery-approach) can exert different effects on motivation during self-regulated learning.

Hidi and Ainley (chapter 4) look at types of interest and their implications for self-regulation. Using a social cognitive theoretical framework, Pajares (chapter 5) writes about perceived self-efficacy, or capabilities for learning or performing tasks, and how self-efficacy motivates self-regulation. Lens and Vansteenkiste (chapter 6) discuss future time perspective as a motivator of self-regulated learning.

Working from an expectancy-value theoretical framework in chapter 7, Wigfield, Hoa, and Klauda discuss the motivational impact of values in self-regulated learning.

Corno (chapter 8) discusses the reciprocal effects between motivation and volitional regulation strategies. Reeve, Ryan, Deci, and Jang (chapter 9) cover intrinsic motivation during self-regulation from a self-determination theoretical perspective. Schunk (chapter 10) examines the motivational impact of attributions on self-efficacy and other achievement outcomes during self-regulated learning. Zimmerman (chapter 11) examines goal setting, a key self-regulated learning process that has strong motivational effects.

Chapter 12 by Winne and Hadwin explores the issue of motivation as an outcome of efforts to self-regulate one's learning. Newman (chapter 13) examines students' willingness to seek help, a key motivational variable that affects self-regulation. In chapter 14, Meece and Painter discuss gender differences as precursors to students' self-regulation and sources of motivation. McInerney (chapter 15) describes cultural group similarities and differences in motivation for self-regulated learning.

Collectively, these chapters show the breadth of interest in motivation and self-regulated learning and suggest many directions for future research. Our hope is that this volume will not only inform readers of the current state of the field but also motivate researchers and practitioners to address the effects of motivational variables during self-regulation.

Acknowledgments

We acknowledge with gratitude many people who have influenced our thinking and helped to make this book become a reality. We express our deepest appreciation to Albert Bandura, who over many years has profoundly affected our interest in self-regulation. His early writings on the topic led us to explore ways to apply self-regulatory processes to educational settings involving learning and motivation. We have also been greatly influenced by the late Paul Pintrich, a friend, colleague, and stellar motivation and self-regulation theorist and researcher. Were Paul alive today, we would be honored to include a chapter by him. We also have benefited from our professional associations with many fine colleagues and students who have assisted with our research and with whom we have had many conversations about self-regulation and motivation. We thank the editorial staff who worked with us at Lawrence Erlbaum and Taylor & Francis: Naomi Silverman—who agreed with us that there was a need for this book—and editorial assistants, Joy Tatusko, Erica Kica; and project editor, Linda Leggio. Finally, we thank our colleagues who authored the chapters in this volume. They are an exceptional group of individuals who continue to advance theory and research on motivation and self-regulated learning.

1

Motivation

An Essential Dimension
of Self-Regulated Learning

Barry J. Zimmerman and Dale H. Schunk

INTRODUCTION

Lexical definitions for self-regulation and close synonyms, such as self-control or self-discipline, all refer to the control of one's present conduct based on motives related to a subsequent goal or ideal that an individual has set for him- or herself (English & English, 1958). Central to these definitions is the role of personal motives regarding one's future (including one's sense of self), although the exact nature of these motives varies from theory to theory, as seen in this volume. A self-regulation analysis broadens conceptions of learning based on reactive outcome measures, such as academic grades or standardized test performance, to include proactive process measures, such as goal setting and strategy use.

Prior books on students' self-regulated learning (SRL) have focused on processes that learners use to activate and sustain not only their behavioral conduct but also their cognitive and affective functioning (Boekaerts, Pintrich, & Zeidner, 2000; Schunk & Zimmerman, 1994, 1998; Zimmerman & Schunk, 2001). Research on these processes has revealed that, in comparison to poor self-regulators, good ones set better learning goals, implement more effective learning strategies, monitor and assess their goal progress better, establish a more productive environment for learning, seek assistance more often when it is needed, expend effort and persist better, adjust strategies better, and set more effective new goals when present ones are completed. These descriptive studies led to interventions

1

to help poorly regulated students overcome deficient processes (e.g., Graham, Harris, & Troia, 1998; Schunk, 1998; Zimmerman, Bonner, & Kovach, 1996). Although SRL interventions produced successful outcomes in classroom settings, they often failed to sustain students' use of these processes in less-structured environments. This limitation has led researchers to focus on students' sources of motivation to self-regulate, such as their goal orientations, attributions, self-efficacy beliefs, outcome expectations, social sources, values, and interests. Not surprisingly, many of these sources of motivation involved self-perceptions of various aspects of one's learning, such as mastery (i.e., goal orientation), personal competence (i.e., self-efficacy), and causality regarding personal outcomes (i.e., attributions).

This chapter focuses on key sources of motivation in SRL. These motives can serve as one or more of the following functions: (a) a precursor to SRL, such as individual differences in interest regarding an academic task such as mathematics; (b) a mediator of SRL, such as whether a training-induced motive leads to improved efforts to SRL; (c) a concomitant of SRL outcomes, such as whether a learning strategy produces changes in intrinsic interest in a task like writing along with improvements in skill; and (d) a primary outcome of SRL, such as whether SRL leads to lower levels of defensiveness about taking courses in a foreign language. In Table 1.1, prominent sources of motivation are listed along with the types of research that have been conducted to date regarding SRL.

In each of the following chapters, the authors provide a distinctive theoretical perspective on the role of motivation in SRL, such as volition, social cognition, goal orientation, self-determination (SD), interest, help seeking, expectancy-value, attributions, as well as others. In this introductory chapter, we discuss key issues regarding the relation between motivation and learning first, and then we briefly survey key sources of motivation that have been linked to students' use of SRL processes.

KEY ISSUES REGARDING MOTIVATION AND LEARNING

One issue concerns why motivation is important during students' efforts to self-regulate their learning. Which aspects of academic learning are influenced by motivational constructs? First, highly motivated students are more attentive to their learning processes and outcomes than poorly motivated students (Bouffard-Bouchard, Parent, & Larivee, 1991). A student can be taught self-monitoring as a cognitive process, but if the student remains motivationally inattentive to his or her feedback, this monitoring is unlikely to be sustained or to enhance learning. Second, students who are motivated to choose a task when given the opportunity display greater progress than unmotivated students (Zimmerman & Kitsantas, 1999). For example, a student who memorizes foreign language words during free time in preference to other activities is more likely to acquire mastery of the language than a less-motivated student. Third, students who are motivated to put forth increased effort to learn a difficult task display higher levels of mastery (Schunk & Hanson, 1985). For example, an American student who comes from a non-English-speaking family will need to exert more effort to succeed in a writing class than a student from an English-speaking family. Fourth, students who are more motivated to persist are more likely to learn on their own than less-persistent classmates (Schunk, 1984). For example, an aspiring news announcer who practices pronunciation skills daily is more likely to develop a high level of elocution than a student who practices only weekly. Finally, students who are highly motivated experience greater satisfaction and positive affect when given the opportunity to learn than poorly motivated students (Zimmerman & Kitsantas, 1999). For example, a student who is motivated to pursue a career in math is more likely to feel satisfied when receiving a good math test score than a student who does not expect to use math in his or her chosen career. Clearly, motivational processes play a vital role in initiating, guiding, and sustaining student efforts to self-regulate their learning.

A second key issue that emerges during SRL instructional interventions involves potential conflicts between learning and motivation. Use of self-regulatory processes, such as self-questioning during reading, usually requires additional time and effort. How does an instructor motivate a passive student to expend the extra effort needed to implement self-regulatory processes? Although self-regulatory training can enhance many forms of motivation, the effectiveness of this training in producing personal success is seldom instant. It usually requires diligent practice. However, SRL interventions can be designed to enhance students' motivation concomitantly, such as their self-efficacy beliefs (Schunk & Pajares, 2005) as well as their learning outcomes. There is growing evidence that students' SRL processes and motivational beliefs are reciprocally interactive. But, what leads to self-enhancing cycles of SRL and motivation rather than conflicting, self-defeating cycles?

One possible answer to this "chicken-and-egg" dilemma for enhancing self-sources of motivation involves the use of social resources, such as parental or instructor modeling, praise, or rewards (e.g., academic grades). Some theorists view these social resources as external to a learner's control, whereas other theorists, such as social cognitive (e.g., Schunk & Zimmerman, 1997; Zimmerman, 2000) and Vygotskian theorists (e.g., McCaslin & Hickey, 2001), view social sources as interdependent with self-sources of motivation. For example, there is a growing body of research indicating that learners' adaptive help seeking is an important skill (see chapter 13, this volume). Surprisingly, poor learners are reluctant to seek help in a dependent manner because it can expose their limitations. However, students with favorable motivational beliefs, such as a mastery goal orientation (Newman, 1994), are willing to seek assistance because they are confident that it will lead to more adaptive cycles of learning. This is a good example of how social forms of support can enhance SRL learning and motivational beliefs rather than detract from them.

A third key issue concerns how learners' motivation can be enhanced to ensure long-term SRL outcomes. Historically, educators have embraced efforts to make the curriculum more motivating by selecting interesting instructional tasks, providing praise or tangible rewards for success, or giving students more autonomy. Each of these approaches to motivation has been hypothesized to have a positive immediate impact on learning. Making a learning task more interesting and engaging is attractive to teachers as well as students, but there are aspects of learning that can be described by many viewers as boring and repetitive, such as memorizing words of a new language. Teachers or students who seek to avoid those aspects of learning may preclude the emergence of long-term forms of motivation (e.g., self-efficacy regarding a career) that are less dependent on external support (Blumenfeld, 1992). Similar concerns have been raised about the use of tangible rewards (Deci & Ryan, 1987). Some parents and teachers feel that if rewards are used to motivate learning, then students will become unwilling to engage in tasks that do not offer such benefits. However, giving students the autonomy to choose preferred learning tasks may lead to "cherry-picking" easy tasks that are superficially fun but do not develop important competencies. Research studies show that setting difficult goals can significantly increase students' motivation and performance (Locke & Latham, 2002).

Research on expert performance (Ericsson, 1997, 2006; Zimmerman, 2006) reveals that the development of high levels of skill involves deliberate practice, which may appear to an outside observer as boring because it involves repetitive efforts to improve certain aspects of one's skill. But, if experts are questioned about their deliberate practice episodes, they typically report high levels of personal motivation. For example, the tennis star Monica Seles described the motivating power of deliberate practice in the following way: "I really never enjoyed playing matches, even as a youngster. I just love to practice and drill and that stuff" (Vecsey, 1999, p. D1). The actress Geena Davis took up archery as a young adult and developed such a high level of skill that she was invited to tryout for the U.S. Olympic team. She described the enjoyment that she derived from deliberate archery practice experiences in the following way: "I guess I just got hooked. It is really fun to try to see how good you can get, and I don't know how good that is. I haven't maxed out. I haven't peaked. I'm trying to get better" (Litsky, 1999, p. D4). These quotations reveal the presence and the nature of long-term forms of motivation, such as perceptions of growing self-efficacy, valuing the task for its inherent properties rather than its instrumental qualities in gaining other outcomes, and the emergence of a mastery learning goal orientation. Clearly, a key question is how do long-term forms of motivation emerge from self-regulatory efforts to learn?

A fourth key issue concerns efforts to deal with motivation as an outcome of efforts to SRL (see chapter 12, this volume). In addition to the role of motivational variables as precursors, mediators, and concomitant outcomes of SRL, they can also serve as the primary outcomes of such self-regulatory processes. Wolters (1999, 2003) identified various self-regulatory strategies for improving students' motivation. These strategies can be used to increase behavioral forms of motivation, such as task persistence, as well as affective forms of motivation, such as elation or self-satisfaction. SRL strategies can also be used to decrease adverse emotional reactions, such as anxiety, and various forms of defensiveness, such as helplessness, procrastination, task avoidance, cognitive disengagement, and apathy (Boekaerts &

Niemivirta, 2000; Garcia & Pintrich, 1994). Because of the perceived effectiveness of these strategies, sport psychologists have employed them widely to help athletes control their motivation and associated emotional reactions during competitive events (Loehr, 1991). These psychologists have used such self-regulatory strategies as verbalizing positive self-directions, setting process rather than outcome goals, and forming images of correct form before executing a particular skill, such as a golf shot, tennis serve, or basketball free throw (Cleary & Zimmerman, 2001). One potential downside of focusing exclusively on motivational outcomes is that students' success in decreasing adverse self-reactions, such as test anxiety, may be short-lived if this intervention does not lead to better study practices as well. It is for this reason that many self-regulation teachers and coaches focus on improving learning outcomes as well as motivational concomitants. Next, we consider some of the key forms of motivation and their relation to specific SRL processes.

ROLE OF KEY MOTIVATIONAL CONSTRUCTS IN SELF-REGULATED LEARNING

Goal Orientation and Self-Regulated Learning

According to most goal orientation theorists (e.g., Ames, Dweck, Elliot, & Harackiewiez; Midgley and colleagues), the purpose of a performance goal orientation is to gain positive judgments of personal competence, whereas the purpose of a learning, mastery, or task goal orientation is actually to increase one's competence. Dweck and her colleagues (see chapter 2, this volume) suggested that a performance goal orientation is based on an entity theory (i.e., intelligence is fixed). This self-theory will motivate confident learners to seek opportunities to demonstrate their prowess but will discourage unconfident learners and lead to feelings of helplessness. In contrast, learning goal orientation is based on an incremental theory (i.e., intelligence is malleable), and this self-theory will motivate both confident and unconfident learners to seek opportunities to improve their abilities. Thus, students' theories of intelligence have clear implications for SRL: Incremental theorists seek self-improvement rather than favorable social comparisons with others.

Although both entity and incremental theories of intelligence are stable over time (Robins & Pals, 2002), they can be induced or taught as concomitant outcomes of learning (Nussbaum & Dweck, 2006). Research also shows that changes in students' goal orientations mediate changes in their learning. For example, Blackwell, Trzesniewski, and Dweck (2003) showed that training-induced goal orientations led to observable changes in students' motivation in class, and these changes were in turn associated with improved achievement. Research studies show that students holding an entity theory were more likely to engage in a form of defensiveness, such as self-handicapping, which refers to purposively setting up barriers to success (Rhodewalt, 1994; Cury, Elliot, Da Fonseca, & Moller, 2006). Grant and Dweck (2003) reported that students with strong learning goals used deep learning strategies more frequently when they studied for a premed course. Students with a learning goal orientation also recovered more quickly from poor performance on the first exam in the course and displayed higher performance by the end of that course than students with a performance goal orientation. Clearly, students' goal orientation is a key precursor as well as a concomitant of their use of SRL processes (see Table 1.1).

TABLE 1.1   Sources of Motivation and Their Role in SRL

| | Self-Regulatory Role | | |
Source of Motivation	Precursor	Mediator	Concomitant or Exclusive Outcomes
Goal orientation	X	X	X
Interests	X	X	X
Self-efficacy	X	X	X
Outcome expectancy	X		
Future time perspective	X		
Task values	X	X	X
Volition	X	X	X
Intrinsic motivation	X	X	X
Causal attributions	X	X	X
Goal setting and self-reactions	X	X	X
Social motivation	X	X	
Gender identity	X		
Cultural identity	X		

Another goal orientation model was formulated by Elliot and Harackiewicz (1996) and their colleagues (see chapter 3, this volume). They distinguished two types of performance goal orientations: approach-performance and avoidance-performance. The former orientation refers to the goal of trying to outperform others and to demonstrate one's competence and superiority, whereas the latter orientation refers to the goal of avoiding failure and looking incompetent. Both Elliot (1999) and Pintrich (2000a, 2000b) theorized that a learning or mastery goal orientation also involves an approach and an avoidance type. An approach-learning goal orientation focuses on mastering tasks, learning, and enhancing understanding, whereas an avoidance-learning orientation focuses on evading learning or misunderstanding, perhaps by adopting a perfectionist self-evaluative standard. An approach-learning goal orientation was measured using rating scale items, such as, "I worry I may not learn all that I possibly could in this class." Elliot and McGregor (2001) found factor analytic support for the presence of the four separable and distinct goal orientations. This two-dimensional (Learning/performance × Approach/avoidance) multigoal orientation perspective seeks to move beyond the dichotomous view that learning goal orientation is good and performance goals are bad to the view that goals may be adaptive or maladaptive depending on the approach/avoidance context (Elliot, 1997; Harackiewicz, Barron, & Elliot, 1998).

In support of this perspective, researchers have found that mastery-approach goals can enhance students' interest and intrinsic motivation, but approach-performance goals may lead to better achievement (Harackiewicz et al., 1998). However, Midgely, Kaplan, and Middleton (2001) questioned the need for a two-dimensional model because the approach/avoidance context of a goal orientation closely parallels Dweck and Leggett's (1988) distinction between high and low confidence in intelligence (that is, self-efficacy), with students who are high in self-efficacy approaching learning tasks and students low in self-efficacy avoiding these tasks. In terms of SRL processes, research studies show that students with a learning-approach goal orientation report more self-monitoring and more use of deep processing strategies during learning than students with a learning-avoidance goal orientation (e.g., Pintrich & DeGroot, 1990; Pintrich & Garcia, 1991). Clearly, students' goal orientations are important precursors to their SRL.

Interests and Self-Regulated Learning

Historically, both teachers and students have attributed differences in academic motivation to the role of interest: Students who are interested in a task or skill are motivated to learn, but students who lack interest will remain disengaged. Pioneering educators, such as Herbart and Dewey, stressed the importance of interest as a precursor to motivation and learning, and interest as a psychological construct continues to attract adherents today. According to contemporary analyses, there are two key forms of interest: situational and individual (see chapter 4, this volume). *Situational interest* is a psychological state characterized by focused attention and a positive affective reaction. This form of interest tends to be task or activity specific in its scope of motivation, and it does not necessarily last over time. Among those who have studied situational interest, reading researchers have discovered how different aspects of texts can generate or sustain learners' interest (Pintrich & Schunk, 2002). These investigations have focused on such textual features as novelty, surprise, complexity, ambiguity, and the inclusion of various themes (death, sex, etc.). Researchers who study situational interests focus mainly on general principles of particular environments, such as how novel examples can make a textbook more interesting.

By contrast, *individual interest* is a relatively enduring predisposition to attend and engage in certain activities (objects, stimuli, ideas). This form of interest is similar to *intrinsic interest*, except that intrinsic interest refers to valuing an activity as a process rather than as a means to an outcome. Researchers who study individual interests focus on student differences and their impact on academic learning and performance. Hidi and Renninger (2006) integrated these two forms of interest within a four-phase model. The first two phases involve situational interest. Phase 1 focuses on a situational interest that is triggered spontaneously, whereas Phase 2 refers to situational interests that are maintained by the environment (others, tasks, etc.). The last two phases involve personal interests. A Phase 3 focus is evident when a student begins to seek repeated engagement with task or activity in the absence of external supports. It is at this point in the development of interest that SRL becomes possible. Phase 4 refers to a well-developed interest when individuals seek repeated opportunities to engage with a task or activity and begin to identify personally with it. Hidi and Ainley see the fourth phase of interest as highly supportive of self-regulated efforts to learn.

There is evidence that both situational and individual forms of interest are positive precursors to SRL. For example, Schiefele (1992) found that college students' personal interest was positively related to such self-regulatory strategies as elaboration, seeking information when confronted with a problem, engagement in critical thinking, and self-reported time and effort expenditure. Research by Sansone, Weir, Harpster, and Morgan (1992) indicates that college students used strategies to improve their interest in academic tasks as well as their performance of these tasks. This indicates that interest can play a concomitant outcome role in motivation as well as a precursor role (see Table 1.1). Interest can also play a differential mediational role in learning depending on how interest is induced. Texts designed to increase students' cognitive interest increased their comprehension and learning, whereas texts designed to increase their emotional interest (e.g., seductive illustrations) failed to produce comprehension or learning (Harp & Mayer, 1997).

Self-Efficacy and Outcome Beliefs in Self-Regulated Learning

Students' willingness to study diligently for a test depends significantly on their beliefs about (a) their SRL capabilities and (b) the outcomes of those capabilities. Bandura (1997) labeled the former beliefs as *self-efficacy*, which refers to judgments of personal capabilities to organize and execute courses of action required to attain designed types of goals. He labeled the latter beliefs as an *outcome expectation*, which refers to judgments of the ultimate outcomes of one's actions. In chapter 5 of this volume, Pajares reports that self-efficacy beliefs are predictive of such motivational outcomes as students' choice of activities, expenditure of effort, and persistence. Efficacious students work harder and persist longer than students who doubt their capabilities. According to Bandura, self-efficacy beliefs are derived from experiences such as verbal persuasion or derision, observing models that succeed or fail, somatic signs of energy or fatigue, and the positive or negative results of personal enactments. Self-efficacy judgments are contextually specific in that they refer to specific performance situations, such as learning a particular type of math problem, rather than to diffuse beliefs of confidence in oneself. In addition to the dependence of self-efficacy judgments on the formal properties of tasks, they depend on conditions of learning and performance, such as whether a student can use a computer when answering a math question on a test.

Pajares reports in chapter 5 that academic self-efficacy beliefs have been found to influence all phases of self-regulation: forethought, performance, and self-reflection. These three phases are similar to the distinction between motivation as a precursor or a mediator and as an exclusive or concomitant outcome of SRL (see Table 1.1). As a precursor to SRL, self-efficacious students use more cognitive and metacognitive strategies than self-doubters, regardless of their level of achievement or ability; self-efficacious students work harder, persist longer, and persevere in the face of adversity than self-doubters. More specifically, students who are high in self-efficacy use more effective self-regulatory strategies. High-efficacy students also monitor their academic work time more effectively, persist longer when confronted with academic challenges, are more reluctant to reject correct hypotheses prematurely, and solve more conceptual problems than low-efficacy students. Students' self-efficacy regarding mathematics has also been positively related to the SRL strategy of reviewing notes and negatively related to nonadaptive forms of help seeking from adults (Zimmerman & Martinez-Pons, 1990). Regardless of students' level of mathematical ability, those who were high in self-efficacy completed more problems correctly and reworked more of the ones they missed than students who were low in self-efficacy (Collins, 1982).

Schunk and his colleagues (1998; see chapter 10, this volume) provided extensive research that training students in the use of advantageous self-regulatory processes led to increases in self-efficacy concomitantly with improved academic achievement outcomes in comparison to students in an untrained control group. Research studies also showed that changes in students' self-efficacy beliefs during SRL mediates increases not only in persistence but also in academic skill (Schunk, 1981).

Bandura (1997) has noted that students' outcome expectancies are also an important source of motivation. For example, a student who is highly self-efficacious about personal writing skills may not seek higher education because of its high cost and the low perceived benefits for graduating with a degree in writing. Frequently, outcome expectancies depend on self-efficacy beliefs. Compared to self-doubting classmates, students who are confident of their skill in biology will be motivated to seek opportunities to take additional courses on this topic, and they will expect to reap personal and professional benefits when they enter the workforce. Researchers have found that outcome expectancies are important precursors of academic achievement (Shell, Murphy, & Bruning, 1989) (see Table 1.1). Although relatively little research has been conducted on outcome expectancies and SRL, research studies show that outcome goals do enhance motivation and achievement for students who achieve mastery over basic skills (see chapter 11, this volume). Dreams of attractive future outcomes may emerge from growing beliefs of personal efficacy based on successful efforts to self-regulate learning.

Future Time Perspective and Self-Regulated Learning

In this volume's chapter 6, Lens and Vansteenkiste discuss the importance of a future time perspective and whether it precludes any role for immediate gratifications. They recommend that present time perspective also be included in a comprehensive account of motivation. However, they caution that the content of the outcomes should also be considered, especially the intrinsic or extrinsic properties. Future goals such as personal development are intrinsically motivating, and future goals such as wealth and fame are extrinsically motivating. This model entails a four-cell design with intrinsic and extrinsic outcomes that occur during the present or the future. In support of this model, Lens and his colleagues (Simons, Dewitte, & Lens, 2000) reported that the lowest levels of task involvement were found for college students who were extrinsically motivated for a present activity when that activity was perceived as instrumental for reaching future extrinsic outcomes. Furthermore, students who believed that the skills that they were developing for a particular academic course would be useful in their professional careers (i.e., a future intrinsic outcome) displayed a wide range of SRL characteristics, such as deep-level learning, persistence, and higher academic achievement. Clearly, a future time perspective is an important precursor to students' use of SRL processes (see Table 1.1).

Task Values and Self-Regulated Learning

According to expectancy-value theory (Eccles, 1983; Eccles, Wigfield, & Schiefele, 1998), values refer to students' need to engage in a particular task, such as math (see chapter 7, this volume). There are four major components of values: attainment value or importance, intrinsic value, utility value or usefulness of the task, and cost. *Attainment value* is defined as the perceived importance of doing well on a given task, such as chemistry, and it is linked to a student's identity, such as perceiving oneself as a future chemist. *Intrinsic value* or *interest* reflects the immediate enjoyment one gains from doing the task. Intrinsic value or interest is similar to the interest construct discussed by Hidi and Ainley in chapter 4 of this volume, and the construct of intrinsic motivation is discussed by Reeve, Ryan, Deci, and Jang in chapter 9. *Importance* or *utility belief* refers to why a task is important to a student in terms of the student's future plans, for instance, taking a math class to fulfill a requirement for a science degree. Here, the activity is not done for its own sake but for another reason, such as a future outcome, and is similar to Lens and Vansteenkiste's notion of a future time perspective (see chapter 6, this volume). *Costs* refer to the perceived consequences of pursuing a valued task, such as the time involved, effort expended, and loss of alternative activities. According to expectancy-value theory, values are only half of the picture. An *expectancy* is defined as one's perceived ability to accomplish an activity. Wigfield and colleagues caution that students may feel competent at a given activity but will not be motivated to learn unless that task has value for them.

There is research indicating that students' values are important precursors to their efforts to self-regulate their learning (see Table 1.1). For example, Battle and Wigfield (2003) demonstrated that when students value a task or activity, they choose to do it more often and perform better. When the activity was seen as having too great a cost, students were less likely to engage in it. In addition to the importance of values as a precursor to SRL, research studies showed (Pintrich & De Groot, 1990) that task values were strongly related to use of cognitive strategies and other self-regulation processes by middle school students. Wolters and Pintrich (1998) also reported that seventh- and eighth-grade students' task value ratings significantly predicted their use of cognitive and self-regulatory strategies, but these ratings did not predict their academic performance, a potential mediation motivational role. Thus, it appears that students who value a task or subject matter area are more likely to report deeper cognitive processing and more strategies to regulate their learning behavior.

In chapter 7 of this volume, Wigfield and his colleagues also address the issue of the effects of self-regulatory processes on students' task values, a concomitant outcome motivational role. For example, Wolters, Yu, and Pintrich (1996) found that students' learning goal orientations and self-evaluations each positively predicted their task values and use of cognitive and self-regulatory strategies. Conversely, students with an extrinsic goal orientation displayed lower task values and poorer SRL. In other research, Wolters (1999) studied students' use of self-regulation strategies to influence motivational outcomes. These strategies included interest enhancement, performance self-talk (good grades), and mastery self-talk (desire to learn). Students who focused on getting good grades increased their task valuing more than students who focused on an inner desire to learn or making the material more interesting. However, students who engaged in goal mastery self-talk reported greater effort and persistence than students who engaged in performance goal self-talk. Interestingly, students who used a mastery goal self-talk motivation strategy also used planning and monitoring learning strategies more often than students engaged in performance goal self-talk. This indicates that students' use of motivation regulation strategies had a mediation effect on their use of SRL processes as well.

Volition and Self-Regulated Learning

Volition is defined as a "dynamic system of psychological control process that protect concentration and directed effort in the face of personal and/or environmental distractions, and so aid learning and performance" (Corno, 1993, p. 16). Following Heckhausen (1991) and Kuhl (1984), Corno distinguishes volition from motivation in chapter 8 of this volume. *Motivation* refers to the predecisonal processes leading to one's choice of goals whereas volition refers to postdecisional processes dealing with the implementation of strategies and attainment of one's goals.

Corno suggests that volition regulation strategies (i.e., a "way") can affect students' motivation and emotions (i.e., a "will") as well as the reverse. This hypothesis is expressed in the title to her chapter: "Helping Students to Find a 'Will' from a 'Way.'" Corno (1993) identified various strategies that self-regulated learners use to control their motivation (that is, setting of goals) as well as their volition processes (i.e., their goal-related intentions and follow-through), such as making a task more meaningful or interesting. These strategies are designed to enhance values, such as those emphasized by expectancy value theorists (see chapter 7, this volume). Among the other strategies designed to enhance motivational outcomes, Corno includes setting self-reward contingencies, visualizing successful outcomes, self-verbalizing encouraging messages, and developing detailed plans. If these strategies lead to the setting of new goals, then they would qualify as motivational according to this model, but if they are designed to enhance attainment of existing goals, then they would be conceptualized as volitional in their focus. It is possible that strategies may have both motivational and volitional impact, such as when a self-reward contingency strategy works so well in math that the student decides to set a higher personal grade goal.

In addition to students' use of strategies to regulate motivational outcomes, their volitional orientation can serve as a precursor to these self-regulatory efforts. Kuhl (1984) found that a positive volitional orientation, which he termed "action control," is a more effective precursor to self-regulatory efforts to learn when compared to an emotional "state" volitional orientation, which involves succumbing to ruminations and vacillation. Research (Oettingen, Honig, & Gollwitzer, 2000) also showed a mediation effect of volitional strategy training. Teaching students a planning strategy induced an action plan, which in turn resulted in a greater number of students completing their homework assignments relative to students in a control group (see Table 1.1).

Intrinsic Motivation and Self-Regulated Learning

Another key motivational construct related to SRL is *intrinsic motivation*, which involves the perceived role of rewards. According to an SD theory (Deci, 1975), rewards have two important properties:

a controlling function (that is, they are contingent on certain behaviors) and an informing function (that is, they provide the recipient with information about personal competence and SD). The relative salience of the two aspects of rewards determines which process will affect a student's motivation. If the controlling aspect is more salient, then students will shift their perceived locus of causality toward external or extrinsic forms of motivation. By contrast, if the informing function is more salient, students will shift their perceived locus of causality toward internal or intrinsic motivation. *Intrinsic motivation* is associated with one's interest, enjoyment, and inherent satisfaction in a task or activity, and Reeve, Ryan, Deci, and Jang discuss in chapter 9 of this volume the importance of intrinsic motivation to students' engagement in SRL.

According to SD theory, *extrinsic motivation* can take one of four forms depending on the perceived locus of causality (ranging from external regulation to integration). *External regulation* is the most external of the four forms of external motivation, and it occurs when students attribute their learning activities and outcomes to the controlling function of rewards. By contrast, *integration* is the most internal form of extrinsic motivation, and it occurs when individuals attribute their activities to their self-schemas and engage in behavior because of its importance to their sense of self. Despite its status as the most internal of the four forms of extrinsic motivation, integration is based on a student's internalized values and goals, whereas intrinsic motivation is based in students' inherent interest in the activity itself. It is hypothesized that internal forms of extrinsic motivation, like intrinsic motivation, can strengthen students' sense of autonomy (i.e., their need to feel a sense of personal control or agency) and willingness to learn in a self-regulated way.

There is growing evidence that intrinsic motivation perceptions are an important precursor of SRL. For example, students who had been experimentally oriented toward an intrinsic goal displayed deeper learning, better performance, and greater persistence at related learning tasks than students who had been oriented toward an extrinsic goal (Vansteenkiste, Simons, Lens, Sheldon, & Deci, 2004). Other research involved instructional procedures that were designed to strengthen students' degree of intrinsic motivation by supporting their need for autonomy. For example, Deci and colleagues (Deci, Schwartz, Sheinman, & Ryan, 1981) found that when teachers were high in autonomy support but low in behavioral control, their students became more intrinsically motivated for learning, felt more competent at learning, and developed a higher level of self-esteem. These are all motivational concomitant outcomes (see Table 1.1). Parents can also have an impact on their children's intrinsic motivation. When parents are autonomy supportive, their children became more intrinsically motivated, and these motivational factors mediated increases in teacher's ratings of students' self-regulatory competence and performance on standardized achievement tests (e.g., Grolnick & Ryan, 1989; Williams & Deci, 1996). Research studies also showed that enhanced autonomy perceptions lead to improved learning. For example, research by Benware and Deci (1984) and by Grolnick and Ryan (1987) showed that students whose perceptions of autonomy had been supported by parents or teachers displayed better conceptual learning and greater enjoyment.

Causal Attributions and Self-Regulated Learning

Another key motivational construct linked to SRL is students' *attributions,* which are perceptions about the causes of their academic outcomes (Weiner, 1992). Like intrinsic motivation beliefs, attributions refer to perceptions of causes of outcomes rather than actual causes, and they are influenced by antecedent personal factors (e.g., self-efficacy beliefs) and environmental conditions (e.g., reward contingencies). In Weiner's attribution model (1992), students' attributions are classified according to three dimensions of causation: locus, stability, and control. Like intrinsic motivation theory, the *locus* dimension refers to whether a cause of a personal outcome is perceived as internal or external. For example, a poor test result could be attributed to a difficult test (i.e., an external cause) or to one's lack of studying (i.e., an internal cause). *Stability* refers to the likelihood that the cause of an outcome will change. For example, attributing poor test results to a lack of ability (i.e., stable and not modifiable) is more devastating to a student's motivation than attributing to a lack of effort (i.e., unstable and modifiable). *Control* refers to the likelihood that the cause is personally controllable. For example, attributing of the poor test results to luck (i.e., low in causal control) is less motivating than attributing these results to the choice of the wrong learning strategies (i.e., high in causal control). From the perspective of Weiner's model, students who attribute causation to internal, changeable, and controllable methods of learning should be more motivated to self-regulate.

In chapter 10 of this volume, Schunk discusses extensive research on the impact of attributions on motivational outcomes. Researchers have found that causal attributions are important precursors of SRL. For example, Schunk and Gunn (1986) studied children who received instruction in long division and engaged in self-regulated practice. Students' attributions of positive outcomes to ability correlated positively with their self-efficacy beliefs, and students' attributions of positive outcomes to luck were negatively correlated with their self-efficacy beliefs. These self-efficacy beliefs were in turn predictive of students' use of effective task strategies and acquisition of math skill. Schunk (1994) also found positive correlations between students' attributions of positive outcomes to ability and their achievement.

Research studies showed that causal attributions are important causes of learning and concomitant motivational outcomes (see Table 1.1). For example, Schunk and Cox (1986) provided subtraction instruction before engaging students in self-regulated practice. Students received effort feedback during the first half of the instructional program, effort feedback during the second half, or no effort feedback. Effort feedback enhanced self-efficacy, skill, and self-regulated practice more than no effort feedback. Effort feedback also led to higher effort attributions than no feedback; students who received effort feedback during the first half of the instructional program judged effort as a more important cause of success than students who received feedback during the second half. These results are consistent with hypotheses derived from Weiner's theory, and they also indicate that attribution judgments are closely related to students' self-efficacy beliefs. There is also evidence that attributions to controllable causes mediate changes induced by strategy training on writing skill acquisition (Zimmerman & Kitsantas, 1999).

Goal Setting, Self-Reactions, and Self-Regulated Learning

An important SRL process is *goal setting*, which is defined as specifying "the object or aim of an action, for example, to attain a specific standard of proficiency, usually within a specified time limit" (Locke & Latham, 2002, p. 705). Goal setting differs from students' goal orientations in that the latter focus on reasons for engaging in academic tasks (i.e., to learn or perform) rather than the self-regulatory act of setting a specific goal that is anchored in context and time. In chapter 11 of this volume, Zimmerman discusses research showing that dimensions of goal setting, such as specificity, closeness in time, difficulty or challenge, can enhance such concomitant motivational outcomes as self-evaluations and self-satisfaction reactions (Bandura & Schunk, 1981; Zimmerman & Kitsantas, 1997, 1999).

Self-reactions are cognitive, affective, and behavioral responses to self-judgments of one's progress in achieving a goal. *Self-satisfaction* refers to cognitive reactions of satisfaction or dissatisfaction and associated emotions regarding one's performance, such as elation or depression. Research had shown that students will choose courses of action that result in self-satisfaction and positive affect and will avoid courses that produce dissatisfaction and negative affect (Bandura, 1991; Boekaerts & Niemivirta, 2000). Good self-regulated learners make self-satisfaction contingent on reaching their learning goals, which helps them motivationally to direct their actions and persist in their efforts (Schunk, 1983). By contrast, poor self-regulated learners do not link self-satisfaction to particular self-evaluative standards of success. Thus, students' perceptions of self-satisfaction are outcomes of two precursor self-regulatory processes: goal setting and self-evaluation. Research (Zimmerman & Kitsantas, 1999) also showed that perceptions of satisfaction mediate increases in self-efficacy for subsequent learning (see Table 1.1).

Self-satisfaction reactions trigger a second form of self-reactions: *adaptive* or *defensive inferences,* which are conclusions about whether a student needs to alter his or her approach during subsequent efforts to learn. Good self-regulated learners make adaptive inferences, such as by modifying a strategy to make it more effective (Cleary & Zimmerman, 2001), whereas poor self-regulated learners resort to defensive reactions (e.g., helplessness, procrastination, task avoidance, cognitive disengagement, and apathy) to protect them from future dissatisfaction and aversive affect (Garcia & Pintrich, 1994).

Social Motivation and Self-Regulated Learning

Although SRL analyses focus on how students can become self-directed agents of their learning, the role of social processes is widely recognized. Social processes are recognized as both precursors of children's self-regulatory development (McCaslin & Hickey, 2001; Schunk & Zimmerman, 1997; Zimmerman, 2002) and as vital components of current efforts to self-regulate (Karabenick, 1998; Newman, 1994). An important topic related to SRL and social motivation is help seeking. Many readers may question whether help seeking is a form of self-regulation and instead view it as the absence of self-regulation, but there is evidence that help seeking is correlated with use of nonsocial strategies for learning (Zimmerman & Martinez-Pons, 1986, 1988). In chapter 13 of this volume, Newman distinguishes between adaptive forms of help seeking and nonadaptive forms based on the use of self-regulatory processes by adaptive help seekers, and he reports that help seeking is an important precursor of academic attainment (see Table 1.1). He identifies three important self-evaluative criteria that are used by adaptive help seekers when they encounter academic difficulties: (a) the necessity of the request for help, (b) the content of the request, and (c) the target of the request. Adaptive help seekers ask for help only when it is necessary, when their request is specific in form, and when it is addressed to a person who is knowledgeable.

Students' willingness to seek help depends on their motivational beliefs as well as social support from their teachers, who are the principal sources of assistance in research on help seeking. The decision to seek help can be daunting for a student because such requests can lead to rejection or ridicule rather than assistance or praise. Newman suggests in this volume that students need high levels of self-esteem to admit their limitations to others and high levels of self-efficacy to enlist help on difficult assignments. These self-beliefs are enhanced in supportive classroom environments where the benefits of seeking help from one's teacher outweigh the costs. In the early years, students perceive that the benefits of help seeking exceed the liabilities, whereas in later elementary and middle school years and beyond, students perceive that the liabilities of help seeking take precedence (Newman, 1990). Researchers have found that students' goal orientation influences their judgments of the costs and benefits of help seeking (Newman, 1998). There is research that students' training designed to encourage help seeking as a mediating variable leads to positive academic outcomes (see Table 1.1). Newman and Schwager (1995) reported that teaching students to value learning more than performance during math problem solving led them to seek more adaptive forms of help seeking that were designed to correct errors.

Gender, Gender Identity, and Self-Regulated Learning

There are interesting gender differences in motivation related to students' use of SRL processes. Although a student's gender in a biological sense is not generally assumed to be a direct source of differences in academic motivation, gender identity can become a source of motivational differences if the person perceives males or females as a group to be better or worse in some form of competence or use of an SRL process.

In chapter 14 of this volume, Meece and Painter discuss gender differences as precursors to students' use of certain forms of SRL and to their sources of motivation (see Table 1.1). For example, the impact of male students' interest in math on their achievement in this academic subject is stronger than that of female students (Schiefele, Krapp, & Winteler, 1992). There are corresponding differences in self-efficacy in math and science. Boys have reported higher self-efficacy beliefs than girls about their performance in math and science. There are also gender differences in self-efficacy for using computers, with males surpassing females. By contrast, the direction of gender-related differences in self-efficacy are reversed in the case of language arts (Pajares & Valiante, 1997, 2001). Even though girls reported lower levels of self-efficacy in science than boys, there is research that girls focused more on their learning strategy and less on their ability in science than boys (Anderman & Young, 1994). Although gender identity has seldom been assessed directly in research on SRL (for example, personal acceptance of gender-related stereotypes), gender differences do figure prominently as precursors of learning and motivational outcomes.

Culture, Ethnic Identity, and Self-Regulated Learning

The issue of cultural or ethnic group differences in students' use of SRL processes and motivation has received relatively little study to date, which may be partly because of the difficulty of defining culture or ethnicity operationally. This difficulty stems from the fact that culture has a subjective as well as objective or material side (Triandis, 2002). *Material culture* refers to the physical properties of group members' appearance, home, and community, whereas *subjective culture* refers to the values, traditions, and beliefs that mediate the behavior of members of a particular cultural group. In chapter 15 of this volume, McInerney describes cultural group differences as well as similarities in their use of a variety of self-regulatory processes.

There is research indicating that cultural group differences are important precursors of students' use of SRL processes. For example, both American and Korean students reported relatively high levels of self-regulation responses during a self-regulation interview, which included such SRL strategies as self-evaluation, goal setting, planning, seeking information, self-monitoring, environmental restructuring, rehearsing and memorizing, seeking peer assistance, and seeking teacher or adult assistance (Gorrell, Hwang, & Chung, 1996). However, on nonschool-based problems, Korean children had higher self-regulation scores than American children, but on school-based problems, American children had higher self-regulation scores. Regarding ethnic differences in motivation, Korean parents reported high expectations for their children's completion of homework assignments, whereas American parents reported high expectations for their children's performance in school. Furthermore, when asked about special ways to improve study at home, students displayed ethnic differences in response. Korean students mentioned active participation in learning more than American students; the American students mentioned help seeking more frequently than Korean students did.

Ethnic differences in students' goal orientation have been reported in research in Australia (McInerney, Hinkley, Dowson, & Van Etten, 1998). Aboriginal Australian students were less likely to believe that their success in school depended on satisfying mastery and performance goal orientation needs than Anglo Australian or immigrant Australian students. Overall, the Aboriginal Australian students were more socially oriented and less individually oriented than students in the other two cultural groups. This was consistent with the Aboriginal cultural values, which emphasize affiliation and social concern more than individual achievement. Clearly, cultural differences are important precursors of students' motivation as well as their use of SRL processes (see Table 1.1).

McInerney (see chapter 15, this volume) also raises important questions about the way that SRL processes and motivational beliefs may emerge cross culturally because of ethnic differences in the nature and valuing of education, the role played by parents and other social agents, and affordances or liabilities of certain cultural and educational settings. Unfortunately, culture has been studied as a descriptive precursor rather than as an explanatory construct (i.e., as a mediator or concomitant outcome) of SRL and motivation. Often, researchers craft cultural explanations for ethnic group differences after they are discovered rather than a priori. Although cultural identity (e.g., personal acceptance of culture-related beliefs) has seldom been assessed directly in research on SRL to date, it could reveal changes in ethnic beliefs as students engage in SRL.

CONCLUSION

In the chapters that follow, internationally prominent researchers discuss important strides that have been made in scientific understanding of relations between students' efforts to self-regulate their learning and key sources of motivation that initiate, mediate, and sustain their efforts to learn. As we enter the 21st century, we increasingly view learning as a lifelong process that involves repeated self-directed efforts to improve one's skill in not only academic and professional areas of functioning but also personal areas of functioning. These systematic efforts to achieve mastery depend on important sources of motivation, ranging from social to personal. Students use self-regulatory processes to guide their learning and provide self-related information that can enhance their personal identity, sense of agency, and motivation toward mastery.

REFERENCES

Anderman, E. M., & Young, A. J. (1994). Motivation and strategy use in science: Individual differences and classroom effects. *Journal of Research in Science Teaching, 31*, 811–831.

Bandura, A. (1991). Self-regulation of motivation through anticipatory and self-reactive mechanisms. In R. A. Dienstbier (Ed.), *Perspectives on Motivation: Nebraska symposium on motivation* (Vol. 38, pp. 69–164). Lincoln: University of Nebraska Press.

Bandura, A. (1997). *Self-efficacy: The exercise of control.* New York: Freeman.

Bandura, A., & Schunk, D. H. (1981). Cultivating competence, self-efficacy, and intrinsic interest through proximal self-motivation. *Journal of Personality and Social Psychology, 41,* 586–598.

Battle, A., & Wigfield, A. (2003). College women's value orientations toward family, career, and graduate school. *Journal of Vocational Behavior, 62,* 56–75.

Benware, C., & Deci, E. L. (1984). The quality of learning with an active versus passive motivational set. *American Educational Research Journal, 21,* 755–766.

Blackwell, L. S., Trzesniewski, K., & Dweck, C. S. (in press). Implicit theories of intelligence predict achievement across an adolescent transition: A longitudinal study and an intervention. *Child Development.*

Blumenfeld, P. C. (1992). Classroom learning and motivation: Clarifying and expanding goal theory. *Journal of Educational Psychology, 84,* 272–281.

Boekaerts, M., Pintrich, P. R., & Zeidner, M. (Eds.). (2000). *Handbook of self-regulation.* San Diego, CA: Academic Press.

Boekaerts, M., & Niemivirta, M. (2000). Self-regulated learning: Finding a balance between learning goals and ego-protective goals. In M. Boekaerts, P. R. Pintrich, & M. Zeidner (Eds.), *Handbook of self-regulation* (pp. 417–451). San Diego, CA: Academic Press.

Bouffard-Bouchard, T., Parent, S., & Larivee, S. (1991). Influence of self-efficacy on self-regulation and performance among junior and senior high-school age students. *International Journal of Behavioral Development, 14,* 153–164.

Cleary, T., & Zimmerman, B. J. (2001). Self-regulation differences during athletic practice by experts, non-experts, and novices. *Journal of Applied Sport Psychology, 13,* 61–82.

Collins, J. L. (1982, March). *Self-efficacy and ability in achievement behavior.* Paper presented at the annual meeting of the American Educational Research Association, New York.

Corno, L. (1993). The best-laid plans: Modern conceptions of volition and educational research. *Educational Researcher, 22,* 14–22.

Cury, F., Elliot, A. J., Da Fonseca, D., & Moller, A. C. (2006). The social-cognitive model of achievement motivation and the 2 × 2 achievement goal framework. *Journal of Personality and Social Psychology, 90,* 666–679.

Deci, E. L. (1975). *Intrinsic motivation.* New York: Plenum.

Deci, E. L., & Ryan, R. M. (1987). *Intrinsic motivation and self-determination in human behavior.* New York: Plenum.

Deci, E. L., Schwartz, A., Sheinman, L., & Ryan, R. M. (1981). An instrument to assess adult's orientations toward control versus autonomy in children: Reflections on intrinsic motivation and perceived competence. *Journal of Educational Psychology, 73*, 642–650.

Dweck, C. S., & Leggett, E. L. (1988). A social-cognitive approach to motivation and personality. *Psychological Review, 95*, 256–273.

Eccles, J. (1983). Expectancies, values, and academic behaviors. In J. T. Spence (Ed.), *Achievement and achievement motives* (pp. 75–146). San Francisco: Freeman.

Eccles, J., Wigfield, A., & Schiefele, U. (1998). Motivation to succeed. In W. Damon (Series Ed.) & N. Eisenberg, (Vol. Ed.), *Handbook of child psychology: Vol. 3. Social emotional, and personality development* (5th ed., pp. 1017–1095). New York: Wiley.

Elliot, A. J. (1997). Integrating "classic" and "contemporary" approaches to achievement motivation: A hierarchical model of approach and avoidance achievement motivation. In P. Pintrich & M. Maehr (Eds.), *Advances in motivation and achievement* (Vol. 10, pp. 143–179). Greenwich: JAI.

Elliot, A. J. (1999). Approach and avoidance motivation and achievement goals. *Educational Psychologist, 34*, 169–189.

Elliot, A. J., & Harackiewicz, J. M. (1996). Approach and avoidance achievement goals and intrinsic motivation: A mediational analysis. *Journal of Personality and Social Psychology, 51*, 1058–1068.

Elliot, A. J., & McGregor, H. A. (2001). A 2 × 2 achievement goal framework. *Journal of Personality and Social Psychology, 80*, 501–519.

English, H. B., & English, A. C. (1958). *A comprehensive dictionary of psychological and psychoanalytical terms.* New York: McKay.

Ericsson, K. A. (1997). Deliberate practice and the acquisition of expert performance: An overview. In H. Jorgensen & A. C. Lehmann (Eds.), *Does practice make perfect?* (pp. 9–51). Stockholm: NIH Publikasjoner.

Ericsson, K. A. (2006). The influence of experience and deliberate practice on the development of superior expert performance. In A. Ericsson, N. Charness, P. Feltovich, & R. Hoffman (Eds.), *Handbook of expertise and expert performance* (pp. 683–703). New York: Cambridge University Press.

Garcia, T., & Pintrich, P. R. (1994). Regulating motivation and cognition in the classroom: The role of self-schemas and self-regulatory strategies. In D. H. Schunk & B. J. Zimmerman (Eds.), *Self-regulation of learning and performance: Issues and educational applications* (pp. 127–153). Hillsdale, NJ: Erlbaum.

Gorrell, J., Hwang, Y. S., & Chung, K. S. (1996, April). *A comparison of self-regulated problem-solving awareness of American and Korean children.* Paper presented at the annual meeting of the American Educational Research Association, New York.

Graham, S., Harris, K. R., & Troia, G. A. (1998). Writing and self-regulation: Cases from the self-regulated strategy development model. In D. H. Schunk & B. J. Zimmerman (Eds.), *Self-regulated learning: From teaching to self-reflective practice* (pp. 20–41). New York: Guilford Press.

Grant, H., & Dweck, C.S. (2003). Clarifying achievement goals and their impact. *Journal of Personality and Social Psychology, 85,* 541–553.

Grolnick, W. S., & Ryan, R. M. (1987). Autonomy in children's learning: An experimental and individual difference investigation. *Journal of Personality and Social Psychology, 52,* 890–898.

Grolnick, W. S., & Ryan, R. M. (1989). Parent styles associated with children's self-regulation and competence in school. *Journal of Educational Psychology, 81,* 143–154.

Harackiewicz, J. M., Barron, K. E., & Elliot, A. J. (1998). Rethinking achievement goals: When are they adaptive for college students and why? *Educational Psychologist, 33,* 1–21.

Harp, S. F., & Mayer, E. (1997). The role of interest in learning from scientific text and illustrations: On the distinction between emotional interest and cognitive interest. *Journal of Educational Psychology, 89,* 92–102.

Heckhausen, H. (1991). *Motivation and action.* Berlin: Springer-Verlag.

Hidi, S., & Renninger, K. A. (2006). The four-phase model of interest development. *Educational Psychologist, 41,* 111–127.

Karabenick, S. A. (Ed.). (1998). *Strategic help seeking: Implications for learning and teaching.* Hillsdale, NJ: Erlbaum.

Kuhl, J. (1984). Volitional aspects of achievement motivation and learned helplessness: Toward a comprehensive theory of action control. In B. A. Maher (Ed.), *Progress in experimental personality research* (Vol. 13, pp. 99–171). New York: Academic Press.

Litsky, F. (1999, August 6). Geena Davis zeros in with bow and arrows. *New York Times,* p. D4.

Locke, E. A., & Latham, G. P. (2002). Building a practically useful theory of goal setting and task motivation: A 35-year odyssey. *American Psychology, 57,* 705–717.

Loehr, J. E. (1991). *The mental game.* New York: Plume.

McCaslin, M., & Hickey, D. T. (2001). Self-regulated learning and academic achievement: A Vytgotskian view. In B. J. Zimmerman & D. H Schunk (Eds.), *Self-regulated learning and academic achievement: Theoretical perspectives* (2nd ed., pp. 227–252). Mahwah, NJ: Erlbaum.

McInerney, D. M., Hinkley, J., Dowson, M., & Van Etten, S. (1998). Aboriginal, Anglo, and immigrant Australian students' motivation beliefs about personal academic success: Are there cultural differences? *Journal of Educational Psychology, 90,* 621–629.

Midgley, C., Kaplan, A., & Middleton, M. (2001). Performance–approach goals: Good for what, for whom, under what circumstances, and at what cost? *Journal of Educational Psychology, 93,* 77–86.

Newman, R. S. (1990). Children's help-seeking in the classroom: The role of motivational factors and attitudes. *Journal of Educational Psychology, 82,* 71–80.

Newman, R. (1994). Academic help-seeking: A strategy of self-regulated learning. In D. H. Schunk & B. J. Zimmerman (Eds.), *Self-regulation of learning and performance: Issues and educational applications* (pp. 283–301). Hillsdale, NJ: Erlbaum.

Newman, R. S. (1998). Students' help seeking during problem solving: Influences of personal and contextual achievement goals. *Journal of Educational Psychology, 90,* 644–658.

Newman, R. S., & Schwager, M. T. (1995). Students' help seeking during problem solving: Effects of grade, goal, and prior achievement. *American Educational Research Journal, 32,* 352–376.

Nussbaum, D., & Dweck, C. S. (2006). *Self-theories and self-esteem maintenance.* Unpublished manuscript, Stanford University, Stanford, CA.

Oettingen, G., Honig, G., & Gollwitzer, P. M. (2000). Effective self-regulation of goal attainment. *International Journal of Educational Research, 33,* 705–732.

Pajares, F., & Valiante, G. (1997). Influence of self-efficacy on elementary students' writing. *Journal of Educational Research, 90,* 353–360.

Pajares, F., & Valiante, G. (2001). Gender differences in writing motivation and achievement of middle school students: A function of gender orientation? *Contemporary Educational Psychology, 26,* 366–381.

Pintrich, P. R. (2000a). An achievement goal theory perspective on issues in motivation terminology, theory, and research. *Contemporary Educational Psychology 25,* 92–104.

Pintrich, P. R. (2000b). The role of goal orientation in self-regulated learning. In M. Boekaerts, P. Pintrich, & M. Zeidner (Eds.), *Handbook of self-regulation* (pp. 451–502). Orlando, FL: Academic Press.

Pintrich, P. R., & De Groot, E. V. (1990). Motivational and self-regulated learning components of classroom academic performance. *Journal of Educational Psychology, 82,* 33–40.

Pintrich, P. R., & Garcia, T. (1991). Student goal orientation and self-regulation in the college classroom. In M. L. Maehr & P. R. Pintrich (Eds.), *Advances in motivation and achievement: Goals and self-regulatory processes* (Vol. 7, pp. 371–402). Greenwich, CT: JAI Press.

Pintrich, P. R., & Schunk, D. H. (2002). *Motivation in education: Theory, research, and applications* (2nd ed.). Upper Saddle River, NJ: Merrill Prentice-Hall.

Rhodewalt, F. (1994). Conceptions of ability, achievement goals, and individual differences in self-handicapping behavior: On the application of implicit theories. *Journal of Personality, 62,* 67–85.

Robins, R. W., & Pals, J. L. (2002). Implicit self-theories in the academic domain: Implications for goal orientation, attributions, affect, and self-esteem change. *Self and Identity, 1,* 313–336.

Sansone, C., Weir, C., Harpster, L., & Morgan, C. (1992). Once a boring task always a boring task? Interest as a self-regulatory mechanism. *Journal of Personality and Social Psychology, 63,* 379–390.

Schiefele, U. (1992). Topic interest and levels of text comprehension. In K. A. Renninger, S. Hidi, & A. Krapp (Eds.), *The role of interest in learning and development* (pp. 151–182). Hillsdale, NJ: Erlbaum.

Schiefele, U., Krapp, A., & Winteler, A. (1992). Interest as a predictor of academic achievement: A meta-analysis of research. In K. A. Renninger, S. Hidi, & A. Krapp (Eds.), *The role of interest learning and development* (pp. 183–212). Hillsdale, NJ: Erlbaum.

Schunk, D. H. (1981). Modeling and attributional feedback effects on children's achievement: A self-efficacy analysis. *Journal of Educational Psychology, 74,* 93–105.

Schunk, D. H. (1983). Goal difficulty and attainment information: Effects on children's achievement. *Human Learning, 2,* 107–117.

Schunk, D. H. (1984). Self-efficacy perspective on achievement behavior. *Educational Psychologist, 19,* 48–58.

Schunk, D. H. (1994). Self-regulation of self-efficacy and attributions in academic settings. In D. H. Schunk & B. J. Zimmerman (Eds.), *Self-regulation of learning and performance: Issues and educational applications* (pp. 75–99). Hillsdale, NJ: Erlbaum.

Schunk, D. H. (1998). Teaching elementary students to self-regulate practice of mathematical skills with modeling. In D. H. Schunk & B. J. Zimmerman (Eds.), *Self-regulated learning: From teaching to self-reflective practice* (pp. 20–41). New York: Guilford Press.

Schunk, D. H., & Cox, P. D. (1986). Strategy training and attributional feedback with learning disabled students. *Journal of Educational Psychology, 78,* 201–209.

Schunk, D. H., & Gunn, T. P. (1986). Self-efficacy and skill development: Influence of task strategies and attributions. *Journal of Educational Research, 79,* 238–244.

Schunk. K. H., & Hanson, A. R. (1985). Peer models: Influence on children's self-efficacy and achievement. *Journal of Educational Psychology, 77,* 313–322.

Schunk, D. H., & Pajares, F. (2005). Competence perceptions and academic functioning. In A. J. Elliot and C. S. Dweck (Eds.), *Handbook of competence and motivation* (pp. 85–104). New York: Guilford Press.

Schunk, D. H., & Zimmerman, B. J. (Eds.). (1994). *Self-regulation of learning and performance: Issues and educational applications.* Hillsdale, NJ: Erlbaum.

Schunk, D. H., & Zimmerman, B. J. (1997). Social origins of self-regulatory competence. *Educational Psychologist, 32,* 195–208.

Schunk, D. H., & Zimmerman, B. J. (Eds.). (1998). *Self-regulated learning: From teaching to self-reflective practice.* New York: Guilford Press.

Shell, D. F., Murphy, C. C., & Bruning, R. H. (1989). Self-efficacy and outcome expectancy mechanisms. *Journal of Educational Psychology, 81,* 91–100.

Simons, J., Dewitte, S., & Lens, W. (2000). Wanting to have versus wanting to be: The effect of perceived instrumentality on goal orientation. *British Journal of Psychology, 91,* 335–351.

Triandis, H. (2002). Subjective culture. In W. J. Connor, D. L. Dinnel, A. Hayes, & D. N. Sattler (Eds.), *Online readings in psychology and culture* (Unit 15, Chapter 1). Bellingham, WA: Center for Cross-Cultural Research, Western Washington University.

Vansteenkiste, M., Simons, J., Lens, W., Sheldon, K. M., & Deci, E. L. (2004). Motivating learning, performance, and persistence: The synergistic effects of intrinsic goal contents and autonomy-supportive contexts. *Journal of Personality and Social Psychology, 87,* 246–260.

Vecsey, G. (1999, September 3). Seles feels windy blast from past. *New York Times,* p. D1.

Weiner, B. (1992). *Human motivation: Metaphors, theories, and research.* Newbury Park, CA: Sage.

Williams, G. C., & Deci, E. L. (1996). Internalization of biopsychosocial values by medical students: A test of self-determination theory. *Journal of Personality and Social Psychology, 70,* 115–126.

Wolters, C. A. (1999). The relation between high school students' motivational regulation and their use of learning strategies, effort, and classroom performance. *Learning and Individual Differences, 11,* 281–301.

Wolters, C. A., & Pintrich, P. R. (1998). Contextual differences in student motivation and self-regulated learning in mathematics, English, and social studies classrooms. *Instructional Science, 26,* 27–47.

Wolters, C. A., Yu, S. L., & Pintrich, P. R. (1996). The relation between goal orientation and students' motivational beliefs and self-regulated learning. *Learning and Individual Differences, 8,* 211–239.

Wolters, C. A. (2003). Regulation of motivation: Evaluating an underemphasized aspect of self-regulated learning. *Educational Psychologist, 38,* 189–205.

Zimmerman, B. J. (2000). Attainment of self-regulation: A social cognitive perspective. In M. Boekaerts, P. Pintrich, & M. Zeidner (Eds.), *Handbook of self-regulation* (pp. 13–39). Orlando, FL: Academic Press.

Zimmerman, B. J. (2002). Achieving self-regulation: The trial and triumph of adolescence. In F. Pajares & T. Urdan (Eds.), *Academic motivation of adolescents* (Vol. 2, pp. 1–27). Greenwich, CT: Information Age.

Zimmerman, B. J. (2006). Development and adaptation of expertise: The role of self-regulatory processes and beliefs. In A. Ericsson, N. Charness, P. Feltovich, & R. Hoffman (Eds.), *Handbook of expertise and expert performance* (pp. 707–724). New York: Cambridge University Press.

Zimmerman, B. J., Bonner, S., & Kovach, R. (1996*). Developing self-regulated learners: Beyond achievement to self-efficacy.* Washington, DC: American Psychological Association.

Zimmerman, B. J., & Kitsantas, A. (1997). Developmental phases in self-regulation: Shifting from process to outcome goals. *Journal of Educational Psychology, 89,* 29–36.

Zimmerman, B. J., & Kitsantas, A. (1999). Acquiring writing revision skill: Shifting from process to outcome self-regulatory goals. *Journal of Educational Psychology, 91,* 1–10.

Zimmerman, B. J., & Martinez-Pons, M. (1986). Development of a structured interview for assessing students' use of self-regulated learning strategies. *American Educational Research Journal, 23,* 614–628.

Zimmerman, B. J., & Martinez-Pons, M. (1988). Construct validation of a strategy model of student self-regulated learning. *Journal of Educational Psychology, 80,* 284-290.

Zimmerman, B. J., & Martinez-Pons, M. (1990). Student differences in self-regulated learning: Relating grade, sex, and giftedness to self-efficacy and strategy use. *Journal of Educational Psychology, 82,* 51–59.

Zimmerman, B. J., & Schunk, D. H. (Eds.). (2001). *Self-regulated learning and academic achievement: Theoretical perspectives* (2nd ed.). Mahwah, NJ: Erlbaum.

2

Self-Theories Motivate
Self-Regulated Learning

Carol S. Dweck and Allison Master

INTRODUCTION

In self-regulated learning, students use their repertoire of strategies to guide and enhance their learning process. Without these strategies, they cannot effectively harness their cognitive skills or their motivation for skill acquisition. Now, it is often assumed that once students have a well-stocked arsenal of strategies, they are all set, but this is far from the case. In our work, we see many highly able students abandon these strategies just when they are most needed. Why does this happen?

Students' use of learning strategies—and their continued use of them in the face of difficulty—is based on the beliefs that these strategies are necessary for learning, and that they are effective ways of overcoming obstacles. Yet, many students do not hold such beliefs. Instead, they believe that if you have high ability you should not need effort or deliberate learning strategies to master new material. They also believe that if you do not have high ability, effort and strategies will not be effective. What is the origin of these ideas?

In this chapter, we show that these ideas grow out of students' theories about their intelligence. Specifically, we show how a fixed view of intelligence discourages students from taking active charge of their learning, whereas a malleable view of intelligence encourages students to undertake, regulate, and motivate their own learning processes.

First, we review research demonstrating that students' theories of intelligence orient them toward or away from learning, particularly in challenging situations. Next, we show how the different theories of intelligence promote or discourage a belief in the efficacy of effort and the use of deliberate strategies on difficult tasks. Finally, we present an intervention in which students were taught an array of study skills and show how the intervention enhanced learning only for students who were also taught a malleable theory of intelligence.

SELF-THEORIES OF INTELLIGENCE: DEFINITIONS AND FREQUENTLY ASKED QUESTIONS

Some students believe that everyone has a deep-seated and unchangeable amount of intelligence. These "entity" theorists agree with the statement, "You have a certain amount of intelligence, and you really can't do much to change it." In contrast, other students believe that intelligence is malleable and can be changed. These "incremental" theorists agree with the statement, "You can always greatly change how intelligent you are." Self-theories have an impact on students by giving different meanings to achievement situations (Molden & Dweck, 2006). In this way, they can shape students' goals and values, change the meaning of failure, and guide responses to difficulty.

Both types of theories tend to be equally popular. About 40% of adults and children endorse an entity theory of intelligence, about 40% endorse an incremental theory, and about 20% are undecided. Similar proportions are typically found in other cultures (Hong, Chiu, Dweck, Lin, & Wan, 1999), although there is some evidence that Asian cultures may foster a greater overall emphasis on effort and self-improvement, which are characteristic of incremental theorists (Heine et al., 2001).

Students' endorsement of a particular theory is relatively stable over time (Robins & Pals, 2002). However, these theories can also be induced or taught, with striking effects. In some studies, students have learned an entity or incremental theory by reading persuasive scientific articles (Hong et al., 1999; Niiya, Crocker, & Bartmess, 2004). In other studies, researchers directly informed participants that the tasks involved either inherent abilities or abilities that could be improved with practice (Martocchio, 1994; Wood & Bandura, 1989). Researchers have also conducted interventions, in which students are taught an incremental theory through workshops (Aronson, Fried, & Good, 2002; Blackwell, Trzesniewski, &

Dweck, 2007). Their academic and motivational outcomes are then compared to a control group who received interventions that did not involve implicit theories. This means that, although self-theories are relatively stable beliefs when left alone, they can also be changed with targeted interventions.

People can hold different types of theories in different domains (Dweck, Chiu, & Hong, 1995). For example, they can believe that intelligence is fixed but athletic ability is malleable or vice versa. Only the relevant theory influences how a person responds in a given situation.

It has been a controversial issue in psychology regarding which theory is "correct." Some researchers argue that intelligence is immutable; others believe that intellectual abilities can be improved (Sternberg, 2005). Clearly, both theories are plausible because people can easily be induced to believe either one. However, increasing evidence suggests that many important abilities can be acquired (Sternberg, 2005). Even Alfred Binet, the inventor of the IQ test, believed that people could literally become more intelligent through education (Binet, 1909/1973). He designed the IQ test not to measure fixed intelligence, but to identify children who needed a different curriculum to advance their intellectual skills.

Self-theories can have a strong impact on how students self-regulate and how effectively they learn. Table 2.1 presents an overview of the beliefs and goals that go along with the entity and incremental self-theories of intelligence. As we examine these, you will see how each self-theory creates its own powerful psychology that can

TABLE 2.1   Self-Theories

	Entity Theory	Incremental Theory
Definition	Intelligence is fixed	Intelligence is malleable
Students' goal	Look smart even if sacrifice learning	Learn new things even if hard or risky
What creates learning?	Native ability	Effort, strategies
What is success?	Being smarter than others	Improvement and mastery
What does failure mean?	Failure means low intelligence	Failure means low effort, poor strategy
What does effort mean?	Effort means low intelligence	Effort activates and uses intelligence

interfere with or promote self-regulated learning (see Molden & Dweck, 2006).

SELF-THEORIES AFFECT ENGAGEMENT WITH LEARNING

Self-Theories and Learning Goals

In this section, you will see how an incremental theory of intelligence orients students toward learning and how, in contrast, an entity theory of intelligence orients students toward documenting their ability.

The first step in self-regulated learning is wanting to learn something. A great deal of research has documented the extent to which holding an incremental theory of intelligence instills "learning goals" in students. In other words, believing that your intelligence can be developed makes you want to do just that. For example, in a study of several hundred students making the transition to junior high school (Blackwell et al., 2007), students holding an incremental theory agreed significantly more than those holding an entity theory that, "It is more important for me to learn things from my schoolwork than it is to get the best grades." This does not mean that grades are unimportant to students with an incremental theory but simply that learning is a priority. Similarly, in a study that tracked several hundred college students across their college years, Robins and Pals (2002) found a significant correlation between holding an incremental theory and valuing learning goals ("The knowledge I gain in school is more important than the grades I receive"). In contrast, there was a significant correlation between holding an entity theory and valuing "performance goals"—that is, having concern about test performance and grades as measures of fixed ability. Thus, the more students have an incremental theory, the more they want to learn in school; the more they have an entity theory, the more they are instead concerned with how intelligent they will appear.

The relationship between self-theories and the valuing of learning has been found across other areas of endeavor as well, not simply in the academic domain. Biddle, Wang, Chatzisaray, and Spray (2003) found that, in the domain of sports, students who hold an incremental theory feel most successful when they improve and master new things, whereas those holding an entity theory feel most successful when they demonstrate their ability by beating out others. This relation also extends to the social sphere. Beer (2002) measured college students' self-theories of shyness, that is, their belief about whether shyness is a fixed trait or can be changed over time through one's efforts. Holding an incremental theory was significantly associated with the tendency to view social situations as learning opportunities—and with the tendency to approach rather than avoid social settings.

Self-Theories and the Desire to Address Deficiencies

Approaching learning opportunities may be especially important when we detect an important deficiency in ourselves, yet these may be the very situations that entity theorists avoid. After all, remedying a deficiency involves admitting and confronting a deficiency, which may be incompatible with entity theorists' goal of being smart.

Hong et al. (1999) provided a striking demonstration of this. They performed a study at the University of Hong Kong, an elite university where everything (classes, exams, and so forth) takes place in English. Yet, not all students arrive at the university proficient in English. Thus, it would be an excellent idea for students who were deficient to remedy this as soon as possible. To find out who would do so, Hong and her colleagues told students that the faculty were thinking of offering an English course to help students gain the language skills they needed to do well in their studies. They were then asked to indicate how likely they were to take such a course. Students with an incremental theory who were deficient in English expressed great interest. However, those with an entity theory were lukewarm about the offering.

This finding suggests that an entity theory makes looking or feeling proficient so important that it blocks the acquisition of true proficiency. These findings were replicated in an experimental situation as well: After doing poorly on a task, entity theorists were significantly less likely than incremental theorists to take a tutorial that would improve their subsequent performance (Hong et al., 1999, Study 3).

We corroborated and extended these findings in three new studies (Nussbaum & Dweck, 2006). College students were put in an entity or incremental "mindset" by reading persuasive articles that espoused either an entity theory or an incremental theory. They then performed very difficult tasks, on which they tended to do quite poorly. In all three studies, students who learned an incremental theory went back and did remedial work. In contrast, those who had been steeped in an entity theory reacted defensively. They made themselves feel better not by repairing their deficiency, but by comparing themselves to students who had done even worse or by redoing something at which they were already good. They restored their confidence but preserved their deficiency.

Does the entity theorists' concern with looking and feeling smart translate into a more general lack of interest in learning-relevant information?

Evidence in the Brain

We turn now to brain research that tracked students' attention to information that would tell them about their ability versus information that would help them learn (Dweck, Mangels, & Good, 2004; Mangels, Butterfield, Lamb, Good, & Dweck, in press). In this research, college students, seated at a computer, were asked challenging general information questions such as, "Who was the Union general at the battle of Gettysburg?" (answer: Meade). They typed in their answers and then, a short time later, received information about whether they were right or wrong, followed a short time later by the correct answer. To which type of information would students pay most attention?

To find this out, electrodes were placed at various sites on the participant's scalp to record activity from different areas of the brain. We were especially interested in activity that reflected students' harnessing of their attention. Would they harness their attention for the ability-related information (the information about whether they were right or wrong) or for the learning-relevant information (information about what the right answer really was)?

We found that everyone showed a clear pattern of attention to the ability-relevant information. After all, even if your main interest is learning, you need to know whether you were right or wrong.

However, for entity theorists, once they had this information, their job was over. They showed no harnessing of attention for learning-relevant information—even when they had gotten the answer wrong.

In contrast, incremental theorists showed a clear harnessing of attention for the learning-oriented information. And, as a result of this greater attention to learning-relevant information, incremental theorists outperformed entity theorists on the retest (Mangels et al., 2006). Not surprisingly, they were able to correct more of the answers they had missed the first time around.

The findings in this section underscore the importance of students' self-theories in getting them to the first step of self-regulated learning: deciding to—having motivation to—learn. The entity theory, with its emphasis on validating one's fixed intelligence, makes learning a less-important, often-threatening, enterprise. The incremental theory, with its emphasis on the growth of intelligence, makes learning of paramount importance.

SELF-THEORIES AFFECT BELIEFS ABOUT AND REGULATION OF LEARNING PROCESSES

Even if we get entity theorists to engage in learning, their self-theory can work against effective self-regulated learning. This is because their emphasis on native ability makes them feel that ability alone should bring about learning without much in the way of learning-directed effort or strategies. As a result, they are less likely to engage in the sustained effort or strategic planning that characterizes effective learning. Table 2.2 provides an overview of the ways in which self-theories affect self-regulation and learning.

TABLE 2.2   Impact of Self-Theories

	Entity Theory	Incremental Theory
Approach to challenging material	Lower-level strategies, shallower processing	More self-regulation of learning and motivation
Strategy after failure	Less effort, more defensiveness	More effort, self-improvement
Self-handicapping	More	Less
Performance after difficulty	Impaired	Equal or improved
Grades in difficult courses	Lower	Higher

Belief in Effort

In several studies (Blackwell et al., 2007; Dweck & Leggett, 1988; Hong et al., 1999), we have found that entity theorists believe that having ability is a sufficient condition for learning—that if you have ability, you should not need effort. They agree with statements like, "Things come easily to people who are true geniuses," "If you're good at something, you shouldn't have to work hard at it."

Entity theorists also believe that the fact of having to work hard at a task means you are not good at it. They agree with statements like, "If you have to work hard at something, you're probably not very good at it" or "To tell the truth, when I work hard at my school-work, it makes me feel like I'm not smart." This means that when tasks are difficult and require effort—even if they are difficult for everyone—entity theorists feel inept. In contrast, incremental theorists recognize that effort is necessary even when ability is present: "Even geniuses have to work hard for their great accomplishments" or "Even if you're good at something, working hard makes you better at it."

In short, entity theorists view effort as unnecessary if you have ability, and undermining if you do not. It is perhaps not surprising that entity theorists say that one of their main goals in school is to exert as little effort as possible (Blackwell et al., 2007). Because studying and learning often require sustained effort, this is not good news for self-regulation. Incremental theorists, on the other hand, understand that effort is an important part of achievement, regardless of one's level of ability.

Effort as Explanation and Remedy

Consistent with incremental theorists' belief in the importance of effort, they often see effort as the explanation for poor outcomes and as the remedy for them as well. In the study by Blackwell et al. (2007), incremental theorists explained a poor showing on an initial course exam in terms of their insufficient effort or their inappropriate study strategies. As a result, they said that they would study harder and study in new ways in the future.

Entity theorists, instead, were more likely than incremental theorists to blame their ability for their poor showing. In line with this, they were more likely to say that they would study less for the next exam, try not to take that course in the future, and consider cheating on future tests. In some sense, they were opting out of self-regulated learning.

In this same study, adolescent students were followed over their first 2 years of junior high school. Although entity and incremental theorists entered junior high with equivalent math achievement, incremental theorists increasingly outperformed entity theorists in math over the next 2 years. Path analyses showed that this widening gap was a function of incremental theorists' greater emphasis on learning, their stronger beliefs in effort, and their more effort-oriented reactions to difficulty. Thus, these different beliefs have real consequences for the acquisition of skills over time.

In short, incremental theorists' emphasis on effort is a boon to their skills. It encourages them to face and remedy their deficiencies, it leads them to persevere in the face of difficulty, and it contributes to their earning higher grades during a challenging school transition.

Using Strategies to Enhance
Learning (and Motivation)

However, it is not sheer effort that produces effective learning. Students must also learn how to select strategies that will bring success and to alter their strategies when they are not working.

In a study of students' self-theories of sports ability, Ommundsen (2003) found that holding an incremental theory predicted strategy change in the face of difficulty ("If the activities or exercises are difficult to understand, I change the way I approach them"), continued effort in the face of difficulty, and deeper processing during learning.

Grant and Dweck (2003) studied college students in their premed chemistry course—the all-important course that was the gateway to the premed curriculum. It was a highly difficult course with stringent grading practices. As one might expect, virtually all students were eager to do well; however, not all students were particularly strategic in their studying. In this study, we measured students' goals for their schoolwork, which, as we discussed, are often linked to their theories of intelligence. We found that strong learning goals predicted higher course grades, and that this was because the students with strong learning goals used deeper learning strategies as they grappled with the material. For example, they searched for themes or principles that cut across units, or they pinpointed material that was especially difficult to understand and stayed with it until they had mastered it.

Thus, although students with strong learning goals were no more skilled than other students when they entered the course, their greater use of self-regulated learning resulted in better performance. Another interesting finding emerged. Many students had difficulty finding their footing in the course and did quite poorly on the first exam. Those with strong learning goals learned from this experience and tended to recover on the next exams. Those with strong performance goals (particularly the goal of looking smart in their schoolwork) did not tend to recover. They continued doing poorly on subsequent exams. In other words, their initial performance spoke to them about their ability, and rather than finding ways to improve, they became locked into disappointing performance.

Yet another interesting finding emerged. We found that strong learning goals encouraged not only deeper study strategies, but also greater self-regulation of motivation. Students with strong learning goals reported that they made sure to psych themselves up for studying or found ways to maintain their interest in the material. This means that they did not leave themselves at the mercy of random forces, such as how interesting the teacher or textbook were or how much they happened to feel like studying as a test rolled around. Instead, they saw themselves as in control of their motivation and, accordingly, took charge.

Thus, when students believe they can play a role in the acquisition of ability, they do things to make this happen. When they think, instead, that ability is something you just have and that (if you have it) will lead you automatically to good performance, then they will do far less in the way of active self-regulated learning.

In contrast to the take-charge incremental approach, excuses seem to be a hallmark of an entity theory approach to learning. Entity theorists, rather than doing everything in their power to ensure success, often focus their energies on finding reasons that their poor performance does not reflect on their ability. For example, Rhode-walt (1994) and Cury, Elliot, Da Fonseca, and Moller (2006) found a significant relationship between holding an entity theory and engaging in self-handicapping. *Self-handicapping* involves behaviors that can undermine your performance—like partying the night before an exam or intentionally starting a paper at the last possible moment—but that leave you with a face-saving excuse in the event that you do not do well. This means that in an entity theory framework preventing a negative impression of one's ability can be more important than actually succeeding.

DOES TEACHING AN INCREMENTAL THEORY PROMOTE SELF-REGULATED LEARNING?

In this section, we ask whether fostering an incremental theory results directly in greater self-regulated learning. Table 2.3 presents a summary of practices that can promote an incremental, as opposed to an entity, theory.

Praise

What is the effect of praising intelligence? Of praising effort? Which inspires the greatest desire to learn? Which fosters the most hardy confidence and persistence? Which leads to better performance? In a series of studies (Mueller and Dweck, 1998), we decided to find out (see also Kamins & Dweck, 1999, for related studies with younger children). Late grade school students were given a series of problems from a nonverbal IQ test, the Raven's Progressive Matrices Test

TABLE 2.3   Practices That Promote an Incremental versus Entity Theory

	Entity Theory	Incremental Theory
Praising	For person: talent, intelligence, etc.	For process: effort, strategy, etc.
Portraying genius	As inborn and effortless	As achieved through passion and effort
Portraying challenge	As something poor students encounter	As a value and a way to learn
Portraying effort	As necessary for the less able students	As necessary for everyone
Portraying the brain	As static	As growing with learning

(Ravens, 1976). After the first set of problems, students were praised for their performance: one third of the students were given intelligence praise (Wow, you got ___ right! That's a really good score. You must be smart at this.), one-third got effort praise (Wow, you got ___ right! That's a really good score. You must have worked really hard.), and the remaining third were simply complimented on their performance (Wow, you got ___ right! That's a really good score.).

We wanted to look at the effects of intelligence versus effort praise because the self-esteem movement was in its heyday, and many of its adherents were advocating intelligence and talent praise. They believed that this would give children confidence, stoke their motivation, and enhance learning. Parents also believed this. In a survey we conducted, we found that over 80% of parents agreed that it was necessary to praise their children's intelligence to give them confidence and help their achievement.

However, having studied motivation for many years, we knew that it was the students with an entity theory—the more vulnerable students—who were already overconcerned with their intelligence and overly focused on measuring and validating it. We therefore worried that praising intelligence might send the wrong message, namely, that your intelligence is what adults value, that they define your success in terms of your intelligence, and that they can read your intelligence from your performance. In contrast, effort (or strategy) praise would convey that process is what is valued, and that it is the process in which you engage—rather than simply the inherent ability you have—that increases your skills and brings success.

First, our results showed that the intelligence praise induced an entity theory relative to the other forms of praise, and that the effort praise induced an incremental theory. This means that simply praising children's intelligence conveys to them that their intelligence is a fixed trait.

In line with this, the intelligence praise oriented students toward performance goals (the goal of demonstrating their intelligence), whereas the effort praise turned them toward learning goals. That is, the majority of the children who were praised for their intelligence, when asked what type of task they wanted next, wanted an easier task on which they could do well and not a harder task from which they could learn something. They wanted to keep on looking smart. The children who had been praised for their effort overwhelmingly wanted a challenging task from which they could learn.

Next, we gave students a much harder set of problems, of which they were able to solve only a few. Students who had been praised for intelligence reported a steep decline in their enjoyment and in their desire to take any of the problems home to practice. They also lost their confidence, thinking that the difficulty meant they had low ability, not high. The students praised for effort, however, remain engaged. They showed no decline in their liking for the problems or their eagerness to take them home. In fact, we noticed that a number of the effort-praised children said that the hard ones were their favorite problems.

Finally, we gave students a third set of problems, which were matched in difficulty to the first set, the one on which they had done fairly well. How would their experience with the challenging problems affect them? Would they profit from their experience with challenging problems, perhaps learning new strategies, or would they be debilitated by their encounter with difficulty?

The effort-praised students, in line with their learning goals and their continued motivation, showed a significant increase in performance from the first to the third trial and achieved the highest performance of any group. Thus, it appears that the effort praise led them to develop problem-solving strategies that served them well, boosting their performance on this IQ test. In contrast, the intelligence-praised group showed a significant decrease in their performance from the first to the third trial—even though the trials were matched in difficulty—and ended up performing worse than the other groups. Thus, intelligence praise, often believed to motivate performance or enhance learning, actually lowered performance on the IQ test.

It is important to note that the students in the three different groups started off with equivalent performance and were simply randomly chosen to receive one type of praise. This means that any differences in later performance were caused by the repercussions of the praise they received. Although future research on the impact of praise needs to track its effects on effort and learning strategies more directly, it is likely that the performance differences arose from differences in both (that is, both the effort students put into the task and the learning strategies they employed and developed during the task).

Praising effort is just one way of portraying effort as something that is valued. When teachers talk about geniuses in math, science, or other fields, they should be careful how they portray them. In our research (Good, Dweck, & Rattan, 2006), we have found that talking about math geniuses as people who solved incredibly hard problems "naturally" fostered an entity theory in students by conveying that genius is inborn and expresses itself effortlessly. In contrast, portraying math geniuses as people who fell in love with math and committed great effort to it fostered an incremental theory.

Teachers should also be careful not to praise students unduly when they do something quickly and easily for this also can convey that being smart is about doing things without effort. Instead, teachers should say that the material was too easy for the student and instead offer something that is more challenging and that the student "can learn from." In this way, teachers are conveying that what they value (and what the students should value) are challenging tasks that require effort and that will teach them something.

The praise studies suggest that experiences that foster different self-theories might well promote or discourage self-regulated learning. In the next studies, we directly taught students an incremental theory of intelligence and examined its impact.

Brainology Intervention I

Self-theories have the most impact when students confront difficulty. This is when self-regulated learning strategies are most needed, and it is when students with an incremental theory of intelligence embrace them, but students with an entity theory seem to abandon them. The transition to junior high school is a time of great challenge for many students. The work often becomes substantially harder, the grading often becomes more stringent, and the environment typically becomes less nurturing. The pressure is also greater because students may often feel that these grades are predictive of their future grades.

We have indeed shown that the math grades of entity and incremental theorists diverge over the junior high school years, and that this divergence results from their differing orientations toward learning, their different beliefs about effort, and their different strategies in the face of difficulty (Blackwell et al., 2007). However, we were also interested in whether teaching an incremental theory would boost students' math grades.

To address this issue, Blackwell et al. (2007) designed an intervention for students in their first year of junior high. It was administered during the second semester, when there was already clear evidence of declining grades, especially in math. Students were randomly assigned to either the experimental or the control group, both of which received an eight-session intervention built around study skills. For the experimental group, however, two of the eight sessions taught students an incremental theory.

In these sessions, students learned about the brain and how it forms new connections every time they learn something new. Over time, they were taught, you and your brain can become smarter. Students engaged in activities that illustrated this concept. For example, they worked on a "neural network maze" that showed how learning makes your brain smarter. They had discussions that reinforced the concept, for example, discussions about times when something was hard for them but they mastered it through effort and became good at it. They also learned how to apply this concept to their schoolwork, for example, what to do when they run into difficulty and are tempted to label themselves and give up.

The control group also received a substantial intervention. Like the experimental group, these individuals were given lessons in study skills, which included goal setting, time management, breaking large assignments into smaller chunks, reading comprehension strategies, math problem-solving and study strategies, memory tips, use of index cards to capture and review important information, test preparation strategies, and test-taking tips. They were also given a kit (with highlighter, index cards, etc.) to help them implement the study strategies. Our idea was that students also need motivation to put such knowledge into practice. Study skill training alone does not provide that, and in line with this, we found that the control group continued to show a decline in their math grades.

In contrast, those in the experimental group showed a rebound in their math grades such that by the end of the semester their math grades were significantly higher than those in the control group. Thus, the combination of tutoring in study skills and the teaching of an incremental theory worked to reverse the decline in their grades.

To determine whether the incremental intervention also brought about observable changes in classroom behavior, teachers were asked whether they noticed any changes in motivation among their students. Teachers did not know the students' group assignments or even that there were two different groups. Nonetheless, the teachers singled out 27% of the students in the group that had received the incremental intervention (as opposed to only 9% of those in the control group) and described the positive changes in motivation that they had observed. Interestingly, the teachers' reports emphasized changes in students' valuing of learning and progress, in the effort students were willing to exert, and in the self-regulation in which the students were engaging. For example, students were now asking for guidance with studying or were handing in papers or homework early to obtain feedback and to make revisions. Here are some examples:

> L., who never puts in any extra effort and often doesn't turn in homework on time, actually stayed up late working for hours to finish an assignment early so I could review it and give him a chance to revise it. He earned a B+ on the assignment (he had been getting Cs and lower).

> M. was [performing] far below grade level. During the past several weeks, she has voluntarily asked for extra help from me during her lunch period in order to improve her test-taking performance. Her grades drastically improved from failing to an 84 on the most-recent exam.

> Several students have voluntarily participated in peer tutoring sessions during their lunch periods or after school. Students such as N. and S. were passing when they requested the extra help and were motivated by the prospect of sheer improvement.

Brainology Intervention II

Encouraged by the success of the incremental intervention but discouraged by the workforce required to administer it, we developed a computer-based workshop. In this workshop, students learned all about the brain. Specifically, they were taken on an online visit to a state-of-the-art brain lab. There, they learned about the structure and function of the brain (how thinking occurs, how learning and memory work), and they were able to do virtual experiments on the brain. In this context, they learned that there were things they could do to make their brains work better (diet, sleep, study habits and strategies). They also learned the incremental lesson that as they used their brains to learn effectively their neurons would form new connections and, over time, they would become smarter.

Students were able to apply these ideas as they followed animated teen characters through their school days and through interactive activities and exercises. They also kept their own online study journals.

We tested this Brainology workshop in 20 New York City schools with seventh-grade students. There were 20 comparable control schools that received an excellent study skills workshop (but without the Brainology concepts) and another 20 comparable schools that we simply monitored. We are also following the students over their next year of school to see whether the benefits lasted. We are still assembling the data on students' grades, but we are able to say that virtually every student reported benefiting academically from the workshop, saying that it had improved their study habits, persistence, enjoyment, or grades.

Students were asked: Have you changed your mind about anything because of the Brainology program? Is there anything you will do differently after what you learned in the program? What is it? Here are a few (anonymous) responses from students who pinpointed changes in self-regulated learning or in their model of how learning takes place:

> After Brainology, I now have a new look at things. Now, my attitude towards the subjects that I have trouble in [is] I try harder to study and master the skills that I have problems in. ... I have been using my time more wisely, studying every day and reviewing the notes that I took on that day. I am really glad that I joined this program because it increased my intelligence about the brain.

> What I learn different is that you could be scared sometimes in a school subject but do not give up keep studying and you could find your way through it.

> The Brainology program kind of made me change the way i work and study and practice for school work now that i know how my brain works and what happens when i learn.

> Thank you for making us study more and helping us build up our brain! I actually picture my neurons growing bigger as they make more connections.

Teachers told us how formerly turned-off students were now talking the Brainology talk. For example, they had learned that when they studied well and learned something, they transferred it from temporary storage (working memory) to more permanent storage (long-term memory). Now, they were saying to each other: "I'll have to put that into my long-term memory." "Sorry, that stuff is not in my long-term memory." "I guess I was only using my working memory."

Teachers also reported that even many of the most able students profited a great deal from the workshop. They had been coasting through math over the previous years in their nontracked, mixed-level classes. Then, in seventh grade, they were surprised by the newness of the algebra curriculum, and many of them stumbled as they called on their relatively unused study skills. Teachers reported that the parts of the Brainology curriculum relating to study skills and different ways of learning were extremely useful to this segment of their student body and not simply to students who had been doing poorly.

In summary, our interventions that taught an incremental theory of intelligence appear to have given students the motivation to put their study skills into practice.

CONCLUSION

In this chapter, we have shown how self-theories affect self-regulated learning. First, an incremental theory of intelligence enhances the motivation to learn, whereas an entity theory of intelligence puts a premium on looking smart. In fact, you have seen how students with an entity theory will pass up important opportunities to learn if they might reveal a deficiency. This is because in the entity theory framework, smart people should not have deficiencies.

Next, the incremental theory puts the spotlight on the *process* of learning—the effort and strategies that play a role in knowledge acquisition—whereas the entity theory fosters the idea that achievement should flow naturally from ability with little effort or strategy required. As a result, those with an incremental theory often do better in difficult courses, especially ones that require self-regulated learning to do well. Interestingly, students with an incremental theory regulate not only their learning strategies, but also their interest and motivation—taking command of the different processes required to learn successfully.

Finally, we showed how teaching an incremental theory promotes self-regulated learning and results in higher grades. In a sense, learning an incremental theory puts students in charge of their minds and how they develop. It thus motivates them to put their repertoire of learning skills into practice. A workshop that simply taught students new study skills had little effect on their motivation or achievement.

In short, the research on self-theories demonstrates that having learning skills is not the same as using them. Entity theorists may have learning skills in their repertoire but may not use them. This could occur because they feel smart people do not need them or because they lose heart in the face of difficulty and do not think learning strategies would help. Or, they become defensive when things are challenging, and they do not want to try. This is why it is so important to ensure that students have not only the learning strategies they need but also the motivation to apply them.

REFERENCES

Aronson, J., Fried, C., & Good, C. (2002). Reducing the effects of stereotype threat on African American college students by shaping theories of intelligence. *Journal of Experimental Social Psychology, 38,* 113–125.

Beer, J. S. (2002). Implicit self-theories of shyness. *Journal of Personality and Social Psychology, 83,* 1009–1024.

Biddle, S., Wang, J., Chatzisaray, N., & Spray, C. M. (2003). Motivation for physical activity in young people: Entity and incremental beliefs about athletic ability. *Journal of Sports Sciences, 21,* 973–989.

Binet, A. (1973). *Les idées modernes sur les enfants* [Modern ideas on children]. Paris: Flammarion. (Original work published 1909)

Blackwell, L. S., Trzesniewski, K., & Dweck, C. S. (2007). Implicit theories of intelligence predict achievement across an adolescent transition: A longitudinal study and an intervention. *Child Development, 78,* 246–263.

Cury, F., Elliot, A. J., Da Fonseca, D., & Moller, A. C. (2006). The social–cognitive model of achievement motivation and the 2 × 2 achievement goal framework. *Journal of Personality and Social Psychology, 90,* 666–679.

Dweck, C. S., Chiu, C., & Hong, Y. (1995). Implicit theories and their role in judgments and reactions: A world from two perspectives. *Psychological Inquiry, 6,* 267–285.

Dweck, C. S., & Leggett, E. L. (1988). A social–cognitive approach to motivation and personality. *Psychological Review, 95,* 256–273.

Dweck, C. S., Mangels, J., & Good, C. (2004). Motivational effects on attention, cognition, and performance. In D. Y. Dai & R. J. Sternberg (Eds.), *Motivation, emotion, and cognition: Integrated perspectives on intellectual functioning* (pp. 41–55). Mahwah, NJ: Erlbaum.

Good, C., Dweck, C. S., & Rattan, A. (2006). *Talking about genius: The impact of genius as natural versus genius as effort-based on students' reactions to difficult math problems.* Unpublished manuscript, Columbia University, New York.

Grant, H., & Dweck, C. S. (2003). Clarifying achievement goals and their impact. *Journal of Personality and Social Psychology, 85,* 541–553.

Heine, S. J., Kitayama, S., Lehman, D. R., Takata, T., Ide, E., Leung, C., et al. (2001). Divergent consequences of success and failure in Japan and North America: An investigation of self-improving motivations and malleable selves. *Journal of Personality and Social Psychology, 81,* 599–615.

Hong, Y. Y., Chiu, C., Dweck, C. S., Lin, D., & Wan, W. (1999). Implicit theories, attributions, and coping: A meaning system approach. *Journal of Personality and Social Psychology, 77,* 588–599.

Kamins, M., & Dweck, C. S. (1999). Person versus process praise and criticism: Implications for contingent self-worth and coping. *Developmental Psychology, 35,* 835–847.

Mangels, J. A., Butterfield, B., Lamb, J., Good, C. D., & Dweck, C. S. (2006). Why do beliefs about intelligence influence learning success? A social–cognitive–neuroscience model. *Social, Cognitive, and Affective Neuroscience, 1,* 75–86.

Martocchio, J. J. (1994). Effects of conceptions of ability on anxiety, self-efficacy, and learning in training. *Journal of Applied Psychology, 79,* 819–825.

Molden, D. C., & Dweck, C. S. (2006). Finding "meaning" in psychology: A lay theories approach to self-regulation, social perception, and social development. *American Psychologist, 61,* 192–203.

Mueller, C. M., & Dweck, C. S. (1998). Intelligence praise can undermine motivation and performance. *Journal of Personality and Social Psychology, 75,* 33–52.

Niiya, Y., Crocker, J., & Bartmess, E. N. (2004). From vulnerability to resilience: Learning orientations buffer contingent self-esteem from failure. *Psychological Science, 15,* 801–805.

Nussbaum, D., & Dweck, C. S. (2006). *Self-theories and self-esteem maintenance.* Unpublished manuscript, Stanford University, Stanford, CA.

Ommundsen, Y. (2003). Implicit theories of ability and self-regulation strategies in physical education classes. *Educational Psychology, 23,* 141–157.

Raven, J. C. (1976). *Standard progressive matrices.* Oxford, U.K.: Oxford Psychologists Press.

Rhodewalt, F. (1994). Conceptions of ability, achievement goals, and individual differences in self-handicapping behavior: On the application of implicit theories. *Journal of Personality, 62,* 67–85.

Robins, R. W., & Pals, J. L. (2002). Implicit self-theories in the academic domain: Implications for goal orientation, attributions, affect, and self-esteem change. *Self and Identity, 1,* 313–336.

Sternberg, R. J. (2005). Intelligence, competence, and expertise. In A. Elliot & C. S. Dweck (Eds.), *The handbook of competence and motivation* (pp. 15–30). New York: Guilford Press.

Wood, R., & Bandura, A. (1989). Impact of conceptions of ability on self-regulatory mechanisms and complex decision making. *Journal of Personality and Social Psychology, 56,* 407–415.

3

Self-Regulation of Achievement Goal Pursuit

James W. Fryer and Andrew J. Elliot

INTRODUCTION

The process of self-regulated learning (Zimmerman, 1989) is characterized by students taking a proactive approach to their own education through the utilization of knowledge and the strategic oversight and adjustment of their affect, cognition, and behavior in education-relevant settings. Achievement goal pursuit (Dweck, 1986; Elliot, 1997; Nicholls, 1984) represents an important aspect of self-regulation as goals provide a clear picture of the situation-specific strategies that students plan to use as well as the outcomes they seek to attain or avoid. Although the achievement goal approach to achievement motivation and the social-cognitive approach to self-regulation represent two diverse traditions of educational research, the process of achievement goal pursuit is analogous to the goal-setting and strategic planning processes described in the self-regulation literature (Zimmerman, 1998). In addition, external factors such as teacher behaviors and classroom characteristics have been found to have effects on both the development of self-regulated learning (Schunk, 1998; Schunk & Zimmerman, 1997; Zimmerman, 1989) and the adoption of achievement goals (Ames & Archer, 1988; Church, Elliot, & Gable, 2001; Roeser, Midgley, & Urdan, 1996; Urdan & Turner, 2005). We believe that an integration of the achievement goal approach to achievement motivation and the social-cognitive model of self-regulation would benefit both of these influential traditions. A broad integration of these traditions is beyond the scope of this or any single chapter; our aim here is much more modest. Specifically, we focus on incorporating an important feature of the social-cognitive model of self-regulation—the cyclical nature of achievement striving—into the achievement goal approach to achievement motivation.

We begin this chapter with an overview of the achievement motivation and achievement goal conceptualizations that drive our empirical work. We then proceed to describe research that we have conducted on achievement goal stability and change over time, research that highlights the benefits of attending to the issue of self-regulation in the achievement goal literature. We end with a discussion of practical considerations facing researchers interested in applying the knowledge learned from achievement goal regulation to real-world classrooms and schools.

THE HIERARCHICAL MODEL OF ACHIEVEMENT MOTIVATION

The hierarchical model of achievement motivation (Elliot, 2006; Elliot & Church, 1997) describes how goals arise from a foundation of distal motivation-relevant influences, such as the motive dispositions need for achievement (McClelland, Atkinson, Clark, & Lowell, 1953) and fear of failure (Birney, Burdick, & Teevan, 1969). Motives derive their energy from the anticipation of affect that will be experienced during or after the achievement situation (Elliot, 1997; McClelland, 1951; Murray, 1938), and goal formation occurs to provide a direction for the energy supplied by motives. Whereas the foundational concerns underlying goal adoption provide a reason and an energy source for behavior (Elliot & Thrash, 2001), goals themselves elucidate concrete aims for behavior within the context of the specific situation. *Broad concerns*, such as motives, represent what an individual tends to do in a typical achievement situation; in comparison, *goals* represent what a person plans to do in a particular achievement situation. The specificity inherent in the achievement goal construct affords improved predictive power over more general, distal constructs, which serve to energize or instigate behavior. However, goals do not fully mediate the relationship between these foundational influences and achievement outcomes; rather, goals combine with their underlying reasons to form "goal complexes" (Elliot & Thrash, 2001), which are then active throughout the entire achievement situation. Individuals may endorse similar patterns of goals, but the processes and outcomes associated with these goals differ depending on the reasons underlying and accompanying the goals.

Other wide-ranging intraindividual and environmental influences, such as school climates (Ames & Archer, 1988), peers (Wentzel, 2005), implicit theories (Dweck, 1999), early relations with caregivers (Elliot & Thrash, 2004), and neurological sensitivities (Elliot & Thrash, 2002), also influence achievement goal endorsement. In each case, these factors not only have a direct influence on achievement goal adoption but also continue to exert an influence on the experience of achievement goal pursuit throughout task engagement (McGregor & Elliot, 2002). This hierarchical motivational model has been validated not only in academic contexts but also in athletic contexts (Conroy & Elliot, 2004; Elliot & Conroy, 2005) and not only in the achievement domain but also in the social domain (Elliot, Gable, & Mapes, 2006).

The 2 × 2 Achievement Goal Framework

Achievement goals are the conceptual centerpiece of the hierarchical model of achievement motivation. Achievement goals are conceptualized as cognitive representations of positive or negative competence-relevant possibilities that are used to guide behavior (Elliot & Thrash, 2001; see also Elliot & Fryer, in press, on the issue of how the goal construct is best conceptualized). These goals may be organized in terms of two aspects of competence: its definition (i.e., whether an absolute/intrapersonal or normative standard is used to evaluate competence) and its valence (i.e., whether the focus is on a positive possibility or a negative possibility). Crossing these aspects of competence gives way to four different achievement goals: mastery-approach (focused on a positive absolute or intrapersonal standard), performance-approach (focused on a positive normative standard), mastery-avoidance (focused on a negative absolute or intrapersonal standard), and performance-avoidance (focused on a negative normative standard; see Table 3.1 for a summary). This conceptualization of achievement goals is labeled the 2 × 2 achievement goal framework (Elliot, 1999; Elliot & McGregor, 2001; see also Elliot & Harackiewicz, 1996, on the trichotomous achievement goal framework; see Elliot, 1999, on considerations regarding a 3 × 2 achievement goal framework).

TABLE 3.1 Focus of the Goals in the 2 × 2 Achievement Goal Framework

Achievement Goal	Focus
Mastery-approach	Focus on a positive absolute or intrapersonal standard
Performance-approach	Focus on a positive normative standard
Mastery-avoidance	Focus on a negative absolute or intrapersonal standard
Performance-avoidance	Focus on a negative normative standard

Each of the achievement goals in the 2 × 2 model is associated with a unique profile of antecedents and consequences (Moller & Elliot, 2006; Van Yperen, 2006). Mastery-approach goals are widely regarded as the most positive form of achievement goal. These goals are grounded in need for achievement (Elliot & Church, 1997), approach temperament (Elliot & Thrash, 2002), and an incremental theory of ability (VandeWalle, 1997) and give rise to positive processes and outcomes such as the deep processing of material (Elliot, McGregor, & Gable, 1999), challenge appraisals (McGregor & Elliot, 2002), decreased procrastination (Wolters, 2004), increased self-regulation (Pajares & Valiante, 2001), adaptive help seeking (Linnenbrink, 2005), less-disruptive behavior (Kaplan, Gheen, & Midgley, 2002), long-term retention of material (Elliot & McGregor, 1999), persistence (Elliot et al., 1999), enjoyment of the learning process (Pekrun, Elliot, & Maier, 2006), and intrinsic motivation (Harackiewicz, Barron, & Elliot, 1998). The literature yields inconsistent results regarding the relationship of mastery-approach goals and performance attainment (Harackiewicz, Barron, Pintrich, Elliot, & Thrash, 2002; Midgley, Kaplan, & Middleton, 2001), and an important issue for the field is to identify the conditions responsible for the discrepancies observed in the literature (e.g., Grant & Dweck, 2003; Senko & Harackiewicz, 2005a).

Performance-avoidance goals, in contrast, are widely thought to be highly problematic in achievement situations. Fear of failure serves as the underlying motive disposition for performance-avoidance goals (Elliot & Church, 1997), and these goals also emerge from avoidance temperament (Elliot & Thrash, 2002), insecure attachment (Elliot & Reis, 2003), an entity theory of ability (Cury, Elliot, Da Fonseca, & Moller, 2006), and a perception of the achievement environment as harshly evaluative (Church et al., 2001). Performance-avoidance goals lead to the surface processing of material (Elliot et al., 1999), evaluation anxiety (Elliot & McGregor, 1999), self-handicapping (Urdan, 2004), the avoidance of help seeking (Middleton & Midgley, 1997), depression (Sideridis, 2005), disengagement (Wolters, 2004), and decreased performance attainment (Elliot, Shell, Bouas Henry, & Maier, 2005). No research to date has linked adaptive processes or outcomes to performance-avoidance goals, and theorists are in agreement that performance-avoidance goals should be discouraged at all costs.

Performance-approach goals have a more complex profile of antecedents and consequences than the two previous goals, partly because of their grounding in both need for achievement and fear of failure (Elliot & Church, 1997) and both approach and avoidance temperament (Elliot & Thrash, 2002). Mastery-approach and performance-approach goals are comparable in that they both give rise to positive processes such as persistence, effort, and challenge appraisals (Elliot et al., 1999; Lopez, 1999; McGregor & Elliot, 2002). However, performance-approach goals also share similarities with performance-avoidance goals as both are linked to the surface processing of material (Elliot et al., 1999), threat appraisals (McGregor & Elliot, 2002), and the avoidance of help seeking (Karabenick, 2003). The knotty issue facing achievement goal researchers is that performance-approach goals have been consistently shown to facilitate performance (Elliot et al., 2005; see Moller & Elliot, 2006) but may exact certain costs, particularly in the long run, on outcomes such as intrinsic motivation and well-being (Elliot & Moller, 2003; Midgley et al., 2001). A critical issue for the achievement goal literature is to determine whether it is possible for individuals to reap the benefits of performance-approach goals in the short run without also encountering possible long-term problems that may result from extended pursuit of performance-approach goals.

Mastery-avoidance goals are the most recent addition to the achievement goal literature as initially only performance-based goals were bifurcated regarding the approach-avoidance distinction. As with performance-avoidance goals, fear of failure is the sole motive disposition underlying mastery-avoidance goal endorsement (Elliot & McGregor, 2001); these goals also emerge from an entity theory of ability (Cury et al., 2006), a perception that the achievement environment is engaging (Elliot & McGregor, 2001), and parental worrying about mistakes and failures (Elliot & McGregor, 2001). Mastery-avoidance goals lead to the avoidance of help seeking (Karabenick, 2003) and reduced intrinsic motivation (Cury et al., 2006). It has been thought that mastery-avoidance goals apply primarily to situations in which individuals are primarily concerned about losing their skills. Examples would include elite performers just past the peak of their prime and the elderly as they begin to observe a decline in their skills and abilities (Elliot & McGregor, 2001). However, data from research using novel methodologies suggest that mastery-avoidance goal endorsement may be more prevalent than initially thought (Van Yperen, 2006). Because of its relatively recent addition to the achievement goal literature, research on mastery-avoidance goals is sparse compared to the other three types of achievement goals. However, mastery-avoidance goals have ample conceptual and empirical support (e.g., Conroy, Kaye, & Coatsworth, 2006; Cury et al., 2006), and these goals deserve increased attention in the achievement goal literature.

Level of Analysis and Multiple Goals

A number of different conceptualizations of achievement goals have been offered over the years (for reviews, see Elliot, 2005; Pintrich, 2000). These conceptualizations differ somewhat across research groups, traditions, and disciplines. In particular, some theorists focus on general patterns of goal pursuit across situations, and some attend to goal pursuit that is specific to a given situation. As such, the extant achievement goal literature varies regarding the level of specificity at which goals are assessed. At their broadest level, goal orientations can be viewed as similar to motives in that they can be described in terms of a deeply ingrained disposition from which competence-relevant behavior originates. However, goals are susceptible to momentary fluctuations in personal concerns and environmental influences, and situation-specific goals may be better predictors of achievement outcomes than general goal orientations (Elliot, 2005). As such, the achievement goal construct seems better suited to a concrete, rather than a general (that is, dispositional), level of analysis (see Elliot & Fryer, in press).

In addition, it is important to note that goal adoption is not conceptualized as limited to only one goal at a time. Similarly, goal endorsement is not a matter of either choosing or not choosing to pursue a particular goal. Rather, individuals can provide varying levels of commitment to many different achievement goals at the same time. An individual can encounter multiple influences in an achievement situation, some of which may even be contradictory (for example, an environment that supports outperforming others, coupled with a personal emphasis on intrapersonal striving). Because these underlying influences affect behavior through the endorsement of achievement goals (Elliot & Church, 1997), multiple influences and foundations should lead to the endorsement of multiple goals.

The multiple goal approach has been validated in a number of different studies (e.g., Barron & Harackiewicz, 2001; Linnenbrink, 2005; Pintrich, 2000; Wentzel, 1993). Although experimental research typically provides participants with one achievement goal to focus on, field studies allow researchers to measure the naturally occurring endorsement of multiple achievement goals in real-world situations. This approach brings conceptual and empirical flexibility to the study of achievement goals by allowing investigation of the processes and outcomes associated not only with single goals, but also with clusters of achievement goal endorsements. Knowledge of the additive, interactive, and potentially competing effects that follow from the endorsement of multiple goals (see Barron & Harackiewicz, 2001) expands our view of the way that individuals are motivated in achievement settings.

The Cyclical Nature of Goal Endorsement

The affects, cognitions, and behaviors associated with different achievement goals have received substantial empirical attention, but the majority of research only considers goals for a single achievement task. Achievement tasks are sometimes encountered as a solitary event, but more often than not they are encountered in sequence. For example, it is common for college students to encounter a series of three or four examinations in their lecture-based courses. Individuals may endorse the same goals across each encounter with the task, or they may vary over time in their goal pursuit. Although this issue of goal stability and change is clearly important, it has received little attention in the achievement goal literature to date.

In contrast to the achievement goal literature, the cyclical nature of the pursuit of achievement is explicitly attended to in research on the social-cognitive model of self-regulation (Zimmerman, 1998, 2000). Initially, goal setting occurs in the forethought phase and is influenced by an individual's goal orientations and self-efficacy beliefs. The performance/volitional control phase details processes

Figure 3.1   The cyclical nature of achievement goal endorsement. Achievement tasks are often encountered in sequence, and the consequences that result from goal adoption at an initial time also serve as the antecedents for goal adoption at a later time. Environmental and personal characteristics are constant influences on achievement goal endorsement.

such as attentional focusing and self-monitoring that are activated during the achievement situation. Once performance is complete, the goals an individual has set for the task can be evaluated during the self-reflection phase, and the judgments made during this evaluation influence the goal-setting process in subsequent forethought phases. All of the phases and processes of the social-cognitive model are highly intertwined, and this presents educators multiple entry points through which self-regulation interventions can take place. Students repeatedly encounter competence-relevant situations throughout their education, and the recursive nature of the social-cognitive model clearly accommodates this pattern of events.

It is evident that the achievement goal approach would benefit greatly by similarly accounting for the cyclical nature of achievement striving in its conceptual framework, its research methodologies, and its application to the classroom (see Figure 3.1). Our research (Fryer & Elliot, in press) has attempted to incorporate the recursive nature of goal endorsement laid out in the social-cognitive model of self-regulation into the achievement goal literature by detailing the nature of stability and change in achievement goal endorsement over time.

Previous Research on Achievement Goal Stability and Change

Research on the temporal patterns and processes of achievement goal endorsement is at an early stage. Previous achievement goal research has found goals to be quite stable, as measured by rank-order intercorrelations of goals across time (e.g., E. M. Anderman & Midgely, 1997; L. H. Anderman & Anderman, 1999; Bong, 2005; Elliot & McGregor, 2001; Meece & Miller, 2001; Middleton, Kaplan,

& Midgely, 2004; Seifert, 1996; Senko & Harackiewicz, 2005b; Stipek & Gralinski, 1996; Wolters, Yu, & Pintrich, 1996). A subset of the studies referenced has also analyzed changes in mean-level endorsements over time (e.g., E. M. Anderman & Midgely, 1997; L. H. Anderman & Anderman, 1999; Bong, 2005; Meece & Miller, 2001; Seifert, 1996; Senko & Harackiewicz, 2005b). This second type of analysis focuses on change in the absolute endorsement of a particular goal at the sample level. The mean-level results in the existing literature are not as uniform as the rank-order results because of differences in the nature of the assessments (goals vs. goal orientations), the ages of the students in the samples (elementary through college students), and the time frames over which the research occurred (within a school year vs. across important academic transitions). The lack of coherence in the mean-level results also suggests that absolute goal endorsement may not be as resistant to change as one might be tempted to conclude from the rank-order correlational data.

In our research (Fryer & Elliot, in press), we conducted three studies in college classroom settings in which participants' achievement goals were assessed prior to each of three examinations over the course of a semester. We found not only strong evidence of stability in goal endorsement but also considerable evidence of goal change. In line with previous research, the rank ordering of goals was highly stable, suggesting that individuals within a sample tend to maintain similar orderings regarding endorsement of a particular type of achievement goal over time. The mean-level analyses provided our first evidence of goal revision; we observed decreases in mastery-approach goals, increases in performance-avoidance goals, and no significant changes for either performance-approach or mastery-avoidance goals. The presence of both rank-order stability and mean-level change is not paradoxical; rather, it is perfectly reasonable for the two to coexist. The rank-order and mean-level analyses focus on different aspects of goal endorsement (rank order and absolute level, respectively) and provide complementary, not contradictory, information on the question of goal stability and change.

Novel Possibilities for Examining Achievement Goal Stability and Change

However, two additional possibilities remain for self-regulation of achievement goals that are not accounted for by the previous analyses. First, the rank-order and mean-level analyses aim to describe stability and change within *samples*, but results from such analyses can obscure patterns of stability and change within *individuals* over time. It is possible that the lack of significant mean-level change observed for performance-approach and mastery-avoidance goals is partly because of the multiple influences that underlie adoption of those goals (Elliot & Church, 1997). That is, the greater variability in the goal complexes associated with these goals (Elliot & Thrash, 2001) leads to the null results observed for the sample. Second, both rank-order and mean-level analyses focus on only one type of achievement goal at a time, which does not account for self-regulatory behavior involving multiple goals (Barron & Harackiewicz, 2001; Pintrich, 2000). Examining the patterns of multiple goals, as opposed to focusing solely on individual achievement goals, increases the possible variability in goal endorsement over time. In addition, consideration of multiple goals reveals information regarding the range of strategies students consider, as well as the various thoughts and emotions they experience, throughout an achievement situation. The combinations of goals endorsed could include goals that augment each other through certain shared characteristics (such as the challenge appraisals linked to mastery-approach and performance-approach goals; Elliot & Reis, 2003; McGregor & Elliot, 2002) as well as goals that activate conflicting processes (such as deep processing for mastery-approach goals and shallow processing for performance-avoidance goals; Elliot et al., 1999). Examining multiple goals at the same time not only greatly increases the complexity of the achievement goal approach but also provides a more comprehensive description of the potential opportunities through which a student can engage in self-regulatory practices.

To address these possibilities for self-regulation, we made use of two additional analytic approaches in our research (Fryer & Elliot, in press), both of which are novel to achievement goal research. The first analysis focuses on the Reliable Change Index (RCI; Christensen & Mendoza, 1986; Jacobson & Truax, 1991). This analysis provides evidence regarding whether any change observed in achievement goal endorsement over time is merely random variation or represents a genuine shift in goal endorsement. The RCI is similar to mean-level analysis in that both examine absolute levels of goal endorsement. However, it differs in that it measures change at the level of the individual, and it can reveal possibilities for change that have been obscured by focusing exclusively on the sample level (Roberts, Walton, & Viechtbauer, 2006). It is also possible to aggregate individual-level RCI results to make statements about the presence of reliable change within a sample (Roberts, Caspi, & Moffitt, 2001).

The second analysis novel to achievement goal research is ipsative stability (i.e., Cronbach & Gleser, 1953; Robins, Fraley, Roberts, & Trzesniewski, 2001). Ipsative stability analysis differs from the three analyses described in that it assesses the cluster of achievement goal endorsements within an individual over time. Ipsative stability analysis yields a correlation coefficient that is essentially the same as a standard Pearson product moment coefficient, only it focuses on the configuration of achievement goals within an individual instead of the rank ordering of individuals within a sample.

The reliable change results corresponded to and extended the scope of the changes we found for mean-level endorsement. For this analysis, the majority of the sample showed decreases in mastery-approach goal endorsement and increases in performance-avoidance goal endorsement comparable to the mean-level change results. Although no significant mean-level change was observed for performance-approach or mastery-avoidance goals, reliable change was observed for endorsement of these goals in both directions, indicating that the sample-level analyses obscured considerable individual-level change. Plus, in all three studies, nearly every participant showed reliable change on at least one goal.

The ipsative stability results were similar to those from the rank-order correlations; the majority of coefficients were very high, indicating substantial stability for the configurations of achievement goals within individuals. However, many individuals still exhibited low (and even negative) coefficients, indicating that for those individuals a substantial revision of achievement goal endorsement took place. In general, the analysis of configurations of achievement goals evidenced a level of stability similar to what has been observed for rank-order correlations of single goals, although evidence of configural change was observed as well.

In sum, the primary contribution of our research is that we have integrated standard approaches to goal stability and change with novel approaches to this issue. We have done so by focusing on different levels of analysis (sample level vs. individual level), different scopes (one goal at a time vs. the configuration of all goals), and different types of information (rank order vs. absolute endorsement).

This use of multiple methods yields a more complete assessment of goal stability and change than that presently available and therefore provides a more comprehensive assessment of the possibilities for self-regulation of achievement goals over time.

PRACTICAL IMPLICATIONS

Environmental Influences on Achievement Goal Endorsement

The research that we have just overviewed clearly shows that regulation of achievement motivation can occur at the person level. However, it is important to note that regulation of achievement motivation can take place at the system level as well. Regulation at the system level entails administrators and teachers overseeing and adjusting classroom and school structures in an attempt to facilitate students' adoption of beneficial achievement goals and diminish students' adoption of detrimental achievement goals.

Research at the system level lags behind research at the person level in the achievement goal literature. One thing that has been clearly documented is that students' perceptions of teachers, classrooms, and schools have an important influence on achievement goal adoption (e.g., Ames & Archer, 1988; Church et al., 2001; Roeser et al., 1996; Urdan & Turner, 2005; Young, 1997). What is less clear is the extent to which objective characteristics of achievement environments (operationalized as consensual perceptions) also influence achievement goal adoption, either directly or via student perceptions (see Urdan & Turner, 2005). Clearly, this is an important area for future research.

Few extant studies have reported experimental intervention research focused on achievement goals (e.g., Ames, 1992; Harwood & Swain, 2002; Meece & Miller, 1999), and currently none exist that have used the trichotomous or 2 × 2 frameworks. Nevertheless, it is widely accepted in the achievement goal literature that encouraging teachers and administrators to foster certain types of achievement goals over others is extremely important (Maehr & Midgley, 1996). Our argument regarding the cyclical nature of achievement goal endorsement suggests that the consequences that result from goal adoption at an initial time also serve as the antecedents for goal adoption at a later time. As such, interventions focused on the processes and outcomes associated with achievement goals can yield benefits as positive and as strong as interventions aimed at modifying achievement goals themselves.

For example, as mentioned, mastery-approach goals have been linked to adaptive help-seeking behavior (Linnenbrink, 2005; A. R. Ryan & Pintrich, 1997). Students who avoid seeking help may do so because of the threat to self-esteem they would experience by asking others for help (Karabenick, 2004). Teachers can encourage help-seeking behavior by setting up classroom activities for which seeking help is necessary to complete the task; help can be received from peers, the teacher, or other classroom resources. Mastery-approach goals have also been linked to intrinsic motivation (Harackiewicz et al., 1998). Self-determination theory (Deci & Ryan, 1985) provides us with ample research on the relationship between intrinsic motivation and autonomy or the experience of choice. Tasks that are assigned tend to be viewed as less interesting than tasks that are chosen (Deci & Ryan, 2000), even when a limited number of choices is provided. Any opportunity for educators to provide students with options and the ability to make their own choices (such as the tasks they would like to do during the day, the topics they would like to research for an upcoming project, etc.) can encourage the development of interest, which can promote the future adoption of mastery-approach goals (Church et al., 2001).

Environmental influences on goal adoption are inherently complex, in part because the student brings personal perceptual predilections to the achievement situation (Elliot & Moller, 2003). As an example, one popular classroom practice is putting student work on display. This practice can signal to students that normative competence will be rewarded in that environment, which can lead to a shift in student goal endorsement. Of course, this is not to say that identifying outstanding work in a classroom results in an automatic induction of performance-approach goals; rather, the same classroom can be interpreted by one student as promoting a mastery-based approach and by another as favoring a performance-based approach. If the rationale for displaying student work is explicitly based on improvement over past performance or on attainment of a task-based standard (e.g., successful completion of a project), then the display of work may be likely to promote mastery-approach goal adoption. The challenge for teachers and administrators is to consider the differences in students' perceptions when shaping their classroom and school environments. The challenge for researchers is to document more clearly the influence that objective shifts in classroom and school environments have on students' perceptions, achievement goal adoption, and, of course, actual achievement-relevant outcomes.

Which Goals to Promote?

If teachers and administrators can shape their classrooms and schools to promote student endorsement of certain types of achievement goals, then which types of goals should be encouraged? As noted, many studies over the past 25 years have identified an overwhelmingly positive nomological network for mastery-approach goals (or conceptual equivalent; for a review, see Meece, Anderman, & Anderman, 2006). Even when considering the ongoing discussion regarding the positive effects of performance-approach goals (Harackiewicz, Barron, Pintrich, et al., 2002; Midgley et al., 2001), it is clear that mastery-approach goals are the most favorable to encourage to generate and maintain long-term student interest (Harackiewicz, Barron, Tauer, & Elliot, 2002) and well-being (Kaplan & Maehr, 1999; Pekrun et al., 2006). Even if mastery-approach goals do not lead to the same level of performance outcomes as performance-approach goals, given the potential long-term problems with performance-approach goal pursuit, it would be prudent to err on the side of caution regarding the promotion of performance-approach goals in the classroom until further research provides clear guidance (Elliot & Moller, 2003; Elliot et al., 2005).

However, achievement goal research utilizing a multiple-goal approach (Barron & Harackiewicz, 2001; Fryer & Elliot, in press; Pintrich, 2000) suggests that because it is possible for an individual to endorse multiple forms of achievement goals in a situation, one can promote the adoption of mastery-approach goals without explicitly seeking to exclude performance-approach goals. The best practical recommendations to yield the most positive pattern of outcomes for students may involve creating an environment emphasizing mastery-approach goals (i.e., encouraging interest in the material, improvement over past exam performances, etc.) while not actively dissuading low-to-moderate levels of normative comparison in the classroom. High levels of competition between students, as well as the unlikely scenario of an environment that explicitly promotes competition, would certainly not be beneficial to student outcomes in the long run. However, normative comparison naturally tends to emerge in classroom contexts, and allowing it to do so, while monitoring its level to make sure it does not overwhelm mastery concerns, may represent an optimal balance. This may particularly be the case as students progress into the upper levels of the educational system because an exclusive focus on the benefits of mastery-approach goals may be ideal primarily in the early years of schooling.

One particularly important issue for teachers and administrators to attend to is the tendency for some students to respond poorly to mistakes and failures. During a student's tenure in the educational system, it is certain that, at some point, the student will experience failure. Of course, the "failure" feedback does not necessarily have to be exclusively negative; what matters most is the way the student construes or defines the failure experience (e.g., as a disastrous event with negative implications for self-worth or as an opportunity for learning and development; see Covington, 1992; Elliot & Thrash, 2004). Even the brightest and most capable students in any class are susceptible to experiencing failure, depending on the expectations they have set for themselves or have adopted or internalized from external sources (Eccles, 1993; R. M. Ryan, Sheldon, Kasser, & Deci, 1996). Optimally, teachers and administrators would bear in mind the important impact of failure experiences in their classrooms and schools and would create their achievement environments accordingly. This is especially critical in the present evaluation-focused ethos of high-stakes testing.

The challenge of creating an environment in which failure can be seen as a tool for learning may be the most difficult of all because fear of failure has strong developmental roots in early experiences (Birney et al., 1969). One strategy that educators can take is highlighting historical instances relevant to the subject matter when the experience of failure provided information necessary for future success. Students may find some comfort in numerous anecdotes from inventors such as Thomas Edison, knowing that such famous individuals persevered and flourished through countless (and likely spectacular) failures. Indeed, the iterative nature of the scientific process itself, in which hypotheses are generated, tested, and revised based on new information, can show the positive possibilities that can arise from failure.

In short, the challenge for achievement goal researchers is not only to determine which goals and combinations of goals provide the best achievement outcomes but also to identify what educators can do to create the conditions that promote these goals in their classrooms and schools. Eventually, perhaps, the achievement goal literature can become as generative for intervention work as the social-cognitive model of self-regulation has already been (for reviews, see Boekaerts & Corno, 2005; Schunk, 1995).

CONCLUSION

The achievement goal approach to achievement motivation is popular in educational psychology, and research in this tradition has produced much knowledge regarding the way students are energized and directed in classroom and school environments. However, achievement goal research has largely overlooked the important issue of how individuals regulate their achievement strivings over time. We think the achievement goal literature would do well to attend more rigorously to this and other issues central to the social-cognitive model of self-regulation.

REFERENCES

Ames, C. (1992). Achievement goals and the classroom motivational climate. In D. H. Schunk & J. L. Meece (Eds.), *Student perceptions in the classroom* (pp. 327–348). Hillsdale, NJ: Erlbaum.

Ames, C., & Archer, J. (1988). Achievement goals in the classroom: Students' learning strategies and motivation processes. *Journal of Educational Psychology, 80,* 260–267.

Anderman, E. M., & Midgley, C. (1997). Changes in achievement goal orientations, perceived academic competence, and grades across the transition to middle-level schools. *Contemporary Educational Psychology, 22,* 269–298.

Anderman, L. H., & Anderman, E. M. (1999). Social predictors of changes in students' achievement goal orientations. *Contemporary Educational Psychology, 24,* 21–37.

Barron, K. E., & Harackiewicz, J. M. (2001). Achievement goals and optimal motivation: Testing multiple goal models. *Journal of Personality and Social Psychology, 80,* 706–722.

Birney, R., Burdick, H., & Teevan, R. (1969). *Fear of failure.* New York: Van Nostrand Reinhold.

Boekaerts, M., & Corno, L. (2005). Self-regulation in the classroom: A perspective on assessment and intervention. *Applied Psychology: An International Review, 54,* 199–231.

Bong, M. (2005). Within-grade changes in Korean girls' motivation and perceptions of the learning environment across domains and achievement levels. *Journal of Educational Psychology, 97,* 656–672.

Christensen, L., & Mendoza, J. L. (1986). A method of assessing change in a single subject: An alteration of the RC index. *Behavior Therapy, 17,* 305–308.

Church, M. A., Elliot, A. J., & Gable, S. L. (2001). Perceptions of classroom environment, achievement goals, and achievement outcomes. *Journal of Educational Psychology, 93,* 43–54.

Conroy, D. E., & Elliot, A. J. (2004). Fear of failure and achievement goals in sport: Addressing the issue of the chicken and the egg. *Anxiety, Stress & Coping: An International Journal, 17,* 271–285.

Conroy, D. E., Kaye, M. P., & Coatsworth, J. D. (2006). Coaching climates and the destructive effects of mastery–avoidance achievement goals on situational motivation. *Journal of Sport and Exercise Psychology, 28,* 69–92.

Covington, M. V. (1992). *Making the grade: A self-worth perspective on motivation and school reform.* New York: Cambridge University Press.

Cronbach, L. J., & Gleser, G. C. (1953). Assessing similarity between profiles. *Psychological Bulletin, 50,* 456–473.

Cury, F., Elliot, A. J., Da Fonseca, D., & Moller, A. C. (2006). The social-cognitive model of achievement motivation and the 2 × 2 achievement goal framework. *Journal of Personality and Social Psychology, 90,* 666–679.

Deci, E. L., & Ryan, R. M. (1985). *Intrinsic motivation and self-determination in human behavior.* New York: Plenum.

Deci, E. L., & Ryan, R. M. (2000). The "what" and "why" of goal pursuits: Human needs and the self-determination of behavior. *Psychological Inquiry, 11,* 227–268.

Dweck, C. (1986). Motivational processes affecting learning. *American Psychologist, 41,* 1040–1048.

Dweck, C. S. (1999). *Self-theories: Their role in motivation, personality, and development.* New York: Psychology Press.

Eccles, J. S. (1993). School and family effects on the ontogeny of children's interests, self-perceptions, and activity choices. In J. Jacobs (Ed.), *Nebraska Symposium on Motivation, 1992: Developmental perspectives on motivation* (pp. 145–208). Lincoln: University of Nebraska Press.

Elliot, A. J. (1997). Integrating "classic" and "contemporary" approaches to achievement motivation: A hierarchical model of approach and avoidance achievement motivation. In P. Pintrich & M. Maehr (Eds.), *Advances in motivation and achievement* (Vol. 10, pp. 143–179). Greenwich, CT: JAI.

Elliot, A. J. (1999). Approach and avoidance motivation and achievement goals. *Educational Psychologist, 34,* 169–189.

Elliot, A. J. (2005). A conceptual history of the achievement goal construct. In A. Elliot & C. Dweck (Eds.), *Handbook of competence and motivation* (pp. 52–72). New York: Guilford Press.

Elliot, A. J. (2006). The hierarchical model of approach-avoidance motivation. *Motivation and Emotion, 30,* 111–116.

Elliot, A. J., & Church, M. A. (1997). A hierarchical model of approach and avoidance achievement motivation. *Journal of Personality and Social Psychology, 72,* 218–232.

Elliot, A. J., & Conroy, D. E. (2005). Beyond the dichotomous model of achievement goals in sport and exercise psychology. *Sport and Exercise Psychology Review, 1,* 17–25.

Elliot, A. J., & Fryer, J. W. (in press). The goal concept in psychology. In J. Shah & W. Gardner (Eds.), *Handbook of motivational science.* New York: Guilford Press.

Elliot, A. J., Gable, S. L., & Mapes, R. R. (2006). Approach and avoidance motivation in the social domain. *Personality and Social Psychology Bulletin, 32,* 378–391.

Elliot, A. J., & Harackiewicz, J. M. (1996). Approach and avoidance achievement goals and intrinsic motivation: A mediational analysis. *Journal of Personality and Social Psychology, 51,* 1058–1068.

Elliot, A. J., & McGregor, H. A. (1999). Test anxiety and the hierarchical model of approach and avoidance achievement motivation. *Journal of Personality and Social Psychology, 76,* 628–644.

Elliot, A. J., & McGregor, H. A. (2001). A 2 × 2 achievement goal framework. *Journal of Personality and Social Psychology, 80,* 501–519.

Elliot, A. J., McGregor, H. A., & Gable, S. (1999). Achievement goals, study strategies, and exam performance: A mediational analysis. *Journal of Educational Psychology, 91,* 549–563.

Elliot, A. J., & Moller, A. C. (2003). Performance–approach goals: Good or bad forms of regulation? *International Journal of Education Research, 39,* 339–356.

Elliot, A. J., & Reis, H. T. (2003). Attachment and exploration in adulthood. *Journal of Personality and Social Psychology, 85,* 317–331.

Elliot, A. J., Shell, M. M., Bouas Henry, K., & Maier, M. A. (2005). Achievement goals, performance contingencies, and performance attainment: An experimental test. *Journal of Educational Psychology, 97,* 630–640.

Elliot, A. J., & Thrash, T. M. (2001). Achievement goals and the hierarchical model of achievement motivation. *Educational Psychology Review, 13,* 139–156.

Elliot, A. J., & Thrash, T. M. (2002). Approach–avoidance motivation in personality: Approach and avoidance temperaments and goals. *Journal of Personality and Social Psychology, 82,* 804–818.

Elliot, A. J., & Thrash, T. M. (2004). The intergenerational transmission of fear of failure. *Personality and Social Psychology Bulletin, 30,* 957–971.

Fryer, J. W., & Elliot, A. J. (in press). Stability and change in achievement goals. *Journal of Educational Psychology.*

Grant, H., & Dweck, C. S. (2003). Clarifying achievement goals and their impact. *Journal of Personality and Social Psychology, 85,* 541–553.

Harackiewicz, J. M., Barron, K. E., & Elliot, A. J. (1998). Rethinking achievement goals: When are they adaptive for college students and why? *Educational Psychologist, 33,* 1–21.

Harackiewicz, J. M., Barron, K. E., Pintrich, P. R., Elliot, A. J., & Thrash, T. M. (2002). Revision of achievement goal theory: Necessary and illuminating. *Journal of Educational Psychology, 94,* 638–645.

Harackiewicz, J. M., Barron, K. E., Tauer, J. M., & Elliot, A. J. (2002). Predicting success in college: A longitudinal study of achievement goals and ability measures as predictors of interest and performance from freshman year through graduation. *Journal of Educational Psychology, 94,* 562–575.

Harwood, C., & Swain, A. (2002). The development and activation of achievement goals within tennis: II. A player, parent, and coach intervention. *Sport Psychologist, 16,* 111–137.

Jacobson, N. S., & Truax, P. (1991). Clinical significance: A statistical approach to defining meaningful change in psychotherapy research. *Journal of Consulting and Clinical Psychology, 59,* 12–19.

Kaplan, A., Gheen, M., & Midgley, C. (2002). Classroom goal structure and student disruptive behaviour. *British Journal of Educational Psychology, 72,* 191–212.

Kaplan, A., & Maehr, M. L. (1999). Achievement goals and student well-being. *Contemporary Educational Psychology, 24,* 330–358.

Karabenick, S. A. (2003). Seeking help in large college classes: A person-centered approach. *Contemporary Educational Psychology, 28,* 37–58.

Karabenick, S. A. (2004). Perceived achievement goal structure and college student help seeking. *Journal of Educational Psychology, 96*, 569–581.

Linnenbrink, E. A. (2005). The dilemma of performance-approach goals: The use of multiple goal contexts to promote students' motivation and learning. *Journal of Educational Psychology, 97*, 197–213.

Lopez, D. F. (1999). Social cognitive influences on self-regulated learning: The impact of action-control beliefs and academic goals on achievement-related outcomes. *Learning and Individual Differences, 11*, 301–319.

Maehr, M. L., & Midgley, C. (1996). *Transforming school cultures*. Boulder, CO: Westview Press.

McClelland, D. C. (1951). *Personality*. New York: Dryden Press.

McClelland, D. C., Atkinson, J. W., Clark, R. A., & Lowell, E. L. (1953). *The achievement motive*. New York: Appleton-Century-Crofts.

McGregor, H. A., & Elliot, A. J. (2002). Achievement goals as predictors of achievement-relevant processes prior to task engagement. *Journal of Educational Psychology, 94*, 381–395.

Meece, J. L., Anderman, E. M., & Anderman, L. H. (2006). Classroom goal structure, student motivation, and academic achievement. *Annual Review of Psychology, 57*, 487–503.

Meece, J. L., & Miller, S. D. (1999). Changes in elementary school children's achievement goals for reading and writing: Results of a longitudinal and an intervention study. *Scientific Studies of Reading, 3*, 207–229.

Meece, J. L., & Miller, S. D. (2001). A longitudinal analysis of elementary school students' achievement goals in literacy activities. *Contemporary Educational Psychology, 26*, 454–480.

Middleton, M. J., Kaplan, A., & Midgley, C. (2004). The change in middle school students' achievement goals over time. *Social Psychology of Education, 7*, 289–311.

Middleton, M. J., & Midgley, C. (1997). Avoiding the demonstration of lack of ability: An underexplored aspect of goal theory. *Journal of Educational Psychology, 89*, 710–718.

Midgley, C., Kaplan, A., & Middleton, M. (2001). Performance-approach goals: Good for what, for whom, under what circumstances, and at what cost? *Journal of Educational Psychology, 93*, 77–86.

Moller, A. C., & Elliot, A. J. (2006). The 2 × 2 achievement goal framework: An overview of empirical research. In A. Mitel (Ed.), *Focus on educational psychology research* (pp. 307–326). New York: Nova Science.

Murray, H. (1938). *Explorations in personality*. New York: Oxford University Press.

Nicholls, J. (1984). Achievement motivation: Conceptions of ability, subjective experience, task choice, and performance. *Psychological Review, 91*, 328–346.

Pajares, F., & Valiante, G. (2001). Gender differences in writing motivation and achievement of middle school students: A function of gender orientation? *Contemporary Educational Psychology, 26*, 366–381.

Pekrun, R., Elliot, A. J., & Maier, M. A. (2006). Achievement goals and discrete achievement emotions: A theoretical model and prospective test. *Journal of Educational Psychology, 98*, 583–597.

Pintrich, P. R. (2000). Multiple goals, multiple pathways: The role of goal orientation in learning and achievement. *Journal of Educational Psychology, 92*, 544–555.

Roberts, B. W., Caspi, A., & Moffitt, T. E. (2001). The kids are alright: Growth and stability in personality development from adolescence to adulthood. *Journal of Personality and Social Psychology, 81*, 670–683.

Roberts, B. W., Walton, K. E., & Viechtbauer, W. (2006). Patterns of mean-level change in personality traits across the life course: A meta-analysis of longitudinal studies. *Psychological Bulletin, 132*, 1–25.

Robins, R. W., Fraley, R. C., Roberts, B. W., & Trzesniewski, K. H. (2001). A longitudinal study of personality change in young adulthood. *Journal of Personality, 69*, 617–640.

Roeser, R. W., Midgley, C., & Urdan, T. C. (1996). Perceptions of the school psychological environment and early adolescents' psychological and behavioral functioning in school: The mediating role of goals and belonging. *Journal of Educational Psychology, 88*, 408–422.

Ryan, A. R., & Pintrich, P. R. (1997). "Should I ask for help?" The role of motivation and attitudes in adolescents' help seeking in math class. *Journal of Educational Psychology, 89*, 329–341.

Ryan, R. M., Sheldon, K. M., Kasser, T., & Deci, E. L. (1996). All goals are not created equal: An organismic perspective on the nature of goals and their regulation. In P. Gollwitzer & J. Bargh (Eds.), *The psychology of action: Linking cognition and motivation to behavior* (pp. 7–26). New York: Guilford.

Schunk, D. H. (1995). Self-efficacy, motivation, and performance. *Journal of Applied Sport Psychology, 7*, 112–137.

Schunk, D. H. (1998). Teaching elementary students to self-regulate practice of mathematical skills with modeling. In D. Schunk & B. Zimmerman (Eds.), *Self-regulated learning: From teaching to self-reflective practice* (pp. 137–158). New York: Guilford.

Schunk, D. H., & Zimmerman, B. J. (1997). Social origins of self-regulatory competence. *Educational Psychologist, 32*, 195–208.

Seifert, T. L. (1996). The stability of goal orientations in grade five students: Comparison of two methodologies. *British Journal of Educational Psychology, 66*, 73–82.

Senko, C., & Harackiewicz, J. M. (2005a). Achievement goals, task performance, and interest: Why perceived goal difficulty matters. *Personality and Social Psychology Bulletin, 31*, 1739–1753.

Senko, C., & Harackiewicz, J. M. (2005b). Regulation of achievement goals: The role of competence feedback. *Journal of Educational Psychology, 97*, 320–336.

Sideridis, G. D. (2005). Goal orientation, academic achievement, and depression: Evidence in favor of a revised goal theory framework. *Journal of Educational Psychology, 97*, 366–375.

Stipek, D., & Gralinski, J. H. (1996). Children's beliefs about intelligence and school performance. *Journal of Educational Psychology, 88*, 397–407.

Urdan, T. (2004). Predictors of academic self-handicapping and achievement: Examining achievement goals, classroom goal structures, and culture. *Journal of Educational Psychology, 96*, 251–264.

Urdan, T., & Turner, J. C. (2005). Competence motivation in the classroom. In A. Elliot & C. Dweck (Eds.), *Handbook of competence and motivation* (pp. 297–317). New York: Guilford Press.

Van Yperen, N. W. (2006). A novel approach to assessing achievement goals in the context of the 2 × 2 framework: Identifying distinct profiles of individuals with different dominant achievement goals. *Personality and Social Psychology Bulletin, 32*, 1432–1445.

VandeWalle, D. (1997). Development and validation of a work domain goal orientation instrument. *Educational and Psychological Measurement, 57*, 995–1015.

Wentzel, K. R. (1993). Motivation and achievement in early adolescence: The role of multiple classroom goals. *Journal of Early Adolescence, 13*, 4–20.

Wentzel, K. R. (2005). Peer relationships, motivation, and academic performance at school. In A. Elliot & C. Dweck (Eds.), *Handbook of competence and motivation* (pp. 279–296). New York: Guilford Press.

Wolters, C. A. (2004). Advancing achievement goal theory: Using goal structures and goal orientations to predict students' motivation, cognition, and achievement. *Journal of Educational Psychology, 96*, 236–250.

Wolters, C. A., Yu, S. L., & Pintrich, P. R. (1996). The relation between goal orientation and students' motivational beliefs and self-regulated learning. *Learning and Individual Differences, 8*, 211–238.

Young, A. J. (1997). I think, therefore I'm motivated: The relations among cognitive strategy use, motivational orientation, and classroom perceptions over time. *Learning and Individual Differences, 9*, 249–283.

Zimmerman, B. J. (1989). A social–cognitive view of self-regulated academic learning. *Journal of Educational Psychology, 81*, 329–339.

Zimmerman, B. J. (1998). Developing self-fulfilling cycles of academic regulation: An analysis of exemplary instructional models. In D. Schunk & B. Zimmerman (Eds.), *Self-regulated learning: From teaching to self-reflective practice* (pp. 1–19). New York: Guilford.

Zimmerman, B. J. (2000). Attaining self-regulation: A social-cognitive perspective. In M. Boekaerts, P. Pintrich, & M. Zeidner (Eds.), *Handbook of self-regulation* (pp. 13–39). San Diego, CA: Academic Press.

4

Interest and Self-Regulation:
Relationships between Two Variables
That Influence Learning*

Suzanne Hidi and Mary Ainley

INTRODUCTION

Interest and self-regulation are concepts that in the last two decades have received considerable attention in educational, developmental, and social psychology. At first, the two concepts were examined independently by researchers. More recently, the empirical investigations and the theoretical conceptualizations of self-regulation and interest started to overlap. Consequently, it seems appropriate to consider how research findings from the two areas are related and how they can best inform each other.

In this chapter, interest is construed as a psychological state having both affective and cognitive components with the additional premise that, as interest develops, it also becomes a predisposition to reengage with content (Hidi & Renninger, 2006; Renninger, 2000). In addition, the physiological aspects of experiencing interest are acknowledged. A variety of other definitions of interest can be found in the literature, ranging from a fundamentally cognitive conceptualization of interest as a motivational belief (e.g., Zimmerman, 2002), to a fundamentally affective conceptualization of interest as

---

* We gratefully acknowledge comments and questions from Pietro Boscolo, Ann Renninger, Dale Schunk, and Barry Zimmerman. We also thank Keri Cull for her editorial assistance.

a basic emotion (e.g., Panksepp, 2000; Silvia, 2001; Tomkins, 1962). Izard (1977) went as far as calling interest the most frequently experienced positive emotion. Fredrickson and Branigan (2000) also made a strong case for the inclusion of interest among the basic, positive emotions. They noted that the emotion of interest tends to arise in any context that (a) offers change, novelty, a sense of possibility (Izard, 1977), or mystery (Kaplan, 1992) and (b) is appraised as important and requiring effort and attention (Ellsworth & Smith, 1988). Hidi (2006) argued that, if we only consider the moment in which the psychological state of interest is triggered, interest may be appropriately referred to as an emotion. However, as interest develops and is maintained, both affect and cognition become important components of the process (Hidi & Berndorff, 1998; Hidi & Renninger, 2006; Hidi, Renninger, & Krapp 2004, Krapp, 2000, 2002; Renninger, 1990, 2000; Sansone & Thoman, 2005). Furthermore, the relative strength of the two components changes over time, with cognition gaining importance as interest develops (Krapp, 2002; Renninger, 2000).

The definition of self-regulation in the literature has been less contentious because, in general, it was understood that self-regulation refers to the ways in which individuals regulate their thoughts and actions. Self-regulation of learning refers specifically to those self-generated operations that focus on individuals' acquisition of academically relevant knowledge and skills (Schunk & Zimmerman, 1994, 1997). Whereas earlier self-regulation research focused on individuals' ability to be active participants of their own cognitive, motivational, and behavioral processes (Boekaerts, 1997; Zimmerman & Bandura, 1994), more recently the capacity to regulate affect has been included as a critical aspect of self-regulation (Boekaerts, 2002, 2006; Pintrich & Zusho, 2002; Zimmerman, 2002). Researchers have also emphasized that self-regulation tends to be exercised by individuals to attain their goals (e.g., Zimmerman, 1989; Pintrich & Schunk, 1996).

Although many of the empirical investigations of interest and self-regulation were distinct, links have been made between the two conceptual frameworks (Renninger & Hidi, 2002; Renninger, Sansone, & Smith, 2004; Sansone & Thoman, 2005). Some interest researchers have demonstrated that self-regulation is an integral part of individual interest development (e.g., Hidi & Renninger, 2006; Hidi et al., 2004; Renninger, 2000; Renninger & Hidi, 2002).

Others have focused on showing that the ability to increase interest can be a powerful aspect of self-regulation (e.g., Sansone & Harackiewicz, 1996; Sansone & Smith 2000; Sansone & Thoman, 1995; Sansone, Weir, Harpster, & Morgan, 1992). Among those investigators who focused on self-regulation, there were a number who noted that possessing self-regulatory skills does not guarantee that individuals apply such skills in the face of difficulties, boredom, or competing attractions (Bandura, 1997; Zimmerman & Bandura, 1994) and pointed to interest as a motivational factor that can facilitate the development and maintenance of self-regulation (e.g., Pintrich & Zusho, 2002; Zimmerman, 2002; Zimmerman & Bandura, 1994).

Empirical investigations of cognitive performance and academic learning demonstrated that interest and self-regulation have similar positive influences. Interest, whether addressed as situational interest, individual interest, or the affective state of interest, has been found to play an important role in learning and development. Studies showed that interest positively influences attentional processes, the quantity and level of learning, and learners' selection of learning strategies and their achievement goals, including choices they make during task performance (see Ainley, Corrigan, & Richardson, 2005) and in selecting academic courses (Harackiewicz, Barron, Tauer, & Elliott, 2002). Importantly, persistence and positive affect have been strongly associated with interested activity (see Hidi & Renninger, 2006, for a review of the literature). Correspondingly, the beneficial results of self-regulation on individuals' performance in both academic and nonacademic areas have been demonstrated by many researchers, who reported that good self-regulators perform better than poor self-regulators (see Pintrich, 2000; Pintrich & Zusho, 2002; Zimmerman & Bandura, 1994, for instance). The role of self-regulation in achieving academic excellence has been emphasized (Zimmerman, 2001, 2002), and experts in such diverse areas as academic writing and sports have been shown to perform at their optimal level when they use self-regulatory techniques (Hidi & Boscolo, 2006; Kitsantas & Zimmerman, 2002; Pintrich, 2004; Zimmerman & Kitsantas, 1997, 2006).

In addition to leading to similar outcomes, both the development of self-regulation and the development of interest have been characterized as having four levels. In the case of self-regulation, observation of modeling, emulation of performance, self-control, and self-regulation have been called the four hierarchical levels of development (e.g., Schunk & Zimmerman, 1997; Zimmerman & Schunk, 2004). The four levels of interest development, which have been referred to as phases, include triggered situational interest, maintained situational interest, emerging individual interest, and well-developed individual interest (Hidi & Renninger, 2006). Whereas in the case of self-regulation, the four levels refer to the development of self-regulatory skills, the four phases of interest development that are discussed further here, describe how the psychological state of interest can develop into a well-developed individual interest. Notwithstanding differences in their conceptualizations, both developmental models can be characterized by a similar underlying trend of evolving from an external to a more internal focus. Self-regulatory skill development is presumed to go from reactivity to proactivity, from goals set externally to those self-generated. Interest development has been described as starting with external input that triggers interest and progressing to more and more self-generated processes in the later phases of development.

Finally, both interest and self-regulation have been associated with *self-efficacy*, defined as an individual's perceived capability to perform at a level of proficiency (Bandura, 1986). As our subsequent review demonstrates, the concepts of interest, self-regulation, and self-efficacy are not only closely related but also may be associated developmentally. In the following sections, we review some of the relevant theoretical and empirical work and consider how individuals' interest and self-regulation are associated with each other as well as with perceptions of self-efficacy. Subsequently, current research indicating that interest is a mediator of self-regulatory processes is reported. Finally, the educational implications of the findings and future directions of ways in which interest and self-regulation research could be best combined are discussed.

SELF-REGULATION RESEARCH,[1] MOTIVATION, AND INTEREST

Zimmerman and Bandura (1994) pointed out that research that initially investigated the processes through which individuals regulate their own learning was focused on cognitive factors such as metacognitive strategies, mnemonic encoding, and the like. With the advent of the social cognitive theory of self-regulation, the focus shifted to a wider lens; social, motivational, and affective aspects of individuals' functioning have been added to the mainly cognitive perspective (Boekaerts, 2002; Pintrich, 2004; Schunk & Zimmerman, 1994, 1997; Zimmerman, 2000a). Researchers have shown that self-regulation can be taught through these aspects (e.g., Boekaerts, 1997). Four progressive levels in the development of self-regulation have been hypothesized by Zimmerman and colleagues (e.g., Zimmerman, 2002; Zimmerman & Kitsantas, 1999; Zimmerman & Schunk, 2004). The first level involves the learner observing a model; the second level involves emulation, which is students' attempt to copy the model's performance. At the third level of self-regulation, the learner's self-control becomes important as the learner plans strategies and self-monitors the progress that is measured by how well it matches or surpasses the model. Finally, at the fourth level, the student adapts personal performance to various internal and external conditions.

In the area of self-regulation, several researchers acknowledged a close association between self-efficacy and self-regulation (Zimmerman, 2002). Zimmerman and Bandura (1994) noted that children who had strong beliefs in their academic self-efficacy were more likely to self-regulate and performed better than students with feelings of low self-efficacy. Based on experimental and correlational research (e.g., Harter, 1998; Pintrich, 1999; Schunk, 1994), Pintrich and Zusho (2002) concluded that judgments of self-efficacy are positively correlated with self-regulation and actual performance. In other words, across various domains and tasks, students who believe in their abilities to perform are more likely to use self-regulatory strategies. Zimmerman (2000a, 2000b) also discussed that feelings of self-efficacy interact with self-regulated processes. More specifically, he concluded that self-efficacy beliefs provide students with motivation for their learning through such self-regulatory processes as goal setting, self-monitoring, self-evaluation, and strategy use.

In social cognitive theory, learning and motivation are related to a triadic model of person, behavior, and environment with reciprocal influences (e.g., Bandura, 1986; Zimmerman & Schunk, 2004). Self-regulation has also been viewed within the triadic model. Specifically, self-regulation is related to the operations of a set of psychological subfunctions (e.g., Bandura, 1991). Activities that have been included as subfunctions ranged from goal setting, motivating one's effort, self-monitoring, and self-judging one's activities to employing appropriate strategies for performance (Zimmerman & Bandura, 1994). It is within some of the subfunctions that the importance of interest has been acknowledged by researchers. Zimmerman (2000a, 2002) postulated that self-regulatory processes and associated self-motivational beliefs influence learning in three successive phases of forethought, performance, and self-reflection, and each phase can be characterized by various subprocesses of self-regulation. Self-motivational beliefs, one of the two major categories of the forethought phase, include interest. Self-efficacy, outcome expectations, and goal orientation are the other motivational constructs that are referred to as *self-motivational beliefs*. More specifically, Zimmerman defined *interest* as a belief that results in valuing an activity or skill for its inherent properties rather than for its ultimate end and concluded that interested students are more likely to be motivated to plan and use learning strategies needed for self-regulation than individuals without such interest. This conceptualization of interest, as it is demonstrated in the subsequent sections of this chapter, is quite different from the way in which interest is defined by most interest researchers, who do not consider interest to be primarily a cognitive variable such as a belief (Hidi & Renninger, 2006).

In Zimmerman's (2002) model (see Zimmerman, 2002, Figure 1.1), motivation in general and interest more specifically have not been considered as central to the performance phase. Two major categories have been included in this phase: self-control and self-observation. *Self-control* refers to operations that center on one's concentration, screening out other processes, events, and distracting stimuli. Attention focusing is one form of self-control that has been postulated to contribute to improving one's concentration. It is important to note that, according to interest theory, interest plays a central role in focusing attention. The impact of interest on attention has been well documented in the literature (e.g., Hidi, 1995, 2001; Hidi et al., 2004; McDaniel, Waddill, Finstad, & Bourg, 2000; Renninger & Wozniak, 1985; Tomkins, 1962). In addition, monitoring interest as it is triggered and maintained across a task is providing insight into the ways interest supports achievement goals, self-efficacy, and self-beliefs (e.g., Ainley & Patrick, 2006; Hidi et al., 2006). As far as the third phase of Zimmerman's self-regulation model, referred to as *self-reflection*, is concerned, he acknowledged a role for affective factors, noting that individuals' self-satisfaction, which is an aspect of this phase, is likely to be influenced by their interest, perceived value, and importance.

In their article on the development of self-regulation, Pintrich and Zusho (2002), similarly to Zimmerman's model, considered triggered interest, along with other affective reactions, to be most important for the "forethought, planning, and activation phase" (p. 252). They concluded that interest and value beliefs are motivational factors that influence the development of self-regulated learning. Pintrich and colleagues (see Pintrich & Zusho, 2002, for a review) found that individuals who were interested in an activity or task or perceived it as more valuable (important or useful) were more likely to use self-regulatory strategies. Based on these findings, Pintrich and Zusho (2002) suggested that high interest and value beliefs may lead students to goals for learning that downplay the costs and highlight the benefits of self-regulation.

Models of self-regulation typically focused on individuals' motivation in terms of goals (Sansone & Harackiewicz 1996; Sansone & Thoman, 2005; Schunk & Zimmerman, 1994). More specifically, motivation has been seen as dependent on how much individuals value goals and expect to attain them (Sansone & Thoman, 2005). Boekaerts (1997) went as far as to stipulate that the capacity to represent a goal mentally is a necessary condition for self-regulation. However, there are other ways to conceptualize important aspects of motivated self-regulation. From interest researchers' point of view, a child may become interested in an activity without having, or prior to having, cognitively represented goals, resulting in increased self-regulation (Hidi & Renninger, 2006). Sansone and Harackiewicz (1996) reviewed the function of interest and goals in self-regulation and suggested that whereas short-term goals may be sufficient to energize behavior, when goals are no longer firm or require choices among multiple options, experiencing the positive "phenomenal state of interest"[2] may be necessary for goal-directed action to continue. Furthermore, experiencing this state of interest may be critical for the initiation and persistence of behavior as well as to individuals' ability to maintain motivation to reach desired goals.

Thus, Sansone and Harackiewicz (1996) proposed a model in which individuals' motivation for self-regulation derives not only from their motivation to reach a goal but also from their phenomenal state of interest while working toward their goal. They maintained that:

> Once an individual begins an activity, the extent to which he or she feels
> like continuing may exert a greater influence on subsequent behaviors
> (such as persistence, degree of effort, attention, and so on) than the
> initial motivation to reach the goal. In other words, outcome-derived
> motivation may be necessary to maintain performance over time. For
> example, a child may begin reading because he or she is motivated by the
> goal of developing reading skills. However, whether he or she continues
> to read over the long term may depend on the degree of enjoyment expe-
> rienced in the process of building those skills. (p. 208)

Sansone and Harackiewicz also noted that individuals who have
similar goals may experience different task involvement and develop
different levels of interest.

Sansone and Thoman (2005) reiterated that motivated self-regulation should not be seen as dependent only on how much individuals value goals and expect to attain them. Rather, they argued, the
type of motivation that arises from an activity—or as they refer to
it, from the process of goal pursuit—should also be recognized as an
important aspect of self-regulation. Experiencing interest is such a
motivator, albeit one that has been missing from some of the goal-
based models of self-regulation.

In summary, most self-regulation researchers have considered
motivation in general, and interest in specific, through a cognitive
perspective, operating through individuals' belief systems and leading to basically cognitive changes in goal structures and evaluations.
In the following section, the position that interest is more fundamentally related to self-regulation than previously acknowledged is
supported. Although individuals can self-regulate under certain circumstances even if they have no interest in an activity, interest experience should facilitate self-regulation and its development. Sansone
and Thoman (2005) consider interest as a necessary component
within a goal-based model of self-regulation. However, it is more
likely that, provided relevant self-regulatory skills are in place, interest is a sufficient condition. That is, once interest is present, existing
self-regulatory skills are activated, even if the activity is not in the
service of clear outcome goals (Renninger & Hidi, 2002).

INTEREST RESEARCH AND SELF-REGULATION

There are two groups of studies in the area of interest research
that have linked interest and self-regulation. In the first group of

studies, researchers argued that as individual interest develops in an activity, self-regulation also develops as an integral aspect of the performance, and that interest is one of the mediating variables of self-regulatory processes (Ainley & Chan, 2006; Ainley & Patrick, 2006; Hidi & Renninger, 2006; Renninger & Hidi, 2002; Sansone & Thoman, 2005). In the other line of research, investigators demonstrated that individuals can increase their interest in activities through self-regulation. That is, they have shown that self-regulation through a variety of strategies can help people create and maintain more interesting engagements (e.g., Sansone & Harackiewicz, 1996; Sansone et al., 1992). Before the findings of these two groups of studies are reviewed, we briefly consider how interest differs from other motivational variables.

Interest: A Unique Motivational Variable

As indicated in the beginning of this chapter, Hidi and Renninger (2006) defined interest as a psychological state that, in later phases of development, is also a predisposition to reengage with particular classes of objects, activities, ideas, and so on, referred to as *content*. The development of interest as a predisposition results from continued exposure to and reengagement with content and is an outcome of positive affect, increased knowledge, and stored value. They also discussed several ways in which interest can be distinguished from other motivational variables.[3] Specifically, the three important distinctions that support viewing interest as a unique motivational variable are as follows: First, interest includes both affective and cognitive components as separate but interactive systems, and thus interest is not considered simply as an outcome of cognitive operations and their representations (e.g., Ainley, Hidi, & Berndorff, 2002; Hidi et al., 2004; Krapp, 2002; Renninger, 1990, 2000). Whereas the affective tone associated with interest is positive, interest can also have implications for negative affective experiences (Hidi & Harackiewicz, 2000; Hidi & Renninger, 2006; Iran-Nejad, 1987; Renninger & Hidi, 2002). However, for interest to develop, the affective component has to change from negative to positive.

Second, both cognitive and affective systems involved in experiencing interest have biological roots (Hidi, 2003, 2006). Neuroscientific evidence of the existence of approach circuits in the brain (e.g.,

Davidson, 2000) and of seeking behavior in humans and animals (e.g., Panksepp, 1998, 2000; Panksepp & Moskal, 2004) indicate that interested activities have a biological foundation in all mammals. Panksepp and colleagues (e.g., Panksepp, 1998; Panksepp & Moskal, 2004) argued that the seeking system—an evolutionary and genetically ingrained brain system—"is a biological foundation of the psychological state of interest in the sense that the person is engaged physically, cognitively, or symbolically with the object of his or her interest" (Hidi & Renninger, 2006, p. 112). Having neuroscientific support for the psychological state of interest suggests specificity of brain reactions when an individual is engaged in interesting activities and is processing interesting content.

Third, interest is the outcome of an interaction between a person and a particular content (Hidi & Baird, 1986; Krapp, 2000; Krapp, Hidi, & Renninger, 1992; Renninger & Wozniak, 1985; Schiefele, Krapp, Prenzel, Heiland, & Kasten, 1983). Whereas the potential for interest resides in the person, the content and the environment may determine the direction of interest and contribute to its development. For example, other individuals, the organization of the environment, and a person's own efforts, such as self-regulation, can support interest development (Renninger, 2000; Renninger & Hidi, 2002; Renninger et al., 2004; Sansone & Smith, 2000; Sansone et al., 1992; Schraw & Dennison, 1994). This interactive view means that interest is always considered to be content specific rather than a predisposition that applies across all activities (Krapp, 2000; Krapp & Fink, 1992; Renninger, 1989, 1990, 2000). Even those students who generally are highly motivated to achieve would have interests only for a discrete set of specific content areas (Renninger, Ewen, & Lasher, 2002).

The Four Phases of Interest Development and Their Effect on Self-Regulation

Representing the development of interest from a psychological state to a predisposition, Hidi and Renninger (2006) proposed the four-phase model of interest development (see Table 4.1). The model builds on and extends previous conceptualizations of situational and individual interest that have been central to educational research in the area (e.g., Ainley et al., 2002; Alexander & Jetton,

1996; Harackiewicz et al., 2002; Hidi & Baird, 1986; Hidi, 1990, 2001; Krapp, 2002, 2005; Krapp et al., 1992; Renninger, 1990, 2000; Schraw & Lehman, 2001). *Situational interest* is a psychological state that is characterized by focused attention and an affective reaction that tends to be positive. It is most commonly generated by particular conditions or objects in the environment, and it may or may not last over time. *Individual interest* is a relatively enduring predisposition to attend to certain content (objects, stimuli, ideas) or to engage in certain activities. Hidi and Renninger (2006) noted that individual interest can also refer to the psychological state associated with an activated predisposition.

Situational interest, as well as individual interest, has been found to have a positive impact on cognitive performance. Focusing attention, narrowing inferences, and increasing persistence, effort, and learning are some of the benefits associated with interested engagements (see Hidi & Renninger, 2006, for a review of the literature). Both situational and individual interest have two phases. In the case of situational interest, the first phase involves the triggering of interest, and the subsequent phase involves the maintenance of interest (see Hidi & Baird, 1986; Mitchell, 1993, for instance). The two phases of individual interest are emerging and well-developed individual interest (Renninger, 2000). It is important to note that experiencing individual interest can coincide with phases of situational interest.

The four-phase model of interest development identifies situational interest as the basis for individual interest development and integrates the four phases that are considered distinct and sequential (Alexander, 1997, 2004; Alexander & Jetton, 1996; Hidi & Anderson, 1992; Krapp, 2002; Renninger, 2000; Schraw & Lehman, 2001; Silvia, 2001). Interest builds on what an individual perceives, feels, cognitively represents, and considers for further engagement (Renninger, 1990, 2000). The progressive development is postulated to depend on interest as supported and sustained in each previous phase, either by the person or through efforts of others. Interest development can be influenced by experience, temperament, and genetic predisposition. Importantly, as Renninger (2000) argued, at any of the phases of interest development, without personal effort or support from others, interest can become dormant, regress, or disappear altogether.

According to the model, each phase of interest development involves varying amounts of affect, knowledge, and value. More

TABLE 4.1 Four Phases of Interest Development

	Phase 1: Triggered Situational Interest	Phase 2: Maintained Situational Interest	Phase 3: Emerging Individual Interest	Phase 4: Well-Developed Individual Interest
Definition	Psychological state that results from short-term changes in affective and cognitive processing	Psychological state subsequent to the triggered state; involves focused attention and persistence over an extended episode in time or reoccurrence	Psychological state as well as the beginning phase of a relatively enduring predisposition to seek repeated engagements with particular classes of content	Psychological state as well as a relatively enduring predisposition to reengage with particular content over time
Developmental progression	May be a precursor to maintained situational interest	May be a precursor to emerging situational interest	May be a precursor to well-developed individual interest	
Type of support needed	Typically, but not exclusively, externally supported; learning environments and instructional conditions, such as puzzles, group work and computers, etc., can trigger situational interest	Typically, but not exclusively, externally supported; instructional conditions that provide meaningful and personally involving activities, such as cooperative groups work, one-to-one tutoring, etc.	Beginnings of self-generation, although external support from peers, experts, environmental challenges, etc., contribute to the development of emerging individual interest	Self-generated to a large degree, external support may be helpful to maintaining well-developed interest

| Characteristics | Focused attention and affective reaction; the affective reaction initially may be negative | Continued attention and affective reaction; if the affective reaction is negative, it must change before individual interest can develop | Positive feelings and beginning of accumulation of content-related knowledge and value; beginning of self-regulation: self-reflections that result in curiosity questions about content | Positive feelings, increased knowledge and stored value, over and beyond those of emerging individual interest; increased self-regulation and higher levels of self-reflection |

Note: It is important to recognize that a person's situational interest can be triggered and maintained in the phases of emerging and well-developed individual interest.

Source: Hidi & Renninger, 2006.

specifically, knowledge and value increase as interest develops together with the increasing self-regulation that becomes an integral part of the third and fourth phases of interest development. Hidi and Renninger (2006) summarized the four-phase model as follows:

> Each phase of the four-phase model of interest development is characterized by affect and each phase also includes some form of knowledge or cognitive processing although these components are more pronounced in the later phases of interest. Once the first phase of triggered situational interest has been elicited, it can last for short or long periods of time and may provide a basis for a person to begin forming a connection to content. In the second phase of interest, maintained situational interest, a person is typically supported by the environment (others, tasks, etc.) to continue to develop a basis for connecting to content and to find ways to relate this information to other available information. In this phase, as interest is sustained, a person is also beginning to develop value for content. In the third phase of emerging individual interest, a person begins to seek repeated engagement with content, continues to reengage content with or without explicit external supports and consolidates related knowledge. He or she begins to pose curiosity questions, a process that leads to self-regulated activity, accumulation of more information, and increased valuing. In the fourth phase of well-developed individual interest, the person continues to seek repeated opportunities for reengagement. Curiosity questions, self-regulations, valuing, and the ability to attenuate frustration and sustain creative thinking inform this reengagement. (pp. 119–120)

Most relevant to the present discussion is the link between interest and self-regulation that is an integral part of the third and fourth phase of interest development. In the third phase, several aspects related to self-regulatory behavior emerge. For example, interest in this phase is typically—although not exclusively—self-generated, individuals are likely to persevere when confronted with difficulty, and their interaction with the content of interest begins to lead to some reflections and the generation of relevant curiosity questions (Renninger, 2000). As persons deal with such curiosity questions, they may exceed or redefine task demands (Renninger & Hidi, 2002; Renninger et al., 2004). These questions are accompanied by efforts to self-regulate and identify with the content (Krapp, 2002, 2003).

When an individual's ability to self-regulate and identify with the content increases, the individual moves into the final phase of development. Well-developed individual interest is characterized by more positive feelings, increased knowledge, and value for particular contents of interest than those of the phase of emerging individual interest. Most significantly, well-developed individual interest promotes self-regulation (Lipstein & Renninger, 2006; Renninger & Hidi, 2002; Renninger et al., 2004; Sansone & Smith, 2000); enables people to be involved in long-term constructive and creative endeavors as suggested by Izard and Ackerman (2000) and Tomkins (1962); and contributes to quantitatively and qualitatively superior strategies for task performance (Alexander & Murphy, 1998).

The four-phase model of interest development is based on empirical studies (see Hidi & Renninger, 2006). Research that supports the model continues to accumulate. For example, Nolen (2007) reported a 3-year longitudinal study of Grade 1 through Grade 3 children's motivation for literacy activities. Content analyses of interviews with the children and their teachers were supplemented by class observations. The results supported the four-phase model's description of how situational interest develops into individual interest. The data also showed that children developed increasingly complex ideas about their motivation for reading and writing. Notably, in children's perceptions, interest as the salient motivator emerged for both reading and writing, whereas the importance of mastery peaked at Grade 2, when children have acquired the basic skills of reading and writing.

Ainley and colleagues (Ainley & Chan, 2006; Ainley & Patrick, 2006) demonstrated empirically that interest can play a mediating role in relation to self-regulatory processes. Their research is summarized next.

Interest as a Mediator of Self-Efficacy and Self-Regulatory Activities

Interest and self-efficacy were reported as significantly correlated in several studies (e.g., Bandura & Schunk, 1981; Zimmerman & Kitsantas, 1997, 1999). Hidi, Berndorff, and Ainley (2002) investigated how to improve students' emotional and cognitive experiences during argument writing and how their interest and self-efficacy were related within the writing situation. The authors suggested that as both interest and self-efficacy are content/domain specific, they may be related to the same knowledge base, and their development may be interrelated and reciprocal. On one hand, when individuals receive feedback from their own activities, the information may strengthen their self-efficacy by suggesting to them that they are competent and can continue to learn (Bandura, 1986). Engaging in and continuing to work with interesting activities may provide individuals with such information. Research findings that demonstrated that interested engagements tend to be focused, persistent, and effortful, although they tend to feel effortless, and to produce positive emotions (Ainley et al., 2005; Hidi, 2001; Renninger, 2000; Renninger & Hidi, 2002; Renninger & Leckrone, 1991) suggested that individuals involved in such activities improve their performance and have a corresponding increase in their self-efficacy. One the other hand, self-efficacious individuals who perceive themselves as capable of dealing with a given task are likely to be motivated to engage in that task and are likely to exhibit increased effort, persistence, and positive emotional reactions (e.g., Bandura, 1997; Zimmerman, 2000b). Such engagements would be likely to have a positive impact on a person's interest even in the case of tasks that initially might have seemed boring.

The findings of Hidi et al. (2002) indicated that the students' genre-specific self-efficacy in writing was closely associated with genre-specific affect (liking), and that both of these factors were also positively correlated with measures of general interest in writing. In a follow-up study, which focused on science-related expository writing, the results again demonstrated a positive association between interest in the topic and self-efficacy for the writing task; both factors positively influenced writing performance (Hidi, Ainley, Berndorff, & Del Favero, 2006). Ainley and colleagues (Ainley & Chan, 2006; Ainley & Patrick, 2006) have been studying the relationship between self-efficacy and interest, specifically to identify the on-task contingencies between these processes, and in this way extend the understanding of self-regulated learning. The tasks used have generally been writing tasks administered online, with students presented a topical or social issue. In addition, students have been provided with on-screen access to information resources related to the topics and were able to take notes from that information to assist them in their writing. When they were ready to start writing on the topic, the resource information disappeared, although students could use their notes to support their writing. Because the whole task was administered on-line, students could be prompted to report on their self-evaluations and reactions before, during, and after their task, as follows:

In the writing tasks, self-efficacy for writing on the topic was assessed by asking students to rate their confidence that they would be able to produce a good piece of writing once they knew what the topic was and what was required of them. When they had finished and had submitted their writing, they rated their confidence in the quality of what they had produced. Ratings of the triggered state of interest were also made prior to commencement of the task, after students had been working on the task for a set period (on-task state of interest), and again when students had finished writing. All of the ratings were made using single-item scales. The appropriateness of using these single-item scales for measuring states such as efficacy and interest has been argued elsewhere (see Ainley & Patrick, 2006; Goetz, Frenzel, Pekrun, & Hall, 2006).

Findings from these empirical studies generally confirm the proposition that the state of interest activated by the task topic and maintained by continued interaction with the task supports and may mediate the effect of self-efficacy on other self-regulatory processes. More particularly, the topic of the writing task in combination with students' individual interest in writing triggers a certain state of interest. Simultaneously, the nature of the writing task and topic trigger a certain level of self-efficacy. Across the course of the task, the effect of self-efficacy on later processing is supported by and often mediated by the level of interest maintained across the task. Hidi et al. (2006) also demonstrated that although pretask self-efficacy predicted students' confidence in the quality of their writing at the end of the task, on-task interest added to the amount of variance explained.

In a further study with eighth-grade girls, Ainley and Chan (2006) were able to demonstrate that these effects met criteria for mediation effects (partial mediation rather than full mediation) as assessed by the Sobel test (Baron & Kenny, 1986; Preacher & Leonardelli, 2001). When on-task interest was included in the model predicting from pretask efficacy to students' confidence in the quality of their writing, on-task interest was a significant predictor, and the prediction from self-efficacy was significantly reduced. An important point to be stressed here is that students' posttask judgments—their reflections of their performance—are a source of the mastery information that feeds into their further efficacy beliefs (Bandura, 1997). These findings suggest that the state of focused attention, concentration, and positive affect represented by these on-task interest measures operates to support learning and achievement by mediating the effects of prior states (e.g., self-efficacy) and general predispositions (e.g., individual interest) on learning.

A further demonstration of these effects has been shown in a smaller, more intensive, unpublished study, in which two classes of senior secondary students ($N = 29$, roughly half male and half female; mean age 16.5 years) were given the task of writing a 400- to 600-word paper on a topical issue concerning future development plans in their city (Scoble, 2005). In this particular study, students also made ratings of their interest and efficacy in relation to the writing genre (argumentative essays) before commencing the task and again at the end of the task. Although efficacy ratings for the writing genre remained relatively stable across the task, efficacy ratings for writing on the specific topic (the blueprint for development of their city) showed significant change across the course of the task. Again, it was found that the level of interest sustained across the task added to the explained variance in efficacy beliefs expressed as confidence in the quality of their writing. Both high levels of interest in the topic sustained across the task and high levels of confidence in writing on the topic were associated with higher quality essays when assessed by classroom teachers using their normal grading criteria. Interest in the task supported and maintained the effects of self-efficacy.

The mediation effects demonstrated have not been confined to individual interest and self-efficacy. In a study that included measures of achievement, goal orientations, and on-task goals, both interest in the topic when first presented and the on-task state of interest were shown to mediate how achievement goal orientations were manifested in on-task goals (see Ainley & Patrick, 2006). In sum, the state of interest as positive, focused attention and arousal mediates effects of associated self-regulatory processes such as self-efficacy and achievement goals.

The Role of Positive Affect in the Relation between Interest and Self-Regulation

Fredrickson (1998) suggested that positive emotions, in addition to making people feel good and improving their subjective life experiences, have the potential to broaden people's way of thinking and help them build physical, intellectual, and social resources. She identified specific positive emotions as joy, interest, contentment, and love. In subsequent work, Fredrickson and Branigan (2000) maintained that, in contrast to negative emotions that spark tendencies for physical actions, positive emotions spark changes primarily in cognitive activities by widening the array of thoughts that come to people's mind and their choices of activities. More specifically, building on Izard's (1977) position, the authors argued that experiencing the positive emotion of interest sparks thought-action tendencies that are aimed at increasing experience with and knowledge of the target of interest. They concluded that interest leads not only to short-term exploration but also, over time, to increased personal knowledge and cognitive abilities; thus, interest can be seen as a mental resource (Hidi, 1990) that contributes to future endeavors.

In addition, citing empirical evidence, Fredrickson and Branigan (2000) pointed out that the positive influence of positive emotions on cognition has been linked to physiological changes, such as increases in brain dopamine levels (e.g., Ashby, Isen, & Turken, 1999), and that the broadened thought-action repertoire of positive emotions is physiologically incompatible with the narrowed thought-action repertoire of negative emotions. In other words, researchers demonstrated an "undoing effect" of positive emotions on negative emotions. The importance of the positive affect that interest generates for knowledge acquisition and cognitive performance suggests that performing activities that individuals are interested in is likely to help build self-efficacy and facilitate the development and the continued practice of self-regulatory skills. Thus, self-regulatory skills that are taught or exercised together with interested engagements should have definite advantages over situations lacking interest.

Increasing Interest through Self-Regulation

Sansone and Thoman (2005) argued that there are two classes of potential interest-enhancing strategies: intrapersonal and interpersonal (see also Sansone & Smith, 2000). The groundbreaking research on enhancing interest through intrapersonal (also referred to as intraindividual) self-regulation has been conducted by Sansone and colleagues. In one of the first articles that examined the link between interest and self-regulation, Sansone et al. (1992) proposed that as an individual starts to participate in an activity, initial judgment of the interest level of the activity tends to determine the continuation or cessation of that activity. If interest is at a low level, then the person may discontinue the activity or, alternatively, may decide to work on generating more interest by modifying the activity or the goals related to the activity. Such modification may depend on opportunity and availability in the environment and requires self-regulation, which can result in a change of the definition of the activity. In their investigations, Sansone et al. (1992) focused on this type of self-regulatory mechanism. In the first of three consecutive studies, they compared college students' reactions to three novel tasks that had to be performed repeatedly and varied in how interesting they were. The most interesting task was a hidden word task, followed by a lettering task, and the least interesting was a copying task. Students were asked to generate specific strategies to make performing their task more interesting. The data showed that students' perceptions of the tasks corresponded to the experimental variations in interest level, and that they had both declarative and procedural knowledge about strategies to regulate their interests. Thus, the results indicated that, at least by the time students are undergraduates, they process fairly sophisticated self-regulatory processes that are responsive to differences in interest levels generated by task variations.

In their second study, the researchers compared undergraduate students' actual performance on the more interesting hidden word task with that of the boring copying task, predicting that more interest-enhancing strategies would be carried out in the case of the less-interesting task. The experimenters also varied the conditions under which students participated in the copying task; only those experimental variables are included in this discussion that are pivotal to the present topic. Half of the subjects were told that there would be health benefits associated with performing the (boring) activity on a regular basis. The other half of the students performing the copying task were not given any specific reason for their activity. The results showed that the students used strategies to make uninteresting tasks more interesting, and through such self-regulated interest enhancement, the likelihood of performing initially boring activities could be increased. The data also indicated that both cognitive and behavioral components of self-regulatory processes were involved.

In the third and final study of the series, based on the assumption that beliefs about the effectiveness of a strategy are important indicators of strategy use (Bandura, 1986; Schunk, 1991), individuals' beliefs about various self-regulatory strategies for maintaining motivation for three everyday activities (reading, listening to music, and exercising) were examined. Subjects were asked to rate the effectiveness of five strategies that could motivate them to perform the three activities. The five strategy types were rewarding oneself ("reward"), obtaining information that performing the activity was good for them ("good for you"), making the activity more interesting ("interest"), obtaining feedback that they performed the activity well ("positive competence feedback"), and using no additional strategies ("none"). Even though students perceived and defined the three activities differently, as reflected by their evaluations of the activities and their beliefs in certain types of self-regulatory strategies to best maintain performance, increasing interest was rated the most effective motivating strategy across the three activities. That is, students recognized that regulating their interest level is an important motivating strategy, over the long-term, for leisure activities as well as for more common, everyday activities.

Sansone et al. (1992) argued that the combined results of the three studies supported the importance of interest in self-regulating motivation and demonstrated that self-regulatory strategies can increase interest and contribute to continued engagement. Sansone and Thoman (2005) noted that there have been a number of other research studies that also supported the intrapersonal regulation of interest. For example, Nolen (2001) demonstrated that children as early as in kindergarten may attempt, on an elementary level, to self-regulate their interest. She reported on kindergarten children's emergent motivation to read and write and quoted one of the children (Kevin), who had to practice writing, as follows: "I'm going to have to do this for a long time? So that maybe I'd better start making this fun" (Nolen, 2001, p. 112). Meyer and Turner (2002; cf. Sansone & Thoman, 2005) noted that some fifth graders intentionally increased the challenge of a writing task to make it more interesting.

To test the assumption that people who approach an activity with interpersonal goals experience greater interest in situations in which such goals can be satisfied, Isaac, Sansone, and Smith (1999) examined how social factors such as other people's presence contributed to the interest level of activities. The results of the study showed that persons with higher interpersonal orientation indicated greater interest in a task and were more likely to engage in similar tasks when working in the presence of another person. Sansone and Thoman (2005) completed a study in which they asked undergraduate students questions regarding interpersonal regulation of their interest. The results showed that over half of the subjects preferred to work with others and tended to find working on something with another person more interesting.

The above-reviewed literature demonstrates that individuals' interest can be increased through self-regulation, although the age at which this type of self-regulation systematically occurs has not been established (Sansone & Thoman, 2005). However, the findings of intrapersonal and interpersonal regulation of interest further support the existence of a reciprocal relation between interest and self-regulation.

EDUCATIONAL IMPLICATIONS

In their case study, Renninger and Hidi (2002) demonstrated that tasks for which a student had well-developed interest did not need external input to ensure persistence the same way that was required for tasks that involved only situational interest. In these cases, teacher and parent input was needed involving reminders or support to meet goals and responsibilities. The researchers also showed that the individual could be supported to develop interest and work with subject content for which the person previously had less interest. Importantly, other investigations demonstrated that classroom teachers' interest and ability to communicate is likely to result in increasing their students' interest and love for subject matter (Long & Murphy, 2005; Sloboda & Davidson, 1995; Sosniak, 1990).

As indicated by the four-phase model of interest development, external support is most important in the early phases of interest development, when educators need to help students experience positive feelings and develop beliefs of self-efficacy about their work with content. Hidi and Renninger (2006) reviewed a variety of studies indicating how educators can facilitate individuals' positive affective responses to tasks. The methods included offering choices in tasks (Flowerday & Schraw, 2003); developing content-related knowledge and promoting a sense of autonomy (Deci, 1992); building feelings of competence (Hidi, 2001; Hoffman & Häussler, 1998; Renninger & Hidi, 2002; Schraw, Flowerday, & Lehman, 2001); and working with peers (Blumenfeld et al., 1991; Hidi, Weiss, Berndorff, & Nolan, 1998; Isaac et al., 1999). All these methods involve teachers organizing the environment to support the development of positive feelings that, according to Hidi and Renninger (2006), is a critical condition for subsequent interest development. We have also noted that interest can be triggered by negative affect, and that for interest to develop, negative feelings about the content must change. Given this type of situation, it is critical for teachers to provide opportunities that support such change (Renninger & Hidi, 2002). Interestingly, Renninger and Lipstein (2006) reported findings from a discourse analysis of students who described their interest as changed (e.g., going from triggered to maintained interest), indicating that choice, particular forms of pedagogy (e.g., group work), and so forth only work if students perceive them as opportunities. When conditions are imposed by others, it may get students to the task but will not guarantee that students engage with the task in a way that supports them to ask curiosity questions and begin the process of self-regulating their learning.

As mentioned, Zimmerman and colleagues (e.g., Schunk & Zimmerman, 1997; Zimmerman, 2000a, 2002), who have identified hierarchical levels in learners' development of self-regulation, also postulated that external influences are most relevant in the early phases of development. Researchers found that the initial form of learning at the observational level involves the presence of models that the learner can observe repeatedly. Furthermore, the persistence of a model affects the perseverance of the observer, and the preference shown by the model increases the observer's valuations of the activity. In the next stage, referred to as the *emulation level,* when learners try to duplicate the actions of the model, external influences remain essential as guidance, and feedback and social reinforcement are the postulated sources of motivation for self-regulatory skills to develop further.

Whereas both interest and self-regulation are more internally driven in the later phases of their development, continued external support remains important for both. Hidi and Renninger (2006) emphasized that emerging and well-developed individual interest is typically but not exclusively self-generated, and continued external support could be beneficial. Similarly, Zimmerman (2002) noted that, even though social support is systematically reduced as learners acquire self-regulatory skills, they continue to depend on social resources and social learning experiences.

Both interest and self-regulation researchers have emphasized that content knowledge is necessary for development and for shifting from external to internal support. For example, Renninger (2000) pointed to the importance of increasing knowledge in shifting from external to internal support. She argued that only on the basis of such knowledge can students generate self-reflective "curiosity questions." These types of questions, which may be externally provided in the early phases of interest development, need to be student generated with the advent of individual interest development. The importance of self-generated curiosity questions, according to Renninger, lies in the role they play in connecting individuals' understanding to other—perhaps more advanced—perspectives. These types of connections can lead students to reconsider what they had previously understood and to seek new information. Boekaerts (1997) also emphasized the importance of content knowledge and warned that self-regulation without it is characterized by complex, deliberate, effortful processing dependent on external control. Thus, more habitual and automatic self-regulation requires sufficient content knowledge. Boekaerts (1997) further argued that students who lack positive appraisal patterns—a concept that includes interest—need to rely on willpower to imitate and maintain their activities. This conclusion corresponds to interest researchers' argument that the presence of interest reduces the need to consciously and effortfully persist in an activity (e.g., Hidi & Renninger, 2006; Renninger & Hidi, 2002). Rather, interested engagements may result in automatic attention, persistence, and maintenance of activity (Hidi, 1995, 2000, 2001, in press).

CONCLUSION

Interest and self-regulation share several characteristics. They both facilitate learning and optimal levels of performance and thus are necessary components of academic success. Their developmental trajectories have similar trends, relying on external input and support in the early phases/levels and graduating to more internal, self-generated processes. Judgments of self-efficacy have been positively correlated with both interest and self-regulation. From a developmental point of view, interest researchers demonstrated that self-regulation is an integral aspect of later phases of interest development.

Researchers of self-regulation acknowledged that developing self-regulation and using the skill, once acquired, requires motivation that interest can contribute. However, generally they have not considered that interest can play a unique role in the development of self-regulatory skills. Self-regulation can be taught without considering the interest level of the learner, just as expertise can be achieved without well-developed individual interest (Hidi & Renninger, 2006). However, interest researchers' empirical investigations and theoretical analyses of the concept of interest presented in this chapter, suggest that the development of self-regulatory skills can be greatly enhanced through activities that are accompanied by individuals' emerging or well-developed interest. More specifically, self-regulation in such cases may occur without conscious goal direction, with less effort, or more automatically. The combination of interest and self-regulation has the potential to facilitate learning of the broad range of skills and competencies students need for productive and creative futures.

NOTES

1. This entire book is about self-regulation, and our discussion is not intended to be an exhaustive review of the literature on the topic. Rather, we focus on articles that seem to be most relevant to how self-regulation researchers view the link between self-regulation and interest.
2. The term *phenomenal state of interest* was explicated by Harackiewicz and Sansone (1991). They defined it as increased positive affect experienced during an activity (e.g., excited, energetic, etc.) and distinguished it from *subsequent interest*, which they measured by task attitudes. In the interest literature, other terms have also been used to describe these two forms of interest. The phenomenal state of interest corresponds to the psychological state of interest (see Hidi & Renninger, 2006 for a review) and is conceptually similar to actualized interest (Krapp et al., 1992) and to the affective state of interest (Ainley et al., 2005). Subsequent stages of interest that Harackiewicz and Sansone proposed to measure through task attitudes, have been traditionally represented in the literature as either topic interest (e.g., Schiefele & Krapp, 1996) or as a form of emerging individual interest (e.g., Renninger, 2000).
3. The observant reader may notice that the terms *intrinsic* and *extrinsic motivation* are not mentioned in this chapter. This omission is not because of neglect but rather because of the recognition that, although the conceptual differences between the two forms of motivation are easily understood and can be manipulated experimentally, intrinsic and extrinsic motivation are unlikely to operate independently of each other in real-life situations (Hidi & Harackiewicz, 2000) and are unlikely to involve exclusive physiological mechanisms.

REFERENCES

Ainley, M., & Chan, J. (2006, April). *Emotions and task engagement: Affect and efficacy and their contribution to information processing during a writing task.* Paper presented at the meetings of the American Educational Research Association, San Francisco.

Ainley, M., & Patrick, L. (2006). Measuring self-regulated learning processes through tracking patterns of student interaction with achievement activities. *Educational Psychology Review, 18,* 267–286.

Ainley, M., Corrigan, M., & Richardson, N. (2005). Students, tasks and emotions: Identifying the contribution of emotions to students' reading of popular culture and popular science texts. *Learning and Instruction, 15,* 433–447.

Ainley, M., Hidi, S., & Berndorff, D. (2002). Interest, learning, and the psychological processes that mediate their relationship. *Journal of Educational Psychology, 94,* 545–561.

Alexander, P. A. (1997). Mapping the multidimensional nature of domain learning: The interplay of cognitive, motivational, and strategic forces. In M. L. Maehr & P. R. Pintrich (Eds.), *Advances in Motivation and Achievement* (Vol. 10, pp. 213–250). Greenwich, CT: JAI.

Alexander, P. A. (2004). A model of domain learning: Reinterpreting expertise as a multidimensional, multistage process. In D. Y. Dai & R. J. Sternberg (Eds.), *Motivation, emotion, and cognition: Integrative perspectives on intellectual functioning and development* (pp. 273–298). Mahwah, NJ: Erlbaum.

Alexander, P. A., & Jetton, T. L. (1996). The role of importance and interest in the processing of text. *Educational Psychology Review, 8,* 89–121.

Alexander, P. A., & Murphy, P. K. (1998). Profiling the differences in students' knowledge, interest, and strategic processing. *Journal of Educational Psychology, 90,* 435–447.

Ashby, F. G., Isen, A. M., & Turken, A. U. (1999). A neuropsychological theory of positive affect and its influence on cognition. *Psychological Review, 106,* 529–550.

Bandura, A. (1986). *Social foundations of thought and action: A social cognitive theory.* Englewood Cliffs, NJ: Prentice Hall.

Bandura, A. (1991). Self-regulation of motivation through anticipatory and self-reactive mechanisms. In R. A. Dienstbier (Ed.), *Perspectives on motivation: Nebraska Symposium on Motivation* (Vol. 38, pp. 69–164). Lincoln: University of Nebraska Press.

Bandura, A. (1997). *Self-efficacy: The exercise of control.* New York: Freeman.

Bandura, A., & Schunk, D. H. (1981). Cultivating competence, self-efficacy, and intrinsic interest through proximal self-motivation. *Journal of Personality and Social Psychology, 41,* 586–598.

Baron, R. M., & Kenny, D. A. (1986). The moderator-mediator variable distinction in social psychological research: Conceptual, strategic, and statistical considerations. *Journal of Personality and Social Psychology, 51,* 1173–1182.

Blumenfeld, P., Soloway, E., Marx, R., Krajcik, J., Guzdial, M., & Palincsar, A. (1991). Motivating project-based learning: Sustaining the doing, supporting the learning. *Educational Psychologist, 26,* 369–398.

Boekaerts, M. (1997). Self-regulated learning: A new concept embraced by researchers, policy makers, educators, teachers, and students. *Learning and Instruction, 7,* 161–186.

Boekaerts, M. (2002). Bringing about change in the classroom: Strengths and weaknesses of the self-regulated learning approach—EARLI Presidential Address, 2001. *Learning and Instruction, 12,* 589–604.

Boekaerts, M. (2006). Self-regulation with a focus on the self-regulation of motivation and effort. In W. Damon & R. M. Lerner (Gen. Eds.), (Vol. 4). *Handbook of child psychology in practice* (6th ed., pp. 345–377). New York: Wiley.

Davidson, R. J. (2000). The neuroscience of affective style. In M. Gazzaniga (Ed.), *The new cognitive neurosciences* (pp. 1149–1162). Cambridge, MA: MIT Press.

Deci, E. L. (1992). The relation of interest to the motivation of behavior: A self-determination theory perspective. In K. A. Renninger, S. Hidi, & A. Krapp (Eds.), *The role of interest in learning and development* (pp. 43–70). Hillsdale, NJ: Erlbaum.

Ellsworth, P. C., & Smith, C. A. (1988). Shades of joy: Patterns of appraisal differentiating pleasant emotions. *Cognition and Emotion, 2,* 301–331.

Flowerday, T., & Schraw, G. (2003). Effect of choice on cognitive and affective engagement. *Journal of Educational Research, 96,* 207–215.

Fredrickson, B. L. (1998). What good are positive emotions? *Review of General Psychology, 2,* 300–319.

Fredrickson, B. L., & Branigan, C. (2000). Positive emotions. In T. J. Mayne & G. A. Bonanno (Eds.), *Emotions* (pp. 123–151). New York: Guilford.

Goetz, T., Frenzel, A., Pekrun, R., & Hall, N. C. (2006). The domain specificity of academic emotional experiences. *Journal of Experimental Education, 75*(1), 5–29.

Harackiewicz, J., & Sansone, C. (1991). Goals and intrinsic motivation: You can get there from here. *Advances in Motivation and Achievement, 7,* 21–49.

Harackiewicz, J. M., Barron, K. E., Tauer, J. M., & Elliot, A. J. (2002). Predicting success in college: A longitudinal study of achievement goals and ability measures as predictors of interest and performance from freshman year through graduation. *Journal of Educational Psychology, 94*, 562–575.

Harter, S. (1998). The development of self-representations. In W. Damon (Series Ed.) & N. Eisenberg (Vol. Ed.), *Handbook of child psychology: Vol. 3. Social, emotional, and personality development* (5th ed., pp. 553–617). New York: Wiley.

Hidi, S. (1990). Interest and its contribution as a mental resource for learning. *Review of Educational Research, 60*, 549–571.

Hidi, S. (1995). A re-examination of the role of attention in learning from text. *Educational Psychology Review, 7*, 323–350.

Hidi, S. (2001). Interest, reading and learning: Theoretical and practical considerations. *Educational Psychology Review, 13*, 191–210.

Hidi, S. (2003, August). *Interest: A motivational variable with a difference.* Plenary address presented at the 10th Biennial Meeting of the European Association for Learning and Instruction, Padova, Italy.

Hidi, S. (2006). Interest: A motivational variable with a difference. *Educational Research Review, 1*, 69–82.

Hidi, S., Ainley, M., Berndorff, D., & Del Favero, L. (2006). The role of interest and self-efficacy in science-related expository writing. In S. Hidi & P. Boscolo (Eds.), *Motivation and interest in writing* (pp. 201–216). Amsterdam: Elsevier.

Hidi, S., & Anderson, V. (1992). Situational interest and its impact on reading and expository writing. In K. A. Renninger, S. Hidi, & A. Krapp (Eds.), *The role of interest in learning and development* (pp. 215–238). Hillsdale, NJ: Erlbaum.

Hidi, S., & Baird, W. (1986). Interestingness—A neglected variable in discourse processing. *Cognitive Science, 10*, 179–194.

Hidi, S., & Berndorff, D. (1998). Situational interest and learning. In L. Hoffman, A. Krapp, K. A. Renninger, & J. Baumert (Eds.), *Interest and learning: Proceedings of the Seeon Conference on Interest and Gender* (pp. 74–90). Kiel, Germany: IPN.

Hidi, S., Berndorff, D., & Ainley, M. (2002). Children's argument writing, interest and self-efficacy: An intervention study. *Learning and Instruction, 12*, 426–446.

Hidi, S., & Boscolo, P. (2006). Motivation and writing. In C. MacArthur, S. Graham, & J. Fitzgerald (Eds.), *Handbook of writing research* (pp. 144–197). New York: Guilford.

Hidi, S., & Harackiewicz, J. (2000). Motivating the academically unmotivated: A critical issue for the 21st century. *Review of Educational Research, 70*, 151–179.

Hidi, S., & Renninger, K. A. (2006). The four-phase model of interest development. *Educational Psychologist, 41,* 111–127.

Hidi, S., Renninger, K. A., & Krapp, A. (2004). Interest, a motivational variable that combines affective and cognitive functioning. In D. Y. Dai & R. J. Sternberg (Eds.), *Motivation, emotion, and cognition: Integrative perspectives on intellectual functioning and development* (pp. 89–115). Mahwah, NJ: Erlbaum.

Hidi, S., Weiss, J., Berndorff, D., & Nolan, J. (1998). The role of gender, instruction and a cooperative learning technique in science education across formal and informal settings. In L. Hoffmann, A. Krapp, K. A. Renninger, & J. Baumert (Eds.), *Interest and learning: Proceedings of the Seeon Conference on Interest and Gender* (pp. 215–227). Kiel, Germany: IPN.

Hoffmann, L., & Häussler, P. (1998). An intervention project promoting girls' and boys' interest in physics. In L. Hoffmann, A. Krapp, K. A. Renninger, & J. Baumert (Eds.), *Interest and learning: Proceedings of the Seeon Conference on Interest and Gender* (pp. 301–316). Kiel, Germany: IPN.

Iran-Nejad, A. (1987). Cognitive and affective causes of interest and liking. *Journal of Educational Psychology, 7,* 120–130.

Isaac, J. D., Sansone, C., & Smith, J. L. (1999). Other people as a source of interest in an activity. *Journal of Experimental Social Psychology, 35,* 239–265.

Izard, C. E. (1977). *Human emotions.* New York: Plenum Press.

Izard, C. E., & Ackerman, B. P. (2000). Motivational, organizational, and regulatory functions of discrete emotions. In M. Lewis & J. M. Haviland-Jones (Eds.), *Handbook of emotions* (2nd ed., pp. 253–264). New York: Guilford.

Kaplan, S. (1992). Environmental preference in a knowledge-seeking, knowledge-using organism. In J. H. Barkow, L. Cosmides, & J. Tooby (Eds.), *The adapted mind: Evolutionary psychology and the generation of culture* (pp. 581–598). New York: Oxford University Press.

Kitsantas, A., & Zimmerman, B. J. (2002). Comparing self-regulatory processes among novice, non-expert, and expert volleyball players: A microanalytical study. *Journal of Applied Sport Psychology, 13,* 365–379.

Krapp, A. (2000). Interest and human development during adolescence: An educational-psychological approach. In J. Heckhausen (Ed.), *Motivational psychology of human development* (pp. 109–128). London: Elsevier.

Krapp, A. (2002). Structural and dynamic aspects of interest development. Theoretical considerations from an ontogenetic perspective. *Learning and Instruction, 12,* 383–409.

Krapp, A. (2003). Interest and human development: An educational-psychological perspective. *Development and Motivation* (BJEP Monograph, Series II, 2), 57–84.

Krapp, A. (2005). Basic needs and the development of interest and intrinsic motivational orientations. *Learning and Instruction, 15,* 381–395.

Krapp, A., & Fink, B. (1992). The development and function of interests during the critical transition from home to preschool. In K. A. Renninger, S. Hidi, & A. Krapp (Eds.), *The role of interest in learning and development* (pp. 397–429). Hillsdale, NJ: Erlbaum.

Krapp, A., Hidi, S., & Renninger, K. A. (1992). Interest, learning, and development. In K. A. Renninger, S. Hidi, & A. Krapp (Eds.), *The role of interest in learning and development* (pp. 3–25). Hillsdale, NJ: Erlbaum.

Lipstein, R., & Renninger, K. A. (2006). "Putting things into words": 12–15-year-old students' interest for writing. In P. Boscolo & S. Hidi (Eds.), *Motivation and writing: Research and school practice* (pp. 113–140). Amsterdam: Elsevier.

Long, J. F., & Murphy, P. K. (2005, April). *Connecting through content: The responsiveness of teacher and student interest in a core course.* Paper presented at the meetings of the American Educational Research Association, Montreal, Canada.

McDaniel, M. A., Waddill, P. J., Finstad, K., & Bourg, T. (2000). The effects of text-based interest on attention and recall. *Journal of Educational Psychology, 92,* 492–502.

Meyer, D. K., & Turner, J. C. (2002). Discovering emotion in classroom motivation research. *Educational Psychologist, 37,* 107–114.

Mitchell, M. (1993). Situational interest: Its multifaceted structure in the secondary school mathematics classroom. *Journal of Educational Psychology, 85,* 424–436.

Nolen, S. B. (2001). Constructing literacy in the kindergarten: Task structure, collaboration, and motivation. *Cognition and Instruction, 19,* 95–142.

Nolen, S. B. (2007). The development of motivation to read and write in young children. *Cognition and Instruction.*

Panksepp, J. (1998). *Affective neuroscience: The foundations of human and animal emotion.* New York: Oxford University Press.

Panksepp, J. (2000). Emotions as natural kinds within the mammalian brain. In M. Lewis & J. M. Haviland-Jones (Eds.), *Handbook of emotions* (2nd ed., pp. 137–156). New York: Guilford.

Panksepp, J., & Moskal, J. (2004). Dopamine, pleasure, and appetitive eagerness: An emotional systems overview of the trans-hypothalamic reward system: I. The genesis of additive urges. In S. Bosch (Ed.), *The cognitive, behavioral, and affective neurosciences in psychiatric disorders.*

Pintrich, P. R. (1999). The role of motivation in promoting and sustaining self-regulated learning. *International Journal of Educational Research, 31*, 459–470.

Pintrich, P. R. (2000). The role of goal orientation in self-regulated learning. In M. Boekaerts, P. R. Pintrich, & M. Zeidner (Eds.), *Handbook of self-regulation* (pp. 451–502). San Diego, CA: Academic Press.

Pintrich, P. R. (2004). A conceptual framework for assessing motivation and self-regulated learning in college students. *Educational Psychology Review, 16*, 385–407.

Pintrich, P. R., & Schunk, D. H. (1996). *Motivation in education: Theory, research and applications.* Englewood Cliffs, NJ: Merrill/Prentice Hall.

Pintrich, P. R., & Zusho, A. (2002). The development of academic self-regulation: The role of cognitive and motivational factors. In A. Wigfield & J. S. Eccles (Eds.), *Development of achievement motivation* (pp. 249–284). New York: Academic Press.

Preacher, K. J., & Leonardelli, G. J. (2001, March). Calculation for the Sobel test: An interactive calculation tool for mediation tests [Computer software]. Retrieved on 9/20/2006 from http://www.unc.edu/~preacher/sobel.htm

Renninger, K. A. (1989). Individual differences in children's play interest. In L. T. Winegar (Ed.), *Social interaction and the development of children's understanding* (pp. 147–172). Norwood, NJ: Ablex.

Renninger, K. A. (1990). Children's play interests, representation, and activity. In R. Fivush and K. Hudson (Eds.), *Knowing and remembering in young children* (pp. 127–165). New York: Cambridge University Press.

Renninger, K. A. (2000). Individual interest and its implications for understanding intrinsic motivation. In C. Sansone and J. M. Harackiewicz (Eds.), *Intrinsic and extrinsic motivation: The search for optimal motivation and performance* (pp. 375–407). New York: Academic Press.

Renninger, K. A., & Hidi, S. (2002). Student interest and achievement: Developmental issues raised by a case study. In A. Wigfield & J. S. Eccles (Eds.), *Development of achievement motivation* (pp. 173–195). New York: Academic Press.

Renninger, A., & Leckrone, T. (1991). Continuity in young children's actions: A consideration of interest and temperament. In L. Oppenheimer & J. Valsiner (Eds.), *The origins of action: Interdisciplinary and international perspectives* (pp. 205–238). New York: Springer-Verlag.

Renninger, K. A., & Lipstein, R. (2006). Developing interest for writing: What do students want and what do students need? Special Issue, P. Boscolo (Ed.), *Età Evolutiva, 84*, 65–83.

Renninger, K. A., Ewen, L., & Lasher, A. K. (2002). Individual interest as context in expository text and mathematical word problems. *Learning and Instruction, 12*, 467–491.

Renninger, K. A., Sansone, C., & Smith, J. L. (2004). Love of learning. In C. Peterson & M. E. P. Seligman (Eds.), *Character strengths and virtues: A handbook and classification* (pp. 161–179). Washington, DC: American Psychological Association and New York: Oxford University Press.

Renninger, K. A., & Wozniak, R. H. (1985). Effect of interest on attention shift, recognition, and recall in young children. *Developmental Psychology, 21,* 624–632.

Sansone, C., & Harackiewicz, J. M. (1996). "I don't feel like it": The function of interest in self-regulation. In L. L. Martin & A. Tesser (Eds.), *Striving and feeling: Interactions among goals, affect and self-regulation* (pp. 203–228). Mahwah, NJ: Erlbaum.

Sansone, C., & Smith, J. L. (2000). Interest and self-regulation: The relation between having to and wanting to. In C. Sansone and J. M. Harackiewicz (Eds.), *Intrinsic and extrinsic motivation: The search for optimal motivation and performance* (pp. 341–372). New York: Academic Press.

Sansone, C., & Thoman, D. B. (2005). Interest as the missing motivator in self-regulation. *European Psychologist, 10,* 175–186.

Sansone, C., Weir, C., Harpster, L., & Morgan, C. (1992). Once a boring task always a boring task? Interest as a self-regulatory mechanism. *Journal of Personality and Social Psychology, 63,* 379–390.

Schiefele, U., & Krapp, A. (1996). Topic interest and free recall of expository test. *Learning and Individual Differences, 8,* 141–160.

Schiefele, H., Krapp, A., Prenzel, M., Heiland, A., & Kasten, H. (1983, July–August). *Principles of an educational theory of interest.* Paper presented at the seventh annual meeting of the International Society for the Study of Behavioral Development, Munich, West Germany.

Schraw, G., & Dennison, R. S. (1994). The effect of reader purpose on interest and recall. *Journal of Reading Behavior, 26,* 1–18.

Schraw, G., Flowerday, T., & Lehman, S. (2001). Increasing situational interest in the classroom. *Educational Psychology Review, 13,* 211–224.

Schraw, G., & Lehman, S. (2001). Situational interest: A review of the literature and directions for future research. *Educational Psychology Review, 13,* 23–52.

Schunk, D. H. (1991). Self-efficacy and academic motivation. *Educational Psychologist, 26,* 207–231.

Schunk, D. H. (1994). Self-regulation of self-efficacy and attributions in academic settings. In D. H. Schunk & B. J. Zimmerman (Eds.), *Self-regulation of learning and performance: Issues and educational applications* (pp. 75–99). Hillsdale, NJ: Erlbaum.

Schunk, D. H., & Zimmerman, B. J. (1994). *Self-regulation of learning and performance: Issues and educational applications.* Mahwah, NJ: Erlbaum.

Schunk, D. H., & Zimmerman, B. J. (1997). Social origins of self-regulatory competence. *Educational Psychologist, 32,* 195–208.

Scoble, K. (2005). *Self-efficacy and interest: Their role in an academic writing task.* Unpublished honors thesis, University of Melbourne, Melbourne.

Silvia, P. J. (2001). Interest and interests: The psychology of constructive capriciousness. *Review of General Psychology, 5,* 270–290.

Sloboda, J. A., & Davidson, J. W. (1995). The young performing musician. In I. Deliege & J. A. Sloboda (Eds.), *The origins and development of musical competence* (pp. 171–190). London: Oxford University Press.

Sosniak, L. A. (1990). The tortoise, the hare, and the development of talent. In M. Howe (Ed.), *Encouraging the development of exceptional skills and talents* (pp. 149–164). Leicester, U.K.: British Psychological Society.

Tomkins, S. S. (1962). *Affect, imagery, consciousness: Vol. 1. The positive affects.* New York: Springer.

Zimmerman, B. J. (1989). A social cognitive view of self-regulated academic learning. *Journal of Educational Psychology, 81,* 329–339.

Zimmerman, B. J. (2000a). Attaining self-regulation: A social cognitive perspective. In M. Boekaerts, P. R. Pintrich, & M. Zeidner (Eds.), *Handbook of self-regulation* (pp. 13–39). New York: Academic Press.

Zimmerman, B. J. (2000b). Self-efficacy: An essential motive to learn. *Contemporary Educational Psychology, 25,* 82–91.

Zimmerman, B. J. (2001). Achieving academic excellence: A self-regulatory perspective. In M. Ferrari (Ed.), *Pursuit of excellence* (pp. 85–109). Mahwah, NJ: Erlbaum.

Zimmerman, B. J. (2002). Achieving self-regulation: The trial and triumph of adolescence. In F. Pajares & T. Urdan (Eds.), *Academic motivation of adolescents* (pp. 1–27). Greenwich, CT: Information Age.

Zimmerman, B. J., & Bandura, A. (1994). Impact of self-regulatory influences on writing course attainment. *American Educational Research Journal, 31,* 845–862.

Zimmerman, B. J., & Kitsantas, A. (1997). Developmental phases in self-regulation: Shifting from process to outcome goals. *Journal of Educational Psychology, 8,* 29–36.

Zimmerman, B. J., & Kitsantas, A. (1999). Acquiring writing revision skill: Shifting from process to outcome self-regulatory goals. *Journal of Educational Psychology, 91,* 1–10.

Zimmerman, B. J., & Kitsantas, A. (2006). A writer's discipline: The development of self-regulatory skills. In S. Hidi & P. Boscolo (Eds.), *Motivation and interest in writing* (pp. 51–72). Amsterdam: Elsevier.

Zimmerman, B. J., & Schunk, D. H. (2004). Self-regulating intellectual processes and outcomes: A social cognitive perspective. In D. Y. Dai & R. J. Sternberg (Eds.), *Motivation, emotion, and cognition: Integrative perspectives on intellectual functioning and development* (pp. 323–349). Mahwah, NJ: Erlbaum.

5

Motivational Role of Self-Efficacy Beliefs in Self-Regulated Learning

Frank Pajares

INTRODUCTION

In 1878, philosopher Charles Peirce contended that the sole function of human thought is to produce the beliefs that individuals come to hold about themselves and about their world. These beliefs become rules of action that determine both what people will do and the sub-sequent thoughts that will generate subsequent beliefs. A century later, psychologist Albert Bandura (1977) theorized that the beliefs that people come to hold about their capabilities and about the out-comes of their efforts powerfully influence not only the ways in which they will behave but also the cognitive and affective processes that accompany their functioning. For Bandura, as for the poet Virgil, people who are able are typically those who *believe* they are able.

OVERVIEW OF SOCIAL COGNITIVE THEORY

Soon after taking a position at Stanford University in 1953, Bandura began a program of research in which he focused on the mechanisms that underlie human learning. In 1963, with his doctoral student Richard Walters, Bandura published *Social Learning and Personality Development*, broadening the frontiers of traditional social learning theories with the now-familiar principles of social modeling, observational learning, and vicarious reinforcement. With the publication of

Social Foundations of Thought and Action: A Social Cognitive Theory, Bandura (1986) put forth a cognitive interactional model of human functioning in which cognitive, vicarious, self-regulatory, and self-reflective factors are accorded a central role in the processes of human adaptation and change. Also central to the theory is the concept of *reciprocal determinism*, the view that (a) personal factors in the form of cognition, affect, and biological events, (b) behavior, and (c) environmental influences create interactions that result in a triadic reciprocality. From this perspective, people are viewed as self-organizing, proactive, self-reflecting, and self-regulating rather than as reactive organisms shaped by environmental forces or driven by concealed inner impulses. They are both products and producers of their own environments and of their social systems. For example, how people interpret the results of their own behavior informs and alters their environments and their personal factors, which in turn inform and alter subsequent behavior. Bandura altered the label of his theory from social learning to social "cognitive" both to distance it from prevalent social learning theories of the day and to emphasize that human cognition plays a critical role in people's capability to interpret reality, self-regulate, encode information, and perform behaviors.

Social cognitive theory provides multiple lenses through which to view the manner in which appropriate actions can be undertaken to improve human functioning. In school, for example, teachers can foster the competence of the students in their care by improving their students' emotional states, faulty self-beliefs, or habits of thinking (personal factors) by enhancing their academic skills and self-regulatory practices (behavior) and by altering the social, school, and classroom structures that may work to undermine student success (the environment). Indeed, because of the reciprocal nature of the causes of human functioning, it can be expected that results obtained in one sphere will lead to subsequent changes in another.

Rooted within Bandura's (1986) conception of reciprocal determinism is the understanding that individuals are imbued with the personal factors that define what it is to be human. Primary among these are the capabilities to symbolize, plan alternative strategies (forethought), learn through vicarious experience, self-regulate, and self-reflect. These capabilities provide humans with the cognitive means by which they are influential in determining their own destiny. This is a view of human agency in which individuals are proactively engaged in their own development and can make things happen by their actions. Key to this sense of agency is the fact that individuals possess the self-beliefs that enable them to exercise a measure of control over their thoughts, feelings, and actions, that "what people think, believe, and feel affects how they behave" (Bandura, 1986, p. 25). For this reason, the beliefs that people have about themselves and about their capabilities are critical elements in the exercise of control and personal agency. In 1997, Bandura published *Self-Efficacy: The Exercise of Control*, a landmark volume that situated these self-beliefs within his social cognitive theory.

Self-Efficacy Beliefs

For Bandura (1986), the capability that is most distinctly human is that of *self-reflection* for it is by examining their own thoughts and feelings that people make sense of their experiences, explore their own cognitions and self-beliefs, engage in self-evaluation, and alter their thinking and behavior accordingly. It is also through self-reflection that people make judgments about their capability to accomplish tasks and succeed in the many activities that comprise their lives. These *self-efficacy* beliefs provide the foundation for human motivation, well-being, and personal accomplishment. No matter what other factors may serve as motivators, Bandura (2004) contended, "they are rooted in the core belief that one has the power to effect changes by one's actions" (p. 622). This is because unless people believe that their actions can produce the outcomes they desire, they have little incentive to act or to persevere in the face of difficulties.

Self-efficacy beliefs touch virtually every aspect of people's lives—whether they think productively or self-debilitatingly; how well they motivate themselves and persevere in the face of adversities; their vulnerability to stress and depression; and the life choices they make. People with a strong sense of efficacy approach difficult tasks as challenges to be mastered rather than as threats to be avoided. They have greater intrinsic interest and deep engrossment in activities, and they set themselves challenging goals and maintain strong commitment to them. High self-efficacy also helps create feelings of serenity in approaching difficult tasks and activities. As a consequence, self-efficacy beliefs powerfully influence the level of accomplishment that one ultimately achieves.

It is at this juncture important to extend the caution that self-efficacy should not be confused with *self-concept*, which is a broader evaluation of one's self, often accompanied by the judgments of worth or esteem that typically chaperone such self-views. When individuals tap into these two self-beliefs, they ask themselves quite different types of questions. Self-efficacy beliefs refer to matters related to one's *capability* and revolve around questions of "can" (Can I drive a car? Can I solve this problem?), whereas self-concept beliefs refer to matters related to *being* and reflect questions of "feel" (Do I like myself? How do I feel about myself as a father?). Moreover, one's beliefs about what one can do may bear little relation to how one feels about oneself. Many bright students are able to engage their academic tasks with strong self-efficacy even while their academic skills are a source of low self-esteem, having been labeled by their classmates as nerds or geeks. Alternatively, many academically weak students suffer no loss of self-esteem when such esteem is nourished by achievements on athletic fields or in social arenas.

Self-efficacy beliefs should also not be confused with *outcome expectations*, the judgments of the consequences that a behavior will produce. In fact, efficacy and outcome judgments are sometimes inconsistent. A young man may realize that pleasing social graces and physical attractiveness will be essential for wooing the young lass who has caught his eye, which, in turn, may lead to a romantic interlude. If, however, he has low confidence in his social capabilities and doubts his physical appearance, he will likely shy away from making contact and hence miss a potentially promising opportunity. High self-efficacy and negative outcome expectations are similarly possible. A student highly self-efficacious in her academic capabilities may elect not to apply to a particular university with entrance requirements that discourage all but the hardiest souls. Of course, self-efficacy beliefs help determine the outcomes one expects. Students confident in their social skills anticipate successful social encounters; those confident in their academic skills expect the quality of their work to reap personal and professional benefits. The opposite is true of those who lack confidence. Students who doubt their social skills envision rejection even before they establish social contact; those who lack confidence in their academic skills envision a low grade before they begin an examination.

Since Bandura's (1977) introduction of the construct of self-efficacy, educational researchers have investigated the role that these self-perceptions play in the academic lives of students. Findings have now confirmed that students' academic self-efficacy beliefs powerfully influence their academic attainments independent of possessed knowledge and skills, and that self-efficacy mediates the effect of such knowledge, skills, or other motivational factors on myriad academic outcomes (for reviews of pertinent literature, see Bandura, 1997; Pajares, 1996b, 1997; Schunk & Pajares, 2005).

Sources of Academic Self-Efficacy

As human beings progress from childhood through adolescence and into adulthood, their self-efficacy beliefs are influenced by the people and events that make up their life. Bandura (1986, 1997) hypothesized that these beliefs are developed as one interprets information from four sources, the most powerful of which is the interpreted result of one's own previous attainments, or *mastery experience*. In school, for example, once students complete an academic task, they interpret and evaluate the results obtained, and judgments of competence are created or revised according to those interpretations. When students believe that their efforts have been successful, their confidence to accomplish similar or related tasks is raised; when they believe that their efforts failed to produce the effect desired, confidence to succeed in similar endeavors is diminished. Experienced mastery in a domain often has enduring effects on one's self-efficacy. Students who have earned top marks in science throughout school will likely believe themselves capable in this area for years to come.

The academic success that students experience will certainly influence what they subsequently choose to do and not do, as well as the frame of mind they will bring to these future endeavors. But, it is important to emphasize that people must *interpret* the results of their attainments just as they must make judgments about the quality of the knowledge and skills they possess. Imagine two students who receive a grade of B on an important exam. In and of itself, a B has no inherent meaning and certainly no causal properties. How will receiving such a grade affect a particular youngster? A student accustomed to receiving As on exams in this class and subject and who worked hard and studied for the exam will view the B in ways quite dissimilar from that of a student accustomed to receiving Cs and who worked equally hard. For the former, the B will be received with distress; for the latter, the B is likely to be received with elation. The student accustomed to earning As will have bruised academic confidence; the C-acquainted student is sure to have confidence boosted. As Alfred Schutz (1970) observed, "It is the meaning of our experiences, and not the ontological structure of the objects, which constitutes reality" (p. 230).

In addition to interpreting the results of their actions, students interpret the actions of others, and they alter their efficacy beliefs through the vicarious experience of observing others perform tasks. Observing the successes and failures of peers perceived as similar in capability contributes to beliefs in one's own capabilities ("If he can do it, so can I!"). Although this source of information is usually weaker than is the interpreted result of one's mastery experience, when young people are uncertain about their own abilities or have limited previous experience, they become especially sensitive to it. Vicarious experience also involves the social comparisons that students make with each other. In school, these comparisons take place constantly, and so it is by comparing the results of their own actions with the results obtained by their peers that students create and develop their self-efficacy beliefs. Recall that academic outcomes have little inherent meaning unless they are contextually framed. Until internal standards are developed, the circled "85" obtained on a spelling test acquires meaning only when one becomes aware that most students obtained a lower, or higher, score.

If there is one finding that is incontrovertible in psychology it is that young people learn from the actions of models. Watching classmates solve a challenging mathematics problem, for example, can help other students to believe that they too can solve it. Schunk and his colleagues have shown that *coping models*—those who struggle through problems until they reach a successful end—are more likely to boost the confidence of observers than are *mastery models*—those who respond to mistakes as though they never make them (Schunk, 1983b, 1987; Schunk & Hanson, 1985, 1988). Of course, coping models are especially effective for students who typically have difficulty learning, as competent students may perceive themselves as more similar to mastery models. Modeling can also work to undermine an observer's confidence, particularly when the model fails at a task perceived as easy. Bandura (1997) noted that students seek out models who are competent at tasks to which they aspire—particularly models with status, power, and prestige. Researchers have suggested that models may play a more influential role during such transitional periods as the shift from elementary to middle school (Eccles, Midgley, & Adler, 1984). Television and other media have increased the salience of "symbolic models," who can convey efficacy-relevant information to young people regarding how to approach school, peers, and parents.

Composer and lyricist Stephen Sondheim (1987) cautioned adults to be "careful the things you say. Children will listen." And indeed they do. Self-efficacy beliefs are influenced by the words (and actions) of others, whether these be intentional or accidental. Consequently, the third source of self-efficacy information comes from the verbal messages and social persuasions that people receive. These messages can help one to exert the extra effort and persistence required to succeed, resulting in the continued development of skills and of personal efficacy. Or they can be powerfully disheartening. The verbal and nonverbal messages received from parents, teachers, peers, and significant (or sometimes nonsignificant) others have the power to raise or diminish students' confidence in their academic capabilities.

Persuaders play an important role in the development of a student's self-beliefs because young people depend on others to provide evaluative feedback and judgments about their academic performances, especially when they are not skilled at making accurate self-appraisals. Effective persuaders cultivate students' beliefs in their capabilities while at the same time ensuring that the envisioned success is attainable. And, just as positive persuasions may work to encourage and empower, negative persuasions can work to defeat and weaken self-efficacy beliefs. In fact, it is usually easier to weaken self-efficacy beliefs through negative appraisals than to strengthen such beliefs through positive encouragement. The infamous red pen is likely to weaken self-efficacy beliefs more than will a teacher's positive comments strengthen them.

Physiological and emotional states such as anxiety and stress, along with one's mood, provide information about efficacy beliefs. Typically, optimism and a positive mood enhance self-efficacy, whereas depression, despair, or a sense of despondency diminish it. As with the other sources, it is not the intensity of the physical indicator or mood state itself that is important, but the individual's interpretation of it. Students with strong self-efficacy will view the emotional state as energizing, whereas those beset by self-doubt may regard it as debilitating.

The self-efficacy beliefs that students hold when they approach new tasks and activities serve as a filter through which new information is processed. For example, students with low self-efficacy in mathematics will likely interpret the butterflies that invade their stomachs just before an important math exam as precursors of impending failure. In this case, the self-fulfilling prophecy helps ensure that this interpretation will lead to the very failure feared. Conversely, students confident in their mathematics capability will be impervious to what they interpret as normal "nerves" before an important test and may even find them energizing. Students' emotional states also influence how they interpret the fruits of their labors. A pessimistic attitude can lead students to misconstrue errors as signs of inability, which in turn diminishes their self-efficacy. Engaging a task with a positive outlook and ebullient mood, however, helps ensure that missteps are viewed as temporary setbacks that simply require greater attention and effort.

SELF-EFFICACY AND SELF-REGULATED LEARNING IN ACADEMIC CONTEXTS

Students regulate and manage their academic progress through the process of *self-regulation*, which Zimmerman (2002a) defined as "the self-directive process by which learners transform their mental abilities into academic skills" (p. 65). Self-regulation is a metacognitive process that requires students to explore their thought processes to understand and evaluate the results of their actions and to plan alternative pathways to success. Students must evaluate their behavior if they are to guide subsequent behavior in a process of self-direction and self-reinforcement. This means that self-regulation operates in large part through one's internal standards and is in part informed by evaluative feedback. Successful individuals have a strong self-regulatory repertoire that assists them in staying focused and completing tasks. For example, students who excel in school are able to monitor and regulate their behaviors successfully to accomplish the many tasks required of them. Zimmerman and his colleagues (Zimmerman, 1989, 1990, 1994, 2000, 2002a; Zimmerman,

Bonner, & Kovach, 1996; Zimmerman & Martinez-Pons, 1990) have outlined a number of these practices in school. They include

- Finishing homework assignments by deadlines.
- Studying when there are other interesting things to do.
- Concentrating on school subjects.
- Taking useful class notes of class instruction.
- Using the library for information for class assignments.
- Effectively planning schoolwork.
- Effectively organizing schoolwork.
- Remembering information presented in class and textbooks.
- Arranging a place to study at home without distractions.
- Motivating oneself to do schoolwork.
- Participating in class discussions.

School, of course, is the primary setting in which cognitive capabilities are cultivated and evaluated. It is also the primary setting in which academic self-regulatory skills are developed and maintained, and the use of these skills is intimately connected both with success in school and with the positive self-beliefs that accompany that success. The importance of these self-regulatory skills is that students can use them across tasks, activities, and situations. Effective self-regulatory practices can result in stronger self-efficacy and achievement in various academic areas. Consequently, they are at the heart of improving self-beliefs and school success.

Without the capacity to self-regulate, human beings would "behave like weather vanes, constantly shifting direction to conform to whatever momentary influence happened to impinge upon them" (Bandura, 1996, p. 5515). Students who are incapable of engaging effective self-regulatory practices simply do not know how to self-correct their actions. Although aware of their lack of success, they can neither understand the reasons for their poor performance nor envision the strategies and behavior changes required to alter their fortunes.

Researchers have found that academic self-efficacy beliefs are influential during all phases of self-regulation: forethought, performance, and self-reflection (see Schunk & Ertmer, 2000, for a review; also Zimmerman, 2002a, 2002b). Students who believe they are capable of performing academic tasks use more cognitive and metacognitive strategies, and, regardless of previous achievement or ability, they work harder, persist longer, and persevere in the face of adversity. In one study, children of low, middle, and high mathematics ability but who had, within each ability level, either high or low mathematics self-efficacy were tested on a set of mathematics problems. After receiving the same mathematics instruction, the children were given new problems to solve and an opportunity to rework those they missed. Level of mathematics ability was related to performance, but, regardless of ability level, children with high self-efficacy completed more problems correctly and reworked more of the ones they missed (Collins, 1982).

Students with high self-efficacy also engage in more effective self-regulatory strategies. Confident students monitor their academic work time effectively, persist when confronted with academic challenges, do not reject correct hypotheses prematurely, and solve conceptual problems. And, as students' self-efficacy increases, so does the accuracy of the self-evaluations they make about the outcomes of their self-monitoring (Bouffard-Bouchard, Parent, & Larivée, 1991). In studies of college students who pursue science and engineering courses, high self-efficacy has been demonstrated to influence the academic persistence necessary to maintain high academic achievement (Lent, Brown, & Larkin, 1984). Self-efficacy in mathematics has also been positively related to the strategy of reviewing notes and negatively related to relying on adults for assistance (Zimmerman & Martinez-Pons, 1990).

Pintrich and De Groot (1990) found that academic self-efficacy was related both to cognitive strategy use and to self-regulation through the use of metacognitive strategies. Academic self-efficacy also correlated with academic grades, in-class seat work and homework, test results, and essays and reports. The researchers concluded that self-efficacy played a "facilitative" role in the process of cognitive engagement, that raising self-efficacy might lead to increased use of cognitive strategies and, thereby, higher performance, and that "students need to have both the 'will' and the 'skill' to be successful in classrooms" (p. 38).

Studies tracing the relationship between academic self-efficacy and the self-regulatory strategy of goal setting have demonstrated that self-efficacy and skill development are stronger in students who set proximal goals than in students who set distal goals, in part because proximal attainments provide students with evidence of growing expertise (Bandura & Schunk, 1981, Schunk, 1983a). In addition, students who have been verbally encouraged to set their own goals experience increases in confidence, competence, and commitment to attain those goals (Schunk, 1985). Self-efficacy is also increased when students are provided with frequent and immediate feedback while working on academic tasks (Schunk, 1983b), and when students are taught to attribute this feedback to their own effort, they work harder, experience stronger motivation, and report greater self-efficacy for further learning (Schunk, 1987).

Because self-efficacy beliefs are powerful predictors of motivational and academic practices, Zimmerman and his colleagues have investigated students' confidence that they possess the self-regulated learning strategies required to succeed in school (see Zimmerman & Cleary, 2005). They discovered that this "self-efficacy for self-regulated learning" contributes both to students' motivational beliefs and to the academic success they experience (Zimmerman, 1989, 1994; Zimmerman & Bandura, 1994; Zimmerman & Martinez-Pons, 1990).

Students' self-efficacy beliefs influence their academic motivation through their use of self-regulatory processes such as goal setting, self-monitoring, self-evaluation, and strategy use (Zimmerman, 2000). The more competent that students view themselves, the more challenging goals they select. Zimmerman, Bandura, and Martinez-Pons (1992) demonstrated that students' self-efficacy for self-regulated learning influenced the confidence students had in their academic capabilities and, through that influence, affected the final grades they obtained. Academic self-efficacy influenced achievement directly as well as indirectly by raising students' grade goals. In another study, college students' writing self-efficacy predicted the personal standards they used to judge the quality of the writing they considered self-satisfying as well as their goal setting and writing skill (Zimmerman & Bandura, 1994).

Researchers have also found that students' self-efficacy for self-regulated learning is related to motivation and achievement in academic areas such as language arts, mathematics, and science and for students at all levels of schooling. Students' confidence in their self-regulated learning strategies is positively related to their academic self-concept, self-efficacy, value of school and of particular school subjects, and mastery goal orientations, as well as to myriad academic performances such as essay writing, mathematics problem solving, and science competence. Self-efficacy for self-regulated learning is negatively related with academic and subject-specific anxiety and with performance-avoid goal orientation (Pajares, 1996b; Pajares, Britner, & Valiante, 2000; Pajares & Graham, 1999; Pajares, Miller, & Johnson, 1999; Pajares & Valiante, 1997, 1999, 2001, 2002, 2006).

Researchers have reported that students' academic self-efficacy and motivation can diminish as students progress through school, with the first drop occurring during the middle school years (see Anderman, Maehr, & Midgley, 1999; Jacobs, Lanza, Osgood, Eccles, & Wigfield, 2002). The transition to middle/junior high school often introduces a larger social comparison group, a greater emphasis on grades and competition, and a larger, less-personal environment. Moreover, these environmental changes arrive at a time when young people are undergoing critical developmental changes that may themselves be responsible for the diminishing motivation. Pajares and Valiante (2002) assessed the self-beliefs of 1,257 students in Grades 3 through 11 and found that students' confidence in their self-regulatory learning strategies decreased as students progressed from elementary school to high school. This decrease was even steeper than a similar decrease in students' self-perceptions of their academic competence.

Gender, Self-Efficacy, and Self-Regulated Learning

Gender differences in students' academic self-efficacy and in their self-efficacy to employ self-regulatory strategies are often reported. For example, boys and girls report equal confidence in their mathematics ability during the elementary years, but by middle school, boys begin to rate themselves more efficacious than do girls (Wigfield, Eccles, & Pintrich, 1996). Conversely, in areas related to language arts, male and female students exhibit similar confidence despite the fact that the achievement of female students is typically greater (see Pajares & Valiante, 2006).

When gender differences in the use of, or confidence to use, self-regulated learning strategies have been reported, they typically favor female students. Zimmerman and Martinez-Pons (1990) interviewed students in Grades 5, 8, and 11 to discover whether gender differences could be detected in their use of 14 strategies. Girls displayed more goal-setting and planning strategies, and they kept records and self-monitored more frequently. Girls also surpassed boys in the ability to structure their environment for optimal learning. Pokay and Blumenfeld (1990) investigated the use of self-regulated learning strategies by high school students in geometry and found that, as the semester began, girls reported using more metacognitive, general cognitive, and specific geometry strategies than did boys. Girls also reported stronger effort management. At semester's end, girls continued to report stronger cognitive strategy use.

It is possible, of course, that boys and girls show differences in self-efficacy and self-regulation as a result of factors unrelated to these variables. For example, many gender differences in academic self-beliefs disappear when previous achievement is controlled (Pajares, 1996a). In other words, when researchers analyze the self-beliefs of students at the same level of academic competence, fewer differences in self-belief emerge. Another factor that may be responsible for gender differences is the tendency of boys to be more "self-congratulatory" in their responses and of girls to be more modest (Wigfield et al., 1996). That is, boys are more likely to express confidence in skills they may not possess and to express overconfidence in skills they do possess. Noddings (1996) suggested that boys and girls may use a different metric when providing confidence judgments, adding that these sorts of ratings may represent more of a promise to girls than they do to boys. If this is the case, then actual differences in confidence are masked or accentuated by such response biases.

A third factor potentially at play in creating differences between boys and girls has to do with the manner in which gender differences in self-efficacy and self-regulation beliefs are typically assessed. Traditionally, students are asked to provide judgments of their confidence that they possess certain academic skills or, in the case of self-efficacy for self-regulation, that they can engage specific self-regulatory strategies. Differences in the average level of confidence reported are interpreted as gender differences in self-efficacy. Pajares and his colleagues (Pajares et al., 1999; Pajares & Valiante, 1999) asked elementary and middle school students not only to provide self-efficacy judgments in the traditional manner but also to compare their academic ability versus that of other boys and girls. Although girls outperformed boys in language arts, girls and boys reported equal writing self-efficacy and self-efficacy for self-regulation. When students were asked whether they were better writers than their peers, however, girls expressed that they were better writers than were the boys in their class and even in their school. That is, regardless of the ratings that boys and girls provided on the self-efficacy measures, it was clear that girls considered themselves better writers than the boys.

A fourth factor that may be responsible for gender differences in academic and self-regulatory self-efficacy deals with the nature of the self-belief that may be undergirding those differences. Researchers have found that some gender differences in social, personality, and academic variables may be a function of *gender orientation*—the stereotypic beliefs about gender that students hold—rather than of gender (see Eisenberg, Martin, & Fabes, 1996). Eccles's (1987) model of educational and occupational choice postulates that cultural milieu factors such as students' gender role stereotypes are partly responsible for differences in course and career selection and in confidence beliefs and perceived value of tasks and activities. To determine the degree to which gender differences in self-efficacy may be a function of gender stereotypic beliefs rather than of gender, Pajares and Valiante (2001) asked students to report how strongly they identified with characteristics stereotypically associated with males or females in American society. A feminine orientation was associated with writing self-efficacy and rendered nonsignificant gender differences favoring girls in self-efficacy for self-regulation. These results suggest that some gender differences in academic motivation and in self-regulated learning may in part be accounted for by differences in the beliefs that students hold about their gender rather than by their gender per se.

Education can influence gender differences in a number of ways. In the area of mathematics, for example, differences can arise simply as a result of the context in which mathematical tasks and activities are placed. Girls typically judge their self-efficacy lower than do boys for occupations requiring quantitative skills, but differences disappear when self-efficacy judgments for the quantitative activities are made on stereotypically feminine tasks (Junge & Dretzke, 1995). Well-intentioned teachers may also hold different expectations for boys and girls. In some cases, elementary school teachers—most of whom are women—and well-meaning parents may convey to girls that mathematics may be difficult for them. School counselors also may discourage girls from pursuing scientific or technical occupations (Betz & Fitzgerald, 1987).

IMPLICATIONS FOR PRACTICE

The evidence so far presented supports three conclusions. First, as Bandura (1986) theorized, students' self-efficacy beliefs strongly influence their academic motivation, the self-regulated learning strategies they use in school, and the academic success they ultimately attain. Second, academic and self-regulatory self-efficacy beliefs may diminish for many students as they progress through school, a decrease that tends to begin as students enter middle school. Third, gender differences are often found in students' academic self-efficacy and in their self-efficacy to employ self-regulatory strategies, although these differences may be the function of factors such as previous achievement, exposure to course content, response biases, measurement practices, or gender orientation beliefs.

What, then, are the implications that these findings hold for teachers, parents, and other school practitioners? How can teachers and parents help motivate students to self-regulate? What can schools do to buttress appropriate self-efficacy beliefs and help ensure that students effectively engage self-regulatory practices?

Zimmerman et al. (1996) provided a cyclic model of self-regulatory training in which students call on four interrelated processes as they consider and engage an academic task. First, students examine their potential effectiveness to complete the task successfully by assessing and evaluating the results of previous performances on related tasks and domains. Second, they set learning goals and plan appropriate self-regulatory strategies that will aid them in completing the task. Third, they implement the strategies selected and monitor the effectiveness of these strategies. Finally, they monitor their performance on the task to again examine their potential effectiveness to conquer subsequent tasks. At this point, students reinitiate the cycle as they contemplate a new task.

Central to this cyclic process are students' assessments of their own self-efficacy beliefs. Such assessments have a number of benefits. First, of course, if students are to accurately judge their capability to complete a task successfully, they must proactively make judgments of this capability, which is to say that they must assess their own self-efficacy beliefs about the task and in the domain under consideration. Indeed, "by rating their self-efficacy, students become more finely attuned to the role that judgments of capability can play in guiding their efforts" (Zimmerman et al., 1996, p. 63). It is for this reason that self-efficacy researchers encourage teachers to introduce the concept of self-efficacy to their students and teach them how to calculate it. Such a judgment requires focusing attention on the beliefs that accompany the learning methods that students employ and the strategies they use to maximize their learning.

Adaptive self-efficacy beliefs are essential to engaging, and when necessary altering or adjusting, the self-regulatory behaviors required to master the material at hand. After all, when students do not believe that they possess the capability to master such material, they are unlikely to invest the time and effort in setting the goals and planning the strategies required to succeed. Conversely, confident students may address especially challenging material by investing more time or adjusting their self-evaluative standards. Thus, belief in one's capability is essential to engaging the self-regulatory processes that aid in the effective execution of academic tasks.

There are numerous ways to maximize students' self-efficacy beliefs to help motivate them to engage the self-regulatory practices that will foster learning and achievement (see Pajares, 2005). One lens through which to examine these ways is to think about the sources students use to inform their self-efficacy beliefs. Recall that Bandura (1986, 1997) posited four such sources: mastery experience, vicarious experience, social persuasions, and physiological indexes. Regarding mastery experience, it is important to keep in mind that the impact that such experiences have on self-efficacy beliefs depends on what a student makes of the experiences themselves (Bandura, 1997). For this reason, teachers should help ensure that success experiences are neither forgotten nor minimized. Writing assignments that ask students to reflect on their academic successes, as well as the strategies they used to achieve them, help students maintain a focus on their previous mastery experiences. Daily or weekly journals that include these reflections not only serve as regular reminders that success is attainable but also help keep track of the self-regulatory strategies that students come to associate with their success. These might include the effort they put forth, the resources they used, the time they allocated to the task, and the goals they set. In this day of inexpensive digital and video cameras, another effective way of reminding students of their successful accomplishments is to record them while engaging in the activities. Simply revisiting those images can give students the mental fuel they need to overcome a tough patch.

The fact that previous mastery experiences are the most influential source of self-efficacy information speaks directly to the self-enhancement model of academic achievement that contends that, to increase student achievement in school, educational efforts should focus on enhancing students' self-conceptions. Traditional efforts to accomplish this have included programs that emphasize building self-esteem through praise or self-persuasion methods. Social cognitive theorists shift the emphasis from self-enhancement to skill development—to raising competence through genuine success experiences with the performance at hand, through *authentic* mastery experiences. Students' self-efficacy beliefs develop primarily through actual success on challenging academic tasks. As Bandura (1997) has written,

> let us not confuse ourselves by failing to recognize that there are two kinds of self-confidence, one a trait of personality and another that comes from knowledge of a subject. It is no particular credit to the educator to help build the first without building the second. The objective of education is not the production of self-confident fools. (p. 65)

It is always important to keep in mind Shel Silverstein's (1974) poetic caution that "if the track is tough and the hill is rough, thinking you can just ain't enough" (p. 158).

A second source of self-efficacy information lies in the vicarious experience of observing others. As noted, children learn much from models, and different modeling practices can differently affect students' self-beliefs. Consequently, it is critical that teachers engage in effective modeling practices. *Coping models*—those who good-naturedly admit their errors when they make them or when their students point them out ("Oops, I was a little careless there. Thanks for pointing that out.")—help their students understand that missteps are inevitable, that they can be overcome, and that even authority figures can make them. Conversely, *mastery models*—those who have their authority and ego tied up into their infallibility—respond to errors in a manner that shows they are incapable of making them ("I was just checking to see if you were paying attention."). Such teaching models run the risk of imbuing in their students the idea that making errors is unacceptable and just plain dumb.

Effective models convey not only the success experience itself but also the information required to succeed. Successful models reveal the strategies they use, provide appropriate detail, clarify complex issues, and instruct. Successful models take the time required to explain how to achieve success. Famed educator John Holt (1970) was fond of telling the story of the day he walked in on his 5-year-old niece happily playing with blocks. Attentive uncle that he was, he sat with her and began playing as well. Soon, he had constructed a rather magnificent castle with the multicolored blocks. His niece stared at the wonderful edifice, looked at her uncle, got up, knocked the blocks down in frustration, and stormed off into her bedroom. She never played with the blocks again.

Because one's peers also become models, effective teachers exercise care in academic grouping practices. Students who model excellence can imbue other students with the belief that they also can achieve that excellence. It is important to select peers for classroom models judiciously to ensure that students view themselves as comparable in learning ability to the models. For example, when peer models make errors, engage in coping behaviors in front of students, and verbalize emotive statements reflecting low confidence and achievement, low-achieving students perceive the models as more similar to themselves and experience greater achievement and self-efficacy. To help bring about this recognition, teachers can instruct students in "talk-aloud" techniques that are carried out during group activities.

Of course, comparisons with peer models can be exercises in inefficacy, and teachers have the added responsibility of ensuring that students do not artificially lower their sense of efficacy by way of these comparisons. When teachers create classroom structures that are individualized and tailor instruction to students' academic capabilities, social comparisons are minimized, and students are more likely to gauge their academic progress according to their own standards rather than compare it to the progress of their classmates. To some degree, students will inevitably evaluate themselves in relation to their classmates regardless of what a school or teacher does to minimize or counter these comparisons. However, in cooperative and individualized learning settings, students can more easily select the peer models with whom to compare themselves. Individualized structures that lower the competitive orientation of a classroom and school are more likely than traditional, competitive structures to increase students' self-efficacy beliefs.

Although mastery experience is usually the most powerful source of self-efficacy, students are also attentive, and often quite vulnerable, to the social persuasions they receive from others. As children strive to exercise control over their surroundings, their first transactions are mediated by adults who can either empower them with self-assurance or diminish their fledgling self-beliefs. Young children are not proficient at making accurate self-appraisals, so they must rely on the judgments of others to create their own judgments of confidence and of self-value. In 1902, Cooley used the metaphor of the "looking-glass self" to illustrate the idea that children's sense of self is formed as a result of their perceptions of how others see them. That is, the appraisals of others act as mirror reflections that provide the information children use to define their own sense of self.

Famed educator Maria Montessori (1966) wisely counseled that, "since children are so eager to learn and so burning with love, an adult should carefully weigh all the words he speaks before them" (p. 104). The verbal and nonverbal judgments of others can play a critical role in the development of a young person's self-confidence, and these judgments often become the self-talk that students repeat covertly further down the road. Successful persuaders cultivate young people's beliefs in their capabilities while ensuring that the envisioned success is attainable. Positive persuasions encourage and empower; negative persuasions defeat and weaken self-beliefs. Such persuasions should be genuine, should offer specific information about what was praiseworthy, and should provide avenues for continued improvement. Imagine, for example, that a teacher wishes to praise Vera for her excellent answer to a question posed during class discussion. Compare the typical, general, and nondescript, "That's an excellent response, Vera" (after which the teacher usually moves on to the next issue, saying something like, "Who else can tell me ... ?), with the more specific and useful, "An excellent response, Vera, you recalled that the author wrote that poem after making a difficult and unexpected decision, and you made a great connection between taking an unfamiliar road and making the less likely choice. Continue to connect events in the lives of authors with the stories they are telling us." Clearly, effective praise takes longer to provide, which is precisely why it should be judiciously dispensed.

Effective persuasions should not be confused with knee-jerk praise or empty inspirational homilies. Praise and encouragement should be delivered honestly and in their proper measure when they are deserved. It is of course important that young people feel positively about themselves and about their capabilities, and teachers and parents play a critical role in nurturing these positive self-beliefs. But heed carefully Erik Erikson's (1959/1980) caution that young people "cannot be fooled by empty praise and condescending encouragement. Their identity gains real strength only from wholehearted and consistent recognition of real accomplishment ... a strong ego does not need, and in fact is immune to, any attempt at artificial inflation" (p. 95). Praising a young person for a job well done is an important way of showing encouragement and support. Providing praise when it is undeserved, however, is dishonest and manipulative, not to mention counterproductive. When capable students accomplish competent work with minimal effort, knee-jerk praise sends the peculiar message that putting forth minimal effort is praiseworthy. Self-efficacy is unaffected when praise is perceived as undeserved, and adults who provide such praise soon lose credibility. Moreover, in such situations the student is clearly underchallenged, and teachers and parents are better served by raising standards and expectations and challenging the young person to meet these expectations.

As teachers and parents hone their persuasive skills, they do well to foster in young people the belief that competence or *ability* is a changeable, controllable aspect of development. This means that they should encourage effort, perseverance, and persistence as ways to overcome obstacles. Praising with statements such as "You are so smart!" or "How bright you are!" can often have the opposite effect intended. Praising for "smarts" tells young people that success is a matter of intellectual ability (which one either has or does not have). How can young people develop confidence in an ability they believe is beyond their control? Praising for effort tells students that the harder the students work the more they will accomplish and the smarter they will get. Whether at home or at school, rather than praising for ability, it is wise practice to praise the genuine effort and persistence a student puts forth.

But let us emphasize that this should not be understood to mean that adults should not be attentive to a young person's capabilities, skills, talents, and gifts. After all, the simple statement "I believe you can do this" conveys confidence in the very capabilities and skills required to accomplish the task successfully. Telling young people that we believe they "can do this" expresses both our belief that they will put forth the effort required to do it and our honest assessment that they have the capability to accomplish the task. If we believe that either is lacking, we have no business providing such empty (and dishonest) encouragement. Our efforts as persuaders should never be guided by impression management. Rather, they should be guided by the desire to provide authentic and encouraging feedback founded on our honest appraisal of the matter at hand. In fact, evaluative feedback that highlights a young person's capabilities helps raise self-efficacy in powerful ways.

A fourth source of self-efficacy beliefs lies in the physiological indexes that students experience as they attend to tasks and activities, and this source also provides insights about how to foster and nurture self-efficacy beliefs. Students appraise their self-efficacy in part by the emotional feelings they experience as they contemplate an action. Teachers can help students read their own emotional feelings and teach them that, if they find themselves experiencing undue anxiety when faced with a task, this is an appropriate time to discuss their feelings with a teacher, parent, or counselor. Students can also be asked to reflect on the anxieties they feel when writing in their journals. Also, when students fear failure, they can engage in all sorts of self-handicapping strategies to avoid feeling the anxiety that accompanies this fear. For example, they may put forth little or no effort on a task in which they have little confidence of success. When one puts forth minimal effort and fails, it hurts less when one explains the failure by claiming that "I didn't do well because I didn't try. I could do well if I wanted to. I just don't want to." Other self-handicapping strategies include self-deprecating talk, deliberate procrastination, setting goals so high and unattainable that failure can be self-viewed as "failing with honor," and setting goals so easy that one cannot fail. Making students aware of the self-handicapping strategies they regularly use to decrease anxiety is a critical first step in teaching them how to circumvent such strategies.

Self-efficacy beliefs can differ as a function of gender, sometimes to the detriment of girls in some areas of mathematics, science, and technology and other times to the detriment of boys in some areas of language arts. But, social cognitive theory does not endow gender with motivating properties. Rather, environmental and personal factors other than gender are posited to be at work in creating motivational and self-regulatory differences in individuals. Researchers have also observed that areas such as mathematics, science, and technology are typically viewed by students as male domains (see Eisenberg et al., 1996). In these areas, a masculine orientation is associated with confidence and achievement because masculine self-perceptions are imbued with the notion that success in these areas is a masculine imperative. Conversely, language arts is typically viewed by students, particularly young students, as a female domain (Eccles, 1987). As a consequence, a feminine orientation is associated with motivational beliefs related to success in skills such as writing or poetry. One challenge before educators is to alter students' views of academic subjects so that they are perceived as relevant and valuable both to girls and to boys. A challenge for all educators, and for the broader culture, is to continue to expound and model gender self-beliefs that encompass both the feminine expressiveness and the masculine instrumentality that are critical to a balanced self-view.

There are a number of strategies that teachers can use to help alter stereotypical gender views of academic subjects and careers. One oft-used and effective strategy is to arrange for professional men and women to speak to students about academic fields and careers. For example, successful female computer programmers, mathematicians, doctors, physicists, architects and engineers, sports announcers, and industry leaders serve as wonderful models that help girls and young women appreciate that success in these fields is not a masculine imperative. Similarly, male nurses, social workers, kindergarten and elementary school teachers, poets, and executive secretaries can broaden the horizons of boys and young men who might otherwise view these domains as not appropriate for them. Language arts teachers can help break down stereotypes by judiciously selecting books and short stories in which feminine expressiveness and masculine instrumentality are portrayed as valuable qualities that all individuals can and should possess. In group activities, teachers can assign stereotypically masculine tasks and activities to girls and vice versa.

Few educational sights are sadder than seeing capable students who have come to believe that they cannot learn. Students who lack confidence in skills they possess are less likely to engage the self-regulatory strategies required to succeed or to select subsequent tasks in which those skills are required, and they will more quickly give up in the face of difficulty. Researchers have also demonstrated that self-efficacy beliefs influence the choice of majors and career decisions of college students (Hackett, 1995). In some cases, underestimation of capability, not lack of competence or skill, is responsible for avoidance of math-related courses and careers, and this is more likely to be the case with women than with men. Zimmerman and Martinez-Pons (1990) expressed concern regarding situations in which girls display greater self-regulated learning strategies but express lower confidence in their academic capabilities than do boys. Efforts to identify and alter students' inaccurate judgments, in addition to continued skill improvement, are an educational imperative.

Gender differences in self-efficacy can be minimized or eliminated when students derive clear performance information about their capabilities or progress in learning. Schunk and Lilly (1984) had middle school students judge their self-efficacy for learning a novel mathematical task, after which they received instruction and opportunities to practice the task. Students received feedback by checking answers to alternate problems. Although girls initially judged their self-efficacy lower than did boys, following instruction girls and boys did not differ in achievement or self-efficacy. The feedback conveyed to students that they were learning and raised girls' self-efficacy to that of boys.

Zeldin and Pajares (2000) explored the personal stories of women who excelled at careers in areas of mathematics, science, and technology to better understand the ways in which their self-efficacy beliefs influenced their academic and career choices. They found that the messages the women received from significant others in their lives, as well as the vicarious experiences they underwent, nourished the self-efficacy beliefs of girls and women as they set out to meet the challenges required to succeed in male-dominated academic domains. Findings suggested that girls develop higher self-efficacy beliefs and engage more self-regulatory strategies in homes and classrooms in which parents and teachers stress the importance and value of academic skills, encourage girls to persist and persevere in the face of academic and social obstacles, and break down stereotypical conceptions regarding academic domains. Parents and teachers should also convey the message that academic success is a matter of desire, effort, and commitment rather than of gender or established social structure. They should also provide models that validate that message. All who would seek to be caring agents in the lives of young women should be especially reflective and proactive in this regard, especially because individuals often convey stereotypical and maladaptive messages to girls in unintentional but subtle ways.

CONCLUSION

Many psychologists contend that individuals perform the bulk of their actions on autopilot, as it were, making use of "automatic self-regulation" (Bargh & Chartrand, 1999). That is, the self-regulatory processes that individuals use to make most of their decisions soon become habitual and are exercised primarily unconsciously. Self-efficacy beliefs and self-regulatory strategies soon become habits of thought and action that are developed like any habit of conduct, and thus they too tend to become automatic mental processes. What this means is that people are, in later life, slaves to the self-regulatory practices and self-beliefs that they obtained during their youth. These mental habits exert a powerful influence on the choices that people make and on the success or failure they experience. For William James (1899/1958), the critical challenge that parents and educators face is making children's effective academic and self-regulatory beliefs and practices automatic and habitual as early as possible. According to James, when sound self-regulatory practices are handed over to "the effortless custody of automatism," higher powers of mind can be freed to engage other tasks. This is not, of course, to suggest that students should be encouraged to engage their academic tasks in rote ways that minimize active cognition and ongoing reflection. Indeed, experts often try to avoid automatic self-regulation during practice because proactively self-monitoring one's cognitions and outcomes is essential to improving the effectiveness of self-regulatory processes such as goal setting and strategy use (Ericsson, 1996).

Teachers do well to take seriously their share of responsibility in nurturing the mental habits of their pupils, for it is clear that these habits can have beneficial or destructive influences. Teachers who provide children with challenging tasks and meaningful activities that can be mastered, and who chaperone these efforts with support and encouragement, help ensure that their students will develop the robust sense of self-efficacy required to rely on their own initiative and engage the world on their own. Researchers have long known that the earlier a belief is incorporated into a belief system, the more difficult it is to alter (Pajares, 1992). Newly acquired beliefs are most vulnerable to change. In fact, people tend to hold on to beliefs based on incorrect or incomplete knowledge, even after correct explanations are presented to them. This is true also of self-efficacy beliefs and of regulatory strategies. Those that are developed early persevere and self-perpetuate. For these reasons, educators face the critical challenge of making their students' positive self-beliefs and self-regulatory strategies automatic and habitual as early as possible, and teachers are influential in helping students to develop the self-belief and self-regulatory habits that will serve them for a lifetime.

REFERENCES

Anderman, E. M., Maehr, M. L., & Midgley, C. (1999). Declining motivation after the transition to middle school: Schools can make a difference. *Journal of Research and Development in Education, 32,* 131–147.

Bandura, A. (1977). Self-efficacy: Toward a unifying theory of behavioral change. *Psychological Review, 84,* 191–215.

Bandura, A. (1986). *Social foundations of thought and action: A social cognitive theory.* Englewood Cliffs, NJ: Prentice Hall.

Bandura, A. (1996). Social cognitive theory of human development. In T. Husen & T. N. Postlethwaite (Eds.), *International encyclopedia of education* (2nd ed., pp. 5513–5518). Oxford, U.K.: Pergamon Press.

Bandura, A. (1997). *Self-efficacy: The exercise of control.* New York: Freeman.

Bandura, A. (2004). Swimming against the mainstream: The early years from chilly tributary to transformative mainstream. *Behaviour Research and Therapy, 42,* 613–630.

Bandura, A., & Schunk, D. H. (1981). Cultivating competence, self-efficacy, and intrinsic interest through proximal self-motivation. *Journal of Personality and Social Psychology, 41,* 586–598.

Bandura, A., & Walters, R. H. (1963). *Social learning and personality development.* New York: Rinehart and Winston.

Bargh, J. A., & Chartrand, T. L. (1999). The unbearable automaticity of being. *American Psychologist, 4,* 462–479.

Betz, N. E., & Fitzgerald, L. F. (1987). *The career psychology of women.* Orlando, FL: Academic Press.

Bouffard-Bouchard, T., Parent, S., & Larivée, S. (1991). Influence of self-efficacy on self-regulation and performance among junior and senior high-school aged students. *International Journal of Behavioral Development, 14,* 153–164.

Collins, J. L. (1982, March). *Self-efficacy and ability in achievement behavior.* Paper presented at the meeting of the American Educational Research Association, New York.

Cooley, C. H. (1902). *Human nature and the social order.* New York: Scribner.

Eccles, J. S. (1987). Gender roles and women's achievement-related decisions. *Psychology of Women Quarterly, 11,* 135–172.

Eccles, J. S., Midgley, C., & Adler, T. (1984). Grade-related changes in the school environment: Effects on achievement motivation. In J. Nicholls (Ed.), *Advances in motivation and achievement: The development of achievement motivation* (Vol. 3, pp. 283–331). Greenwich, CT: JAI Press.

Eisenberg, N., Martin, C. L., & Fabes, R. A. (1996). Gender development and gender effects. In D. C. Berliner & R. C. Calfee (Eds.), *Handbook of educational psychology* (pp. 358–396). New York: Simon and Schuster Macmillan.

Ericsson, K. A. (1996). The acquisition of expert performance: An introduction to some of the issues. In K. A. Ericsson (Ed.), *The road to excellence* (pp. 1–50). Hillsdale, NJ: Erlbaum.

Erikson, E. (1980). *Identity and the life cycle.* New York: Norton. (Original work published 1959)

Hackett, G. (1995). Self-efficacy in career choice and development. In A. Bandura (Ed.), *Self-efficacy in changing societies* (pp. 232–258). New York: Cambridge University Press.

Holt, J. (1970). *What do I do on Monday?* New York: Dutton.

Jacobs, J. E., Lanza, S., Osgood, W., Eccles, J. S., & Wigfield, A. (2002). Changes in children's self-competence and values: Gender and domain differences across grades 1 through 12. *Child Development, 73,* 509–527.

James, W. (1958). *Talks to teachers.* New York: Norton. (Original work published 1899)

Junge, M. E., & Dretzke, B. J. (1995). Mathematical self-efficacy gender differences in gifted/talented adolescents. *Gifted Child Quarterly, 39,* 22–26.

Lent, R. W., Brown, S. D., & Larkin, K. C. (1984). Relation of self-efficacy expectations to academic achievement and persistence. *Journal of Counseling Psychology, 31,* 356–362.

Montessori, M. (1966). *The secret of childhood.* New York: Ballantine Books.

Noddings, N. (1996, April). *Current directions in self research: Self-concept, self-efficacy, and possible selves.* Symposium presented at the meeting of the American Educational Research Association, New York.

Pajares, F. (1992). Teachers' beliefs and educational research: Cleaning up a messy construct. *Review of Educational Research, 62,* 307–332.

Pajares, F. (1996a). Role of self-efficacy beliefs in the mathematical problem-solving of gifted students. *Contemporary Educational Psychology, 21,* 325–344.

Pajares, F. (1996b). Self-efficacy beliefs in academic settings. *Review of Educational Research, 66,* 543–578.

Pajares, F. (1997). Current directions in self-efficacy research. In M. Maehr & P. R. Pintrich (Eds.), *Advances in motivation and achievement.* (Vol. 10, pp. 1–49). Greenwich, CT: JAI Press.

Pajares, F. (2005). Self-efficacy beliefs during adolescence: Implications for teachers and parents. In F. Pajares & T. Urdan (Eds.), *Adolescence and education. Vol. 5: Self-efficacy beliefs of adolescents* (pp. 339–367). Greenwich, CT: Information Age.

Pajares, F., Britner, S. L., & Valiante, G. (2000). Relation between achievement goals and self-beliefs of middle school students in writing and science. *Contemporary Educational Psychology, 25,* 406–422.

Pajares, F., & Graham, L. (1999). Self-efficacy, motivation constructs, and mathematics performance of entering middle school students. *Contemporary Educational Psychology, 24,* 124–139.

Pajares, F., Miller, M. D., & Johnson, M. J. (1999). Gender differences in writing self-beliefs of elementary school students. *Journal of Educational Psychology, 91,* 50–61.

Pajares, F., & Valiante, G. (1997). Influence of self-efficacy on elementary students' writing. *Journal of Educational Research, 90,* 353–360.

Pajares, F., & Valiante, G. (1999). Grade level and gender differences in the writing self-beliefs of middle school students. *Contemporary Educational Psychology, 24,* 390–405.

Pajares, F., & Valiante, G. (2001). Gender differences in writing motivation and achievement of middle school students: A function of gender orientation? *Contemporary Educational Psychology, 26,* 366–381.

Pajares, F., & Valiante, G. (2002). Students' self-efficacy in their self-regulated learning strategies: A developmental perspective. *Psychologia, 45,* 211–221.

Pajares, F., & Valiante, G. (2006). Self-efficacy beliefs and motivation in writing development. In C. A. MacArthur, S. Graham, & J. Fitzgerald (Eds.), *Handbook of writing research* (pp. 158–170). New York: Guilford Press.

Peirce, C. (1878). How to make our ideas clear. *Popular Science Monthly, 12,* 286–302.

Pintrich, P. R., & De Groot, E. V. (1990). Motivational and self-regulated learning components of classroom academic performance. *Journal of Educational Psychology, 82,* 33–40.

Pokay, P., & Blumenfeld, P. C. (1990). Predicting achievement early and late in the semester: The role of motivation and use of learning strategies. *Journal of Educational Psychology, 82,* 41–50.

Schunk, D. H. (1983a). Developing children's self-efficacy and skills: The roles of social comparative information and goal setting. *Contemporary Educational Psychology, 8,* 76–86.

Schunk, D. H. (1983b). Reward contingencies and the development of children's skills and self-efficacy. *Journal of Educational Psychology, 75,* 511–518.

Schunk, D. H. (1985). Self-efficacy and classroom learning. *Psychology in the Schools, 22,* 208–223.

Schunk, D. H. (1987). Peer models and children's behavioral change. *Review of Educational Research, 57,* 149–174.

Schunk, D. H., & Ertmer, P. A. (2000). Self-efficacy and academic learning: Self-efficacy enhancing interventions. In M. Boekaerts, P. R. Pintrich, & M. Zeidner (Eds.), *Handbook of self-regulation* (pp. 631–650). San Diego, CA: Academic Press.

Schunk, D. H., & Hanson, A. R. (1985). Peer models: Influence on children's self-efficacy and achievement. *Journal of Educational Psychology, 77,* 313–322.

Schunk, D. H., & Hanson, A. R. (1988). Influence of peer-model attributes on children's beliefs and learning. *Journal of Educational Psychology, 81,* 431–434.

Schunk, D. H., & Lilly, M. W. (1984). Sex differences in self-efficacy and attributions: Influence of performance feedback. *Journal of Early Adolescence, 4,* 203–213.

Schunk, D. H., & Pajares, F. (2005). Competence beliefs in academic functioning. In A. J. Elliot & C. Dweck (Eds.), *Handbook of competence and motivation* (pp. 85–104). New York: Guilford Press.

Schutz, A. (1970). *On phenomenology and social relations.* Chicago: University of Chicago Press.

Silverstein, S. (1974). *Where the sidewalk ends.* New York: HarperCollins.

Sondheim, S. (1987). *Into the woods: 1987 original Broadway cast* [CD]. New York: RCA Victor.

Wigfield, A., Eccles, J. S., & Pintrich, P. R. (1996). Development between the ages of 11 and 25. In D. C. Berliner & R. C. Calfee (Eds.), *Handbook of educational psychology* (pp. 148–185). New York: Simon and Schuster Macmillan.

Zeldin, A. L., & Pajares, F. (2000). Against the odds: Self-efficacy beliefs of women in mathematical, scientific, and technological careers. *American Educational Research Journal, 37,* 215–246.

Zimmerman, B. J. (1989). A social cognitive view of self-regulated academic learning. *Journal of Educational Psychology, 81,* 329–339.

Zimmerman, B. J. (1990). Self-regulating academic learning and achievement: The emergence of a social cognitive perspective. *Educational Psychology Review, 2,* 173–201.

Zimmerman, B. J. (1994). Dimensions of academic self-regulation: A conceptual framework for education. In D. H. Schunk & B. J. Zimmerman (Eds.), *Self-regulation of learning and performances: Issues and educational implications* (pp. 3–21). Hillsdale, NJ: Erlbaum.

Zimmerman, B. J. (2000). Attaining self-regulation: A social cognitive perspective. In M. Boekaerts, P. R. Pintrich, & M. Zeidner (Eds.), *Handbook of self-regulation* (pp. 13–39). San Diego, CA: Academic Press.

Zimmerman, B. J. (2002a). Achieving self-regulation: The trial and triumph of adolescence. In F. Pajares & T. C. Urdan (Eds.), *Adolescence and education* (Vol. 2, pp. 1–28). Greenwich, CT: Information Age.

Zimmerman, B. J. (2002b). Becoming a self-regulated learner: An overview. *Theory Into Practice, 41,* 64–70.

Zimmerman, B. J., & Bandura, A. (1994). Impact of self-regulatory influences on writing course attainment. *American Educational Research Journal, 31,* 845–862.

Zimmerman, B. J., Bandura, A., & Martinez-Pons, M. (1992). Self-motivation for academic attainment: The role of self-efficacy beliefs and personal goal setting. *American Educational Research Journal, 29,* 663–676.

Zimmerman, B. J., Bonner, S., & Kovach, R. (1996). *Developing self-regulated learners: Beyond achievement to self-efficacy.* Washington, DC: American Psychological Association.

Zimmerman, B. J., & Martinez-Pons, M. (1990). Student differences in self-regulated learning: Relating grade, sex, and giftedness to self-efficacy and strategy use. *Journal of Educational Psychology, 82,* 51–59.

Zimmerman, B. J., & Cleary, T. J. (2005). Adolescents' development of personal agency: The role of self-efficacy beliefs and self-regulatory skill. In F. Pajares & T. Urdan (Eds.), *Adolescence and education. Vol. 5: Self-efficacy beliefs of adolescents* (pp. 339–367). Greenwich, CT: Information Age.

6

Promoting Self-Regulated Learning
A Motivational Analysis*

Willy Lens and Maarten Vansteenkiste

INTRODUCTION

Learning can be defined as a complex cognitive, motivational, and hence emotional process. The regulation of learning can therefore refer to each of these three components separately or to the molar learning activity. The distinction between metacognitive, meta-motivational and metaemotional processes (Boekaerts, Pintrich, & Zeidner, 2000) refers to conscious or implicit regulatory cognitive processes that are intended and used (or not) to control these three components of academic learning and achieving. Self-regulated (or self-regulating) learners are then students who are able to control these different cognitive-motivational processes to facilitate their own learning process and who are thus likely to perceive themselves at the helm or as the masters of their own learning process (Zimmerman & Schunk, 2001). Self-regulating learners experience themselves as origins, as agents and not as pawns (deCharms, 1968, 1984).

But who or, better, what is the "self" in "self-control" or "self-regulation"?[1] It cannot be a homunculus, an autonomous, independent decision taker (Shallice & Burgess, 1993; Wegner & Wheatley, 1999). The self in the concept self-regulated learning or the self that controls and regulates its actions is nothing else than a variety of

---

* The contribution by Maarten Vansteenkiste was supported by the Fund for Scientific Research—Flanders.

implicit and explicit covert psychological processes by which learners intentionally steer their cognitive, motivational, and emotional functioning during academic learning and performances. The regulating self is a set of executive functions, which is intentionally activated by an individual to have an impact on his or her thoughts, actions, and emotions. "Self-regulation involves the self acting on itself to alter its own responses" (Schmeichel & Baumeister, 2004, p. 84; see also Cervone, Shadel, Smith, & Fiori, 2006). The *self* in self-regulation is rather the *subject* (the I) than the *object* (the me) of these regulatory processes. The individual learner can (fail to) acquire, develop, and apply the skills that monitor and control the learning process. The objects of the regulatory processes are the different behavioral, motivational, and emotional aspects of the learning process (e.g., being task oriented and not performance oriented, the use of deep vs. superficial study strategies, procrastination, time management, perseverance, choices, effort, concentration, intrinsic enjoyment rather than test anxiety).

These regulatory processes, of course, have their own determinants and correlates (Dewitte & Lens, 1999b). To be able to foster self-regulated learning among students, one must not only know and understand the regulatory processes (e.g., delay of gratification) as such but also have insight in their determinants. For example, learners' ability to delay gratification is a function of length of future time perspective (FTP), as seen in the following illustration:

> The psychological distance toward a future goal, say 5 years from now, is shorter for individuals with a long FTP than for individuals with a short FTP. The decrease in anticipated rewarding value of that goal because of its delay will be less steep for people with a long FTP. When encountering an approach-approach conflict between a smaller but immediate reward or satisfaction (e.g., going to the movies tonight) or studying as an important instrumental activity for achieving the future goal, people with a long FTP will have less difficulty to keep going for the important goal in the future. Anticipating the highly valued future outcomes (e.g., going to college, becoming a well-trained plumber) of present learning activities enhances effort and persistence.

Here, we suggest, along with others (Heckhausen & Dweck, 1998), that the use of self-regulated learning strategies is a motivationally driven process; that is, the extent to which students will make use of self-regulation will to a large extent depend on their motivational resources. Indeed, whereas some students seem to use self-regulated learning strategies spontaneously to improve their learning and academic achievement (e.g., they smoothly apply regulatory skills to continue studying rather than doing something else), others need to deliberately focus on its use, and still others fail to apply self-regulatory strategies at all. Differences in the smooth versus reluctant versus nonuse of self-regulatory strategies are to a certain extent a function of learners' motivational resources. By using controllable or autonomous motivational processes, students can learn to affect their self-regulated learning and hence to enhance their achievement (Vansteenkiste, Lens, & Deci, 2006; Zimmerman & Martinez-Pons, 1990; Zimmerman & Schunk, 2001).

Because we approach the topic of self-regulated learning from a motivational perspective, we focus our discussion in the remaining part of this chapter on the motivational determinants of self-regulated learning. The proposed general model of the current chapter is graphically depicted in Figure 6.1.

In general, we discuss how students can control the amount of time they spend studying via motivational processes such as goal setting and motivational planning. The proverb, "Practice makes perfect," does indeed not hold for all moments and not for everybody, but it is certainly true that many students are underachieving because they do not spend enough time in lecture halls and study rooms (Lens & Decruyenaere, 1991). Their immediate, and even more so their cumulative, educational achievement would profit

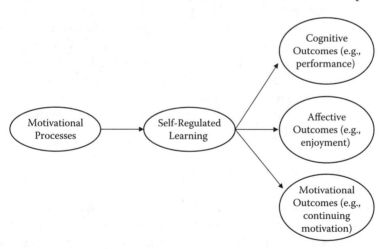

Figure 6.1 Proposed integrative model, which indicates how motivational processes facilitate self-regulated learning, which in turn results in various positive learning outcomes.

greatly from devoting more time to their study career, which is a function of their study motivation (Atkinson & Birch, 1978).

The present chapter is divided in two sections differentiated from each other on the basis of the type of motivational determinants that are studied. Whereas the first section focuses on motivational processes that deal with the "how" of self-regulated learning, the second set of motivational processes focuses on the energetic basis of the self-regulated learning. The how of learning pertains to those motivational processes that might best be used by students to achieve a greater sense of self-regulated learning. In this respect, we discuss relevant findings from action identification theory (Vallacher & Wegner, 1985) and research on implementation intentions (Gollwitzer, 1999). As explained in more detail, students' self-regulatory activity will to a certain extent depend on the level at which they have identified a particular action. The second section focuses on the motivational processes that provide individuals with the necessary energy to initiate and sustain their self-regulated learning. These motivational processes are more global in nature as they pertain to the reason why learners are studying. In this respect, we discuss our own empirical work based on the dynamics of action (Atkinson & Birch, 1970); expectancy-value theory (Eccles & Wigfield, 2002; Feather, 1982); FTP theory (Husman & Lens, 1999; Lens, 1986; Lens & Moreas, 1994; Uchnast, 2006; Zaleski, 1994); achievement-goal theory (Elliot, 1999); and self-determination theory (SDT; Deci & Ryan, 2000, 2002). Our goal is not to provide an in-depth account of these motivational frameworks, but we rather limit our discussion of these frameworks to their need to provide an overview of our empirical work (Lens & Vansteenkiste, 2006). Furthermore, with respect to self-regulated learning, the current discussion primarily focuses on *persistence*, which refers to the continued engagement in the learning activity.

MICROMOTIVATIONAL PROCESSES

Students can influence the time they spend studying (or they can be helped to do so) (a) by defining their learning activities at either a rather high or a low level of action identification, depending on the difficulty of the learning task, and (b) by elaborating goal intentions into specific action intentions and by developing implementation intentions for those intended or planned actions.

Level of Action Identification

One manifestation of volitional problems might be procrastination. According to Lay (1986), *procrastination* refers to a frequent failure at doing what ought to be done to reach goals, to postponing activities one had planned to do at a particular moment. Many students fail an exam because they did not start studying on time. At the beginning of the semester, they formulated the best intentions but failed in enacting them. There may be several reasons for procrastinating studying, such as important or more interesting competing activities, fear of failure, or the need for arousal or excitement. But, procrastinating students do not necessarily lack intellectual abilities or motivation (Depreeuw & Lens, 1998; Ferrari, 2001). Dewitte and Lens (2000c) found no differences in the number of formulated study intentions between procrastinating and nonprocrastinating students. Procrastinating students, however, failed to enact their intentions. Based on these findings, Dewitte and Lens (2000c) hypothesized that procrastination may result from failing volitional or self-regulatory processes. For example, when translating motivational goals into behavioral intentions, procrastinating students may generate unadaptive mental representations of the actions to be performed or identify an action in a less-than-optimal way.

In this respect, Vallacher and Wegner (1985, 1987) showed that the level of an action identification (ranging from very general to very specific) is relevant for the enactment of a behavioral intention and that it depends on the skills of the actor (or the difficulty of the task) which level of action identification is more optimal. To guarantee enactment, a researcher with high statistical proficiency may plan to "analyze her data" (i.e., a general or high action identification level), while her beginning master student would better plan to run an analysis of variance (i.e., a specific or low action identification level). Enactment is much less sure in the second case.

Assuming that many study activities are difficult for many students, Dewitte and Lens (2000b) tested the hypothesis that a stable low or specific level of action identification promotes self-regulated learning, as manifested, for instance, through continued persistence at the learning activity. Focusing on procedural details should enhance persistence in a difficult learning task. It was found that, in comparison with students with an intermediate action identification level, students with a low action identification level were indeed significantly more persistent and scored significantly higher on difficult questions requiring creative thinking. For the easier, reproductive question, the action identification level did not matter; regardless of one's action identification level, students obtained equally high scores for reproductive learning.

Dewitte and Lens (2000b) also found that procrastinators did better on the reproductive question when they had an intermediate mental representation than when they had a low one. For nonprocrastinating students, the difference was in the opposite direction. Academic procrastinators seem to have difficulties maintaining an autonomous, volitional mind-set. To maintain their study behavior, they have to rely on the self-controlling strategy of identifying what they are doing or have to do on a higher, more general level. As expected, Dewitte and Lens (200b) also found that procrastinating students lack high and low action identities. Students with few low action identities procrastinated more than people with many low action identities. Students with few high action identities procrastinated more than those with many high action identities. Procrastination was hence related to both a lack of a broad action perspective on behaviors and a lack of specific or low action identification levels.

To summarize, a high action identification level seems to help students to maintain their self-regulated learning. Specifically, a high identification level keeps students focused on the activity itself (e.g., to become a psychologist) and enhances their motivation to persist, not to give in to competing alternative activities (e.g., going to the movies). When, however, the ongoing task becomes difficult, students might better switch to a low action identification level and focus on procedural details of the ongoing action to maintain their self-regulated learning (e.g., first multiply and then divide; Dewitte & Lens, 1999a).

Dewitte and Lens (2000b) also found that students' abilities and the subjective difficulty of the task matter. When learning tasks are really challenging for a given student (i.e., difficult but manageable), students will spontaneously use self-regulatory strategies. For instance, they will have no problem freely persisting at the activity until the activity is terminated. When students are confronted with tasks that are too easy (and therefore dull) or too difficult because the tasks demands exceed the learner's abilities, students will need to use self-controlling or self-regulatory strategies deliberately so that they are able to persist at the activity. This does also mean that not all students who score low on a questionnaire measuring the frequency of self-controlling strategies are unmotivated and poor learners (Wolters, 2000).

Dewitte and Lens (2000a, exp. 4) found that people who enjoyed solving word anagrams and who were strongly focused on that task persisted longer when they used no volitional strategies than when they did apply regulating strategies. For participants who did not enjoy the task, the reverse pattern was found. Identifying an action at a lower level or adopting a narrower task orientation will more easily engender intrinsic motivation and allow a flow experience. Such students rather may need self-regulatory strategies to refrain from (always) studying, to interrupt ongoing learning activities (Kuhl & Beckman, 1985, 1994) when necessary.

Implementation Intentions

Corresponding to the distinction between goals (as end states) and goal-oriented actions, Gollwitzer (1999) makes a distinction between goal intentions and implementation intentions. Goal intentions refer to goal setting (e.g., I plan to lose weight), and from research on goal-setting theory (Locke & Latham, 2002) we know that the probably of enactment increases the more specific the goal is (e.g., I want to lose 10 pounds before the end of the year). Implementation intentions refer to the planned goal-directed actions and to the temporal and situational circumstances in which the intended action will be performed (e.g., I want to lose 10 pounds before the end of the year by not eating fast food anymore and by doing physical exercises at least 30 minutes each morning). It has repeatedly been shown that the probability of persisting at one's goals, and hence, displaying self-regulated learning, can significantly be increased by formulating specific implementation intentions (see Gollwitzer, 1999, for an overview). The formulation of specific implementation intentions equally leads to greater successful enactment of goal-directed actions and attainment of one's goals.

Dewitte, Verguts, and Lens (2003) found, however, in three experimental studies that goal difficulty plays a moderating role in the behavioral effects of implementation intentions. More specifically, they found that when the focus was on the outcome of goal-directed action rather than on the goal-directed actions themselves, implementation intentions specifying when or in what conditions the relevant actions were to be performed did not enhance enactment. When the focus was on the goal-directed actions, they replicated the positive effect of forming implementation intentions. Specifying when or where a goal-directed action should be enacted only enhances persistence, which reflects self-regulated learning, when the enacted goal is rather easy. In those cases, the subject knows what to do to reach the goal. When they do not know well what to do to reach a goal, as is often the case for really difficult goals (e.g., a student making a PowerPoint presentation when the student never has seen one and does not know how to do it), implementation intentions (e.g., I'll make the PowerPoint presentation this weekend at home) will not foster much enactment and persistence at the goal unless one first learns how it has to be done. Persistence can then be enhanced by acquiring the skill and especially the habit of formulating implementation intentions for actions that belong to the student's repertoire and that are instrumental for the goal.

MACROMOTIVATIONAL PROCESSES

Competing Interests Matter

To understand and predict students' persistence at learning activities (Figure 6.2), most contemporary motivational models consider the strength of students' motivation for their schoolwork. However, study persistence might be affected not only by the amount of study motivation, but also by the motivation to engage in competing alternative activities, as suggested more than three decades ago by Atkinson and Birch in their *Dynamics of Action* (1970). Atkinson

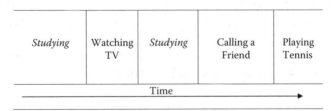

Figure 6.2 Learning activities are episodes in a continuous stream of activities and changes in activity. Before and after study time, students do other things in which they are interested and that motivate them. The end of one activity defines the beginning of another one.

and Birch (1970, 1978) argued that the basic phenomenon to be explained by motivational psychology is not a series of isolated, episodic actions but a continuous stream of activities and changes in activities. When we look at a particular action as integrated in such a stream of activities, it becomes evident that the initiation of an activity (e.g., studying for an exam) defines at the same time the end or persistence of the foregoing activity (e.g., going for a run), and that the end of that activity coincides with the initiation of the following activity. Atkinson and Birch (1978) further assumed that a change from one activity to another expresses a change in the strength of underlying behavioral tendencies or motivations. The strongest tendency is expressed in action. A change in activity will follow when an originally subdominant behavioral tendency becomes dominant or stronger than all other competing motivational tendencies, irrespective of the absolute strength of those tendencies. This means that the initiation of an activity at a certain moment in time and the duration or persistence of that action depend not only on the strength of the motivation for that action but also on the number and the strength of competing action tendencies. Self-regulation to make more time available for studying can then imply that students limit the number and strength of their interests in other activities. This can, for example, mean that there are in their study environment no strong instigations for competing motivational tendencies, such as a television set, DVD or CD player, and the like. Controlling their learning environment allows students to control the strength of their motivation to study compared to the strength of competing motivations, and by doing so they can make more time available for learning.

Creten, Nijsmans, Lens, Douterlungne, and Cossy (1998; Creten, Lens, & Simons, 2001) analyzed the reasons 9th- to 12th-grade students in vocational high schools gave for their (lack of) motivation. Participants were asked to indicate how much effort they spent for three different courses (i.e., a general theoretical course, a French language course, and a practical course). The students who reported very little or little effort in one of these courses were then asked to select one or more reasons from a list of 10 reasons to explain their low effort. For all three courses, the highest percentages were found for the category "other things to do" (percentages ranged from 41.1% to 52.9%), suggesting that for many students other activities (e.g., leisure) are more important and might prevent them from initiating their schoolwork. A small group said that they worked hard for school because they had "nothing else to do," reflecting some sense of boredom (percentages ranged from 2.6% to 5.8%). These data indicate that the presence of competing activities might indeed lead students to procrastinate in studying and hence interfere with their investment in studying.

Lens, Lacante, Vansteenkiste, and Herrera (2005) discussed empirical evidence showing that not only the amount of time one spends on competing activities matters in predicting students' persistence, motivation and, learning, but also the content or the type of competing activity matters. They reported that both students' motivation and attitude toward schooling are differently related to the amount of time spent at leisure versus work (i.e., student job) activities. Time spent on working activities is inversely related to study motivation, attitude toward schooling, persistence, and academic achievement, so that the more time students spent working during the week, the less they adopted a positive attitude toward schooling, the less they persisted, and the lower grades they obtained. Such relationships were not found for leisure time engagement. Spending some time on leisure time activities did not seem to interfere with optimal learning. Students with a leisure time engagement of 1 to 4 hours a week had a significantly more positive attitude toward schooling compared to students spending no time at leisure activities. Students' attitude and motivation were only significantly lower if they devoted more than 5 hours a week to leisure.

Thus, although the number of competing activities and time spent on these competing activities seem to interfere with study motivation, persistence, and optimal academic achievement, this general conclusion does not hold for all types of competing activities. Spending some time in leisure activities is optimally motivating, presumably because it fills students' energetic resources, allowing them to turn again toward their study activities.

Instrumental Motivation and Self-Regulation: Goal Content Matters

Classrooms are no playgrounds but workshops. Learning needs not only to be fun as such (intrinsic motivation) but also to be useful for the future. Schooling is by definition future oriented, it has utility value; it is instrumental for future educational and professional goals and for life in general (extrinsic motivation).

As discussed, when students are asked to define what they are doing when they are studying, their definitions can vary from broad (e.g., I am studying in order to become a psychologist; I study to make sure that I pass the exams), to intermediate (e.g., I am trying to understand the difference between mediation and moderation), to low or a specific definition (e.g., I am reading when I am studying). Dewitte and Lens (2000c) found that most students' definitions of studying that they identified as high action identification level referred to achieving a further goal for which studying was instrumental. Many of us are familiar with parents' and teachers' good advice to do one's best at school, as this is so important for one's future. Schooling and education in general are future oriented. Many students are highly motivated for their schoolwork because of further educational and professional goals.

Those future goals are for them additional sources of motivation, and as such perceived instrumentality may motivationally affect the initiation, the persistence, and perhaps the quality of learning activities. Instrumental motivation necessarily represents extrinsic motivation as students perceive their studying as means toward achieving a particular outcome (i.e., a future goal) that is separated from the activity itself. This does not, however, imply that students cannot be simultaneously intrinsically motivated, in which case students derive a sense of intrinsic enjoyment of engaging in the learning activity (Ryan & Deci, 2000).

The concept of instrumental motivation is highly similar to Eccles's (Eccles & Wigfield, 2002; Wigfield & Eccles, 1992) concept of utility value, which she described as the importance of a task for a future goal. Utility value is contrasted with interest value, which Eccles described as the inherent and immediate enjoyment from engaging in an activity. Thus, the concepts of utility value or instrumental motivation and intrinsic value are very much in line with the classic definitions of extrinsic and intrinsic motivation (Eccles & Wigfield, 2002).

Assuming that at each moment in time the total strength of students' motivation can be conceived of as the sum of an intrinsic and an extrinsic component, students can increase their motivation for schoolwork by developing longer educational plans and projects in which more immediate educational goals also function as means toward future goals. Most of our goals are indeed not final goals (or end goals) but subgoals. For most of our goals, we can easily answer the question, Why do you want to achieve that goal?

> Why are you studying chemistry? Because I want to succeed in the exam.
> Why do you want to succeed in the exams? Because I want to graduate.
> Why do you want to graduate? Because I want to enter medical school.
> Why? Because I want to become a medical doctor.
> Why a doctor? Because I want to do something useful for the very poor people in developing countries.
> Why? Because that would make my life meaningful (end goal).

Linking a specific study activity not only to more limited immediate goals (e.g., passing the exams) but also to more molar but still subgoals or intermediate goals in the near or distant future and even to important life goals (see the preceding example) enhances motivation and commitment for the present learning activity because its instrumental value increases as a function of the number and importance of further goals that are contingent on immediate goal achievement (De Volder & Lens, 1982; Miller, DeBacker, & Greene, 1999; Raynor, 1981; Simons, Vansteenkiste, Lens, & Lacante, 2004).

Striving for goals in the more distant future (e.g., to become a medical doctor) does not necessarily mean a delay of gratification (Bembenutty & Karabenick, 1998; Mischel, 1981). Achieving subgoals can be rewarding in itself because such goals have a reinforcing value when they satisfy important needs. For example, to succeed in a difficult exam can be rewarding because it satisfies the needs for achievement and competence. Second, given that achieving subgoals has instrumental value, it will be rewarding because it is perceived as moving one step closer to other subgoals and to the distant end goal. Preparing an exam for a compulsory course in which one is not interested can be frustrating, especially on a beautiful summer day. But, seeing the contingency between preparing that exam now and becoming a medical doctor in 8 years will lower the frustration and may even result in feeling good while preparing for such an exam. Formulating and striving for important goals in the distant future does, in our view, not necessarily exclude immediate gratifications. One can at the same time be future oriented and enjoy the present.

This is a rather intriguing statement, which has been examined in various correlational and experimental studies at our center. Indeed, if instrumental motivation is a form of extrinsic motivation, then it is important to know if this also implies that the utility value of a learning or achievement task will undermine the intrinsic motivation or task orientation in the same way as extrinsic rewards do under certain circumstances (Deci, 1975; Deci & Ryan, 1985). Does a focus on the future (i.e., instrumentality) preclude one to stay focused on one's present behavior (i.e., task orientation) and to derive a sense of enjoyment from engagement in the activity at hand (i.e., intrinsic motivation)? In already published and ongoing research, we distinguish different types of instrumental relationships between a present task and a future goal, and we analyze their motivational effects in general and effects on intrinsic motivation and task orientation in particular (see Lens, 2001; Lens, Herrera, & Lacante, 2004; Lens & Rand, 1997; Lens, Simons, & Dewitte, 2001, 2002; Simons, Dewitte, & Lens, 2000, 2003, 2004; Vansteenkiste, Simons, Lens, Soenens, et al., 2004; Vansteenkiste, Simons, Soenens, & Lens, 2004).

Studying and performing well in school can be instrumental for different types of goals. Achievement goal theory (Elliot, 1999, 2005), for example, distinguishes two types of task and performance goals (i.e., approach vs. avoidance). SDT (Deci & Ryan, 2002) makes a distinction between intrinsic and extrinsic goals and between autonomous versus controlled reasons for pursuing goals. Empirical research on motivation in education has shown the differential effects of goal content and their underlying reasons on learning, persistence, and academic achievement (Vansteenkiste et al., 2006). This means that students can strongly affect their learning through the type of goals they set for themselves in the near and distant future.

It became clear from our empirical studies that, from a motivational point of view, we must distinguish different types of perceived instrumental links between present actions or immediate subgoals on one hand and future outcomes on the other, and that especially the content or type of the future goals (intrinsic vs. extrinsic) is particularly relevant for the motivational consequences in the present.

Future Intrinsic versus Future Extrinsic Goals

Not all goals are created equal: Intrinsic goals are better than extrinsic goals. Not only the quantity, but also the quality of students' motivation matters. By setting intrinsic goals rather than extrinsic goals, students can enhance their learning.

The differentiation between intrinsic and extrinsic goals is made within SDT (Deci & Ryan, 2000). Intrinsic goals, such as community contribution, health, personal growth, and affiliation are differentiated from extrinsic goals such as fame, financial success, and physical appearance. Consistent with SDT (Ryan & Deci, 2000), which assumes that learners—as everybody else—are active and growth-oriented individuals who are endowed with a set of basic psychological needs (i.e., autonomy, competence, and relatedness), the former goals are labeled *intrinsic* because they are satisfying in their own right, and they provide direct satisfaction of the basic psychological needs. Hence, they are expected to be positively related to psychological well-being, greater persistence, and better learning. In contrast, extrinsic goals have an "outward" orientation (Williams, Cox, Hedberg, & Deci, 2000) or a "having" orientation (Fromm, 1976; Van Boven & Gilovich, 2003) that is concerned with external manifestations of worth rather than with basic need satisfaction. When people are focused on extrinsic goals, they tend to be more oriented toward interpersonal comparisons (Patrick, Neighbours, & Knee, 2004; Sirgy, 1998), contingent approval (Kernis, 2003), and acquiring external signs of self-worth (Kasser, Ryan, Couchman, & Sheldon, 2004), which are likely to detract their attention from the learning activity at hand (Vansteenkiste, Matos, Lens, & Soenens, in press) and to undermine their well-being (Kasser & Ryan, 1996).

Simons et al. (2000) reported on four correlational studies in which they found that stressing the personally important future consequences of present learning tasks enhanced task involvement and decreased a less-adaptive performance-approach orientation, even when the present motivation was extrinsic. Lowest scores for task involvement were found for students who were extrinsically motivated for a present activity that was perceived as instrumental for reaching extrinsic future goals.

Simons et al. (2004) found that first-year college students who were convinced that the capacities and knowledge that they were developing in a particular course would be very useful in their future professional life and who were motivated by intrinsic future goals (e.g., personal development) scored significantly higher for task orientation, deep-level learning, intrinsic motivation, persistence, and academic achievement than students who perceived the abilities and knowledge they had to develop now as useless for the future and who were motivated by future extrinsic goals.

Vansteenkiste, Simons, Soenens et al. (2004) created four experimental conditions to manipulate the content of the future goal of a present physical activity. More specifically, participants in the future intrinsic goal condition were told that doing Tae Bo helps individuals remain physically fit and healthy. Participants in the future extrinsic goal condition were told that doing Tae Bo was instrumental to become or stay physically attractive to others. Further, participants in the future content-free goal condition were told that "doing Tae Bo is important for your future"; no specific future goal was mentioned. Participants in the control group were not provided with any future reference. The authors reasoned that framing an activity in terms of extrinsic goal attainment would detract individuals' attention from the activity at hand and hence result in poorer performance. In contrast, intrinsic goal framing, because of its closer link with basic need satisfaction, should result in more optimal learning and performance as such goals direct individuals' attention to the activity at hand. In line with these predictions, it was found that framing a physical exercise activity in terms of a future intrinsic goal (i.e., health and physical fitness) has a positive effect on effort expenditure, autonomous exercise motivation, performance, and long-term persistence compared to the no-goal control group and the extrinsic goal-framing group. In contrast, framing a physical exercise activity in terms of a future extrinsic goal (i.e., physical appearance and attractiveness) undermined those outcomes compared to a no-future-goal control group.

Furthermore, providing a vague reference to the future importance of the current exercise activity (i.e., "do your best for the current exercising, it is so important for your future"), in contrast to expectations based on FTP theory (Lens, 1986), does not result in better learning and performance outcomes compared to a no-goal control group. Thus, this study led to the following two important conclusions: If learners themselves or socializing agents (e.g., teachers, parents, etc.) want to promote learning by referring to the future importance of the learning activity, then they can better formulate

intrinsic goals, and they need to set for themselves or provide concrete rather than vague future goals.

Also, Vansteenkiste, Simons, Lens, Soenens et al. (2004) tested
the importance of the type or the content of future goals students
are pursuing. They created three experimental conditions. In the
future intrinsic goal condition, first-year students in a teacher training college were told that "reading the text could provide you some
information about how to teach your future toddlers some simple
ecological strategies so that they can do something for the environment," which was intended to represent the intrinsic goal of contributing to the community. In the future extrinsic goal condition, they
were told that "reading the text might provide you some information
about how to save money on your future job by recycling materials,"
which was intended to represent the extrinsic goal of attaining mon-
etary benefit. Finally, in the double-goal condition participants were
told that their current task engagement served both types of future
goals. Based on expectancy-value accounts, it was predicted that
providing two instead of one single future goal should result in more
optimal learning and performance as the activity will be perceived
as more instrumental and as containing a higher utility value. However, based on SDT, a set of conflicting hypotheses was formulated.
Specifically, because extrinsic goals yield an outward-oriented focus,
they preclude task absorption and should undermine learning and
performance. Hence, adding an extrinsic goal to an already-present
intrinsic goal should forestall the learning process compared to a
single intrinsic goal condition.

The data show that framing a learning activity in terms of both
an intrinsic and an extrinsic future goal facilitated a mastery orientation, performance, and persistence; it decreased a performance-
approach orientation compared to the single future extrinsic goal
condition. However, in line with SDT and contrary to what could be
expected based on expectancy-value theories, it was also found that
the double-goal framing resulted in a less-optimal pattern of outcomes compared to the single future intrinsic goal condition. "Less"
(one intrinsic goal vs. one intrinsic plus one extrinsic goal) is indeed
sometimes "more" (higher quality of motivation; more adaptive
outcomes). Finally, it was found that the effects of the goal content
on performance and persistence were fully mediated by the degree
of task orientation. Framing a learning activity in terms of a future

intrinsic goal enhances a task orientation, and extrinsic future goals seem to distract students from the learning task.

These findings provide evidence that so-called extrinsic motivations (derived from intrinsically motivated future activities as well as from anticipated intrinsic future goals) may even enhance intrinsic motivation and optimal goal orientation (i.e., task orientation).

Autonomous versus Controlled Regulation

Not only *what* type of goals (intrinsic vs. extrinsic) students strive for is important, but also their reasons for doing so (autonomous vs. controlled reasons), or *why* they do so, matter.

In addition to studying the type of goals people hold, SDT conceptualizes students' reasons for engaging in a learning activity. In doing so, it is maintained that learners have the natural inclination to engage in learning activities that are experienced as self-chosen or volitional (deCharms, 1968; Deci & Ryan, 1985; Ryan & Deci, 2000). Deci and Ryan (1985) suggested that intrinsically motivated behavior is the prototype of self-determined or autonomous activity, because students' interests are fully involved in a self-catalyzing chain of activities. When intrinsically motivated, students enjoy the process of studying itself without engaging in the learning to obtain an outcome that is separable from the activity itself, as in the case of extrinsic motivation. Although extrinsically motivated behaviors are carried out to achieve an instrumental end (Ryan & Deci, 2000), according to SDT, they can still differ in their degree of relative autonomy or self-determination, depending on the extent to which initially externally regulated reasons for acting have been gradually 'taken in' or internalized (Ryan & Connell, 1989; Schafer, 1968). Because this internalization process can be more or less successful, three different types of extrinsic motivation are differentiated: external, introjected, and identified.

In the case of *external regulation*, people's behavior is regulated by pressuring contingencies that are overtly external to the individual, such as the promise of a reward or the threat of a punishment. In this case, the behavioral regulation has not been internalized. *Introjected regulation* describes behaviors that are motivated by internal prods and pressures such as self-worth-related contingencies and feelings of guilt and shame. Although the behavioral regulation resides within the person in the sense that it no longer requires overtly external contingencies, it is also characterized by a pressured demand of oneself, and the behavioral regulation has only been partially internalized. Finally, *identified regulation*, as a third type of extrinsic motivation, is considered an internalized type of extrinsic motivation that occurs when the value of the behavior is recognized as personally valuable (Deci, Eghrari, Patrick, & Leone, 1994). When people manage to concur with or endorse the personal relevance of the behavior, they are more likely to engage in the activity with a sense of willingness and volition. For this reason, identified regulation is in empirical research often combined with intrinsic motivation to form an autonomous motivation composite (e.g., Vansteenkiste, Lens, Dewitte, De Witte, & Deci, 2004). Autonomous motivation is then contrasted with controlled motivation, which contains both external and introjected regulation. In short, SDT differentiates between autonomously motivated behaviors that are enacted with a sense of volition and psychological freedom and controlled behaviors that are typically executed with a sense of resistance, pressure, or obligation.

A variety of both correlational and experimental research (see Reeve, Deci, & Ryan, 2004, for an overview) has documented the advantages of autonomous compared to controlled motivation for studying. Specifically, because studying out of choice and personal endorsement provides one with the necessary energy to persist in the face of setbacks, autonomous motivation should predict better performance and less dropout. Also, because individuals are willingly engaging in the learning activity, they should be more fully absorbed in it and remain more concentrated when studying. In contrast, in the case of controlled motivation, studying will require considerable energy and effort because the studying is not self-initiated. As such pressures will be experienced as mentally draining and ego depleting, studying out of controlled motivation is more likely to foster dropout and to interfere with a concentrated engagement in the learning activity. A number of different studies have provided evidence for these hypotheses. Specifically, autonomous motivation has been found to predict deep-level learning (Grolnick & Ryan, 1987), higher academic competence (Soenens & Vansteenkiste, 2005), better time management, higher concentration (Vansteenkiste, Zhou, Lens, &

Soenens, 2005), higher grades (Black & Deci, 2000), and lower drop-out rates (Vallerand, Fortier, & Guay, 1997). In contrast, controlled motivation has been found to predict maladaptive coping (Ryan & Connell, 1989), more test anxiety (Vansteenkiste et al., 2005), more procrastination (Sénécal, Julien, & Guay, 2003), lower performance, and less persistence (Vansteenkiste, Simons, Lens, Sheldon, & Deci, 2004). Notably, these effects not only emerged among Western samples but also were equally found in Eastern samples (e.g., Vansteenkiste, Lens, Soenens, & Luyckx, in press; Vansteenkiste et al., 2005).

To be really self-regulating with respect to their learning, students should develop autonomous motivation. They should either be intrinsically motivated or try to identify with and finally integrate the originally externally controlling reasons for their learning.

PRACTICAL IMPLICATIONS

In the following, we provide a number of practical suggestions that can be derived from the present work and be implemented by the learners themselves or—originally and temporarily—by teachers, parents, or other socializing agents to foster self-regulated learning that leads to persistent learning, task orientation, deep-level information processing and subjective well-being. To foster self-regulated learning, learners and teachers do well by

- Defining learning activities at a high level (e.g., becoming a car mechanic) if the activity is easy and defining it at a low level (e.g., understanding the mechanics of automatic transmission) if the activity is difficult.
- Formulating specific implementation intentions to enact their academic goals (e.g., when and where will I study what, and how will I do that?).
- Organizing one's learning environment in such a way that the instigations for doing something other than studying is minimal.
- Creating or making more time available for study (if necessary) by reducing the number or strength of competing but less-important alternative interests.
- Engaging in some leisure time activity as such activities—in contrast to engaging in student jobs—might provide them with renewed energy to continue their studies.

- Setting a specific instead of vague ("schooling is important for your future") future goal when trying to increase the perceived utility value of the present learning activity.
- Setting immediate and future intrinsic goals such as self-development or the development of competencies and skills, community contribution, and affiliation (e.g., helping other students with learning difficulties) instead of extrinsic goals such as financial success and fame.
- Fostering an autonomous or volitional engagement instead of a controlled or pressured engagement in the learning activity as the former will provide students with the necessary energetic resources to freely persist at the requested activities, to more deeply process the learning material, and as a result to achieve better grades.

CONCLUSION

Self-regulated learning refers both to *what* learners are doing (i.e., that they are learning rather than doing something else) and *how* they are learning (e.g., deep vs. superficial information processing; degree of elaboration; learning details or only main ideas; using study aids or not; being highly concentrated and mindful or not). For a motivational psychologist, the first aspect is probably more interesting than the second one, although different types of approach and avoidance motivation differentially affect the learning process and the well-being of learners (Vansteenkiste et al., 2006). Self-regulating students are—among many others things—able to manage their use of time and to control the amount of time they spend on their study or career. For (too) many youngsters, attending classes and studying are something they are forced to do, without much of a choice. They *must* go to school, do their homework, and learn their lessons. They experience themselves as externally controlled pawns in the hands of teachers and parents, which of course undermines their intrinsic interest and well-being (deCharms, 1976, 1984). To become self-regulating learners, they should develop autonomous motivation.

It was our aim to discuss part of our correlational and experimental research to show how different motivational processes affect the regulation of students' learning (persistence and performance). These studies were based on different motivational theories (e.g., dynamics of action, expectancy-value theory, achievement-goal theory, goal-setting theory, SDT).

First, it was found that students can control their study persistence not only via the strength of their motivation to study but also by controlling the number, strength, and content of competing motivational interests. Second, persistence can be enhanced or thwarted by how students define what they are doing when they are studying. It has been shown that the action identification level, in interaction with the experienced difficulty of the learning task, has a significant effect on the implementation of action intentions or not (i.e., procrastination). Third, and most important, it was found that—in line with achievement-goal theory and SDT—not only the quantity but also the quality of students' motivation matters. Not all types of motivation are created equal. The content of students' immediate and future goals matters (e.g., task goals vs. performance goals; intrinsic vs. extrinsic goals). Finally, in addition to the goal content, the reasons students have for trying to achieve those different goals are important for persistence, satisfaction, and performance. See the difference made in SDT between the what (goal content) and the why (volitional, autonomous vs. controlled) of motivated behavior. Empirical evidence shows the adaptive consequences of learning goals and intrinsic goals that are pursued for autonomous, volitional reasons. Learners can easily be coached to change from helpless "pawns" into self-regulated and intrinsically or autonomously motivated learners by helping them to set for themselves particular types of goals in the present and the future and to create for them an autonomy-supporting learning environment.

NOTE

1. Although some authors (e.g., Kuhl & Fuhrman, 1998, p. 15) make a distinction between self-control ("volition supporting the maintenance of an active goal") and self-regulation ("maintaining one's actions in line with one's integrated self"), many others—including us—use the terms of self-regulation and self-control interchangeably (see also Carver, 2004; Schmeichel & Baumeister, 2004).

REFERENCES

Atkinson, J. W., & Birch, D. (1970). *The dynamics of action.* New York: Wiley.

Atkinson, J. W., & Birch, D. (1978). The dynamics of achievement-oriented activity. In J. W. Atkinson & J. O. Raynor (Eds.), *Personality, motivation, and achievement* (pp. 143–197). Washington, DC: Memishere.

Bembenutty, H., & Karabenick, S. A. (1998). Academic delay of gratification. *Learning and Individual Differences, 10,* 329–346.

Black, A. E. & Deci, E. L. (2000). The effect of student self-regulation and instructor autonomy support on learning in a college-level natural science course: A self-determination theory perspective. *Science Education, 84,* 740–756.

Boekaerts, M., Pintrich, P. R., & & Zeidner, M. (Eds.). (2000). *Handbook of self-regulation.* San Diego, CA: Academic Press.

Carver, C. S. (2004). Self-regulation of action and affect. In R. F. Baumeister & K. D. Vohs (Eds.), *Handbook of self-regulation: Research, theory, and applications* (pp. 13–61). New York: Guilford Press.

Cervone, D., Shadel, W. G., Smith, R. E., & Fiori, M. (2006). Self-regulation: Reminders and suggestions from personality science. *Applied Psychology: An International Review, 55,* 333–385.

Creten, H., Lens, W., & Simons, J. (2001). The role of perceived instrumentality in student motivation. In A. Efklides, J. Kuhl, & R. M. Sorrentino (Eds.), *Trends and prospects in motivation research* (pp. 37–45). Dordrecht, The Netherlands: Kluwer Academic.

Creten, H., Nijsmans, I., Lens, W., Douterlungne, M., & Cossey, H. (1998). *Algemene vakken en beroepsleerlingen: Op dezelfde golflengte? Motivatie van leerlingen en functioneren van leerkrachten algemene vakken in het beroepssecundair onderwijs.* Leuven, Belgium: Department ofPsychology and HIVA.

deCharms, R. (1968). *Personal causation.* New York: Academic Press.

deCharms, R. (1984). Motivation enhancement in educational settings. In R. E. Ames & C. Ames (Eds.), *Research on motivation in education. Vol. 1: Student motivation* (pp. 275–310). New York: Academic Press.

deCharms, R. (1976). *Enhancing motivation: Change in the classroom.* New York: Irvington.

Deci, E. L. (1975). *Intrinsic motivation.* New York: Plenum Press.

Deci, E. L., Eghrari, H., Patrick, B. C., & Leone, D. L. (1994). Facilitating internalization: The self-determination perspective. *Journal of Personality, 62,* 119–142.

Deci, E. L., & Ryan, R. M. (1985). *Intrinsic motivation and self-determination in human behavior.* New York: Plenum.

Deci, E. L., & Ryan, R. M. (2000). The "what" and "why" of goal pursuits: Human needs and the self-determination of human behavior. *Psychological Inquiry, 11,* 227–268.

Deci, E. L., & Ryan, R. M. (Eds.). (2002). *Handbook of self-determination research.* Rochester, NY: University of Rochester Press.

Depreeuw, E., & Lens, W. (1998). *Procrastination in higher education students: Conceptual analysis and exploration of personal and contextual factors.* Paper presented at the Sixth WATM Conference, Thessaloniki, Greece.

De Volder, M., & Lens, W. (1982). Academic achievement and future time perspective as a cognitive-motivational concept. *Journal of Personality and Social Psychology, 42,* 566–571.

Dewitte, S., & Lens, W. (1999b). Volition: Use with measure. *Learning and Individual Differences, 11,* 321–333.

Dewitte, S., & Lens, W. (1999a). Determinants of the action identification level and its influence on self-control. *Psychologica Belgica, 39,* 1–14.

Dewitte, S., & Lens, W. (2000a). *Does goal awareness enhance self-control? Required effort moderates the relation between the level of action identity and persistence.* Unpublished research report no. 93, Research Center for Motivation and Time Perspective, University of Leuven, Belgium.

Dewitte, S., & Lens, W. (2000b). Exploring volitional problems in academic procrastinators. *International Journal of Educational Research, 33,* 733–750.

Dewitte, S., & Lens, W. (2000c). Procrastinators lack a broad action perspective. *European Journal of Personality, 14,* 121–140.

Dewitte, S., Verguts, T., & Lens, W. (2003). Implementation intentions do not enhance all types of goals: The moderating role of goal difficulty. *Current Psychology: Developmental, Learning, Personality, Social, 22,* 73–89.

Eccles, J. S., & Wigfield, A. (2002). Motivational beliefs, values, and goals. *Annual Review of Psychology, 53,* 109–132.

Elliot, A. J. (1999). Approach and avoidance motivation and achievement goals. *Educational Psychologist, 34,* 169–189.

Elliot, A. J. (2005). A conceptual history of the achievement goal construct. In A. Elliot & C. Dweck (Eds.), *Handbook of competence and motivation* (pp. 52–72). Andover, NJ: Guilford Press.

Feather, N. T. (1982). *Expectations and actions: Expectancy-value models in psychology.* Hillsdale, NJ: Erlbaum.

Ferrari, J. R. (2001). Procrastination as self-regulation failure of performance: Effects of cognitive load, self-awareness, and time limits on "working best under pressure." *European Journal of Personality, 15,* 391–406.

Fromm, E. (1976). *To have or to be?* New York: Continuum.

Gollwitzer, P. M. (1999). Implementation intentions: Strong effects of simple plans. *American Psychologist, 54,* 493–503.

Grolnick, W. S., & Ryan, R. M. (1987). Autonomy in children's learning: An experimental and individual difference investigation. *Journal of Personality and Social Psychology, 52,* 890–898.

Heckhausen, J., & Dweck, C. S. (Eds.). (1998). *Motivation and self-regulation across the life span.* Cambridge, U.K.: Cambridge University Press.

Husman, J., & Lens, W. (1999). The role of the future in student motivation. *Educational Psychologist, 34,* 113–125.

Kasser, T., & Ryan, R. M. (1996). Further examining the American dream: Differential correlates of intrinsic and extrinsic goals. *Personality and Social Psychology Bulletin, 22,* 280–287.

Kasser, T., Ryan, R. M., Couchman, C. E., & Sheldon, K. M. (2004). Materialistic values: Their causes and consequences. In T. Kasser & A. D. Kanfer (Eds.), *Psychology and consumer cultures: The struggle for a good life in a materialistic world* (pp. 11–28). Washington, DC: American Psychological Association.

Kernis, M. (2003). Toward a conceptualization of optimal self-esteem. *Psychological Inquiry, 14,* 1–26.

Kuhl, J., & Beckman, J. (1985). *Action control: From cognition to behavior.* Berlin: Heidelberg.

Kuhl, J., & Beckman, J. (Eds.). (1994). *Volition and personality: Action versus state orientation.* Seattle, WA: Hogrefe and Huber.

Kuhl, J., & Fuhrmann, A. (1998). Decomposing self-regulation and self-control: The volitional components inventory. In J. Heckhausen & C. S. Dweck (Eds.), *Motivation and self-regulation across the life span* (pp. 15–49). Cambridge, U.K.: Cambridge University Press.

Lay, C. H. (1986). At last, my research article on procrastination. *Journal of Research in Personality, 20,* 474–495.

Lens, W. (1986). Future time perspective: A cognitive-motivational concept. In D. R. Brown & J. Veroff (Eds.), *Frontiers of motivational psychology* (pp. 173–190). New York: Springer-Verlag.

Lens, W. (2001). How to combine intrinsic task-motivation with the motivational effects of the instrumentality of present tasks for future goals. In A. Efklides, J. Kuhl, & R. M. Sorrentino (Eds.), *Trends and prospects in motivation research* (pp. 23–36). Dordrecht: Kluwer Academic Publishers.

Lens, W., & Decruyenaere, M. (1991). Motivation and demotivation in secondary education: Student characteristics. *Learning and Instruction, 1,* 145–159.

Lens, W., Herrera, D., & Lacante, M. (2004). The role of motivation and future time perspective in educational counseling. *Psychologica* (Special Issue), 169–180.

Lens, W., Lacante, M., Vansteenkiste, M., & Herrera, D. (2005). Study persistence and academic achievement as a function of the type of competing motivational tendencies. *European Journal of Psychology of Education, 20*, 275–287.

Lens, W., & Rand, P. (1997). Combining intrinsic goal orientations with professional instrumentality/utility in student motivation. *Polish Psychological Bulletin, 28*, 103–123.

Lens, W., & Moreas, M.-A. (1994). Future time perspective: An individual and a societal approach. In Z. Zaleski (Ed.), *Psychology of future orientation* (pp. 23–38). Lublin, Poland: Towarzystwo Naukowe KUL.

Lens, W., Simons, J., & Dewitte, S. (2001). Student motivation and self-regulation as a function of future time perspective and perceived instrumentality. In S. Volet & S. Järvelä (Eds.), *Motivation in learning contexts: Theoretical advances and methodological implications* (pp. 233–248). New York: Pergamon.

Lens, W., Simons, J., & Dewitte, S. (2002). From duty to desire: The role of students' future time perspective and instrumentality perceptions for study motivation and self-regulation. In F. Pajares & T. Urdan (Eds.), *Academic motivation of adolescents* (Vol. 2, pp. 221–245, in the Adolescence and Education Series). Greenwich, CT: Information Age Publishing.

Lens, W., & Vansteenkiste, M. (2006). Motivation: About the "why" and "what for" of human behavior. In K. Pawlik & G. d'Ydewalle (Eds.), *International conceptual history of psychology* (pp. 249–270). Hove, U.K.: Psychology Press.

Locke, E. A., & Latham, G. P. (2002). Building a practically useful theory of goal setting and task motivation. A 35-year odyssey. *American Psychologist, 57*, 705–717.

Miller, R. B., DeBacker, T. K., & Greene, B. A. (1999). Perceived instrumentality and academics: The links to task valuing. *Journal of Instructional Psychology, 26*, 250–260.

Mischel, W. (1981). Objective and subjective rules for delay of gratification. In G. d'Ydewalle & W. Lens (Eds.), *Cognition in human motivation and learning* (pp. 33–58). Leuven & Hillsdale, NJ: Leuven University Press & Erlbaum.

Patrick, H., Neighbours, C., & Knee, C. R. (2004). Appearance-related social comparisons: The role of contingent self-esteem and self-perceptions of attractiveness. *Personality and Social Psychology Bulletin, 30*, 501–514.

Raynor, J. O. (1981). Future orientation and achievement motivation: Toward a theory of personality functioning and change. In G. d'Ydewalle & W. Lens (Eds.), *Cognition in human motivation and learning* (pp. 199–231). Leuven & Hillsdale, NJ: Leuven University Press & Erlbaum.

Reeve, J., Deci, E. L., & Ryan, R. M. (2004). Self-determination theory: A dialectical framework for understanding socio-cultural influences on student motivation. In D. M. McInerney & S. Van Etten (Eds.), *Big theories revisited* (pp. 31–60). Greenwich, CT: Information Age.

Ryan, R. M., & Connell, J. P. (1989). Perceived locus of causality and internalization: Examining reasons for acting in two domains. *Journal of Personality and Social Psychology, 57,* 749–761.

Ryan, R. M., & Deci, E. L. (2000). Self-determination theory and the facilitation of intrinsic motivation, social development, and well-being. *American Psychologist, 55,* 68–78.

Schafer, R. (1968). *Aspects of internalization.* New York: International Universities Press.

Schmeichel, B. J., & Baumeister, R. F. (2004). Self-regulatory strength. In R. F. Baumeister & K. D. Vohs (Eds.), *Handbook of self-regulation: Research, theory, and applications* (pp. 84–98). New York: Guilford Press.

Senécal, C., Julien, E., & Guay, F. (2003). Role conflict and academic procrastination: A self-determination perspective. *European Journal of Social Psychology, 33,* 135–145.

Shallice, T., & Burgess, P. (1993). Supervisory control of action and thought selection. In A. Baddeley & L. Weiskrantz (Eds.), *Attention: selection, awareness, and control* (pp. 171–187). Oxford, U.K.: Clarendon Press.

Simons, J., Dewitte, S., & Lens, W. (2000). Wanting to have versus wanting to be: The effect of perceived instrumentality on goal orientation. *British Journal of Psychology, 91,* 335–351.

Simons, J., Dewitte, S., & Lens, W. (2003). "Don't do it for me, do it for yourself." Stressing the personal relevance enhances motivation in physical education. *Journal of Sport and Exercise Psychology, 25,* 145–160.

Simons, J., Dewitte, S., & Lens, W. (2004). The role of different types of instrumentality in motivation, study strategies, and performance: Know why you learn, so you'll know what you learn! *British Journal of Educational Psychology, 74,* 343–360.

Simons, J., Vansteenkiste, M., Lens, W., & Lacante, M. (2004). Placing motivation and future time perspective theory in a temporal perspective. *Educational Psychology Review, 16,* 121–139.

Sirgy, M. J. (1998). Materialism and quality of life. *Social Indicators Research, 43,* 227–260.

Soenens, B., & Vansteenkiste, M. (2005). Antecedents and outcomes of self-determination in three life domains: The role of parents' and teachers' autonomy support. *Journal of Youth and Adolescence, 34,* 589–604.

Uchnast, Z. (Ed.). (2006). *Psychology of time: Theoretical and empirical approaches.* Lublin, Poland: Wydawnictwo KUL.

Vallacher, R. R., & Wegner, D. M. (1985). *A theory of action identification.* Hillsdale, NJ: Erlbaum.

Vallacher, R. R., & Wegner, D. M. (1987). What do people think they're doing? Action identification and human behavior. *Psychological Review, 94,* 3–15.

Vallerand, R. J., Fortier, M. S., & Guay, F. (1997). Self-determination and persistence in a real-life setting: Toward a motivational model of high-school drop-out. *Journal of Personality and Social Psychology, 72,* 1161–1176.

Van Boven, L., & Gilovich, T. (2003). To do or to have? That is the question. *Journal of Personality and Social Psychology, 85,* 1193–1202.

Vansteenkiste, M., Lens, W., & Deci, E. L. (2006). Intrinsic versus extrinsic goal contents in self-determination theory: Another look at the quality of academic motivation. *Educational Psychologist, 41,* 19–31.

Vansteenkiste, M., Lens, W., Dewitte, S., De Witte, H., & Deci, E. L. (2004). The "why" and "why not" of job search behavior: Their relation to searching, unemployment experience, and well-being. *European Journal of Social Psychology, 34,* 345–363.

Vansteenkiste, M., Lens, W., Soenens, B., & Luyckx, K. (2006). Autonomy and relatedness among Chinese sojourners and applicants: Conflictual or independent predictors of well-being and adjustment. *Motivation and Emotion, 30,* 273–282.

Vansteenkiste, M., Matos, L., Lens, W., & Soenens, B. (in press). Understanding the impact of intrinsic versus extrinsic goal framing on exercise performance: The conflicting role of task and ego involvement. *Psychology of Sport and Exercise.*

Vansteenkiste, M., Simons, J., Lens, W., Sheldon, K. M., & Deci, E. L. (2004). Motivating learning, performance, and persistence: The synergistic effects of intrinsic goal contents and autonomy-supportive contexts. *Journal of Personality and Social Psychology, 87,* 246–260.

Vansteenkiste, M., Simons, J., Lens, W., Soenens, B., Matos, L., & Lacante, M. (2004). Less is sometimes more: Goal-content matters. *Journal of Educational Psychology, 96,* 755–764.

Vansteenkiste, M., Simons, J., Soenens, B., & Lens, W. (2004). How to become a persevering exerciser? Providing a clear, future intrinsic goal in an autonomy supportive way. *Journal of Sport and Exercise Psychology, 26,* 232–249.

Vansteenkiste, M., Zhou, M., Lens, W., & Soenens, B. (2005). Experiences of autonomy and control among Chinese learners. Vitalizing or immobilizing? *Journal of Educational Psychology, 97,* 468–483.

Wegner, D. M., & Wheatley, T. P. (1999). Why it feels as if we're doing things: Sources of the experience of will. *American Psychologist, 54,* 480–492.

Wigfield, A., & Eccles, J. (1992). The development of achievement task-values: A theoretical analysis. *Developmental Review, 12,* 265–310.

Williams, G. C., Cox, E. M., Hedberg, V. A., & Deci, E. L. (2000). Extrinsic life goals and health-risk behaviors among adolescents. *Journal of Applied Social Psychology, 30,* 1756–1771.

Wolters, C. (2000). The relation between high school students' motivational regulation and their use of learning strategies, effort, and classroom performance. *Learning and Individual Differences, 11,* 281–299.

Zaleski, Z. (Ed.). (1994). *Psychology of future orientation* (pp. 23–38). Lublin, Poland: Towarzystwo Naukowe KUL.

Zimmerman, B., & Martinez-Pons, M. (1990). Student differences in self-regulated learning: Relating grade, sex, and giftedness to self-efficacy and strategy use. *Journal of Educational Psychology, 82,* 51–59.

Zimmerman, B. J., & Schunk, D. H. (2001). Reflections on theories of self-regulated learning and academic achievement. In B. J. Zimmerman & D. H. Schunk (Eds.), *Self-regulated learning and academic achievement: Theoretical perspectives* (2nd ed., pp. 289–307). Mahwah, NJ: Erlbaum.

7

The Role of Achievement Values in the Regulation of Achievement Behaviors*

*Allan Wigfield, Laurel W. Hoa,
and Susan Lutz Klauda*

INTRODUCTION

In this chapter, we review research on how children's valuing of achievement tasks may influence the ways in which they regulate their behavior in achievement situations. In doing so, we attempt to link research based primarily in an expectancy-value model of achievement motivation and behavior developed by Eccles, Wigfield, and their colleagues (e.g., Eccles, 1993; Eccles [Parsons] et al., 1983; Wigfield, 1994; Wigfield & Eccles, 1992, 2000, 2002) with the growing body of research on students' self-regulation. Our general premise is that the different ways in which children do (or do not) value the achievement activities that they are doing likely has an impact on the quality and quantity of their use of different self-regulatory strategies as they do these activities. We review the research relevant to this general premise and discuss in some detail a specific example from the area of reading comprehension instruction of how teachers can foster children's self-regulation by increasing their valuing of reading. We begin by defining achievement values in the Eccles and Wigfield expectancy-value model.

* Much of the research on children's achievement values discussed in this chapter was supported by grant HD-17553 from the National Institute of Child Health and Human Development (NICHD). Other research discussed in this chapter was supported by grant MH-31724 from the National Institute for Mental Health, HD-17296 from NICHD, grant BNS-8510504 from the National Science Foundation, and grants from the Spencer Foundation.

DEFINING ACHIEVEMENT VALUES

Eccles and Wigfield's expectancy-value model of achievement behavior and choice has been discussed in some detail in a variety of publications [e.g., Eccles, 1993; Eccles (Parsons) et al., 1983; Wigfield & Eccles, 1992, 2000, 2002; Wigfield, Tonks, & Eccles, 2004]. Here, we focus primarily on the achievement values construct in the model, but because students' expectancies for success also are important to their regulation of achievement behavior, we define this construct. We focus on these two constructs because in this model they are the ones linked most directly to children's achievement behaviors and choices and thus to the regulation of achievement behavior.

Expectancies for success are defined as children's beliefs about how well they will do on future tasks; these expectancies are closely tied to their beliefs about their ability to accomplish different tasks, but because they focus on the future, the two types of beliefs have been distinguished conceptually. The subjective value of a task or activity to an individual depends in part on the nature of the task and on the needs, goals, and broader personal values held by the individual [Eccles (Parsons) et al., 1983; Wigfield & Eccles, 1992]. As stated by Eccles (Parsons) et al. (1983), "The degree to which the task is able to fulfill needs, facilitate reaching goals, or affirm personal values determines the value a person attaches to engaging in that task" (p. 89).

Both expectancies and values are essential to achievement behavior and choice; however, in this model expectancies for success are tied most directly to performance and achievement values most closely to the choice of which activities individuals do. As many researchers have noted, when individuals believe they can accomplish an activity, they are more likely to engage in it and persist at it (Bandura, 1997; Schunk & Pajares, 2002; Wigfield & Eccles, 2002). However, the extent to which the activity is valued plays a crucial role in activity choice. Individuals may feel competent at a given activity but not engage in it because it has no value for them. Because expectancies and values themselves are related, each can have indirect influences on the performance and choice outcomes.

Eccles (Parsons) et al. (1983) proposed four major components of achievement values: attainment value or importance, intrinsic value, utility value or usefulness of the task, and cost [see Eccles (Parsons) et al., 1983, and Wigfield & Eccles, 1992, for more detailed discussion of these components]. These components are presented in Table 7.1. Building on E. Battle's (1965, 1966) work, Eccles et al. defined *attainment value* as the importance of doing well on a given task. More broadly, attainment value also deals with identity issues; tasks are important when individuals view them as central to their own sense of themselves. *Intrinsic value* reflects the enjoyment one gains from doing the task; this component is similar in certain respects to the constructs of intrinsic motivation (see Ryan & Deci, 2002; Harter, 1981) and interest (see Hidi, chapter 4, this volume; Renninger & Hidi, 2002). When one intrinsically values an activity, the person does it because it is enjoyable, not as a means to another end. By contrast, *utility value* or *usefulness* refers to how a task fits into an individual's future plans, for instance, taking a math class to fulfill a requirement for a science degree. Here, the activity is not done for its own sake but for another reason. *Cost* refers to what the individual has to give up to do a task (e.g., do I do my math homework or call my friend?), as well as the anticipated effort one will need to put into task completion. The cost aspect has been the least studied of these components of task value, but as we discuss in this chapter, it likely has important implications for the regulation of behavior (see A. Battle & Wigfield, 2003).

In original statements of the expectancy-value model, competence beliefs were posited to predict both expectancies for success and achievement values. Relations between expectancies and values

TABLE 7.1   Components of Achievement Task Values in Eccles and Wigfield's Expectancy–Value Model

Value Component	Definition	Example
Attainment value	Importance of the activity to the individual	I value AP courses because I see myself as a capable student
Interest value	Enjoyment obtained from doing an activity	I love reading novels
Utility value	Usefulness of the activity to the individual	I am taking this math class because I want to be a doctor
Cost	Perception of amount of effort needed for the activity and how that has an impact on other valued activities	I don't have time to do my homework because I'd rather go out with my friends

themselves were not specified. However, researchers have found that children's competence and expectancy beliefs relate positively to their subjective values (e.g., E. Battle, 1966; Eccles & Wigfield, 1995), with the relations apparent as early as first grade (Wigfield et al., 1997). These findings contrast with Atkinson's (1957) assertion that the most valued tasks are the ones that are difficult for individuals to do (i.e., tasks on which individuals have low expectancies for success). It appears that, for real-world achievement tasks, individuals value the tasks at which they think they can succeed. It also appears that changes in children's expectancy beliefs predict change in children's valuing of different achievement activities (Jacobs, Lanza, Osgood, Eccles, & Wigfield, 2002). These findings have important implications for students' regulation of their achievement behavior, as we discuss.

We noted that children's achievement values relate to and predict their choices of which activities to do; thus, values are one cause of behavioral choice. It also is important to point out that the individual's valuing of a task depends in part on the nature of the task or activity and the contexts in which it occurs. Brophy (1999) discussed how children's valuing of activities is facilitated when the activities are meaningful to them, are connected to other things they do, and are authentic. Brophy also emphasized teachers' roles in scaffolding children's valuing of learning, helping them to appreciate and recognize as authentic different activities that they do. Thus, children's achievement values should be viewed both as possible causes of subsequent behaviors and as effects of the nature of different activities and the contexts in which they occur.

*Theoretical Perspectives on Relations
of Students' Achievement Values to
the Regulation of Their Behavior*

There are a variety of models of self-regulation and self-regulated learning (see Boekaerts, Pintrich, & Zeidner, 2000). We focus (briefly) here on certain social cognitive models of self-regulated learning that are prominent in the educational psychology field. In their models of self-regulation, Pintrich and Zusho (2002), Schunk and Ertmer (2000), and Zimmerman (2000) discussed separate phases of self-regulation. It is important to note that these phases are not necessarily always sequential and may not occur in every learning situation, but they are a useful way to organize the types of regulatory actions that can occur during learning. In each of these phases, students must regulate their cognition, motivation and affect, behavior, and the contexts in which the learning is occurring.

The first phase is forethought and planning; the individual plans his or her course of action, and various motivational beliefs, values, and goals are activated. When individuals are positively motivated for an activity, they are more likely to plan carefully for it and actually engage in it. Next is performance in the learning situation; this phase also involves monitoring of both performance and motivation and attempts to control these things. For instance, by monitoring their performance students can decide when they may need to change the strategies they are using. During the performance phase, students can control their motivation in a variety of ways; for example, they can change their goals for certain learning outcomes or can value or devalue the outcome depending on how well they are doing and how important the outcome remains for them. The third phase is reflections on performance, which occur after the learning activities are completed. During reflection, the student attempts to understand why different outcomes occurred, manage his or her emotions with respect to the achievement outcomes, adjust his or her goals, and otherwise engage in self-evaluation and reflection about the learning situation just experienced. These reflections can influence the student's approach to the next task or activity undertaken in this domain of learning. If the reflections are positive, then students will be more likely to approach related tasks positively and enthusiastically than if their reflections on previous performance are negative.

Motivation generally and achievement values in particular play prominent roles in these models. Indeed, Zimmerman (2000) stated, "Because the most effective self-regulatory techniques require anticipation, concentration, effort, and careful self-reflection, they are used only when the skill or its outcome is highly valued" (p. 27). Importantly, motivation must be considered at each phase of the self-regulatory process (Pintrich & Zusho, 2002). Pintrich and Zusho suggested that during forethought/planning, the learner's goals for learning, beliefs about one's capability to complete the activity successfully, and valuing of the activity are activated. Similarly, both Zimmerman (2000) and Schunk and Ertmer (2000) noted that the value of an activity plays an important part in the forethought or preengagement phase of self-regulation; when activities are valued, students will devote more time both to planning for them and doing them. During performance, students must monitor their motivation and affect and keep them directed in positive ways if they are to be successful in achievement situations (see Wolters, 2003). During reflection, motivation for subsequent activities can be influenced by how one reacts to performance in the current learning situation, as just discussed.

Rheinberg, Vollmeyer, and Rollet (2000) also incorporated values into their model of self-regulation. They specified four different questions individuals pose to themselves concerning potential links of their actions to desired outcomes. The first two are expectancy-related questions: Does the situation determine the outcome, and can my actions have an impact on the outcome? If the answer to the first question is no and to the second question is yes, then an individual proceeds to the next two questions, which reflect the extent to which they value the activity. The first "values" question asks whether the consequences are personally important. If the answer is yes, then the individual considers whether there are desired consequences that may come from one's action in the learning situation. If the answer to this question is yes, then action is undertaken. Thus, in this model the importance of outcomes has a crucial impact on students' engagement in activities and regulation of their behavior to attain an outcome.

Rheinberg et al. (2000) further discussed two kinds of values in their model: incentives based on what the student considers to be important and incentives related to the activity itself. The first of these has some resemblance to attainment and utility value, and the second has some similarities to the notion of interest in certain activities or situational interest (see further discussion of situational interest in the next section).

Motivation is not only included in different models of self-regulation, but also is something that itself needs to be regulated during learning activities along with cognition, affect, and context (see Pintrich & Zusho, 2002). Wolters (2003) focused specifically on the regulation of motivation in learning situations. He defined as motivational issues choice of task, effort, and persistence at the task or tasks chosen. He then defined regulation of motivation as the individual's attempt to manage or control his or her choices, effort, and persistence. Importantly, such strategies are *self-regulatory* when they are under the student's control or direction. Wolters viewed motivation regulation as one part of the overall process of self-regulation and discussed specific ways students can regulate their self-efficacy, goals, and interest in the activities they are doing. For example, students can regulate their self-efficacy by attempting not to give in to self-doubt and self-criticism when facing challenging activities. Students can regulate their interest by varying the ways in which they are doing a task or activity, taking breaks to refresh themselves, or connecting what they are learning to other things they have learned. We return to studies of students' management of their motivation (specifically their valuing of the learning activity) in the next section.

As Wolters (2003) noted, one essential part of behavioral regulation tied directly to motivation is choice of whether to continue to do different activities; such choices often can be complex in real-world achievement situations, in which there are many uncertainties about probable outcomes (see Byrnes, 1998; Busemeyer & Townsend, 1993, for discussion of complex decision making under uncertainty). The decision about whether to continue or discontinue an activity often comes as individuals reflect back on their performance (see Schunk & Ertmer, 2000; Zimmerman, 2000). Carver and Scheier (2000) discussed how information processing through feedback loops, affective reactions, and expectancies for success provide the basis for deciding whether to continue doing an activity. As discussed next, we have found that children's valuing of different activities predicts their choices about which activities to pursue, often more strongly than expectancies for success. Thus, we would argue that the role of values in such decision making needs to be considered more carefully in models of self-regulation.

Relations of Achievement Values to the Regulation of Achievement Behavior: Research Findings

Research within Eccles and Wigfield's expectancy-value model has shown that individuals' expectancies for success and achievement values predict their achievement outcomes, including their performance, persistence, and choices of which activities to do [e.g., Durik, Vida, & Eccles, 2006; Eccles 1993; Eccles (Parsons) et al., 1983; Meece, Wigfield, & Eccles, 1990]. For instance, students' achievement task values predict both intentions and actual decisions to keep taking mathematics and English and to engage in sports activities. The relations are evident in children as young as those in first grade, although the relations strengthen across age [Eccles, 1984; Eccles (Parsons) et al. 1983; Eccles & Harold, 1991; Meece et al., 1990; Wigfield, 1997]. These relations also are robust over time; Durik et al. (2006) reported that the importance children gave to reading in fourth grade related significantly to the number of English classes they took in high school. Also, children's interest in reading measured in fourth grade indirectly predicted (through interest measured in tenth grade) high school leisure time reading, career aspirations, and course selections.

A. Battle and Wigfield (2003), in one of the few studies to include the cost component of achievement values, found that attainment and utility value were positive predictors of college students' intentions to enter graduate school, but the perceived psychological cost of graduate school attendance was a negative predictor. Thus, with respect to self-regulation, findings from this research show that when students value something they choose to do it more and likely perform better. When the activity is seen as having too great a cost, they will be less likely to engage in it.

Understanding how individuals' values relate to these relatively general choice and performance outcomes is important, but the models of the regulation of achievement behavior discussed here propose more specific ways in which students regulate their behavior at different phases of self-regulation. Unfortunately, to date there is a dearth of empirical research on this topic. There is a more expansive field of related research, however, on relations among values, goals, interest, motivation, and self-regulation, which can contribute to our emerging understanding of how values relate to regulation of behavior. In this section, we review these relevant studies along with extant research on values and self-regulation. There also is work on relations of volitional strategies, motivation, and self-regulation; see Corno's chapter 8 in this volume for discussion of that work.

One of the first empirical studies to examine the relations among motivation, values, and self-regulation was Pintrich and De Groot's (1990) correlational study. They measured a range of motivational, cognitive, and self-regulation variables using the Motivated Strategies for Learning Questionnaire (MSLQ) and investigated how they related to academic performance for seventh graders. In this study, intrinsic values (beliefs about importance of and interest in a task) were strongly related to seventh-grade students' reported use of cognitive strategies and self-regulation. Thus, when students reported believing that their schoolwork was important, they indicated use of such metacognitive strategies as planning and comprehension monitoring and use of such effort management strategies as persistence and diligence to master difficult or tedious material. It is important to note that intrinsic value was not directly related to performance outcomes; rather, cognitive strategy use and self-regulation significantly predicted academic performance, with value related to cognitive engagement and regulation. This finding suggests that the role of values in the regulation of achievement behavior is to determine (in part) the extent to which the individual engages cognitively in the activity and regulates this activity, with these two variables relating more directly to performance.

Wolters and his colleagues (e.g., Wolters, 1999, 2003; Wolters & Pintrich, 1998; Wolters & Rosenthal, 2000; Wolters, Yu, & Pintrich, 1996) have done much research on values, goals, motivation, and self-regulated learning. Wolters and Pintrich (1998) examined the relation between motivational components, including task value, and self-regulation in seventh- and eighth-grade students. Task value and strategies for self-regulation of learning were measured with self-report questionnaires, and performance was measured with teachers' grade reports. Results indicated that task value strongly predicted use of cognitive and self-regulatory strategies, yet task value did not significantly predict performance. Thus, it appears that students who value a task or subject are more likely to report deeper cognitive processing and more strategies to regulate their learning behavior. However, task value itself is not directly related to academic achievement; these results replicate those reported by Pintrich and De Groot (1990).

What are some of the specific motivational predictors of achievement values? Wolters et al. (1996) examined this question using self-reported information about goal orientations, motivation, and self-regulated learning from seventh- and eighth-grade students. They measured three goal orientations: learning goal orientation (focus on mastery of material), extrinsic goal orientation (focus on grades, avoiding punishment), and relative ability orientation (focus on competition, social comparison). Learning goal and relative ability orientations both positively predicted students' task value and use of cognitive and self-regulatory strategies. An extrinsic goal orientation was negatively related with task value and self-regulated learning. Therefore, students who focused either on learning material for its own sake or on social comparison had higher levels of interest, perceived greater utility, and regulated their learning behavior more than students focused on grades. Although this study did not directly relate values to self-regulation, it appears that students with intrinsic and utility value for learning tasks also regulate their behavior, and those who lack task value do not frequently engage in self-regulation.

Wolters and Rosenthal (2000) corroborated these results with respect to goal orientations in a study that also examined the relations of task value with five strategies for the regulation of motivation. These strategies were (a) self-consequating, by which students give themselves reinforcement or punishment as they work toward an academic goal; (b) environmental control, by which students make their surroundings conducive to task completion; (c) performance self-talk, in which goals are emphasized that focus on good grades and rewards; (d) mastery self-talk, for which motivation comes from a desire to master the material; and (e) interest enhancement, by which students make a task more interesting and enjoyable. Students completed self-report questionnaires assessing their use of these motivation regulation strategies and task values, and performance was obtained from school records. In this study with eighth-grade students, task value was significantly related to self-consequating, environmental control, mastery self-talk, and interest enhancement. Task value was not related to performance self-talk, for which the focus is on grades. In general, students who highly valued a task stated that they employed many self-regulatory strategies to accomplish that task. Results from regression analyses indicated that task value predicted students' reported use of self-consequating, mastery self-talk, and interest enhancement. Thus, it appears that when students value an academic activity, this may prompt them to engage in motivation regulation strategies to enhance their interest and desire to master the material and think about consequences for completing or not completing the activity.

In related work, Wolters (1999) examined relations between regulation of motivation and learning strategies in ninth- and tenth-grade students. Some of the motivation regulation strategies studied were interest enhancement, performance self-talk (good grades), and mastery self-talk (desire to learn). Students reported focusing on getting good grades to increase motivation more often than focusing on an inner desire to learn or making the material more interesting. However, mastery self-talk better predicted effort and persistence than performance self-talk. In addition, students who reported mastery self-talk stated that they used planning and monitoring strategies more than students with performance self-talk. Hence, learning material because of wanting to learn it (intrinsic value) was associated with the use of self-regulatory strategies to enhance learning.

There is some research that links interest, values, and self-regulation (see chapter 4, this volume, for a detailed discussion of the role of interest in self-regulated learning). To note, there are distinctions in the literature between personal and situational interest (see Hidi & Harackiewicz, 2001). *Personal,* or *individual, interest* is a relatively stable predisposition or personal characteristic oriented toward a domain over time. *Situational interest* refers to interest stimulated by an environmental event. Schiefele (1999) has asserted that personal interest is defined in part by value-related attributes or the personal significance and importance of a domain. Thus, interest and attainment value work together to influence motivation. Intrinsic and utility value are also related to interest; for example, a student might read a text with the goal of better understanding another text that is the true object of interest. These interests and values can provide motivation to impel behavior. Personal interest is related to the use of learning strategies, persistence, and cognitive engagement (Schiefele, 1999). Renninger and Hidi (2002) suggested that situational interest in a task can lead students to recognize attainment, intrinsic, and utility value of that task, particularly in an environment that provides and supports situational interest.

More empirical research is needed to understand further the role of achievement values in the regulation of specific types of behavior. It is particularly important to note that to date most of the empirical research has been correlational, so we currently lack knowledge about the causal direction of these relationships. We discussed that students' valuing of different tasks can be influenced by task characteristics and is predictive of future involvement with the task. A similar point applies to relations of students' task values and their regulation of behavior; such relations likely are bidirectional. As just reviewed, students' valuing of an activity can have an impact on the extent to which they engage in self-regulatory strategies. Engagement in these strategies may also have an impact on their valuing of the activity. By effectively regulating one's achievement behavior, doing well on an activity becomes more likely, which could increase the value of the activity for the individual. For example, a self-regulated student who studies hard and effectively for a geometry final and does well on it may come to value geometry more and see possibilities for mathematics careers not previously thought feasible.

Developmental Issues and Self-Regulation of the Educational Context

There are at least two developmental issues important to consider as we think about how children's values relate to their self-regulation and learning. The first is how the relations of values and regulatory processes change over time. Children only gradually learn how to regulate their achievement behavior (see Zimmerman, 2000, for discussion of different levels of self-regulatory behavior in learning settings). Given this, it is possible that relations between children's valuing of different tasks and how they regulate their behavior while doing those tasks may be weak at first and gradually grow in strength as children develop. Ultimately, children may regulate their behavior to the greatest extent when they value the tasks they are doing. As just noted, effective regulation of certain achievement behaviors leading to success on a task or activity also could increase a child's valuing of that activity.

Second, there is a large body of work showing that children's valuing of different academic activities decreases over time (Fredricks & Eccles, 2002; Jacobs et al., 2002; Wigfield, Eccles, Mac Iver, Reuman, & Midgley, 1991; Wigfield et al., 1997; see Wigfield, Eccles, Schiefele, Roeser, & Davis-Kean, 2006, for review). Most children come to school excited about learning, curious about many different topics, and interested in what they are learning at school. As they go through the school years, this excitement disappears for many children, and school becomes more like a workplace than an exciting place to learn new things. The observed decline in many children's valuing of achievement may have an impact on the ways in which they regulate their achievement behaviors. First, if children begin to devalue academic activities, in that their interest in and perceived importance of them decreases, then children will choose to do them less. This may become particularly true as other activities become more appealing to them. Recall that the cost aspect of achievement values refers to how much engaging in one activity makes it difficult to engage in another activity. The cost of engaging in academic activities becomes higher as other activities become more appealing. Second, if academic activities become less valued, then students may not work as hard at them or monitor their performance as carefully as they might otherwise, and so on. As discussed, when one is interested in a text or activity, deep processing is more likely to occur; lack of interest (or other forms of value) may undermine the types of deep cognitive processing that leads to stronger learning.

These kinds of problems may become particularly acute for students who become apathetic about learning; by definition, apathetic students are those who see little value in academic learning. As Zimmerman (2000) put it, "When a skill or its outcomes are not perceived as valuable, there is no incentive to self-regulate" (p. 27). Apathetic students are not likely to be engaged in learning and even less likely to engage in the types of self-regulatory strategies that can lead to learning. Brophy (2004) discussed how apathetic students do not have fully developed schemas for how to learn or to be motivated to learn and so do not see school tasks as learning opportunities but instead as tasks imposed on them that they do not want to do. According to Brophy, socializing apathetic students' motivation to learn can be a difficult process. To reconnect apathetic students and other students who devalue learning, teachers must focus on students' motivation as well as cognition in their teaching (see Ames, 1992; Stipek, 1996, 2002). The reading comprehension instruction program discussed in the next section focuses on both motivational and cognitive aspects of reading.

The term *self-regulation* by its very definition focuses on the individual, and thus it is tempting to think that models of self-regulation do not attend to the learning context in much detail. This actually is not the case; social cognitive models of self-regulation give the learning context an important role in the self-regulatory process. For instance, Pintrich (2000; Pintrich & Zusho, 2002) included the learning context as one of the main areas of self-regulation, along with behavior, motivation/affect, and cognition. The learning context can have an impact on self-regulation in at least two broad ways. First, students often attempt to control or regulate their learning environments; this is the sense in which the learning context is an area of self-regulation. Second, the nature of the learning context can facilitate or undermine students' attempts to regulate their achievement behaviors, depending on the nature of the context, the tasks and activities included, and teachers' approaches to them. For instance, learning contexts that are completely teacher centered likely will not foster students' own self-regulatory skills. We turn next to a discussion of a reading comprehension instructional program that attempts to foster students' motivation for reading and regulation of their reading behavior to build students' engagement in reading.

INSTRUCTIONAL PRACTICES TO FOSTER STUDENT ENGAGEMENT AND SELF-REGULATION: CONCEPT-ORIENTED READING INSTRUCTION

Concept-Oriented Reading Instruction, or CORI, is a reading comprehension instructional program in which teachers seek to help students become skilled at comprehending diverse types of reading materials and foster students' motivation to become independent readers who strive for deep comprehension of what they read. To achieve these aims, teachers provide instruction in a variety of strategies for reading comprehension while implementing five instructional practices grounded in research on achievement motivation to enhance children's motivation for reading and engagement in reading activities. Another central feature of the CORI program is that reading instruction is integrated with instruction in a domain such as science or social studies to provide meaningful content for the reading instruction (see Guthrie, Wigfield, & Perencevich, 2004a, and Swan, 2003, for detailed overviews of CORI).

In the theoretical framework underlying CORI, it is the joint implementation of strategy instruction and motivational practices that is viewed as facilitating students' engagement in reading and thereby their growth in comprehension (Guthrie & Wigfield, 2000). In Guthrie and Wigfield's view, engaged readers are motivated, knowledgeable, socially interactive, and strategic as they read. Here, we focus specifically on the practices for fostering student motivation because these are the practices most likely to augment the value that students place on reading as an activity in itself and promote the development of independent, self-regulated reading. (For more information about the comprehension strategies, see Guthrie & Taboada, 2004.)

The five motivational practices (see Table 7.2) that teachers implement in CORI classrooms directly support development of students' valuing of reading and help students become strategic, independent, and therefore self-regulated readers. The first motivational practice, hands-on activities, means that CORI teachers involve students in scientific experiments, observations, and modeling of natural processes closely tied to the conceptual theme of the unit the teachers are presenting (Guthrie, 2004; Guthrie, Wigfield, & Perencevich, 2004b). For instance, when the theme is hidden worlds of the woodland and wetland, students simulate the effects of pollution on wetlands by exposing celery plants grown in the classroom to several different substances. Teachers use such hands-on activities, particularly at the start of a unit, to stimulate students to form their own questions about the focal topic or foster their personal, unique interests within the larger theme. The activities are designed not to provide all the information students need to answer their questions, but rather to encourage them to do further reading on the topic. In this way, students may develop greater value for reading as a major means to satisfying their curiosities.

Second, throughout each instructional unit, CORI teachers emphasize conceptual knowledge goals and the relatedness of all activities to the one central theme (Guthrie, 2004; Guthrie, Wigfield, & Perencevich, 2004b). This conceptual focus and provision of explicit purposes for learning may help students develop a sense that what they are doing in school has long-term meaning and relevance

TABLE 7.2   Effects of Engaging Instructional Practices on Students' Valuing and Self-Regulation of Reading

Instructional Practice	Impact on Value and Self-Regulation
Hands-on activities	Stimulate situational and personal interest in the topic studied
Conceptual knowledge goals	Provide purposes for learning and authenticate the learning activities, thus increasing attainment value
Provision of interesting texts	Increases students' intrinsic valuing of reading
Autonomy support	Increases attainment value and students' regulation of their achievement activities
Collaboration support	Increases students' interest value and coregulation of achievement activities

and foster a mastery-oriented rather than a performance-oriented learning orientation (Guthrie, Wigfield, & Perencevich, 2004b).

The third CORI motivational practice, the provision of interesting texts, has special importance in generating and sustaining the value that students place on reading and hence in facilitating their self-regulation. In CORI, in contrast with traditional reading curricula, students are not given basal readers, and in contrast with traditional science curricula, students are not given science textbooks. Instead, a wide variety of information and literary trade books are the primary reading materials. Books of both types are selected that are appropriate for diverse reading levels. Special care is taken to find books for struggling readers that do not sacrifice depth or accuracy for easiness to read (Davis & Tonks, 2004). In addition, many high-quality Web sites have been identified that correspond with each instructional theme and that extend the information available in books or encourage new ways of interacting with it. Employing this variety of reading materials helps students develop greater familiarity with the diversity of reading materials available beyond traditional schoolbooks. Having varied and interesting reading materials in classrooms increases the likelihood that each student will discover materials that capture the student's attention or mesh with their preexisting topic interests or genre preferences and are of appropriate difficulty for their reading level. Thus, the provision of interesting texts likely helps increase the value students place on reading and their likelihood of reading in their free time both inside and outside school.

The fourth motivational practice is autonomy support or affording students some control over what and how they learn (Guthrie, 2004; Guthrie, Wigfield, & Perencevich, 2004b). To a large degree, this means giving students choices and permitting them to make decisions about different aspects of the tasks they are given, such as what specific topics they will research, which books or which sections of books they will read, whether they will work independently or with others, and what form of expression they will use to share what they have learned through reading. However, as discussed in more detail here, teachers need to gauge how much autonomy the class as a whole as well as individual students are ready to assume and to moderate accordingly the significance of the decisions they ask their students to make and the number of options they give them. Students, for instance, only make choices about the foci of their culminating project for CORI once they have received about 8 weeks of CORI and have developed some familiarity with the topics they are studying.

This practice of autonomy support perhaps most directly links to the development of self-regulation in reading. By offering students some control of their reading activities, teachers are conveying to students that they view them as competent both in reading and in making decisions for themselves, which should increase student self-efficacy and consequently the value that they place on reading. Also, students may develop a sense of ownership for the particular choices they make and thus be more invested in ensuring that their choices lead to positive outcomes, like sizable gains in knowledge through their reading or effective products (e.g., posters or "published" books) for sharing their knowledge with others (Au, 1997; Guthrie, Wigfield, & Perencevich, 2004b). Finally, giving choices to students, particularly about which topics they will explore through reading, means that students have the opportunity to do what they find the most interesting of the available options and thus hopefully minimizes the chance that they will become bored, distracted, or frustrated in their work.

The final motivation practice is support for student collaboration (Guthrie, 2004; Guthrie, Wigfield, & Perencevich, 2004b). Teachers do this by regularly providing opportunities for students to work together on CORI activities as pairs, teams, or a whole class. For example, within one lesson teams of about five students discussed with each other the results of their science experiment, and a representative of each team then shared the results with the whole class. Then, pairs of students brainstormed a question relevant to the lesson topic, individually searched for the answer to their joint question in different books, and shared the information they had found with each other and composed an answer together. Although at first glance student collaboration may appear irrelevant to the development of self-regulation, it does potentially play a facilitative role. As Wentzel (1999) contended, when students have group assignments, "the group enforces individual efforts to achieve common goals that represent both social and task-related outcomes" (p. 89); thus, when students have collaborative projects to complete, they may make special effort to ensure that they make a helpful contribution to the group. Also, in a classroom atmosphere that encourages students to consult with one another, even when not explicitly instructed to do so, students may take good advantage of their classmates as knowledge resources when they have difficulty with part of an assignment rather than flounder and lose the motivation or ability to persist at the task (see Webb & Palincsar, 1996, for discussion of how by working together students help regulate each other's achievement behaviors).

The specific ways in which teachers implement each of the five motivational practices in CORI may vary tremendously. A common guiding principle, however, is that they all should be implemented in ways that support, or scaffold, students' development into engaged, self-regulated readers. Scaffolding for motivation and engagement in reading is a process that is similar to the use of scaffolding for cognitive development (Guthrie, Wigfield, & Perencevich, 2004b). That is, it involves the teacher gradually reducing the degree of support provided to the student or transferring responsibility to the student as he or she develops the expertise to work independently in a given area. The only difference is that the focus is on helping students develop the motivation, including the sense of value, they need to become engaged readers and fully use their cognitive abilities, rather than solely the cognitive abilities themselves.

Scaffolding for motivation and engagement entails recognizing the appropriate level of support that students need to engage productively in reading; too much scaffolding may inhibit self-regulation just as much as too little scaffolding (Guthrie, Wigfield, & Perencevich, 2004b). For instance, as alluded to in the discussion of autonomy support, it is critical that teachers do not initially give their students too many choices about what to read. An effective high scaffold for student decision making at the beginning of the program, for example, might be for the teacher to ask students to choose between two books, each focusing on a subtopic of the central theme about which the teacher has just provided significant background information. The teacher might also model the decision-making process by explicitly stating one reason for choosing each book. Gradually, the teacher might reduce the scaffolding for decision making of this sort by increasing the number of book options, providing less background information, and asking students for their reasons for choosing particular books rather than supplying reasons to them. Ultimately, highly self-regulated readers can make their own selections from the full classroom library and base these selections on their well-established interests and long-term goals relevant to the unit theme. Similarly, teachers might initially provide a high scaffold for collaboration support by forming teams of students, assigning students specific roles within their teams, and providing them explicit guidelines for how to work effectively as a group. Eventually, though, students might be encouraged simply to form groups with others with whom they know they can work well and to divide the group work as they see fit.

Lutz, Guthrie, and Davis (2006) have documented how CORI teachers modify their scaffolds during the course of different instructional activities, even within individual lessons, and that these modifications have a strong impact on students' engagement in the activity and regulation of their achievement behaviors. For example, single lessons in two CORI classrooms were described in which the teachers provided strong, varied scaffolding for all students, but only for the first third of the lessons; for the remaining two thirds, the overall level of scaffolding was greatly reduced and consisted primarily of prompts for a few individual students. This pattern of scaffolding appeared to enable students at diverse reading levels to self-regulate their engagement in complex tasks involving searching information books to answer conceptual questions about survival in different habitats.

Research on Concept-Oriented Reading Instruction's Effects on Students' Reading Comprehension and Motivation

Research on earlier versions of CORI showed that students experiencing CORI surpassed students receiving traditional instruction in reading comprehension, strategy learning (Guthrie et al., 1998; Guthrie, Wigfield, Metsala, & Cox, 1999), and reading motivation (Guthrie, Wigfield, & Von Secker, 2000). These studies provided important initial support for CORI's effectiveness.

Guthrie, Wigfield, and their colleagues currently are conducting a study of CORI's effects on third- through fifth-grade children's reading motivation and comprehension (e.g., Guthrie, Wigfield, Barbosa et al., 2004; Guthrie et al., in press; Guthrie et al., 2006; Wigfield, Guthrie, Tonks, & Perencevich, 2004). Some of the children in the study participated in CORI, some were in a reading program that focused on cognitive strategy instruction, and some were in the school district's traditional instruction program. The CORI intervention lasted 12 weeks, and the study had a pretest-posttest matched-groups quasi-experimental design. A variety of reading comprehension, reading motivation, and actual strategy use measures was obtained at pretest and posttest; the reading motivation measures focused on intrinsic motivation and valuing of reading. Strategies measured included activation of background knowledge, generation of questions, and a search for information. Results of these studies showed that, in both third and fourth grade, CORI students surpassed students in the strategy instruction and traditional instruction groups in reading motivation, use of strategies, and reading comprehension. Thus, the CORI instructional program enhanced students' motivation, regulation of their reading behavior (as measured by the use of reading strategies), and their achievement in reading.

CONCLUSION AND DIRECTIONS FOR FUTURE RESEARCH

In this chapter, we reviewed work showing that children's valuing of the achievement activities they do has an important role in the regulation of achievement behavior. Children's valuing of achievement relates positively to their choices of which activities to do, intentions to continue their involvement in different activities, and (self-reported) regulation of their use of different cognitive and other regulatory strategies. We also discussed how instructional programs (specifically, the CORI reading comprehension instructional program) designed to foster children's motivation for reading by increasing their interest in reading and control over their reading activities (among other things) foster both children's valuing of reading and use of cognitive strategies in reading. This research indicates clearly that children's motivation and self-regulation of achievement behavior can be fostered through specific instructional practices, with positive effects on not only motivation and self-regulation but also achievement.

There are a number of important directions for future research on relations of achievement values to self-regulation. First, Eccles, Wigfield, and their colleagues defined and measured different aspects of children's values, including attainment value, interest value, and utility value [Eccles (Parsons) et al., 1983; Wigfield & Eccles, 1992]. Most of the research to date has looked at how composite measures of children's values relate to different outcomes. It would be interesting to assess whether the different aspects of values relate to the regulation of achievement behavior in different ways. For instance, extant research shows that when children are interested in a topic they engage in it more deeply and thus regulate their behavior to complete the activity (Hidi, chapter 4, this volume; Renninger & Hidi, 2002). We predict that children who have high attainment value for an activity also likely engage in such activities deeply and therefore carefully regulate their achievement behaviors. The pattern may be somewhat different for utility value; if one engages in an activity in pursuit of another end, then he or she may regulate "just enough" to accomplish the activity rather than engaging in it as fully as when one values the activity intrinsically.

Second, it would be interesting to look at how children's valuing of different activities relates to their specific regulation of their achievement behaviors in different settings. Much of the work to date has looked at relations of values to relatively general achievement behaviors (e.g., choice, intentions to continue) rather than to specific regulatory behaviors as defined in the different social cognitive models reviewed. Looking at these specific relations would provide a clearer understanding of the relations and may begin to help us understand some of the processes involved in them; this work will help embellish theoretical models of achievement values and of self-regulation. Such work likely will require the development of different types of measures of achievement value that capture their ongoing operation in different achievement contexts.

Third, much of the work on relations of values to different types of regulatory strategies has used self-report measures of both values and self-regulation. It now is important to supplement this work with research using behavioral measures of self-regulation along with (or in place of) the self-report measures of self-regulation. Guthrie, Wigfield, Barbosa, and colleagues' (2004) work using measures of actual strategy use rather than self-reports was an important step in this direction.

Finally, to help foster the development of children's motivation and self-regulation, it is essential to build instructional programs in different instructional areas that do both things. The CORI program has been successful in doing so for elementary school students' reading motivation, strategy use, and comprehension. Programs need to be developed in other subject areas and for children of different ages and levels of schooling to work toward the important goals of enhancing children's valuing of achievement and regulation of behavior to attain high levels of achievement.

REFERENCES

Ames, C. (1992). Achievement goals and the classroom motivational climate. In D. Schunk & J. Meece (Eds.) *Student perceptions in the classroom* (pp. 327–349). Hillsdale, NJ: Erlbaum.

Atkinson, J. W. (1957). Motivational determinants of risk taking behavior. *Psychological Review, 64,* 359–372.

Au, K. H. (1997). Ownership, literacy achievement, and students of diverse cultural backgrounds. In J. T. Guthrie & A. Wigfield (Eds.), *Reading engagement: Motivating readers through integrated instruction* (pp. 168–182). Newark, DE: International Reading Association.

Bandura, A. (1997). *Self-efficacy: The exercise of control.* New York: Freeman.

Battle, A., & Wigfield, A. (2003). College women's value orientations toward family, career, and graduate school. *Journal of Vocational Behavior, 62,* 56–75.

Battle, E. (1965). Motivational determinants of academic task persistence. *Journal of Personality and Social Psychology, 2,* 209–218.

Battle, E. (1966). Motivational determinants of academic competence. *Journal of Personality and Social Psychology, 4,* 534–642.

Boekaerts, M., Pintrich, P. R., & Zeidner, M. (Eds.). (2000). *Handbook of self-regulation.* San Diego, CA: Academic Press.

Brophy, J. E. (1999). Toward a model of the value aspects of motivation for education: Developing appreciation for particular learning domains and activities. *Educational Psychologist, 34,* 75–86.

Brophy, J. E. (2004). *Motivating students to learn* (2nd ed.). Mahwah, NJ: Erlbaum.

Busemeyer, J. R., & Townsend, J. T. (1993). Decision field theory: A dynamic cognitive approach to decision making in an uncertain environment. *Psychological Review, 100,* 432–459.

Byrnes, J. P. (1998). *The nature and development of decision-making: A self-regulation perspective.* Mahwah, NJ; Erlbaum.

Carver, C. S., & Scheier, M. F. (2000). On the structural of behavioral self-regulation. In M. Boekaerts, P. R. Pintrich, & M. Zeidner (Eds.), *Handbook of self-regulation* (pp. 41–84). San Diego, CA: Academic Press.

Davis, M. H., & Tonks, S. (2004). Diverse texts and technology for reading. In J. T. Guthrie, A. Wigfield, & K. C. Perencevich (Eds.), *Motivating reading comprehension: Concept-Oriented Reading Instruction* (pp. 143–172). Mahwah, NJ: Erlbaum.

Durik, A. M., Vida, M., & Eccles, J. S. (2006). Task values and ability beliefs as predictors of high school literacy choices: A developmental analysis. *Journal of Educational Psychology, 98*, 382–393.

Eccles, J. S. (1984). Sex differences in achievement patterns. In T. Sonderegger (Ed.), *Nebraska Symposium on Motivation* (Vol. 32, pp. 97–132). Lincoln: University of Nebraska Press.

Eccles, J. S. (1993). School and family effects on the ontogeny of children's interests, self-perceptions, and activity choice. In J. Jacobs (Ed.), *Nebraska Symposium on Motivation, 1992: Developmental perspectives on motivation* (pp. 145–208). Lincoln: University of Nebraska Press.

Eccles (Parsons), J., Adler, T. F., Futterman, R., Goff, S. B., Kaczala, C. M., Meece, J. L., et al. (1983). Expectancies, values, and academic behaviors. In J. T. Spence (Ed.), *Achievement and achievement motivation* (pp. 75–146). San Francisco: Freeman.

Eccles, J. S., & Harold, R. D. (1991). Gender differences in sport involvement: Applying the Eccles' expectancy-value model. *Journal of Applied Sport Psychology, 3*, 7–35.

Eccles, J. S., & Wigfield, A. (1995). In the mind of the achiever: The structure of adolescents' academic achievement related-beliefs and self-perceptions. *Personality and Social Psychology Bulletin, 21*, 215–225.

Fredricks, J., & Eccles, J. S. (2002). Children's competence and value beliefs from childhood through adolescence: Growth trajectories in two male sex-typed domains. *Developmental Psychology, 38*, 519–533.

Guthrie, J. T. (2004). Classroom contexts for engaged reading: An overview. In J. T. Guthrie, A. Wigfield, & K. C. Perencevich (Eds.), *Motivating reading comprehension: Concept-Oriented Reading Instruction* (pp. 1–24). Mahwah, NJ: Erlbaum.

Guthrie, J. T., & Taboada, A. (2004). Fostering the cognitive strategies of reading comprehension. In J. T. Guthrie, A. Wigfield, & K. C. Perencevich (Eds.), *Motivating reading comprehension: Concept-Oriented Reading Instruction* (pp. 87–112). Mahwah, NJ: Erlbaum.

Guthrie, J. T., Van Meter, P., Hancock, G. R., McCann, A., Anderson, E., & Alao, S. (1998). Does Concept-Oriented Reading Instruction increase strategy-use and conceptual learning from text? *Journal of Educational Psychology, 90*, 261–278.

Guthrie, J. T., Hoa, L. W., Wigfield, A., Tonks, S. M., Humenick, N., & Littles, E. (in press). Reading motivation and reading comprehension growth in the later elementary years. *Contemporary Educational Psychology.*

Guthrie, J. T., & Wigfield, A. (2000). Engagement and motivation in reading. In M. Kamil, P. Mosenthal, P. D. Pearson, & R. Barr (Eds.), *Handbook of reading research* (Vol. 3, pp. 403–422). Mahwah, NJ: Erlbaum.

Guthrie, J. T., Wigfield, A., Barbosa, P., Perencevich, K. C., Taboada, A., Davis, M. H., et al. (2004). Increasing reading comprehension, motivation, and strategy use through Concept Oriented Reading Instruction. *Journal of Educational Psychology, 96,* 403–423.

Guthrie, J. T., Wigfield, A., Humenick, N. H., Perencevich, K. C., Taboada, A., & Barbosa, P. (2006). Influences of stimulating tasks on reading motivation and comprehension. *Journal of Educational Research, 99,* 232–247.

Guthrie, J. T., Wigfield, A., Metsala, J. L., & Cox, K. E. (1999). Motivational and cognitive predictors of text comprehension and reading amount. *Scientific Studies of Reading, 3,* 231–257.

Guthrie, J. T., Wigfield, A., & Perencevich, K. C. (Eds.). (2004a). *Motivating reading comprehension: Concept-Oriented Reading Instruction.* Mahwah, NJ: Erlbaum.

Guthrie, J. T., Wigfield, A., & Perencevich, K. C. (2004b). Scaffolding for motivation and engagement in reading. In J. T. Guthrie, A. Wigfield, & K. C. Perencevich (Eds.), *Motivating reading comprehension: Concept-Oriented Reading Instruction* (pp. 55–86). Mahwah, NJ: Erlbaum.

Guthrie, J. T., Wigfield, A., Von Secker, C. (2000) Effects of integrated instruction on motivation and strategy use in reading. *Journal of Educational Psychology, 92,* 331–341.

Harter, S. (1981). A new self-report scale of intrinsic versus extrinsic orientation in the classroom: Motivational and informational components. *Developmental Psychology, 17,* 300–312.

Hidi, S., & Harackiewicz, J. M. (2001). Motivating the academically unmotivated: A critical issue for the 21st century. *Review of Educational Research, 70,* 151–179.

Jacobs, J., Lanza, S., Osgood, D. W., Eccles, J. S., & Wigfield, A. (2002). Ontogeny of children's self-beliefs: Gender and domain differences across grades 1 through 12. *Child Development, 73,* 509–527.

Lutz, S. L., Guthrie, J. T., & Davis, M. H. (2006). Scaffolding for engagement in elementary school reading instruction. *Journal of Educational Research, 100,* 3–20.

Meece, J. L., Wigfield, A., & Eccles, J. S. (1990). Predictors of math anxiety and its consequences for young adolescents' course enrollment intentions and performances in mathematics. *Journal of Educational Psychology, 82,* 60–70.

Pintrich, P. R. (2000). The role of goal orientation in self-regulated learning. In M. Boekaerts, P. R. Pintrich, & M. Zeidner (Eds.), *Handbook of self-regulation* (pp. 451–502). San Diego, CA: Academic Press.

Pintrich, P. R., & De Groot, E. V. (1990). Motivational and self-regulated learning components of classroom academic performance. *Journal of Educational Psychology, 82,* 33–40.

Pintrich, P. R., & Zusho, A. (2002). The development of academic self-regulation: The role of cognitive and motivational factors. In A. Wigfield & J. S. Eccles (Eds.), *Development of achievement motivation* (pp. 173–195). San Diego, CA: Academic Press.

Renninger, K. A., & Hidi, S. (2002). Student interest and achievement: Developmental issues raised by a case study. In A. Wigfield & J. S. Eccles (Eds.), *Development of achievement motivation* (pp. 173–195). San Diego, CA: Academic Press.

Rheinberg, F., Vollmeyer, T., & Rollet, W. (2000). Motivation and action in self-regulated learning. In M. Boekaerts, P. R., Pintrich, & M. Zeidner (Eds.), *Handbook of self-regulation* (pp. 503–529). San Diego, CA: Academic Press.

Ryan, R. M., & Deci, E. L. (2002). An overview of self-determination theory: an organismic-dialectical perspective. In E. L. Deci & R. M. Ryan (Eds.), *Handbook of self-determination theory research* (pp. 3–33). Rochester, NY: University of Rochester Press.

Schiefele, U. (1999). Interest and learning from text. *Scientific Studies of Reading, 3,* 257–279.

Schunk, D. H., & Ertmer, P. A. (2000). Self-regulation and academic learning: Self-efficacy enhancing interventions. In M. Boekaerts, P. R. Pintrich, & M. Zeidner (Eds.), *Handbook of self-regulation* (pp. 631–649). San Diego, CA: Academic Press.

Schunk, D. H., & Pajares, F. (2002). The development of academic self-efficacy. In A. Wigfield & J. S. Eccles (Eds.), *Development of achievement motivation* (pp. 15–32). San Diego, CA: Academic Press.

Stipek, D. J. (1996). Motivation and instruction. In D. Berliner & R. Calfee (Eds.), *Handbook of educational psychology* (pp. 85–113). New York: Macmillan.

Stipek, D. J. (2002). Good instruction is motivating. In A. Wigfield & J. S. Eccles (Eds.), *Development of achievement motivation* (pp. 309–351). San Diego, CA: Academic Press.

Swan, E. A. (2003). *Concept-Oriented Reading Instruction: Engaging classrooms, lifelong learners.* New York: Guilford.

Webb, N. M., & Palincsar, A. S. (1996). Group processes in the classroom. In D. C. Berliner & R. C. Calfee (Eds.), *Handbook of educational psychology* (pp. 841–873). New York: Macmillan.

Wentzel, K. R. (1999). Social-motivational processes and interpersonal relationships: Implications for understanding motivation at school. *Journal of Educational Psychology, 91,* 76–97.

Wigfield, A. (1994). Expectancy-value theory of achievement motivation: A developmental perspective. *Educational Psychology Review, 6,* 49–78.

Wigfield, A. (1997, April). *Predicting children's grades from their ability beliefs and subjective task values: Developmental and domain differences.* Paper presented at the biennial meeting of the Society for Research in Child Development, Washington, DC.

Wigfield, A., & Eccles, J. (1992). The development of achievement task values: A theoretical analysis. *Developmental Review, 12,* 265–310.

Wigfield, A., & Eccles, J. S. (2000). Expectancy-value theory of motivation. *Contemporary Educational Psychology, 25,* 68–81.

Wigfield, A., & Eccles, J. S. (2002). The development of competence beliefs and values from childhood through adolescence. In A. Wigfield & J. S. Eccles (Eds.), *Development of achievement motivation* (pp. 92–120). San Diego, CA: Academic Press.

Wigfield, A., Eccles, J. S., Mac Iver, D., Reuman, D., & Midgley, C. (1991). Transitions at early adolescence: Changes in children's domain-specific self-perceptions and general self-esteem across the transition to junior high school. *Developmental Psychology, 27,* 552–565.

Wigfield, A., Eccles, J. S., Schiefele, U., Roeser, R., & Davis-Kean, P. (2006). Development of achievement motivation. In W. Damon (Series Ed.) & N. Eisenberg (Vol. Ed.), *Handbook of child psychology* (6th ed., Vol. 3, pp. 933–1002). New York: Wiley.

Wigfield, A., Eccles, J. S., Yoon, K. S., Harold, R. D., Arbreton, A., Freedman-Doan, C., et al. (1997). Changes in children's competence beliefs and subjective task values across the elementary school years: A 3-year study. *Journal of Educational Psychology, 89,* 451–469.

Wigfield, A., Guthrie, J. T., Tonks, S., & Perencevich, K. C. (2004). Children's motivation for reading: Domain specificity and instructional influences. *Journal of Educational Research, 97,* 299–309.

Wigfield, A., Tonks, S., & Eccles, J. S. (2004). Expectancy-value theory in cross-cultural perspective. In D. McInerney & S. Van Etten (Eds.), *Research on sociocultural influences on motivation and learning. Vol. 4: Big theories revisited* (pp. 165–198). Greenwich, CT: Information Age Press.

Wolters, C. A. (1999). The relation between high school students' motivational regulation and their use of learning strategies, effort, and classroom performance. *Learning and Individual Differences, 11,* 281–301.

Wolters, C. A. (2003). Regulation of motivation: Evaluating an underemphasized aspect of self-regulated learning. *Educational Psychologist, 38,* 189–205.

Wolters, C. A., & Pintrich, P. R. (1998). Contextual differences in student motivation and self-regulated learning in mathematics, English, and social studies classrooms. *Instructional Science, 26,* 27–47.

Wolters, C. A., & Rosenthal, H. (2000). The relation between students' motivational beliefs and their use of motivational regulation strategies. *International Journal of Educational Research, 33,* 801–820.

Wolters, C. A., Yu, S. L., & Pintrich, P. R. (1996). The relation between goal orientation and students' motivational beliefs and self-regulated learning. *Learning and Individual Differences, 8,* 211–239.

Zimmerman, B. J. (2000). Attaining self-regulation: A social-cognitive perspective. In M. Boekaerts, P. R. Pintrich, & M. Zeidner (Eds.), *Handbook of self-regulation* (pp. 13–39). San Diego, CA: Academic Press.

8

Work Habits and Self-Regulated Learning:
Helping Students to Find a "Will" from a "Way"

Lyn Corno

INTRODUCTION

This chapter focuses on motivation as a consequence of learning to self-regulate, arguing that a facility for learning is, in itself, a motivator. By engaging productively in academic pursuits, an individual can enjoy being a student and develop confidence about schoolwork. When productive engagement reaches the point at which students are judged publicly to have good work habits, the ramifications are nontrivial. Students with good work habits are recognized and given status as full participants in their school community. What is more, students tend to carry this sort of recognition throughout their school years. To elaborate these points, I first discuss some relevant history and concepts.

DEFINITIONS OF TERMS
AND THEIR THEORETICAL ROOTS

In 1982, as part of a study with colleagues in California, we characterized *self-regulated learning* as "an intentional effort to deepen and manipulate the associative network in a *particular* area (not necessarily academic content), and to monitor and improve that deepening process" (Corno, Collins, & Capper, 1982, p. 3; emphasis in original). The term *associative network* derived from cognitive network theory (e.g., J. R. Anderson & Bower, 1973) and referred to semantic material as content, such as in connected text or lessons, math problems, and the like (i.e., academic work). In keeping with cognitive theory then developing in education (e.g., R. C. Anderson & Spiro, 1977), we assumed that students use self-regulation to organize and acquire knowledge that is nonacademic as well, particularly under conditions involving lack of time, valued goals, and potential distractions (Corno & Mandinach, 1983). In addition, this definition pertained to routines they might apply in experiencing particular content and not to some general disposition or trait.

We also said:

> The self-regulated learner has a "way" to accomplish a range of academic tasks of which he or she is well aware. Such self-knowledge should influence judgment processes in achievement situations. For example, it should raise the likelihood that a student will expect to succeed on classroom tasks. (Corno et al., 1982, pp. 3–4)

Here, we expressed the idea that consciously using self-regulation as a tool for undertaking learning tasks increases control and results in other favorable consequences. These reinforcing consequences should lead students to again call forth self-regulation as the way to accomplish tasks when conditions demand it in the future. Ongoing use of self-regulation in academic settings raises the likelihood that these processes will be tapped "automatically" as conditions dictate. Thus, in routinely applying self-regulation to control action on school-related tasks, students begin to develop academic work habits (see also Corno, 1986).

We based this series of hypotheses on two other streams of theoretical research developing in educational psychology at that time. First, Snow and Lohman (1984) analyzed the information-processing requirements of various standardized tests. They demonstrated that high scores on measures of both general intellectual ability and academic achievement could be mapped onto a small set of cognitive organizing and control operations on content. Students using these operations scored higher on the tests. If general information-processing regularities correlate with intellectual ability as measured by standardized tests, then it is not a big leap to posit that students might improve in school if they learn to process information more effectively when they confront academic work and develop a strategic approach to learning as second nature (Corno, 1981). Could we take low-achieving students and teach them how to be better learners, and would they then use their learning skills proactively to succeed in school? The questions extend beyond the effects of learning strategy instruction to address how internalizing what it means to "learn how to learn" might be used to promote effective academic work habits.

The second stream of investigation we tapped was from Bandura (1977), whose efficacy theory was then just being formulated. Bandura made the case that strong beliefs in personal capabilities influence motivated behavior, including effort and engagement in school. He argued that unless students believe in their abilities and expect success in academic situations, they will have little reason to try to do well in school. Our 1982 study was a preliminary exploration of the relations between student efforts to manage their own learning and motivation processes such as self-efficacy and attributions (see also Corno & Mandinach, 1983). If a realistic appraisal of personal capabilities influences a learner's expectations for success in school, then students who can develop into confident and consistent self-regulated learners ought to be able to tackle almost any task with that adaptive mindset, even if their personal capabilities are average relative to peers (see also Rohrkemper & Corno, 1988). Students with a way to approach complex classroom tasks should ultimately develop a "will" to succeed.

As other authors in this volume have detailed, multiple strands of research followed from this early work, showing that low achievers can learn the strategies of self-regulation, and that they will apply them under the demands of school tasks, supported by a belief in personal agency as Bandura defined it. In addition, the evidence is that better students use self-regulation as appropriate, along a continuum of more or less conscious control, and that many weaker students benefit from instruction in this process (see, e.g., Boekaerts & Corno, 2005; Schunk & Zimmerman, 1998; Winne, 2004).

One more piece of the history is relevant. My colleagues and I integrated modern theory on volition into our research (see, e.g., Corno, 1994). Although motivational processes set the stage for goal pursuits, completing a performance in many cases requires the persistent striving and navigation of obstacles that define volition. According to extant theory, volition comes into play following commitment, supporting task preparation, protecting goals, and influencing task appraisal and continued motivation (Kuhl, 2000). *Volition* reflects an intention to implement or carry out action (Gollwitzer, 1999). It includes the postdecisional self-regulation activities of setting an action plan and prioritizing and activities concerned with implementation, such as bypassing barriers, checking work, managing resources, and budgeting time. Educational settings are sufficiently complex and social that understanding their dynamics requires mapping out volitional processes along with those that are cognitive, affective, and motivational for students and teachers alike.

One illustration of why volition is important in education is provided by a study of "self-discipline." Duckworth and Seligman (2005) created a composite indicator of self-discipline in two independent samples of high school students from the same magnet school. The composite reflected good work habits by combining subjective ratings by students of how they worked (self-reports), objective observation (teacher/parent ratings on the same qualities), and a performance-based measure (a "delay-of-gratification" task) modeled after early work by Mischel and Mischel (1983). The Mischels observed young children using regulatory strategies as a way to avoid temptation in an experimental setting.

Duckworth and Seligman conducted regression analyses of final GPA (grade point average) on a measure of general ability (the Otis-Lennon School Ability Test), prior GPA, and the self-discipline composite. Results showed self-discipline accounted for over twice the variance attributable to the ability measure and 16 to 20% of the variance beyond that accounted for by prior GPA. These authors also reported that highly self-disciplined adolescents outperformed their peers on achievement test scores, high school attendance, and even admission to a selective high school (p. 939), thus suggesting the importance of good academic work habits (see Shoda, Mischel, & Peake, 1990, for an earlier study with similar results). Adding volition to research examining relations among student cognition, affection, and motivation better captures the full range of processes needed to function at the highest levels of academic effort. If work habits and work styles such as those reflected in self-discipline are volition made manifest, then it makes sense for students to hone their volitional competency.

One way for students to strengthen volitional competency is through repeated experience with monitoring volitional states (Corno, 2004). Because academic work requires concentrated attention, the teacher is perhaps the most important source driving motivational and volitional monitoring experiences for students. My colleagues and I have continued since our early work in the 1980s to collaborate with practicing teachers in describing ways that certain educational activities and events can develop good academic work habits in students. One of our findings is that getting students to use self-regulated learning routinely demands a relatively subtle change in teaching practice by which there is a shift in control from teacher to student. However, teachers change their practice only by degrees, and they do so on a need-by-need basis (see Randi & Corno, 1997). In the next section of this chapter, I describe some key aspects of the theory we are developing around work habits, providing grounds for later discussion of supportive teaching practices and how they may be influenced.

A FRAMEWORK FOR THINKING ABOUT WORK HABITS

Good work habits "comprise the strategies and tactics for completing academic tasks that become honed through experience" (Corno, 2004, p. 1671). Psychology treats the concept of habit as so firmly rooted that it operates just beneath conscious awareness or "automatically" (e.g., Bargh, 1997). Definitions consistently show that *habits* are acquired predispositions for certain types of activity (see e.g., Dewey, 1922). Good work habits are cultivated tendencies that contribute to readiness as well as success in school (Stanford Aptitude Seminar, 2002), and teachers understand the need for them.

Among the most difficult problems teachers describe when surveyed are managing, motivating, and addressing the needs of slow learners (Veeman, 1984). Even for students without special learning needs, at every grade level, teachers raise questions about the best ways to motivate work on tasks. They readily share frustrations about students who jump right into assignments only to become distracted as projects stretch out over time or require teamwork. Teachers speak of self-starters who demonstrate planning and follow-through initially but then shy away from risk or veer off course when the going gets rough. Even exceptional students occasionally find it difficult to handle competition between academic and social goals; they also may experience crises of confidence.

Along with a perception that students need better work habits, we find that teachers tend to reward students who display them.

Whether actively participating in class or independently managing homework, students with good work habits receive positive feedback all along the age range. Beyond the public praise, teachers give "hard workers" a variety of opportunities to develop and display leadership. They also recommend self-disciplined students for other honors available in the school. In these ways, teachers confer power and status on students, thus establishing an upward performance trajectory that extends beyond any particular classroom. Of course, good work habits produce more than extrinsic rewards. Better time management allows opportunities for personal pursuits during free time. In addition, students enjoy it when they receive good grades and take pride in helping peers when they are asked.

Perhaps the most subtle aspect of the situation is that experiences pertaining to work habits speak to some students more than others. To say that an experience *speaks* to a student means that it causes a shift in engagement in response to feedback. The student adapts to handle academic tasks in new ways. Consider, for example, students working together in groups. The social context of a group assignment leads some students to take on the role of explainer ("teacher"); others seek assistance (taking the role of "student"). Students who take on either the teacher or the student role provide models of work habits to be perceived and emulated by other members of the group. Yet, some students in the group will never adopt effective work patterns through this form of vicarious learning. They seem to miss the observational opportunities presented, thus reducing the likelihood that habits will develop (Webb & Palincsar, 1996). However, those students who find utility in the positive consequences of good group work habits, and set goals accordingly, should increase their likelihood of school success in the long term. Students who are open to this experience stand to benefit more than those who are not.

THEORETICAL DYNAMICS

Figure 8.1a,b is a schematic of the processes in this hypothesized dynamic system (see, for example, Kelso, 1995, for discussion of properties common to all dynamic systems). The spiral represents a view of how work habits develop over the two scales of time and experience. The spiral dissolves at each end into broken lines, suggesting no definite start or end. Vertical line segments represent

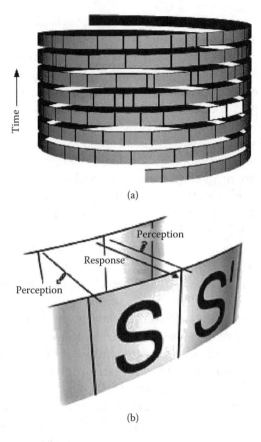

(a)

(b)

Figure 8.1a,b Hypothesized cycle in development of work habits. From *Remaking the Concept of Aptitude: Extending the Legacy of Richard E. Snow,* Figs. 2.3 and 2.4, p. 52, Stanford Aptitude Seminar, 2002, Erlbaum, Mahwah, NJ.

experiences and consequences of good work habits in the spiral. A collection of experiences, cut out of the life span (see Figure 8.1B), can reflect several years of development, a few weeks, or a single classroom session.

Following modern situated aptitude theory (Stanford Aptitude Seminar, 2002), educational experiences are person-environment transactions that alter students' work propensities as well as the situations in which they work (see also Greeno, Collins, & Resnick, 1996). The academic setting provides certain types of experiences—literacy events, public performance requests, group projects, and the like—all opportunities for understanding and developing the types of work habits that contribute to success in school. Because school-aged children spend more time in academic settings (classrooms or school-like events) than in any other type of setting, they receive repeated exposure to a variety of situations with opportunities (e.g., performance requirements, literacy evaluations, requests for abstract thinking) to develop work habits, both good and not so good.

The spiral suggests as well that, as a student repeatedly encounters educational situations with their common elements, there is change in the fund of information or content, academic skills, sense of self as learner, enjoyment of the experience, and so on — a change in the repository of propensities. Accumulated experiences organize and stabilize, reshaping a student's repertoire of propensities, some of which are work habits. The fund of work habits is thus formed and maintained, although new patterns certainly may emerge.

Following theory from Gibson (1979), a situation presents patterns of stimuli or affordances to the student. When the student takes note of or perceives these patterns, the patterns speak to the student, suggesting a response; the student is effectively "in the situation."

To give one example, among its menu of affordances, a conventional classroom consists of repeated instances of the *recitation strategy*, that is, sequences of teacher statements, followed by teacher questions, student responses, and teacher reactions (Bellack, Kliebard, Hyman, & Smith, 1966). When the teacher asks a question, the question speaks to students who perceive the need to respond. If the teacher confirms or disconfirms a student's answer, then there is an incremental effect on the student's propensity to respond the next time he or she is presented with a similar situation. Feedback and other conditions in the situation include the possibility that the student carries on a dialog with the teacher based on his or her answer to the question. In addition to the student's understanding of the material, this dialog adds to his or her evolving relationship with the teacher. Finally, the transaction alters the situation along with the learner. Classmates also react and judge the quality of participation by both student and teacher, thus responding accordingly. A classroom is, after all, a "community of practice" (Brown & Campione, 1994).

Students who are responsive to classroom affordances are *attuned*: They are playing the game by classroom norms, and doing this regularly will nourish them in the long run (Corno & Mandinch, 2004; McCaslin and Good, 1996). Beyond the classroom, academic work habits develop through homework, peer helping, and in other socio-cultural experiences that share properties with school, events that collectively "educate" an individual's attention (Greeno et al., 1996). This is basic theorizing around academic work habits. To apply the theory, we can consider examples of work habits and how they can be developed and supported in students.

A STUDENT'S CHART FOR ACADEMIC WATERS

Figure 8.2 and Table 8.1 show categories of good work habits that have been studied by educational psychologists. We think of these as a way to begin "charting the academic waters"; students who acquire work habits such as these are "on board" and should begin to navigate their way through school.

It is beyond the scope of the present chapter to discuss the ineffective work habits in which many students engage in school, although that is surely a research target. It is also not possible to document all relevant sources for each category depicted; a few selected sources provide support for a category's inclusion. Finally, these lists of work habits should not be seen as exhaustive.

The large circle of Figure 8.2 depicts the learning space as a possible repository for any number of work habits (*acquired predispositions*)

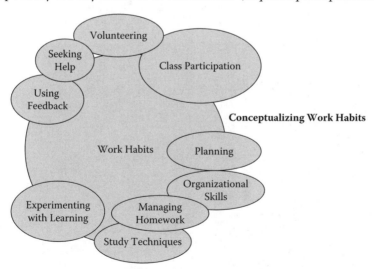

Figure 8.2   Schematic conception of work habits for school.

TABLE 8.1 Categories of Student Work Habits Studied by Educational Psychologists with Examples

	Class Participation	Volunteering	Seeking Help	Using Feedback	Planning	Organization Skills	Managing Homework	Study Techniques	Experimenting With Learning
Examples	Asking questions Answering when called on Focused on lesson	To read or solve problems For leadership roles For community service	Asking for assistance when confused Conferencing with teacher	Compare current/baseline performance Use errors as cues Take pride in success	Goal setting Outcome expected Scheduling	Outline, diagram, review, summarize, mark important points	Arranging the environment, managing time, monitoring and controlling motivation	Paraphrase, teachback, underline, copy notes, form images	Observation, analyze data, interpret evidence, reinvent practices
Sample sources	Corno, 1980; Turner & Patrick, 2004	Eccles & Barber, 1999; Larson, 2000	Newman, 1994; Webb & Palincsar, 1996	Zimmerman, 2004; Elawar & Corno, 1985	Gollwitzer, 1999; Zimmerman, 2000	Palincsar & Brown, 1984; Peterson, 1977	Bryan & Burstein, 2004; Xu, 2004	Pressley et al., 1990; Schoenfeld, 1985	Winne & Jaimeson-Noel, 2003; Winne, 2004

that students might eventually develop, good and bad, throughout their school experiences. The smaller circles in the bottom half of the large circle overlap somewhat and cluster together; they are useful for independent learning. Similarly clustered at the top of the large circle are small circles listing strategies now honed as habits through repeated classroom or "social" learning experiences. These habits "lie in waiting," ready for display whenever conditions to produce them are presented. Because they are habits, appropriate conditions can trigger activity in any category with little conscious effort—one "plans" when given an assignment timeline or experiences a need to feel in better control. It is assumed that any specific habit shown in the figure (e.g., studying) may at first appear in the repertoire of mental resources as a process, tactic, or strategy that gains status as a habit via repetition and responsive use of feedback.

Figure 8.3 shows subcategory possibilities for the work habit of planning. Note that the figure accounts for iteration in planning. Although the specific steps (bottom row) of planning may vary across situations that students encounter, the basic planning schema (*prepare to learn*) remains available for easy access when ingrained as a work habit.

Sources cited in Table 8.1 can be used to produce similar subcategories for each of the other areas. Figure 8.4 shows possibilities for the area of *studying*.

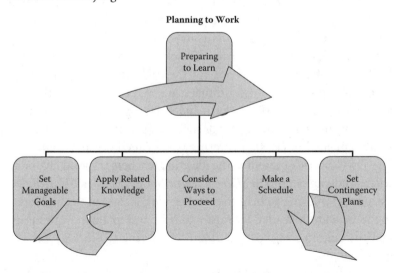

Figure 8.3   Steps in the iterative process of planning.

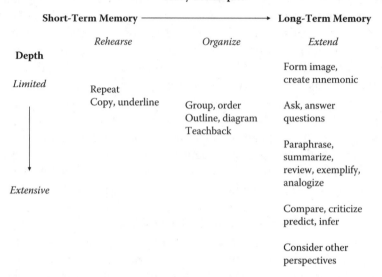

Figure 8.4 Study techniques that can become work habits: rehearsing, organizing, and extending. (After Corno, 1987.)

To illustrate further, consider the categories of *organizing, class participation*, and *volunteering*. Corno (1980) described a curriculum for use by elementary teachers to foster "organizing and participation skills" in students. In student materials for this Learning Skills Program, we referred to *organizing* as "making ideas orderly" and to *participating* as "sharing your ideas." We also used a catchy metaphor, describing two "bags of tricks" for doing well in school. In the case of making ideas orderly, the tricks included goal setting, marking important points, summarizing, and reviewing. In the case of sharing your ideas, the tricks included asking questions, talking to learn (meaning not talking out or socializing, but staying focused on what happened in class), answering when called on, and volunteering. This last trick presented the idea that teachers respond favorably when students offer to help in class without being asked. It included as cues (a) offering to help the teacher with a class project, (b) asking to be a group leader, (c) raising one's hand to answer questions, and (d) volunteering to read aloud or offering to work a problem publicly.

Items in the two bags of tricks derived from related research identifying specific student behavior that positively influenced academic performance or grades (see sources reviewed in Peterson, 1977). These behaviors can be interpreted as representing the good work habits of structuring and prioritizing information taught and displaying engagement through class participation. The curriculum asked teachers to work together with students and their parents to complete specially designed, home-based learning skills exercises. The exercises helped students become attuned to the performance requirements and effort expectations of classrooms and school, and we hoped that by introducing students to these tricks in the early grades that parents might lay a foundation for good academic work habits teachers could reinforce in class.

A series of studies tested the effectiveness of this curriculum in a large sample of third-grade children (Corno, 1980, provides references but see also Harvey, 1982). Both quantitative and qualitative evidence supported the value of introducing children to class participation and memory support skills. Students learned the skills when they used them in the exercises with parents, and teachers were able to reinforce their use in class. Moreover, students who completed all the exercises in the program had significantly higher reading and vocabulary scores than students who did not; there were upward achievement trends within treated classrooms based on completion rates and between treated classrooms and those serving as controls. The treatment effect exceeded 0.75 standard deviations on adjusted class means; in classes where the majority of students completed the full curriculum, reading and vocabulary scores were at nearly the 68th percentile of nontreated classes on a normal distribution.

Despite successes with this curriculum, the idea of using a parent–teacher approach to build work habits failed to catch on beyond these early research studies. For one thing, our research findings never moved to the conduit of teacher professional developers who influence practice. In addition, the program needed additional development before it could easily "travel" (Greeno, 2004). What we have learned over the years about how to do research that influences practice has been detailed elsewhere (see e.g., Corno & Mandinach, 2004; Corno & Randi, 1999; Randi & Corno, 2000).

I retold the story of the Learning Skills Program here to emphasize, for what remains of this chapter, that teachers can develop work habits in many ways: in collaboration with researchers and through direct communication about changes in practice that seem most promising. Rather than hope that research findings are discovered by professional development experts and conveyed to teachers through that pipeline, we have found it useful to work together with teachers directly toward this end.

Presently, we collaborate with teachers to understand their perceptions of students at the same time that we teach them what we know about good work habits. Teachers are developing their own strategies for addressing student work habits; and we are learning some things about how teachers think as they do this. We are also learning about which approaches meet with success for students at different grade levels. At the middle and high school levels, teachers seek to change some bad habits in students as well as to develop good ones. In the next section, I describe general aspects of our current efforts, providing examples that we have found most useful. The final section of the chapter frames some conclusions.

COLLABORATING WITH TEACHERS TO STUDY WORK HABITS

In our current research, we are investigating theoretical relationships among motivational and volitional variables in self-regulated learning while working closely with practicing teachers and their students. We try to present the theoretical concepts from psychology in a framework that allows teachers to provide their own vivid and personal instantiations of key terms and principles. So, for example, when we define a term such as *self-regulated learning* and provide attendant examples from the research literature, we ask teachers to illustrate the same concept using instances from their own teaching experience. Just as students need extended exposure to good work habits to ensure their cultivation, we find that teachers benefit if they experience the semantic framework we want them to learn gradually as we record their own examples. The examples we get from teachers then plug into the materials we discuss as we look at a given teacher's practices.

We define *good work habits* as regular and recurring patterns of self-regulation strategies and tactics such as those listed in Table 8.1. Teacher-provided examples of strategies or tactics in each category (underlined entries) can generate similar examples in discussions with their students. A context for lubricating classroom discussions is a curriculum we developed around "quest literature" (i.e., the journey tale or myth). The curriculum can be used at middle and high school levels and aims to give students a broad understanding of self-regulation in action. The target events for self-regulated learning are therefore "curriculum embedded" (Randi & Corno, 2000).

In our curriculum, the generic quest narrative frames self-regulation strategies as a literary journey. In this refrain, the journey embodies change, growth, and movement toward goals (e.g., *The Odyssey*). We provide assistance to teachers who wish to use our curriculum or adapt it for their purposes (e.g., as part of a humanities or literature course). We talk with teachers about how to personalize the curriculum and the quest-related strategies it offers to polish in students. For example, one teacher developed a variation on this theme for fourth graders she taught in an urban setting (Johnson, 2004).

The experiences teachers devise for their particular students have a common goal: to teach self-regulation strategies and encourage students to apply them naturally when planning for their own challenging quests or events. The teachers understand that work habits can develop into a productive work style, that is, a way of doing things—both in and outside the classroom—that contributes to success across the curriculum. In our discussions with teachers, we consider how small successes carry with them positive consequences and other sorts of rewards that sustain student engagement. We talk about helping students find the motivation (or will) to perform in school. We use *will* in the Bandura sense, that is, as reflecting a budding sense of academic efficacy that students bring to school in the early grades.

Teachers point out that a student's sense of efficacy can be fragile, and even confident learners can falter in the face of disappointing performance. In our discussions with teachers, we reflect on how, unless there is ongoing instruction in work habits even beyond middle school, the upward demands of curriculum and assessment can become increasingly difficult for students to handle. We share with teachers new theorizing about the concept of *aptitude*, which is no longer seen as innate and unchanging (Stanford Aptitude Seminar, 2002).

Contemporary scholars have disputed old claims that standardized tests "measure aptitude" and that people "have aptitude" or not. Rather, *aptitude* is now understood to be a "fit" between demands and preparation. Students display aptitude when they grasp the necessary conditions for success on the tasks assigned in school and then attempt to create those conditions for themselves. Thus, the cultivation of aptitude for schooling is at one level the cultivation of attention to contextual cues (Greeno et al., 1996). When students fail to pick up what a situation demands, or misread what an assignment calls for, their chances for error increase, and their chances for satisfaction and rewards decrease. Put differently, even students with the efficacy or will to perform are only halfway there without a way.

Teachers often tell us that students do not have to fail in school—not in the technical sense of receiving a failing grade—to fail from their own unique perspectives. "Average" grades, if unexpected or anomalous, can be sufficiently disappointing to damage a sense of efficacy in some students. Below-average grades can confirm an already low sense of self. So, in our talks with teachers, we try to press home the complexity of the spiral depicted in Figure 8.1: Processes of motivation and volition rise and fall away in a context of increasing demands and decreasing support. And, although it is the putative role of the teacher to promote student learning in educational situations, students mediate all the instruction they receive. Mediation that includes self-regulation is powerful; it builds self-confidence, leading to other attainments. Weak mediation can have an altogether different outcome (for similar ideas from different perspectives, compare Stanford Aptitude Seminar, 2002, chapter 2, to McVee, Dunsmore, & Gavelek, 2005).

When individual students have trouble with planning and organization, if they fail to review and rehearse, or if they do not ask questions when things are unclear, teachers say the entire class suffers. To be held accountable under such circumstances is dismaying for teachers. It is similarly frustrating for teachers when students do not complete homework (Trautwein, Ludtke, Schnyder, & Niggli, 2006). The need for effective mediation, not only from students but also from parents, is particularly acute in the case of homework, for which students complete assigned tasks more or less on their own. Young students are beginners with homework who must cultivate good habits in that task just like in any other (Corno, 2000).

Our bottom line in working with teachers, then, is that one way to get students engaged with school is to provide them with many opportunities to practice and become versed in the work habits of preparation and follow-through as they are represented in assigned tasks: Having a way to do schoolwork will not always produce a will, but strong volitional competency is one important means to promote the development and maintenance of motivation. Thus, in the practice-oriented activities we conduct with teachers, we are able to weave in ideas from Bandura and Snow, as well as other prominent psychologists, to teach important concepts from the "big theories" extant today (McInerney & VanEtten, 2004). The next section explains, using examples from our research, how teachers can cultivate work habits in students.

GETTING STUDENTS TO DEVELOP GOOD WORK HABITS

To be useful as a basis for developing good work habits, student assignments have to *require* self-regulation. Some aspects of classroom learning provide a good environment to help this along; the limits on work time in the presence of other students mean that individual learners have to ward off intrusions, prioritize work goals, and manage under pressure; this is true as well in cooperative learning. To require volitional control, however, assignments should be just beyond students' current capabilities and likely to be perceived by them as difficult.

One situation we studied provides an example of how this can be done. In planning an eleventh-grade course in U.S. history, the teacher sought, among other goals, to prepare students for a high-stakes history test, the Scholastic Aptitude Test (SAT) II (U.S. history subject area test). Course material was challenging even for the higher-achieving juniors in the course. The teacher also assigned culminating projects at the end of each unit. One project asked students to "enact the roles of delegates from the states at the first Constitutional Convention in 1787" (each student assumed the identity of a different delegate to the convention to espouse his line of reasoning in drafting the U.S. Constitution). The teacher expected students to take seriously these projects and course goals, essentially forming an intention to accomplish them.

But, how does a teacher know which assignments are just beyond students' current volitional capabilities and devise work that will challenge them to apply self-regulation? At course outset, to capture evidence on student work habits, the teacher had his class complete a volitional assessment using an instrument available from McCann and Turner (2004). He also did an in-class exercise in which he asked students to uncover their work habits by sharing how they did their work at home, how they studied, how they coped with distractions, and so forth, which he recorded and discussed. Scores on the two assessments yielded a profile of work habits for each student, indicating who needed help in which aspects of self-regulation and where the teacher should focus his efforts during the year (i.e., a profile of volitional strengths and weaknesses for the class).

The teacher working with a grade-level curriculum team studied student responses on the volitional assessments and devised a series of course activities that required work habits for which his students appeared weak (see Randi, 2004). The team then designed the curriculum to exercise and develop budding work habits, for example:

- Students kept records of time spent preparing for tests or quizzes outside school, numbers of assignments tackled for extra credit, and any ways they sought out assistance in completing homework assignments and projects (e.g., self-management charts).
- Students continued to share with one another and with the teacher information on how they managed their work; they described their work space at home, their habitual work tactics, any strategies they used for action control, and their work styles.
- Students wrote about the ways they planned and prepared for tests and what they to did to stay on task, both in and outside class (e.g., making lists, color-coding notes, drawing up tables, or self-monitoring).
- Stronger students, with good examples from materials they provided, were asked to share their strategies as peer helpers.

When students engaged in these activities, they experienced a range of opportunities to display work habits that were then open to teacher and peer inspection. The teacher used a grading rubric for each major assignment that assessed work habits in addition to other aspects of task performance. The rubric gauged responses of individual students given opportunities to display good work habits.

Measures of "typical" investment (how individual students responded across the range of activities presented) explained some of student successes and failures in handling ongoing course demands throughout the year. Particular features of this or any course and its requirements for self-regulation inevitably elicit atypical investment from some students with identical scores on initial (preinstructional) assessments. To understand the range of volitional competence presented by a given class, the teacher or curriculum team hoping to maximize success for *all* students has to consider both typical and situation-specific response.

To get at situation-specific response, students were asked to reflect on their work habits as course activities progressed, using the tools listed as bullet items above. Of course, there are many ways to accomplish this same objective in class, whether the class learns from one another in small groups or individually. Teachers can present students with problems to solve and other scenarios that prompt evidence of more- and less-productive ways to tackle tasks and invest effort. Teachers can also take notes on work habits that they observe to be developing in individual students throughout the year and productively share these notes with students and parents. It is profitable for parents to take notes as well, especially on how their child completes homework. These notes passed to the teacher will increase the validity of the teacher's own dossiers on students, making steps for intervention more likely to result in positive effects (Corno, 2000; Xu, 2004).

For teachers or school psychologists who wish to work in a more clinical way with individual students to develop good work habits, a useful procedure is to establish what Julius Kuhl (2000) calls *interaction partnerships*. Here, a counselor–student pair agrees to work together to address the complex web of issues related to affect and goal setting that might be compromising the student's productive work habits. The partnership between a counselor and student ensures prompt and directive feedback when the student expresses negative affect or frames unrealistic goals that create problems for work efforts.

Oettingen, Honig, and Gollwitzer (2000) provided an example of the possibilities for establishing interaction partnerships with students. In their research, a simple experimental manipulation produced implementation mind-sets in students. Following an assignment, a partner asks the student to envision a game plan for completing it, that is, to think through when and where he or she could work. "If it's Tuesday at 7 p.m. and I'm home, then I'm going to do my assignment." In the Oettingen et al. (2000) study, this request was sufficient to induce an action plan for completing the task in the majority of student participants. Formation of an action plan in turn resulted in an increase in the number of students actually completing their homework assignments relative to those in control groups.

According to these authors, mentally representing the game plan provides a frame for enactment. That is, when the critical homework situation occurs, the conditions are set so the student does not have to worry about buckling down or exerting self-control. Mental resources are freed for other use. Each time the established situation occurs, the cues stored in memory as a metacognitive schema trigger an implementation mind-set with its associated behavioral routine. Doing homework in a timely way is now a work habit induced by a particular situation.

It is worth reemphasizing that recording a game plan goes beyond merely setting goals. The frame for enactment includes the envisioned conditions for meeting goals (when and where the task is to be carried out). Thus, goal setting is necessary for volitional control to occur, but goals alone are insufficient. Some studies show wide variation in how students engage in maneuvers that effectively protect their academic work time. Another good source is the work of Perry, Phillips, and Dowler (2004), who provided direction on how teachers can help to ensure that habits operating beneath awareness can be drawn out to support more strategic use of self-regulation in students when class lessons present challenges to concentration.

ONCE MORE: WHY WORK HABITS MATTER

This chapter presented a framework for conceptualizing student work habits, including examples of work habits studied by educational psychologists as well as those described by students and teachers themselves. I have considered how theory and research can be applied to motivate students to self-regulate. I have also described the history of our work with teachers on the topic of helping students to develop better work habits for school, providing examples for use by other teachers or curriculum teams who might wish to adopt some of our practices for their own use. Space limits precluded extensive discussion of research supporting this agenda, but there are relevant references for readers' own pursuits.

In explicating how teachers can lead students toward good work habits, I tried to convey a sense of the importance we attach to doing psychologically based professional work *with* rather than *on* teachers — work that is at once theory, research, *and* practice. I would like in closing to reemphasize what I said at the outset of this chapter about why it really matters for students to have good work habits in school.

Students with good work habits tend to be noticed by teachers and others in the larger academic communities they experience as youth. Students who have good work habits are held as examples for other students from their earliest years. Some are raised up as stars, not only to peers but also to siblings. These public or social comparisons are common among teachers and parents alike (McCaslin & Good, 1996). Students with good work habits tend to be offered opportunities for leadership both in and outside the classroom. Leadership begins with even the simplest request from a teacher: "Nina, would you please share what you think of this book with the class?" "P. J., I want you to show Pearson how you take notes on lessons." From there, leadership gradually comes to include a major role in a school play (students with good work habits will learn their lines and not miss rehearsals), or leadership means nomination by an advisor to head the Peer Helping Club (which takes a lot of organizing). Leadership may also be an elected student government position in which the officer has to pursue a prescribed activity agenda. Positions such as these show up as serious commitments to meaningful activities on a students' college or job applications (for a discussion of the importance of productive follow-through in high school activities to success in college, see Willingham, 1985). A full picture of the student depicted in applications, interviews, and letters of recommendation that inevitably points to work habits is considered reflective of *productive motivation*, allowing that student either to shine or not.

It is perhaps an obvious observation that students will vary in their developmental trajectories for good work habits (see Brooks, 2006). So also will the opportunities they are given to display good work habits in school, but educational psychologists can do something to reduce the school variance. To once more evoke the ship metaphor, it seems likely that grade school students who miss the boat for good work habits can make up for lost time if they hop on in high school. Even those late to board in high school (or those who jump ship) may eventually get on board in college. Perhaps the ideas and sources discussed here can be explored in future years to better suggest how.

REFERENCES

Anderson, J. R., & Bower, G. H. (1973). *Human associative memory.* Washington, DC: Winston.

Anderson, R. C., & Spiro, R. J. (Eds.). (1977). *Schooling and the acquisition of knowledge.* Hillsdale, NJ: Erlbaum.

Bandura, A. (1977). Self-efficacy: Toward a unifying theory of behavioral change. *Psychological Review, 84,* 191–215.

Bargh, J. A. (1997). The automaticity of everyday life. In R. S. Wyer (Ed.), *Advances in social cognition* (Vol. 10, pp. 1–61). Mahwah, NJ: Erlbaum.

Bellack, A., Kliebard, R., Hyman, & Smith, F. (1966). *The language of the classroom.* New York: Teachers College Press.

Boekaerts, M., & Corno, L. (2005). Self-regulation in the classroom: A perspective on assessment and intervention. *Applied Psychology: An International Review, 54,* 199–232.

Brooks, D. (2006, May 7). Marshmallows and public policy. *New York Times,* p. 13.

Brown, A. L., & Campione, J. C. (1994). Guided discovery in a community of learners. In K. McGilly (Ed.), *Classroom lessons: Integrating cognitive theory and classroom practice* (pp. 229–272). Cambridge, MA: MIT Press/Bradford Books.

Bryan, T., & Burstein, K. (2004). Improving homework completion and academic performance: Lessons from special education. *Theory Into Practice, 43,* 213–219.

Corno, L. (1980). Individual and class level effects of parent-assisted instruction in classroom memory support strategies. *Journal of Educational Psychology, 72,* 278–292.

Corno, L. (1981). Cognitive organizing in classrooms. *Curriculum Inquiry, 11,* 360–377.

Corno, L. (1986). The metacognitive control components of self-regulated learning. *Contemporary Educational Psychology, 11,* 333–346.

Corno, L. (1987). Teaching and self-regulated learning. In D. C. Berliner & B. U. Rosenshine (Eds.), *Talks to teachers* (pp. 249–267). New York: Random House.

Corno, L. (1994). Student volition and education: Outcomes, influences, and practices. In B. Zimmerman & D. Schunk (Eds.), *Self-regulated learning and academic achievement: Educational applications* (pp. 229–254). New York: Springer-Verlag.

Corno, L. (2000). Looking differently at homework. *Elementary School Journal, 100,* 529–548.

Corno, L. (2004). Work habits and work styles: Volition in education. *Teachers College Record, 106,* 1669–1694.

Corno, L., Collins, K. M., & Capper, J. (1982). *Where there's a way there's a will: Self-regulating the low achieving student* (Report No. TM 820 465). East Lansing, MI: National Center for Research on Teacher Learning. (ERIC Document Reproduction Services ED222499)

Corno, L., & Mandinach, E. B. (1983). Using existing classroom data to explore relationships in a theoretical model of academic motivation. *Journal of Educational Research, 77,* 33–43.

Corno, L., & Mandinach, E. B. (2004). What we have learned about student engagement in the past twenty years. In D. M. McInerney & S. Van Etten (Eds.), *Big theories revisited: Research on sociocultural influences on motivation and learning* (Vol. 4, pp. 299–328). Greenwich, CT: Information Age.

Corno, L., & Randi, J. (1999). A design theory for classroom instruction in self-regulated learning? In C. M. Reigeluth (Ed.), *Instructional-design theory and models: A new paradigm of instructional theory* (Vol. 2, pp. 293–317). Mahwah, NJ: Erlbaum.

Dewey, J. (1922). Habits and will (pp. 15–42). *Human nature and conduct: An introduction to social psychology.* New York: Modern Library.

Duckworth, A. L., & Seligman, M. E. P. (2005). Self-discipline outdoes IQ in predicting academic performance of adolescents. *Psychological Science, 16,* 939–944.

Eccles, J. S., & Barber, B. L. (1999). Student council, volunteering, basketball, or marching band: What kind of extracurricular involvement matters? *Journal of Adolescent Research, 14,* 10–43.

Elawar, M. C., & Corno, L. (1985). A factorial experiment in teachers' written feedback on student homework: Changing teacher behavior a little rather than a lot. *Journal of Educational Psychology, 77,* 162–173.

Gibson, J. J. (1979). *The ecological approach to visual perception.* Boston: Houghton-Mifflin.

Gollwitzer, P. M. (1999). Implementation intentions: Strong effects of simple plans. *American Psychologist, 54,* 493–503.

Greeno, J. (2004). We must be doing something (actually, a lot) right. *Division 15 Newsletter, American Psychological Association, 27*(3), 1, 3, 8.

Greeno, J. G., Collins, A. M., & Resnick, L. (1996). Cognition and learning. In D. C. Berliner & R. C. Calfee (Eds.), *Handbook of educational psychology* (pp. 15–46). New York: Macmillan.

Harvey, P. C. (1982). *Variations on direct instruction in one third grade classroom.* Unpublished doctoral dissertation, Stanford University, Stanford, CA.

Johnson, E. (2004). *The hero in me: Reinforcing self-regulated learning as we connect to literary heroes.* Yale-New Haven Teachers Institute Curriculum Unit. Retrieved on June 5, 2007 from http://www.yale.edu/ynhti/curriculum/units/2004/2/04.02.03.x.html

Kelso, J. A. S. (1995). *Dynamic patterns: The self-organization of brain and behavior.* Cambridge, MA: MIT Press.

Kuhl, J. (2000). The volitional basis of personality systems interaction theory: Applications in learning and treatment contexts. *International Journal of Educational Research, 33,* 665–704.

Larson, R. W. (2000). Toward a psychology of positive youth development. *American Psychologist, 55,* 170–183.

McCann, E. J., & Turner, J. E. (2004). Increasing student learning through volitional control. *Teachers College Record, 106,* 1695–1714.

McCaslin, M., & Good, T. (1996). The informal curriculum. In D. C. Berliner & R. C. Calfee (Eds.), *Handbook of educational psychology* (pp. 622–672). New York: Macmillan.

McInerney, D. M., & Van Etten, S. (Eds.). (2004). *Big theories revisited: Research on sociocultural influences on motivation and learning* (Vol. 4, pp. 299–328). Greenwich, CT: Information Age.

McVee, M. B., Dunsmore, K., & Gavelek, J. R. (2005). Schema theory revisited. *Review of Educational Research, 75,* 531–566.

Mischel, H. N., & Mischel, W. (1983). The development of children's knowledge of self-control strategies. *Child Development, 54,* 603–619.

Newman, R. S. (1994). Adaptive help seeking: A strategy of self-regulated learning. In D. Schunk & B. Zimmerman (Eds.), *Self-regulation of learning and performance: Issues and educational applications* (pp. 283–301). Hillsdale, NJ: Erlbaum.

Oettingen, G., Honig, G., & Gollwitzer, P. M. (2000). Effective self-regulation of goal attainment. *International Journal of Educational Research, 33,* 705–732.

Palincsar, A. S., & Brown, A. L. (1984). Reciprocal teaching of comprehension-fostering and monitoring activities. *Cognition and Instruction, 1,* 117–175.

Perry, N., Phillips, L., & Dowler, J. (2004). Examining features of tasks and their potential to promote self-regulated learning. *Teachers College Record, 106,* 1854–1878.

Peterson, P. L. (1977). Interactive effects of student anxiety, achievement orientation, and teacher behavior on student achievement and attitude. *Journal of Educational Psychology, 69,* 779–792.

Pressley, M., Woloshyn, V., Lysynchuk, L. M., Martin, V., Wood, E., & Willoughby, T. (1990). A primer of research on cognitive strategy instruction: The important issues and how to address them. *Educational Psychology Review, 2,* 1–58.

Randi, J. (2004). Teachers as self-regulated learners. *Teachers College Record, 106,* 1825–1853.

Randi, J., & Corno, L. (1997). Teachers as innovators. In B. Biddle, T. Good, & I. Goodson (Eds.), *The international handbook of teachers and teaching* (Vol. 1, pp. 1163–1221). New York: Kluwer.

Randi, J., & Corno, L. (2000). Teacher innovations in self-regulated learning. In M. Boekaerts, P. R. Pintrich, & M. Zeidner (Eds.), *Handbook of self-regulation* (pp. 651–686). San Diego, CA: Academic Press.

Rohrkemper, M. M., & Corno, L. (1988, January). Success and failure on classroom tasks: Adaptive learning and classroom teaching. *Elementary School Journal,* pp. 297–313.

Schoenfeld, A. H. (1985). *Mathematical problem solving.* Orlando, FL: Academic Press.

Schunk, D. H., & Zimmerman, B. J. (1998). *Self-regulated learning: From teaching to self-reflective practice.* New York: Guilford.

Shoda, Y., Mischel, W., & Peake, P. (1990). Predicting adolescent cognitive and self-regulatory competencies from preschool delay of gratification: Identifying diagnostic conditions. *Developmental Psychology, 26,* 978–986.

Snow, R. E., & Lohman, D. F. (1984). Toward a theory of cognitive aptitude for learning from instruction. *Journal of Educational Psychology, 76,* 347–376.

Stanford Aptitude Seminar: Corno, L., Cronbach, L. J., Kupermintz, H. K., Lohman, D. H., Mandinach, E. B., Porteus, A., et al. (2002). *Remaking the concept of aptitude: Extending the legacy of Richard E. Snow.* Mahwah, NJ: Erlbaum.

Trautwein, U., Ludtke, O., Schnyder, I., & Niggli, A. (2006). Predicting homework effort: Support for a domain-specific, multilevel homework model. *Journal of Educational Psychology, 98,* 438–456.

Turner, J. C., & Patrick, H. (2004). Motivational influences on student participation in classroom learning activities, *Teachers College Record, 106,* 1759–1785.

Veeman, S. (1984). Perceived problems of beginning teachers. *Review of Educational Research, 54,* 143–178.

Webb, N. M., & Palincsar, A. S. (1996). Group processes in the classroom. In D. C. Berliner & R. C. Calfee (Eds.), *Handbook of educational psychology* (pp. 841–876). New York: Macmillan.

Willingham, W. (1985). *Success in college.* New York: College Board.

Winne, P. H. (2004). Putting volition to work in education. *Teachers College Record, 106,* 1879–1887.

Winne, P. H., & Jaimeson-Noel, D. L. (2003). Self-regulating studying by objectives for learning: Students' reports compared to a model. *Contemporary Educational Psychology, 28,* 259–276.

Xu, J. (2004). Family help and homework management in urban and rural secondary schools. *Teachers College Record, 106,* 1786–1803.

Zimmerman, B. J. (2000). Attaining self-regulation: A social cognitive perspective. In M. Boekaerts, P. R. Pintrich, & M. Zeidner (Eds.), *Handbook of self-regulation* (pp. 13–39). New York: Academic Press.

9

Understanding and Promoting Autonomous Self-Regulation:
A Self-Determination Theory Perspective

Johnmarshall Reeve, Richard Ryan, Edward L. Deci, and Hyungshim Jang

INTRODUCTION

The term *self-regulation* has taken on many meanings in psychology (Baumeister & Vohs, 2004) and education (McCaslin et al., 2006), although there is general agreement that self-regulation is a process in which people organize and manage their capacities—that is, their thoughts (e.g., competency beliefs), emotions (e.g., interest), behaviors (e.g., engagement with learning activities), and social-contextual surroundings (e.g., select a quiet, comfortable place to study)—in the service of attaining some desired future state (Pintrich & De Groot, 1990; Zimmerman, 2000). Despite this common ground, theories of self-regulation vary considerably in their specific foci, with some focusing on the "why" of self-regulation, some on the "what," and some on the "how." Briefly, the why, what, and how theories of self-regulation ask the following questions:

- Why theories: For what reasons do people engage in behaviors—because they want to or because they have to?
- What theories: What goals do people seek to attain for themselves?
- How theories: How do people enact effective (rather than ineffective) self-regulation?

The why theories investigate the causes people perceive as underlying their actions. It has been clear for some time that the why underlying behavior has consequences for the quality and consequences of that behavior (e.g., deCharms, 1976). Thus, why theories differentiate between types of motivation or regulation, such as autonomous versus controlled forms (Deci & Ryan, 1985; Ryan & Deci, 2000a). For example, one reason why people engage in behaviors is to actualize their interests and self-endorsed values. The regulation of behavior when people's interests and values are the reason for acting is said to be *autonomous*. From the perspective of self-determination theory (SDT; Deci & Ryan, 1985), this constitutes self-regulation. Other reasons why people engage in behaviors are introjected under interpersonal pressures or directly controlled by forces outside the self. When such forces regulate a person's behavior, their behavior is considered *controlled* rather than autonomous. As such, this does not constitute true self-regulation because the person is regulated by the coercive or seductive forces rather than self-initiated, volitional, or self-endorsed regulation.

What theories of self-regulation are concerned with the content focus of the goals people pursue. These theories specify what it is people are attempting to attain or achieve. For example, people can select a learning goal of improving or, alternatively, a performance goal of outperforming others (Elliot, McGregor, & Thrash, 2002). People can also pursue intrinsic goals or extrinsic goals (Kasser & Ryan, 1996), a distinction we subsequently elaborate. Research of the what variety suggests that different types of goal contents are associated with different qualities of action and different degrees of learning and persistence (e.g., Vansteenkiste, Simons, Lens, Sheldon, & Deci 2004).

Finally, the how theories concern the specific skills and mechanisms people use to regulate themselves toward goals or standards (Boekaerts, Pintrich, & Zeidner, 2000; Carver & Scheier, 1998). In these theories, the goals are typically taken as givens, so the theories do not address types of goals (*what* people pursue) or types of regulation (*why* people behave). Instead, the how theories of self-regulation are concerned with the question of how people effectively (vs. ineffectively) keep themselves on track toward their desired outcomes. Much recent research on self-regulated learning (SRL) has taken this approach, and it has used a social transmission model grounded in either social learning theory (Zimmerman, 2000) or the metaphor of an apprenticeship (Collins, Brown, & Newman, 1989).

In the current chapter, we focus on the why and the what of motivation and self-regulation. To do so, we present an overview of SDT, particularly as it relates to education (e.g., Reeve, Deci, & Ryan, 2004; Ryan & Deci, 2000b). The central concept in an SDT analysis of students' self-regulation is the concept of *autonomous self-regulation.* When autonomous in their self-regulation, students are self-initiating and persistent because the tasks they undertake are perceived as interesting or personally important to them. From the SDT perspective, such self-regulation is associated with autonomous motivation and is characterized by acting with a sense of volition and choice. In contrast, behaviors that are imposed on students—behaviors that the students do not endorse—are not considered self-regulated. Rather, the regulation is controlled by the impositions or their associated contingencies. Beyond this distinction, SDT suggests that goal contents differ in the degree to which they meet or fulfill the psychological needs of students, which in turn predicts both the quality of their engagement and the outcomes it produces for learning and well-being. Finally, the chapter concludes with a section that relates SDT to theories that focus on the how of self-regulation.

SELF-DETERMINATION THEORY

Self-determination theory begins with the assumption that people are by nature active, with an evolved tendency to engage the environment, assimilate new knowledge and skills, and integrate them into a coherent psychological structure. SDT is organized by minitheories, three of which are particularly relevant to the current discussion: cognitive evaluation theory, organismic integration theory, and basic psychological needs theory (see Reeve, Deci, & Ryan, 2004; Ryan & Deci, 2000b). Collectively, these minitheories identify the underlying source of students' autonomous self-regulation and explain how social influences either support or undermine students' capacities for autonomous self-regulation.

Cognitive Evaluation Theory

Cognitive evaluation theory was formulated to explain how aspects of the social environment affect intrinsic motivation (Deci & Ryan, 1985). To be *intrinsically motivated* is to engage in an activity because one finds the activity itself interesting and enjoyable; thus, behavior is motivated by its inherent satisfactions (Ryan & Deci, 2000a). In contrast, *extrinsic motivation* involves doing an activity in an attempt to achieve some separable consequence, for example, to attain a reward or avoid a punishment. Extrinsic rewards originate in the social environment, with a contingency set up by someone else. Initially, studies examined the effects of extrinsic rewards on intrinsic motivation, and more than 100 experiments showed that there is a general tendency for rewards to undermine intrinsic motivation, although positive feedback (which is sometimes referred to as *verbal rewards*) tends to enhance intrinsic motivation, and even tangible rewards can potentially enhance intrinsic motivation when they are used to communicate competence or improvement (see Deci, Koestner, & Ryan, 1999, for an extensive review). In general, the theory says that external factors, including specific events (e.g., the imposition of a goal; Mossholder, 1980) or broader classroom climate factors (Deci, Schwartz, Sheinman, & Ryan, 1981), tend to enhance intrinsic motivation when they provide positive competence information and support people's autonomy. In contrast, external factors tend to undermine intrinsic motivation when they convey incompetence or pressure and control people's behavior.

Organismic Integration Theory

Organismic integration theory investigates the phenomena of internalization and integration. *Internalization* refers to the process through which an individual transforms an externally prescribed regulation or value into an internally endorsed one; *integration* refers to the experience in which an internalized regulation has been fully and coherently assimilated with one's sense of self (Ryan & Deci, 2000a, 2000b). In SDT, the processes of internalization and integration represent "action and development from within," and *within* refers to inner motivations such as basic psychological needs, intrinsic motivation, and the values and regulations that develop over time from internalization experiences and the integration process (Deci

& Ryan, 1991). In school, there are many things in which parents and teachers want students to engage and learn that the students do not find interesting. Parents, teachers, and school psychologists therefore often use extrinsic motivators, such as explicit requests or implicit approval, to achieve this end. More ideally, however, SDT suggests that students not be controlled into action but rather be given the nutriments to internalize a personal value for acting. Students would still be extrinsically motivated because the behaviors are done not because they are interesting and enjoyable but rather because they are instrumental for the students' values and self-selected goals. However, when they have been fully internalized (i.e., integrated), the behaviors are experienced as autonomous because they are wholly self-endorsed.

Organismic integration theory specifies four types of extrinsic motivation, characterized by the degree to which the motivation has or has not been internalized and integrated into the self. *External regulation* means that the regulation is still a function of explicit external contingencies. *Introjected regulation* refers to regulation by partially internalized contingencies that have been stipulated by socializing agents to pressure and control students, typically using contingent self-worth or threats of guilt. Here, the regulation is within the student, but the student has not really accepted it as his or her own but feels controlled by it. *Identified regulation* results when students have identified with the value of an activity and have thus accepted personal responsibility for its regulation. Finally, *integrated regulation* refers to the identification having been fully integrated with other aspects of one's self, so the regulation becomes a part of one's true self.

Basic Psychological Needs Theory

Basic psychological needs theory focuses on the psychological needs for autonomy, competence, and relatedness as the basis of students' autonomous self-regulation. This minitheory was developed to identify students' innate, universal psychological needs as sources of autonomous self-regulation and to investigate the degree to which their satisfaction facilitates learning, development, and well-being. Substantial research has linked basic need satisfaction to intrinsic motivation, autonomous self-regulation, and psychological well-being across cultures and across the life span, as well as to positive classroom functioning and enhanced conceptual learning (Chirkov & Ryan, 2001; Reis, Sheldon, Gable, Roscoe, & Ryan, 2000; Ryan, Deci, & Grolnick, 1995). For instance, one study designed explicitly to test the cross-cultural generalizability of SDT found that Korean high school students, like their Western counterparts, felt highly satisfied when classroom learning experiences nurtured their psychological needs, felt highly unsatisfied when learning activities frustrated their psychological needs, and showed high engagement, achievement, intrinsic motivation, and emotional well-being when teachers supported their autonomy and psychological needs satisfaction in general (Jang, Reeve, & Ryan, 2007).

This minitheory also encompasses the work on intrinsic versus extrinsic goals (Kasser & Ryan, 1996). *Intrinsic goals* are specified as those that relatively directly satisfy the basic psychological needs of autonomy, competence, and relatedness and include goals for personal growth, relationships, and contributing to one's community. *Extrinsic goals* are defined as those that are not inherently need satisfying and usually represent some attempt to gain contingent approval. They include material wealth, being popular or famous, and projecting an attractive image, and they have been associated with poorer performance and lesser well-being.

STUDENT–CLASSROOM DIALECTIC

According to the SDT framework, all students, regardless of their starting points, backgrounds, or abilities, possess inner motivational resources that can potentially allow them to engage constructively and proactively in learning activities. Yet, these inner resources are more or less activated and apparent as a function of the social context, which tends either to support or to thwart students' tendencies toward internalization or intrinsic motivation. The dialectical outcome between students' natural propensities to learn and integrate and the classroom learning environments in which they find themselves is especially important in this regard. Greater autonomy and more positive functioning result only when the context nurtures and supports that tendency, whereas all too often these inherent positive resources are derailed or blocked by excessive controls that thwart autonomy, excessive demands that thwart feelings of competence, or an absence of warmth and care that thwarts relatedness to those who teach.

Figure 9.1 illustrates this person–environment dialectic. The box on the left side of the figure represents the student and defines his or her inner resources. That is, students have basic psychological needs to connect, grow in competence, and develop volitionally that can lead them to engage proactively in the classroom learning environment. The box on the right side of the figure represents the classroom learning environment that can be autonomy-supportive, controlling, or amotivating and thus will either support or thwart these inner resources. The cognitive evaluation and organismic integration minitheories explain the social-related processes through which the classroom learning environment sometimes nurtures but other times thwarts students' inner resources.

Autonomy

Student functioning is most positive within the student–classroom dialectic when students experience high autonomy (Reeve & Jang, 2006; Ryan & Connell, 1989; Ryan & Grolnick, 1986) and when the

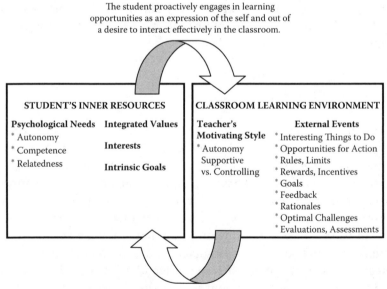

The student proactively engages in learning opportunities as an expression of the self and out of a desire to interact effectively in the classroom.

STUDENT'S INNER RESOURCES

Psychological Needs   Integrated Values
* Autonomy
* Competence   **Interests**
* Relatedness
    Intrinsic Goals

CLASSROOM LEARNING ENVIRONMENT

Teacher's   **External Events**
Motivating Style   * Interesting Things to Do
* Autonomy   * Opportunities for Action
Supportive   * Rules, Limits
vs. Controlling   * Rewards, Incentives
    * Goals
    * Feedback
    * Rationales
    * Optimal Challenges
    * Evaluations, Assessments

The classroom environment sometimes nurtures and enriches the student's inner resources, maintaining intrinsic motivation and facilitating internalization, but other times disrupts and thwarts these natural processes.

Figure 9.1   Student–classroom dialectical framework in self-determination theory.

classroom environment supports their autonomy (Deci et al., 1981; Reeve, Jang, Carrell, Barch, & Jeon, 2004; Roeser, Eccles, & Sameroff, 2002; Vallerand, Fortier, & Guay, 1997).

Autonomy is the inner endorsement of one's actions—the sense that one's actions emanate from oneself and are one's own (Deci & Ryan, 1985). When autonomous, students attribute their actions to an internal perceived locus of causality (deCharms, 1976), feel volitional, and experience a sense of choice over their actions (Reeve, Nix, & Hamm, 2003). An internal locus of causality is the perception that the causal source of one's motivated action is oneself, and that the ensuing action is congruent with and regulated by one's self; its opposite is an external locus of causality and the perception that one's behavior is initiated and regulated by forces outside the self. Feeling volitional or psychologically free involves a sense of a willingness to engage in an activity; its opposite is feeling pressured, coerced, or ego involved. Perceived choice over one's actions reflects an ongoing decision-making flexibility to choose what do to, how to do it, and whether to do it; its opposite is a rigid assignment or sense of obligation. Classroom experiences of autonomy can therefore be measured through students' reports of an internal locus, feeling free, and a perceived choice over their actions.

Autonomy Support

Although teachers cannot directly give students an experience of autonomy, they can provide interpersonal conditions that support students' experience of autonomy. *Autonomy support* is the interpersonal behavior one person provides to nurture another's inner motivational resources and their true self-regulation of action. Autonomy-supportive acts of instruction include fostering inner motivational resources, providing rationales, relying on informational and noncontrolling language, and accepting students' perspectives in ways that nurture, support, and increase students' inner endorsement of their classroom activity (Reeve, Deci, & Ryan, 2004; Reeve, Jang, et al., 2004).

In addition to these general guidelines, Table 9.1 lists 10 specific instructional behaviors that have been validated as autonomy-supportive ways of teaching and motivating students during instruction (Deci, Spiegel, Ryan, Koestner, & Kauffman, 1982; Reeve & Jang,

TABLE 9.1 Empirically Validated Autonomy-Supportive and Controlling Instructional Behaviors

	Autonomy-Supportive Instructional Behaviors
Listening	Time teacher spends listening to students' voice during instruction
Asking what students want, need	Frequency with which teacher asks what the students want or need
Creating independent work time	Time teacher allows students to work independently and in their own way
Encouraging students' voice	Time students spend talking about the lesson during instruction
Seating arrangements	The provision of seating arrangements in which the students—rather than the teacher—are positioned near the learning materials
Providing rationales	Frequency with which teacher provides rationales to explain why a particular course of action, way of thinking, or way of feeling might be useful
Praise as informational feedback	Frequency of statements to communicate positive effectance feedback about the students' improvement or mastery
Offering encouragements	Frequency of statements to boost or sustain students' engagement (e.g., "You can do it")
Offering hints	Frequency of suggestions about how to make progress when students seem stuck
Being responsive	Being responsive to student-generated questions, comments, recommendations, and suggestions
Perspective-taking statements	Frequency of empathic statements to acknowledge the students' perspectives or experiences

	Controlling Instructional Behaviors
Uttering directives/commands	Voicing commands, such as do this, move that, place it here, turn the page, etc.
Uttering should, got to, ought to	Voicing statements that students should, must, have, got to, or ought to think, feel, or do something that they are not currently thinking, feeling, or doing
Telling "the right way"	Verbalizing, or announcing, a particular way of behaving before students have the opportunity to discover an effective way of behaving for themselves
Showing "the right way"	Explicitly displaying, or exhibiting, a particular way of behaving before students have the opportunity to discover an effective way of behaving for themselves
Monopolizing learning materials	The teacher physically holds, possesses, and monopolizes the learning materials
Controlling questions	Communicating directives posed as a question and voiced with the intonation of a question

2006). Acts of instruction such as listening and encouraging students' voice nurture students' inner motivational resources. Acts of instruction such as providing rationales promote students' valuing and internalization processes. Acts of instruction such as offering encouragement and offering hints represent instances of informational, noncontrolling language. Acts of instruction such as responsiveness and communication of perspective-taking statements represent instances of acknowledging and accepting students' perspectives. The bottom half of Table 9.1 provides a list of six specific instructional behaviors that have been validated as controlling (i.e., autonomy-suppressing) ways of teaching and motivating students (Reeve & Jang, 2006). We include them here because many of these acts of instruction represent staples within some forms of classroom instruction and motivational interventions.

CLASSROOM RESEARCH ON SELF-DETERMINATION THEORY

Numerous studies have examined both autonomous self-regulation and intrinsic goal pursuits in the classroom, examining both their antecedents and their consequences. For example, Deci et al. (1981) found that when teachers were high in autonomy support, relative to when teachers were orienting toward controlling student behavior, their students became more intrinsically motivated for learning, felt more competent while learning, and developed higher levels of self-esteem. Further, studies showed that when both parents and teachers were more autonomy supportive, their children or students tended to internalize extrinsic motivation and become more effective in self-regulating their learning and performance (e.g., Grolnick & Ryan, 1989; Williams & Deci, 1996). As well, studies of learning showed that students whose autonomy had been supported demonstrated better conceptual learning and enjoyed the learning more (Benware & Deci, 1984; Grolnick & Ryan, 1987). In short, autonomy-supportive classroom contexts tend to promote students' autonomous self-regulation by helping students set their own goals, direct their own behavior, seek out optimal challenges, pursue their own interests and values, choose their own way of solving a problem, think more flexibly and more actively, persist rather than give up, perform better and more creatively, utilize more mature coping strategies, and experience more positive feelings about themselves and their learning (Reeve, 2002).

Studies have also shown that students learn better and feel better when they pursue intrinsic rather than extrinsic goals and when their teachers facilitate learning associated with intrinsic goals. For example, Vansteenkiste and colleagues (2004) reported three studies in which students learned different text material or activities to attain either an intrinsic or an extrinsic goal. Students in a business class were told that their learning about communications could help them either learn about themselves (an intrinsic goal) or make more money (an extrinsic goal). Those who had been oriented toward the intrinsic goal displayed relatively deeper learning, better performance, and greater persistence. Further, in those studies, when learning tasks were introduced in autonomy-supportive, as opposed to controlling, ways, students also showed more positive learning outcomes. The optimal condition for learning was when students were oriented toward intrinsic goals and teachers were autonomy supportive.

Supporting Intrinsic Motivation

One source of students' autonomous self-regulation is intrinsic motivation. The idea of facilitating intrinsic motivation in the classroom is based on the notion that learning can be interesting, enjoyable, and fun. Intrinsic motivation is a natural process that arises out of students' basic psychological needs (Deci & Ryan, 1985) that allows students to generate their own intentions ("I *want* to read the book [for fun].").

Supporting intrinsic motivation does not mean avoiding external and teacher-initiated events. Much of the research on cognitive evaluation theory detailed how specific external events such as opportunities for choice (Zuckerman, Porac, Lathin, Smith, & Deci, 1978), self-direction (Reeve et al., 2003), optimal challenge (Shapira, 1976), and competence-affirmative feedback (Ryan, 1982; Vallerand & Reid, 1984) preserve autonomy, support perceived competence, and thus enhance students' intrinsic motivation. In addition, research showed that teachers' intentions in using various structures strongly influenced their effects on students' intrinsic motivation. For example, when teachers set limits, provided rewards, or offered feedback with the intention of supporting students' autonomy, these external events had much more positive consequences for intrinsic motivation and engagement than they did when teachers provided these same events with the intention of controlling students' behavior (Koestner, Ryan, Bernieri, & Holt, 1984; Ryan, 1982; Ryan, Mims, & Koestner, 1983). Hence, supporting intrinsic motivation means being attuned to students' psychological needs and offering external events in ways that support students' autonomy, competence, and intrinsic motivation. It also means finding ways to enrich learning opportunities, making them more interesting and relevant to students' lives.

Intrinsic motivation fuels engagement and learning, but it does more. When students are learning out of interest and enjoying their learning activities, they experience what it means to be an origin of their behavior rather than a pawn to social forces. (*Origins* "originate" their own intentional behavior; *pawns*—a metaphor taken from the game of chess—experience powerful people pushing them around; deCharms, 1976.) Intrinsically motivated students learn what it means to seek out, master, and derive pleasure from optimal challenges. They also learn what it means to act in close harmony with their interests and self-endorsed values. Accordingly, classroom opportunities to engage in intrinsically motivated learning help build the type of inner resources that are often described by the phrase "learning to learn."

Supporting Internalization, Identified Regulation, and Integrated Regulation

Two additional forms of autonomous self-regulation are identified regulation and integrated regulation. For example, a student whose attitude would be captured by the statement "I *want* to read the book because it contains meaningful and valuable ideas" is manifesting *identified regulation*. Identified and integrated regulations approximate intrinsic motivation in their degree of autonomy (volition), but they differ in that both are based on the importance of the activity for the student's internalized values and goals, whereas intrinsic motivation is based on students' interest in and enjoyment of the activity itself (Ryan & Deci, 2000a). The study of autonomous types of extrinsic motivation (i.e., identified regulation, integrated regulation) shows that a student's level of self-determined extrinsic motivation for a learning activity forecasts the quality of his or her educational outcomes in much the same way that intrinsic motivation does (Jang, 2007; Reeve, Jang, Hardre, & Omura, 2002; Ryan & Connell, 1989; Ryan & Deci, 2000a).

Internalization occurs as students come to value a behavior or regulation, identify with it, and accept it as their own; integration occurs when students integrate each individual internalized regulation into their larger sense of self (Deci, Eghrari, Patrick, & Leone, 1994; Grolnick & Ryan, 1989; Reeve et al., 2002; Williams & Deci, 1996). To support students' internalization and integration processes, teachers can provide (a) rationales that explain why their recommended way of thinking or behaving might be personally useful for the students, (b) informational rather than pressuring language, (c) acknowledgments of students' negative feelings about undertaking uninteresting or nonvalued endeavors, and (d) high relatedness so students know with confidence that their teacher truly cares about and is looking out for their personal welfare. Collectively, through these aspects of the social context—rationales, nonpressuring language, acknowledging negative feelings, and relatedness—teachers support students' capacity to transform socially valued activities, behaviors, regulations, and values into their sense of self so that these integrated internalizations can act subsequently as inner motivational resources (i.e., the integrated values in Figure 9.1).

In addition to promoting internalization and integration, teachers can suggest "interest-enhancing strategies" to support students' engagement during relatively uninteresting lessons (Jang, 2007; Sansone, Weir, Harpster, & Morgan, 1992). Interest-enhancing strategies include adding a goal to try to reach, doing a repetitive task in different ways, and working in the company of friends. When enacted, these strategies help students self-regulate (enhance) their interest, engagement, perseverance, and emotional well-being (Jang, 2007).

ONE CLASSROOM ILLUSTRATION   Ms. Marcus teaches English at a public high school on the north side of Milwaukee, Wisconsin. The school serves 99% minority students, and the following is a summary of an observer's record of how this autonomy-supportive teacher taught her sixth-period class one winter's day.

From the upbeat preclass mood, it was apparent that Ms. Marcus and her students shared a high-quality relationship. She explained that today's class would feature three events: (a) a question-and-answer session on a reading assignment; (b) a lesson on how to write a good paragraph; and (c) individual writing time. She asked on which activity students wanted to spend the most time, and which activity they wanted at the beginning. The reading was obviously interesting to students, so they chose to begin with the group discussion. Students asked questions and offered comments, but mostly they highlighted how the article related to their personal experiences. Ms. Marcus supplemented the discussion by revealing the author's purpose in writing the article and by noting attractive features of the writing style. After 10 minutes, she asked if students wanted to make the transition to the writing lesson, and they said they did. During the transition, a couple of problems surfaced, such as students talking off topic too much. Ms. Marcus acknowledged that students have interesting things to talk to one another about, but she added that the talking would need to wait until their free time together because she did not want the time spent talking to put their time for individual writing at risk. During the lesson itself, she presented a checklist of a paragraph's strengths and weaknesses, and she framed writing as a problem for each student to solve (e.g., "What are you trying to say in your paragraph?"). The last 15 minutes were devoted to individual work time. Several students said that they wanted to work together (not singly), and she said that they could. Once students made the transition to the writing project, Ms. Marcus added, "I want you to have fun writing your paper, the most fun you've ever had writing, and see if you can improve your skills. Try to become a better writer today than you were yesterday." Several students struggled in their effort to self-regulate the writing, as expressed by their complaints, episodes of frustration, and disengagement (low persistence). She approached one pair of struggling writers and said, "I've noticed that you are having trouble with the project; is there anything I can do to help?" This question and ensuing conversation seemed to help the pair considerably.

By definition, autonomy-supportive instruction is sensitive to and dependent on students' voice and needs, so any representative illustration needs to be offered with that caution in mind. Still, Ms. Marcus's class provides a taste of what autonomy-supportive teachers might say or do during instruction as they strive to identify, nurture, and strengthen students' inner motivational resources and promote a synthesis between learners and their learning environment. The two key features to note are how Ms. Marcus enacted the full range of autonomy-supportive behaviors listed in Table 9.1 and how she helped students cope with four essential self-regulatory tasks.

The first self-regulatory task autonomy-supportive teachers can facilitate is initiating classroom engagement. The motivational goal is to help students adopt an autonomous intention to act, such as "Okay, yes, this is something I want to do." To support the construction of such autonomous intentions, the teacher seeks to build instructional events around students' inner resources by tapping into their interests, preferences, sense of curiosity, and sense of being challenged. In Ms. Marcus's case, she provided an interesting reading for students to discuss, and she began the writing time by encouraging students to have fun and by challenging them to improve. She also welcomed and acted on their many suggestions.

A second self-regulatory task autonomy-supportive teachers can help students with is overcoming their motivational problems. When talking with students about problems such as listlessness or a poor performance, an autonomy-supportive teacher would rely on language that is noncontrolling, informational, and flexible (rather than pressuring, unilateral, and rigid). Ms. Marcus's sentence, "I've noticed that you are having trouble with the project; is there anything I can do to help?" illustrates this nicely and shows that she treats poor performance as a problem to be solved rather than as a target for criticism.

A third self-regulatory task teachers can help students with is supporting their engagement during uninteresting (but important) activities. An autonomy-supportive teacher would offer rationales to explain the activity's value or personal meaning. In Ms. Marcus's case, she explained the reasoning behind why she asked students to refrain from their off-task conversations, as well as why the day's lesson was important and useful.

A fourth self-regulatory task is negotiating the inevitable conflicts that arise during instruction between what teachers want students to do and what students want students to do. Instead of countering students' negative affect and arguing that such an "attitude" is unacceptable, an autonomy-supportive teacher would accept students' negative feelings and resistance as potentially valid reactions to imposed classroom structures. In Ms. Marcus's case, negative affect surfaced only in the last few minutes of class, and she acknowledged and accepted that writing was a difficult task to do well. She further communicated her view that trying to improve oneself had both its negatives (e.g., frustration) but also its positives (e.g., sense of accomplishment).

THEORIES ON THE "HOW" OF SELF-REGULATED LEARNING

Because students' experiences at home, in school, and elsewhere often undermine their intrinsic motivation and interfere with the effective internalization of extrinsic motivation for learning, teachers are often faced with students who show little classroom engagement and little or no willingness to be self-regulating. This has led researchers to develop approaches to teach students the skills necessary for keeping themselves on target with a learning-related goal or activity. In addition, even when there is "the will" to learn, researchers have developed approaches to enhance students' efficacy during the lesson, such as through the acquisition and internalization of more effective strategies and methods for learning. These "how" approaches derive from various perspectives, including behavioral (Mace, Belfiore, & Hutchinson, 2001), social-cognitive (Schunk, 2001; Zimmerman, 2000), and Vygotskian (McCaslin & Hickey, 2001).

Collectively, these approaches to understanding the how of SRL endorse a top-down, socially guided framework that is anchored in the practice of exposing students to highly competent models whose thoughts, cognitions, and behaviors are to be emulated. For example, Zimmerman and Kitsantas (2005) presented a model described as a "social cognitive path to self-regulatory skill" (p. 519). It targets students with novice-like self-regulatory capacities (e.g., vague goals, no self-monitoring, ineffective learning strategies). Through instruction and social guidance, teachers initiate self-regulation interventions. The typical script in these interventions begins with explicit instruction and modeling from the teacher. The students' role is to watch and listen and then emulate what they have seen and heard. During the emulation period, students imitate the teacher, and the teacher provides supplemental instruction along with guidance, scaffolding, and corrective feedback. In doing so, teachers pave the way for students to discern what constitutes expert performance and to practice what they have seen and heard. Over time, teacher-regulated activity matures into coregulated activity as students internalize the teacher's ways of planning, monitoring, and evaluating so that students can become increasingly able to generate their own planning, monitoring, and evaluating. Students also acquire new and more adaptive sources of task-related motivation, such as self-efficacy and an intrinsic valuing of and interest in the task. The ultimate goal is for students to gain the capacity to utilize more adaptive motivation and to enact their newly found self-regulatory skills on their own and in new and less-structured settings (e.g., study hall, at home).

We believe that developing such skills is important for students' regulating their learning activities effectively. However, we also suggest that for students to put the skills to use and take greater responsibility for their learning, they will need to develop autonomous motivations for doing so. Without a meaningful degree of autonomous motivation, it is unlikely that the students will enact the skills with any regularity or effectiveness. An important implication of this is that interveners would do well to focus on the facilitation of autonomy at the same time they are working on teaching the skills. Indeed, it is school personnel who typically decide that a self-regulation intervention is needed, and it is school personnel who conduct the interventions, often as a mandatory activity for students. That creates conditions in which students are likely to feel controlled. Thus, it places considerable responsibility on the interveners to approach the students in a way that will facilitate their autonomous motivation rather than allowing them to fall into a pattern of feeling controlled. This is especially the case because the goal of such interventions is to have students internalize the skill so that the enhanced self-regulatory capacities will be maintained and transferred to new environments.

The SRL researchers characterize "optimal self-regulatory training as initially social in form but becoming increasingly self-directed" (Zimmerman & Kitsantas, 2005, p. 519). That is, although autonomous self-regulation is the destination, the road goes through social regulation, reflecting the ancient Chinese proverb, "Start with your master, end with yourself." SDT research emphasizes that among the crucial ingredients for transforming external regulations into internal, self-endorsed ones is perceived autonomy for the student and autonomy support from the teacher/role model.

Increasingly, within the area of SRL, there seems to be recognition of this important point as SRL researchers offer the following list of what veteran classroom teachers say and do when they successfully promote their students' SRL: encourage autonomy by offering choices; build competence by providing challenge; encourage group work and peer support; build in student self-evaluation; and use feedback that is nonthreatening and mastery oriented (Eisner, 1991; Meyer & Turner, 2002; Patrick & Middleton, 2002; Perry, Nordby, & VandeKamp, 2003; Perry, VandeKamp, Mercer, & Nordby, 2002). As one may recognize, this list of instructional behaviors overlaps considerably with the list of autonomy-supportive instructional behaviors in Table 9.1 and with our general conception of what it means to support autonomy. Hence, SDT provides a theoretical basis for understanding why these practices are crucial to effective interventions. In short, these recent realizations and developments suggest the importance of integrating the SRL and SDT perspectives, a goal that this chapter hopefully has subserved.

REFERENCES

Baumeister, R. F., & Vohs, K. D. (2004). *Handbook of self-regulation: Research, theory, and applications.* New York: Guilford Press.

Benware, C., & Deci, E. L. (1984). The quality of learning with an active versus passive motivational set. *American Educational Research Journal, 21,* 755–766.

Boekaerts, M., Pintrich, P. R., & Zeidner, M. (Eds.). (2000). *Handbook of self regulation.* San Diego, CA: Academic Press.

Carver, C. S., & Scheier, M. F. (1998). *On the self-regulation of behavior.* New York: Cambridge University Press.

Chirkov, V., & Ryan, R. M. (2001). Parent and teacher autonomy-support in Russian and U.S. adolescents: Common effects on well-being and academic motivation. *Journal of Cross Cultural Psychology, 32,* 618–635.

Collins, A., Brown, J. S., & Newman, S. E. (1989). Cognitive apprenticeship: Teaching the crafts of reading, writing, and mathematics. In L. B. Resnick (Ed.), *Knowing, learning, and instruction: Essays in honor of Robert Glaser* (pp. 453–494). Hillsdale, NJ: Erlbaum.

deCharms, R. (1976). *Enhancing motivation: Change in the classroom.* New York: Irvington.

Deci, E. L., Eghrari, H., Patrick, B. C., & Leone, D. R. (1994). Facilitating internalization: The self-determination theory perspective. *Journal of Personality, 62,* 119–142.

Deci, E. L., Koestner, R., & Ryan, R. M. (1999). A meta-analytic review of experiments examining the effects of extrinsic rewards on intrinsic motivation. *Psychological Bulletin, 125,* 627–668.

Deci, E. L., & Ryan, R. M. (1985). *Intrinsic motivation and self-determination in human behavior.* New York: Plenum.

Deci, E. L., & Ryan, R. M. (1991). A motivational approach to self: Integration in personality. In R. Dienstbier (Ed.), *Nebraska Symposium on Motivation: Perspectives on motivation* (Vol. 38, pp. 237–288). Lincoln: University of Nebraska Press.

Deci, E. L., Schwartz, A., Sheinman, L., & Ryan, R. M. (1981). An instrument to assess adult's orientations toward control versus autonomy in children: Reflections on intrinsic motivation and perceived competence. *Journal of Educational Psychology, 73,* 642–650.

Deci, E. L., Spiegel, N. H., Ryan, R. M., Koestner, R., & Kauffman, M. (1982). Effects of performance standards on teaching styles: Behavior of controlling teachers. *Journal of Educational Psychology, 74,* 852–859.

Eisner, E. E. (1991). What really counts in schools. *Educational Leadership, 48,* 10–17.

Elliot, A. J., McGregor, H. A., & Thrash, T. M. (2002). The need for competence. In E. L. Deci & R. M. Ryan (Eds.), *Handbook of self-determination research* (pp. 361–387). Rochester, NY: University of Rochester Press.

Grolnick, W. S., & Ryan, R. M. (1987). Autonomy in children's learning: An experimental and individual difference investigation. *Journal of Personality and Social Psychology, 52,* 890–898.

Grolnick, W. S., & Ryan, R. M. (1989). Parent styles associated with children's self-regulation and competence in school. *Journal of Educational Psychology, 81,* 143–154.

Jang, H. (2006). *Supporting students' motivation, engagement, and learning during an uninteresting activity.* Manuscript submitted for publication.

Jang, H., Reeve, J., & Ryan, R. M. (2007). *Can self-determination theory explain what underlies the productive satisfying learning experiences of collectivistically-oriented South Korean adolescents?* Manuscript submitted for publication.

Kasser, T., & Ryan, R. M. (1996). Further examining the American dream: Differential correlates of intrinsic and extrinsic goals. *Personality and Social Psychology Bulletin, 22,* 280–287.

Koestner, R., Ryan, R. M., Bernieri, F., & Holt, K. (1984). Setting limits on children's behavior: The differential effects of controlling versus informational styles on intrinsic motivation and creativity. *Journal of Personality, 52,* 233–248.

Mace, C. F., Belfiore, P. J., & Hutchinson, J. M. (2001). Operant theory and research on self-regulation. In B. J. Zimmerman & D. H. Schunk (Eds.), *Self-regulated learning and academic achievement: Theoretical perspectives* (2nd ed., pp. 39–66). Mahwah, NJ: Erlbaum.

Meyer, D. K., & Turner, J. C. (2002). Turning the kaleidoscope: What we see when self-regulated learning is viewed with a qualitative lens. *Educational Psychologist, 37,* 27–39.

McCaslin, M., Bozack, A. R., Napoleon, L., Thomas, A., Vasquez, V., Wayman, V., & Zhang, J. (2006). Self-regulated learning and classroom management: Theory, research, and considerations for classroom practice. In C. M. Evertson & C. S. Weinstein (Eds.), *Handbook of classroom management: Research, practice, and contemporary issues* (pp. 223–252). Mahwah, NJ: Erlbaum.

McCaslin, M., & Hickey, D. T. (2001). Self-regulated learning and academic achievement: A Vygoskian view. In B. J. Zimmerman & D. H. Schunk (Eds.), *Self-regulated learning and academic achievement: Theoretical perspectives* (2nd ed., pp. 227–252). Mahwah, NJ: Erlbaum.

Mossholder, K. W. (1980). Effects of externally mediated goal setting on intrinsic motivation: A laboratory experiment. *Journal of Applied Psychology, 65,* 202–210.

Patrick, H. E., & Middleton, M. J. (2002). Using instructional discourse analysis to study the scaffolding of student self-regulation. *Educational Psychologist, 37,* 17–25.

Perry, N. E., Nordby, C. J., & WandeKamp, K. O. (2003). Promoting self-regulated reading and writing at home and school. *Elementary School Journal, 103,* 317–338.

Perry, N., VandeKamp, K. O., Mercer, L. K., & Nordby, C. J. (2002). Investigating teacher-student interactions that foster self-regulated learning. *Educational Psychologist, 37,* 5–15.

Pintrich, P. R., & De Groot, E. V. (1990). Motivation and self-regulated learning components of academic performance. *Journal of Educational Psychology, 82,* 33–40.

Reeve, J. (2002). Self-determination theory applied to educational settings. In E. L. Deci & R. M. Ryan (Eds.), *Handbook of self-determination research* (pp. 183–203). Rochester, NY: University of Rochester Press.

Reeve, J., Deci, E. L., & Ryan, R. M. (2004). Self-determination theory: A dialectical framework for understanding the sociocultural influences on student motivation. In D. McInerney & S. Van Etten (Eds.), *Research on sociocultural influences on motivation and learning: Big theories revisited* (Vol. 4, pp. 31–59). Greenwich, CT: Information Age Press.

Reeve, J., & Jang, H. (2006). What teachers say and do to support students' autonomy during a learning activity. *Journal of Educational Psychology, 98,* 209–218.

Reeve, J., Jang, H., Carrell, D., Barch, J., & Jeon, S. (2004). Enhancing high school students' engagement by increasing their teachers' autonomy support. *Motivation and Emotion, 28,* 147–169.

Reeve, J., Jang, H., Hardre, P., & Omura, M. (2002). Providing a rationale in an autonomy-supportive way as a strategy to motivate others during an uninteresting activity. *Motivation and Emotion, 26,* 183–207.

Reeve, J., Nix, G., & Hamm, D. (2003). The experience of self-determination in intrinsic motivation and the conundrum of choice. *Journal of Educational Psychology, 95,* 375–392.

Reis, H. T., Sheldon, K. M., Gable, S. L., Roscoe, J., & Ryan, R. M. (2000). Daily well-being: The role of autonomy, competence, and relatedness. *Personality and Social Psychology Bulletin, 26,* 419–435.

Roeser, R. W., Eccles, J. S., & Sameroff, A. J. (2002). School as a context of early adolescents' academic and socio-emotional development: A summary of research findings. *The Elementary School Journal, 100,* 443–471.

Ryan, R. M. (1982). Control and information in the intrapersonal sphere: An extension of cognitive evaluation theory. *Journal of Personality and Social Psychology, 43,* 450–461.

Ryan, R. M., & Connell, J. P. (1989). Perceived locus of causality and internalization: Examining reasons for acting in two domains. *Journal of Personality and Social Psychology, 57,* 749–761.

Ryan, R. M., & Deci, E. L. (2000a). Intrinsic and extrinsic motivation: Classic definitions and new directions. *Contemporary Educational Psychology, 25,* 54–67.

Ryan, R. M., & Deci, E. L. (2000b). Self-determination theory and the facilitation of intrinsic motivation, social development, and well-being. *American Psychologist, 55,* 68–78.

Ryan, R. M., Deci, E. L., & Grolnick, W. S. (1995). Autonomy, relatedness, and the self: Their relation to development and psychopathology. In D. Cicchetti & D. J. Cohen (Eds.), *Developmental psychopathology* (Vol. 1, pp. 618–655). New York: Wiley.

Ryan, R. M., & Grolnick, W. S. (1986). Origins and pawns in the classroom: Self-report and projective assessments of individual differences in children's perceptions. *Journal of Personality and Social Psychology, 50,* 550–558.

Ryan, R. M., Mims, V., & Koestner, R. (1983). Relation of reward contingency and interpersonal context to intrinsic motivation: A review and test using cognitive evaluation theory. *Journal of Personality and Social Psychology, 45,* 736–750.

Sansone, C., Weir, C., Harpster, L., & Morgan, C. (1992). Once a boring task always a boring task? Interest as a self-regulatory mechanism. *Journal of Personality and Social Psychology, 63*, 379–390.

Schunk, D. H. (2001). Social cognitive theory and self-regulated learning. In B. J. Zimmerman & D. H. Schunk (Eds.), *Self-regulated learning and academic achievement: Theoretical perspectives* (2nd ed., pp. 125–152). Mahwah, NJ: Erlbaum.

Shapira, Z. (1976). Expectancy determinants of intrinsically motivated behavior. *Journal of Personality and Social Psychology, 34*, 1235–1244.

Vallerand, R. J., Fortier, M. S., & Guay, F. (1997). Self-determination and persistence in a real-life setting: Toward a motivational model of high school dropout. *Journal of Personality and Social Psychology, 72*, 1161–1176.

Vallerand, R. J., & Reid, G. (1984). On the causal effects of perceived competence on intrinsic motivation: A test of cognitive evaluation theory. *Journal of Sport Psychology, 6*, 94–102.

Vansteenkiste, M., Simons, J., Lens, W., Sheldon, K. M., & Deci, E. L. (2004). Motivating learning, performance, and persistence: The synergistic effects of intrinsic goal contents and autonomy-supportive contexts. *Journal of Personality and Social Psychology, 87*, 246–260.

Williams, G. C., & Deci, E. L. (1996). Internalization of biopsychosocial values by medical students: A test of self-determination theory. *Journal of Personality and Social Psychology, 70*, 115–126.

Zimmerman, B. J. (2000). Attaining self-regulation: A social cognitive perspective. In M. Boekaerts, P. R. Pintrich, & M. Zeidner's (Eds.), *Handbook of self-regulation* (pp. 13–39). San Diego, CA: Academic Press.

Zimmerman, B. J., & Kitsantas, A. (2005). The hidden dimension of personal competence: Self-regulated learning and practice. In A. J. Elliot & C. S. Dweck (Eds.), *Handbook of competence and motivation* (pp. 509–526). New York: Guilford Press.

Zuckerman, M., Porac, J., Lathin, D., Smith, R., & Deci, E. L. (1978). On the importance of self-determination for intrinsically-motivated behavior. *Personality and Social Psychology Bulletin, 4*, 443–446.

10

Attributions as Motivators of Self-Regulated Learning

Dale H. Schunk

INTRODUCTION

Ms. Tuttle's U.S. history class was tough; everyone who took it agreed on that point. There was a lot of reading and many assignments, and tests were challenging. Many students felt that they spent more time on her course than on all their other courses combined. At the same time, students generally felt that this course was one of the best they took in high school, and that Ms. Tuttle was an exceptional teacher. Her advice to students was to work hard, keep up with the work, and ask about what you don't understand.

Following an especially difficult unit test, Alysha and Kerri walked out together:

> *Alysha:* That was impossible! I wasn't prepared.
>
> *Kerri:* Me either. I've got to work harder and be better organized for this class.
>
> *Alysha:* Fine to say but how much work is enough? I shouldn't have taken this class; I'm not smart enough in history.
>
> *Kerri:* I'm going to stick with it. I think I can do ok in here but tonight I'm going to figure out a better study schedule for these tests.
>
> *Alysha:* Good luck!

Self-regulation, or *self-regulated learning,* refers to the process by which students activate and sustain cognitions, behaviors, and affects that are systematically directed toward the attainment of goals (Zimmerman, 2000). Self-regulation is a complex process and includes such activities as attending to and concentrating on instruction; organizing, coding, and rehearsing information to be learned; establishing a productive work environment and using resources effectively; holding positive beliefs about one's capabilities, the value of learning, the factors influencing learning, and the anticipated outcomes of one's actions; and experiencing pride and satisfaction with one's goal-directed efforts (Pintrich, 2000).

Motivation is a key process in self-regulation (Pintrich, 2000). Effective self-regulation requires that students regulate not only their actions but also their underlying achievement-related cognitions, beliefs, and affects. As Zimmerman (2000) has shown, the self-regulation of motives occurs before, during, and after learning.

At the same time, motivation also influences self-regulation. This process is evident in the opening scenario. Alysha and Kerri are in a challenging class. Alysha feels the class is beyond her and may not stay in the class. Kerri, on the other hand, feels that effort and self-regulation will help her succeed. She plans to spend some time working out a better study schedule. Thus, Kerri's beliefs are motivating her to be better self-regulated, whereas Alysha's are not.

This chapter focuses on one type of motivator of self-regulated learning: attributions. *Attributions* are beliefs concerning the causes of outcomes (Weiner, 1992). Theory and research substantiate the idea that attributions are important motivators of self-regulated learning, and in turn, the results of one's learning affect future attributions.

The following section discusses a theoretical rationale for the importance of attributions in self-regulated learning. Research evidence then is presented showing the role of attributions in self-regulation. The chapter concludes with examples of how teachers can use attributions to motivate students to engage in better self-regulated learning.

THEORETICAL BACKGROUND

This section is divided into two parts. The first part gives a brief historical background, followed by discussion of a contemporary view of attributions. In the second part, the role of attributions in social cognitive theory is discussed.

Attribution Theory

Historical Views Attribution theory originated with Heider's (1958) *naïve analysis of action,* which examines how people view the causes of important events. Heider believed that people attribute causes to internal and external factors. Internal factors include abilities and motivation; external factors are those in the environment. Abilities and the environment, when combined, constitute the *can* factor; motivation is the *try* factor. One's ability is relative to the environment. Assuming that ability is sufficient to overcome environmental obstacles, then trying (motivation) affects outcomes.

Heider's views were thought provoking but offered little research evidence. Kelley (1967; Kelley & Michela, 1980) developed an attribution theory that provided testable hypotheses. According to Kelley, attributions represent a process by which people decide on the explanation that best fits the event. Often, there are several possible attributions for an outcome. In these cases, people decide which is the most likely.

Rules Guide the Attribution Process *Covariation* means that when an event occurs repeatedly across time, people determine which potential causes consistently accompany that event. For example, over a series of history tests, Jon discovers that when he does not study for a test he gets a low score, but when he studies he gets a higher score. Although there are other potential causes of the test scores (e.g., Jon's mood, the weather, the day of the week the test was given), he is likely to attribute test performance to amount of studying because the other variables were not consistently present on successful testing days.

Discounting means that a given factor will be eliminated as a cause if other, more likely causes are present. Although Jon got his highest test grade when the test was given on Tuesday, he is likely to discount day of the week as a potential cause if he knew that an easy test was given on that day. *Augmentation* refers to the increased likelihood of making an internal attribution for an outcome when powerful environmental influences are present that can inhibit that outcome. If Jon gets a minor boost in his grades from a new method of studying when his classroom was noisy, then he is likely to augment his perceived value of the method because it had to overcome an adverse environment.

Research conducted using Kelley's theory identified how people use rules to form and modify attributions. Much of this research, however, had little relevance to education. Weiner's theory, described next, has direct relevance to achievement behavior and education.

Weiner's Theory   Guided by the work of Heider and Kelley, Weiner and his colleagues developed an attribution theory of achievement behavior (Weiner, 1992; Weiner et al., 1971). Weiner postulated that students attribute their outcomes (successes, failures) to factors such as ability, effort, task difficulty, and luck. These factors are given general weights, and for any outcome two or more factors may be viewed as primarily responsible. Thus, if Jon makes an A on a history test, then he may attribute it to ability (he is good at history) and effort (he studied hard for the test). Although ability, effort, task difficulty, and luck are common attributions for achievement outcomes, they are not the only ones. Students use many other attributions, such as illness, distractions, teacher's attitude, and room conditions.

As shown in Table 10.1, causes can be represented along three dimensions: internal or external to the person; relatively stable or unstable over time; and controllable or uncontrollable by the individual. Effort generally is viewed as internal, unstable, and controllable, whereas ability is seen as internal, stable, and uncontrollable.

People use situational cues to form attributions. When success is attained easily or early in the course of learning or when there are many successes, people will attribute those outcomes to high ability. When people persist despite physical or mental exertion, people will attribute these outcomes to effort. When a task is lengthy and difficult, people will attribute their outcomes to task difficulty. When outcomes seem random—success or failure does not depend on what one does—people will attribute these outcomes to luck.

Attributions influence students' expectations, motivation, and emotions (Weiner, 1979). Stability influences expectancy of success. Assuming that task conditions remain much the same, success

TABLE 10.1   Weiner's Classification of Attributions

	Internal		External	
	Stable	Unstable	Stable	Unstable
Controllable	Effort	Strategy use	Teacher bias	Help from others
Uncontrollable	Ability	Mood	Task difficulty	Luck

attributed to stable causes (e.g., high ability, low task difficulty) should result in higher expectations for future success than success attributed to unstable causes (e.g., high effort, good luck). Locus influences learners' affects and emotions. Learners experience greater pride or shame after succeeding or failing when outcomes are attributed to internal causes. Controllability has diverse effects. Feeling that one can control one's academic outcomes can raise one's motivation and self-regulation to learn, whereas the perception of little control can affect expectations, motivation, emotions, and self-regulation negatively.

Attributions and Social Cognitive Theory

Theoretical Framework   The theoretical framework used for self-regulation and the role of attributions is Bandura's (1986, 1997) *social cognitive theory*, which construes human functioning as a series of reciprocal interactions between personal influences (e.g., thoughts, beliefs), environmental features, and behaviors. To exemplify these interactions, assume that Jon believes that if he studies diligently he can perform well in history. If Jon attributes poor history test results to a lack of effort (a personal process), then he is more likely to study diligently (behavior). Conversely, Jon's environment can affect his attributions and behaviors. When Jon receives encouraging feedback from his history teacher, he may attribute his success to his effort and work harder to succeed. His teacher might further encourage test preparation by allowing students to ask questions and study in class before the test.

The influence of behavior on personal variables can be seen when Jon studies, feels he understands the material, and attributes it to hard work. Behaviors also can affect the environment, as when Jon moves to a quiet place in his house to eliminate distractions from his parents and sister.

Working within a social cognitive framework, Zimmerman (1998, 2000) conceptualized self-regulation as consisting of three phases: forethought, performance control, and self-reflection. The forethought phase precedes actual performance and refers to processes that set the stage for action, such as setting goals and deciding on effective strategies. The performance control phase involves processes that occur during learning and affect attention and action, such as social comparisons, feedback, and use of strategies. During the self-reflection phase that occurs after performance, learners respond to their efforts by evaluating their goal progress, making attributions for performance, and adjusting strategies as needed.

Perceived Self-Efficacy Within this model, a critical variable is *perceived self-efficacy*, or one's beliefs about one's capabilities to learn or perform actions at designated levels (Bandura, 1986, 1997). Self-efficacy is hypothesized to influence choice of activities, effort, persistence, and achievement (Bandura, 1997; Schunk, 2001). Compared with students who doubt their learning capabilities, those with high self-efficacy for acquiring a skill or performing a task participate more readily, work harder, persist longer when they encounter difficulties, and achieve at higher levels.

Learners obtain information to appraise their self-efficacy from their actual performances, vicarious (modeled) experiences, forms of persuasion, and physiological reactions. One's own performances offer reliable guides for assessing self-efficacy. In general, successes raise self-efficacy and failures lower it, although an occasional failure or success after many successes or failures may not have much effect.

Learners also acquire much self-efficacy information vicariously, primarily through exposure to models. Although adult models can teach children skills, children derive the best self-efficacy information from models who are similar to themselves (e.g., peers) (Schunk, 1987). Observing similar others succeed at a task, such as reading aloud in front of the class, may raise observers' self-efficacy. Children are apt to believe that if the peers can succeed, then they can as well. Children may not experience the same sense of self-efficacy from observing a competent adult read to the class. Conversely, observing similar peers have difficulty on a task may lead observers to believe that they also may have trouble, which can lower their self-efficacy.

Students also receive persuasive information from others that can influence their self-efficacy to engage in activities, such as when teachers tell them, "You can do it," or, "Work hard and you'll do well." Such information can raise self-efficacy, but actual performance will validate or invalidate the information. The increased self-efficacy will be substantiated if learners subsequently succeed, but the effect will be short-lived if students subsequently attempt the task and perform poorly.

Finally, physiological reactions (e.g., sweating, heart rate) offer information to gauge self-efficacy. Children who notice that they are less anxious than usual while taking tests may interpret that to mean that they are more skillful, which can promote self-efficacy.

Self-efficacy, however, is not the only influence on achievement. High self-efficacy will not produce competent performance when requisite knowledge and skills are lacking. *Outcome expectations,* or anticipated consequences of actions (e.g., making a high grade on a test after studying hard), are influential because learners engage in activities they believe will lead to positive outcomes (Shell, Murphy, & Bruning, 1989). Even students with high self-efficacy are not apt to attempt a task if they believe that performance will not lead to positive outcomes. *Perceived value,* or the utility of the learning, affects behavior because learners show little interest in activities they do not value (Wigfield & Eccles, 2002). Conversely, students who value an activity and believe that it will lead to positive outcomes (e.g., playing sports leads to social status among peers) may attempt the activity even if they lack self-efficacy for performing well. Assuming that learners hold positive outcome expectations and value the activity, their self-efficacy is predicted to influence their choice of activities, effort, persistence, and achievement (Bandura, 1986).

Within this social cognitive theoretical framework, attributions are seen as important influences on self-efficacy and as key motivators of self-regulation (Table 10.2). Effective self-regulation depends on students making attributions that enhance self-efficacy and motivation. Attributions enter into self-regulation during the self-reflection phase when students compare and evaluate their performance. Whether goal progress is deemed acceptable depends on its attribution. Students who attribute success to factors over which they have

TABLE 10.2   Attributions during Self-Regulated Learning

	Phases		
	Forethought	Performance control	Self-reflection
Key Processes	Self-efficacy	Strategy use	Attributions
	Attributions	Social comparisons	Goal progress
	Goals	Feedback	Strategy change
	Strategy selection		

little control (e.g., luck, task ease) may hold low self-efficacy if they believe they cannot succeed on their own. If they believe they lack ability to perform well, then they may judge learning progress as deficient and be unmotivated to work harder. Conversely, students who attribute success to ability, effort, and effective use of learning strategies should experience higher self-efficacy and remain motivated to continue to learn (Schunk, 1994).

Attributions also come into play during the forethought phase. Prior to the onset of a task, students experience varying degrees of self-efficacy for succeeding. This initial sense of self-efficacy depends heavily on their prior experiences on the same or similar task and their attributions for their prior outcomes. Thus, when Jon gets ready to begin a new history unit he may think back to prior units and how well he performed. Assuming that he attributes his higher grades to effort (and increasing ability) he is apt to feel self-efficacious for succeeding on the new unit.

It is important to note that attributions will have different effects on self-efficacy, motivation, and self-regulation depending on whether they are made for successes or failures. For example, attributing failure to low ability should have negative effects on these outcomes, whereas attributing success to high ability will have positive effects. Attributing failure to low effort may heighten motivation and self-regulation if students believe they are capable of working harder. Attributing success to high effort will sustain self-efficacy, motivation, and self-regulation only if students believe they can maintain the intensity of their effort. If they do not believe they can, then self-efficacy, motivation, and self-regulation may suffer. Thus, it is imperative in attribution research to identify the outcomes for which students make attributions to determine their predicted effects.

RESEARCH EVIDENCE

This section reviews research studies that addressed the role of attributions in motivating students to engage in self-regulated learning and that explored the influences on attributions and self-efficacy among children engaged in academic learning. Collectively, this research evidence highlights the influence of attributions and suggests ways that teachers might help students become self-regulated learners.

Attributional Feedback

An extended body of research has addressed how providing students with attributional feedback influences their attributions, self-efficacy, motivation, and achievement. *Attributional feedback* links students' academic outcomes with one or more attributions. For example, in the opening scenario assume that both Kerri and Alysha make a C on the history test. As the teacher hands back the tests, she might give them attributional feedback by saying, "I know that you can do better if you study the material more." This is an example of effort attributional feedback. Other types of attributional feedback might stress ability (e.g., "You're really good at this."); strategy use (e.g., "You did well because you used a good strategy."); cooperative learning (e.g., "You do well when you work together."); and so forth.

A series of studies demonstrated that attributional feedback affects students' attributions, self-efficacy, self-regulation, and achievement (Schunk, 1983, 1984; Schunk & Cox, 1986; Schunk & Rice, 1986). Schunk (1983) provided children who had poor subtraction skills with instruction and self-directed practice solving over several sessions. Children were assigned to one of four attributional feedback conditions: ability, effort, ability plus effort, none. During the problem solving, ability-feedback children periodically received verbal feedback from the teacher linking their successful problem solving with ability (e.g., "You're good at this."); effort feedback students received effort statements (e.g., "You've been working hard."); ability-plus-effort students received both forms of feedback; and no-feedback students did not receive attributional feedback. Self-efficacy and subtraction skill were assessed following the last instructional session. Children also judged the amount of effort they expended during the sessions; although this is not a pure attribution measure, it reflects the extent that children believed their successes were because of effort.

Ability feedback promoted self-efficacy and skill more than did the other three conditions; those in the effort and ability-plus-effort conditions outperformed the no-feedback group. Those in the three treatment conditions solved more problems during self-directed practice (a measure of motivation during self-regulated learning) than did those in the no-feedback condition. Those in the effort and ability-plus-effort conditions judged effort expenditure greater than did those in the ability group, who judged effort higher than the no-feedback condition.

These findings support the point that the same degree of success attained with less effort strengthens self-efficacy more than when greater effort is required (Bandura, 1997). Ability-plus-effort students may have discounted ability information in favor of effort; they may have wondered how good they were if they had to work hard to succeed. By the third grade, most children can use inverse compensation in judging ability from effort information (i.e., more effort required to succeed implies lower ability) (Schunk, 1994).

Schunk (1984) conducted two studies to determine how the sequence of attributional feedback influenced achievement outcomes. Children with low subtraction skills received instruction and self-regulated practice over sessions. One group (ability–ability) periodically received ability feedback for their successes; a second group (effort–effort) received effort feedback; in a third condition (ability–effort) ability feedback was given during the first half of the instructional program and effort feedback during the second half; for a fourth condition (effort–ability), this sequence was reversed. Self-efficacy, skill, and attribution for problem-solving progress during the instructional sessions were assessed following the last instructional session.

In both studies, children who initially received ability feedback (ability–ability and ability–effort) demonstrated higher self-efficacy and skill than those initially receiving effort feedback. Students initially given ability feedback placed greater emphasis on ability attributions than did students who initially received effort feedback. Early successes constitute a prominent cue for forming ability attributions. Telling students that ability is responsible for their successes supports these perceptions. Students' ability attributions for successes enhance self-efficacy and motivate them to self-regulate their performances to continue to improve. Effort-ability students may have discounted ability feedback; they may have wondered how competent they were because their prior successes were attributed to effort. Although effort feedback raises self-efficacy and skills (Schunk, 1982), its overall effects are weaker than when successes are attributed to ability.

Working with children with learning disabilities, Schunk and Cox (1986) provided subtraction instruction with self-regulated practice. Children received effort feedback during the first half of the instructional program, effort feedback during the second half, or no-effort feedback. Effort feedback enhanced self-efficacy, skill, and self-regulated practice more than no-effort feedback. Effort feedback also led to higher effort attributions than no feedback; students who received effort feedback during the first half of the instructional program judged effort as a more important cause of success than students who received feedback during the second half.

Telling students that effort was responsible for their successes was credible because these students had encountered prior learning difficulties. Effort feedback conveys that students can continue to improve by working hard, which raises self-efficacy and motivation for self-regulation. It was predicted that first-half effort feedback would be more effective than second-half feedback, but the two conditions did not differ. Students' learning disabilities may have forced them to expend effort to succeed during all sessions, so later effort also seemed credible.

Schunk and Rice (1986) gave children with reading problems instruction and practice in identifying important ideas over 15 sessions. One group (ability–ability) periodically received ability feedback for successful comprehension, a second group (effort–effort) received effort feedback, a third group (ability–effort) was given ability feedback during the first 7½ sessions and effort feedback during the second 7½ sessions, and for a fourth group (effort–ability) this sequence was reversed. Although practice was not self-regulated because it was under the direction of a teacher, self-regulatory processes were involved because children were taught a comprehension strategy and were largely on their own during the sessions to apply it.

The four conditions did not differ in comprehension skill, but ability-ability and effort-ability students judged self-efficacy higher at the end of the program than did students in the other conditions. Children who received ability feedback during the second half of the instructional program placed greater emphasis on ability as a cause of success than children who received effort feedback during the second half. Ability-effort students made higher effort attributions than ability–ability children.

It is difficult to reconcile these findings showing benefits of later ability feedback with those of Schunk (1984), who found that early ability feedback was better. These studies differ in type of participants, content, and number and format of instructional sessions. Schunk and Rice's students had severe reading problems and had experienced much school failure. Perhaps early ability feedback had less impact because they discounted it due to their frequent failures but that after continued successes over sessions they were more likely to adopt the ability information.

Relich, Debus, and Walker (1986) explored the influence of attributional feedback during instruction on long division with children who tended to attribute academic failures to low ability and devalue the role of effort. Children received either modeled instruction of division operations or written instruction. Half of the children in each of these conditions received attributional feedback stressing effort and ability for success and failure (e.g., "That's incorrect. I know you have the ability, but you just have to try harder."). All students participated in self-regulated practice over sessions. A control group received only the pretest and posttest, which included self-efficacy, division skill, and attributions.

Attributional feedback raised children's attributions for success and failure to effort and decreased attributions of failure to low ability. Compared with the control condition, children receiving attributional feedback demonstrated higher self-efficacy and skill than did children not receiving feedback. Thus, the feedback apparently led to better self-regulation with corresponding skill acquisition.

Researchers also have explored the role of attributions during self-regulation in the absence of attributional feedback. Butkowsky and Willows (1980) compared good, average, and poor readers' performances on anagrams; during the performances, feedback indicated success or failure. Good and average readers persisted longer than poor readers. Poor readers were more likely to attribute failure to internal and stable causes (e.g., low ability) and less likely to attribute success to ability. Relative to good and average readers, poor readers showed a greater decrease in expectancy of success following failure.

Collins (1982) measured children's self-efficacy for solving mathematical word problems and mathematical ability. Students were classified as high, average, or low ability, and within each level students were classified as high or low in self-efficacy. Students were given word problems to solve—some were unsolvable—and could rework any they missed. Students engaged in self-regulation during the problem solving because students decided how long and in what fashion to work on problems. Regardless of ability level, students with higher self-efficacy spent more time reworking problems they missed than did low-efficacy students. Low-efficacy children made lower ratings of their ability relative to that of peers than did high-efficacy students. High-efficacy students were more likely than low-efficacy students to attribute failure to low effort.

Relation of Attributions to Self-Regulation

Researchers have examined the relation of attributions to self-regulation and achievement outcomes. Much research has obtained positive correlations between ability attributions for success and self-efficacy (Schunk, 1994). Schunk and Cox (1986) found a positive relation between effort attributions for success and self-efficacy. Self-efficacy also correlates positively with attributions of success to task ease and negatively with luck attributions (Schunk & Gunn, 1986). Several studies have found a positive correlation between achievement and attributions to ability (Schunk, 1994).

Schunk and Gunn (1986) used multiple regression to determine the percentage of variance in achievement outcomes accounted for by various predictors. Children received instruction in long division and engaged in self-regulated practice. Ability and luck attributions accounted for significant increments in the explained variability of self-efficacy; the luck effect was in a negative direction. For division skill, self-efficacy and use of effective task strategies accounted for significant increments in variability.

Relich et al. (1986) explored the effects of attributional feedback on attributions, self-efficacy, and achievement; the effects of attributions on self-efficacy and achievement; and the influence of self-efficacy on achievement. Attributional feedback had a significant direct effect on attributions, self-efficacy, and achievement; attributions influenced self-efficacy; and self-efficacy had a direct effect on achievement. Thus, feedback affected achievement directly and indirectly through its effects on attributions and self-efficacy. The effect of attributions on achievement was weak, which suggests that attributions affect achievement indirectly through self-efficacy and motivation during self-regulation.

Schunk and Gunn (1986) found that the largest direct influence on changes in children's division skill was caused by use of effective strategies; skill also was influenced by self-efficacy and effort attributions. The strongest influence on self-efficacy was ability attributions for success, which suggests that instructional variables affect self-efficacy partly through the intervening influence of attributions. The attributions likely affected children's motivation during self-regulated practice.

Strategy attributions can be effective motivators. Zimmerman and Kitsantas (1999) taught high school girls a writing revision strategy. Girls then practiced rewriting sentences under different goal conditions. Outcome-goal students were told to minimize the number of words in their revisions; process-goal students were advised to use the strategy to rewrite sentences; shifting-goal students were told to initially focus on the strategy and then to shift to the outcome goal. The authors found that on measures of writing skill, self-efficacy, and intrinsic interest, the shifting goal was more effective than the process goal, which was better than the outcome goal. Girls also judged attributions for why they did not do better rewriting the last sentence during practice. Their attributions of performance deficiency to poor strategy use related to higher self-efficacy, skill, and interest; attributions to low effort related to lower skill and interest; and attributions to low ability related to low self-efficacy and skill. Strategy attributions for poor performance, which reflect self-regulatory processes, bore the best relation to motivational variables.

MOTIVATING STUDENTS TO ENGAGE IN SELF-REGULATION

There are ways that attributions can be used effectively to help motivate students to engage in self-regulated learning. Based on theory and research, the following three scenarios discuss applications at different educational levels.

Motivating Elementary Students in Mathematics

Attributional feedback has been applied effectively with elementary students to help increase their motivation for self-regulation (Schunk, 1982, 1983, 1984; Schunk & Gunn, 1986; Schunk & Rice, 1986). Elementary-age children have not differentiated the concepts of effort and ability, believing that working harder implies higher ability. Once children differentiate these concepts, they understand that greater effort to attain the same level of performance implies lower ability. Given that children are in transition on their differentiation, both attributions can be used to motivate self-regulation.

The key is to ensure that the attributions are credible to children. Children who have to work hard to succeed and then are told by a teacher that they are smart are apt to discount the feedback. Similarly, they are apt to discount effort feedback (e.g., "You've been working hard.") when they succeed easily and quickly. Rather than rely on one type of attributional feedback, teachers can sequence their feedback to match children's academic outcomes and levels of effort and persistence.

Ms. Gomez teaches fourth grade and is beginning a unit on fractions to include adding, subtracting, multiplying, and dividing fractions with like and unlike denominators. Part of this is review because children previously have worked on adding and subtracting fractions with like denominators. New material includes finding the lowest common denominator (LCD) and multiplying and dividing.

Ms. Gomez begins each arithmetic session by modeling and explaining the particular operation to be mastered that day. She then works more problems at the board by calling on students to answer questions; for example, in the problem $1/3 + 1/4$, what is the LCD? Then, what do we do with the 12? After she has gone through some examples, she breaks students into dyads to solve problems at their desks.

While students are engaged in this small-group problem solving, Ms. Gomez circulates and checks their work. The topic of LCD is difficult for many children to grasp. Ms. Gomez has demonstrated it to the whole class previously using various props and manipulatives, for example, by cutting a pie into sixths and showing how 2/6 is the same as $1/3$. Now, the children must translate that knowledge into symbolic form with numbers.

Effort is the credible attribution at this point, along with correct strategy (e.g., find a number that all denominators divide into evenly). Thus, as she circulates through the room she attributes their success to effort and using the correct strategy (e.g., "That's correct. You used the right step."). If children have difficulty, then she attributes that to their not using the correct strategy (e.g., "No, the LCD for 3 and 4 isn't 6. Remember the rule—figure out what number both 3 and 4 divide into evenly.").

After some time on the group work, Ms. Gomez allows children a few minutes to work problems individually. The individual time is designed to build skills and self-efficacy. She again circulates during this problem solving. Now, she tailors her feedback to children's level of skill acquisition. Regarding those who are succeeding regularly, she provides ability feedback (e.g., "That's correct. You're getting really good at this."). For children who are succeeding but slowly, she continues to emphasize effort (e.g., "That's correct. You're working hard, and it will begin to get easier."). For those still performing incorrect operations, she continues to emphasize strategy (e.g., "Let's remember the rule—find the number that both denominators divide into evenly. You can do that, and then you'll be able to correctly solve the problem.").

Ms. Gomez assigns some homework that is designed as a short review of the day's lesson. With reasonable effort, children should be able to complete the homework in 15 minutes. The next day, she checks children's homework to make sure they completed it and answered most questions correctly. At that time, she tailors her attributional feedback to children's level of skill acquisition. To Kara, who succeeded easily, she remarks, "You're good at this." To Devon, who succeeded with effort, she says, "You worked hard on these." And to Shayna, who is finally understanding the strategy, she says, "That's correct. You are working hard and using the rule correctly."

Ms. Gomez repeats this sequence with each lesson on fractions. She incorporates into the modeling attributional statements that she verbalizes aloud and tells children to use. For example, with the problem $\frac{1}{2} \div \frac{1}{4}$, she verbalizes, "Now I have to be careful and use the correct rule. Remember that to divide we just turn around the second fraction and multiply. So, the problem becomes $\frac{1}{2} \times 4$, or 4×1 divided by 2×1, which is 4 divided by 2 or 2. I need to work hard to remember to use that rule." Then, during the group problem solving she asks children to verbalize aloud (quietly) the rule and to give themselves effort information as they work (e.g., "That's right. Remember to use the right rule. Work hard and I'll get it right."). In this fashion, Ms. Gomez is inculcating in her students a means for providing themselves with attributional feedback that will improve their self-regulated learning.

Motivating Middle School Students in Social Studies

Mr. Langdon teaches eighth-grade social studies. Students are required to complete a major unit on their state's history. This unit requires that students pass a state-mandated test at the end of the year. The unit includes much information about key events in the state's history and many technical terms, such as those referring to acts passed and important people.

For each chapter in the text, Mr. Langdon gives students a list of terms. Students are to write each term on an index card, along with a short definition or description. They then study these terms to learn them. Students also complete workbook exercises and read passages from other sources to complement the text.

The unit requires much memorization as well as understanding of how events served to influence later history. Success in the course requires hard work because students must keep up with the material and learning the key terms. Mr. Langdon believes that all students can perform well in his course, but they must believe that they are capable of learning and attribute their successes to diligence and good time management and planning.

Mr. Langdon teaches his students strategies to use to find meanings and examples for technical terms. These include search strategies in books and on the Internet, as well as strategies for locating information in libraries. He grades students' cards for accuracy and completeness, and students are graded on their tests and quizzes on the material.

For terms that students cannot locate and for those that they define incorrectly, Mr. Langdon asks them to attribute the reasons. They have to state about how long they worked on finding the definition, the sources they consulted, and the search strategies they used. He reviews students' attributions and meets with them to provide feedback. For example, Kyle could not find a definition for a bill introduced by a state senator during the early 1800s and subsequently enacted into law. He responded that he spent 30 minutes searching the textbook and put the bill's name and senator's name in an Internet search. He felt that he did not respond correctly because he did not know where else to search (lack of ability).

Mr. Langdon informed him of two key works describing state legislation and showed him how to access from the Internet documents described in these works. He provided feedback that with necessary effort the next time Kyle should be able to find terms similar to this one.

Mr. Langdon believes that all of his students can be successful at this task and that doing this work helps to develop understanding of key individuals and events in history. His goals are that students' develop effective strategies for locating information, and that they make attributions for their performances that motivate them to engage in effective self-regulation as they complete their assignments. The results pay off. As students learn strategies, they soon are able to define all terms of an assignment. Initially, they attribute more of their failures to low ability in social studies, but as they see that they can succeed, they switch their attributions to improper strategy and insufficient effort. When they incorrectly define terms, they are able to pinpoint where they erred, which typically involves an improper strategy (e.g., assuming that a similar-sounding term means the same thing as the original term). Further, as students see their class performances improve (e.g., better participation, higher grades on tests), they realize the value of the work, and their self-efficacy for continuing to succeed improves. Because finding definitions for terms is largely a self-regulated learning task, attributions and self-efficacy help motivate students to work effectively.

Motivating High School Students in English

Ms. Ming teaches honors English to eleventh-grade students. The course has a heavy workload: Students read books and text selections, write papers of various lengths, take weekly vocabulary quizzes, and spend much time studying literary devices and literary expression.

Ms. Ming is aware that many students approach English with a negative attributional set. They believe that reading, writing, and spelling are heavily influenced by ability, and that there is little that one can do to change that (e.g., "I'm not a good speller."). To counter this negative view, Ms. Ming works with her students to set goals and to make attributions for their performances.

Ms. Ming believes that the development of students' responsibility for their own outcomes is critical. Students who fail to take responsibility for their academic outcomes are at risk for school failure (Zimmerman, 2006). For example, students might attribute low performance to poor teaching or disruptive home environment. Although there may be some truth in such attributions, they do not motivate students to succeed because they reflect factors that are beyond students' control. Instead, taking responsibility requires that students ask teachers about what they do not understand, seek academic help from school counselors, and work to create a more conducive studying environment in their homes.

The personal responsibility training that Ms. Ming uses is patterned after that described by Zimmerman (2006). In teaching literary devices, Ms. Ming explains and demonstrates each device using literary text. Students then complete workbook exercises designed to build their skill in recognizing different devices. In each book they read, students must write a paper and list multiple examples with page numbers for each literary device.

Although some literary devices are fairly easy to comprehend (e.g., simile, metaphor), others present greater challenges (e.g., foreshadowing, irony). Research by Zimmerman (2006) and his colleagues showed that beginning with process goals (e.g., steps one uses to locate a literary device) and moving to outcome goals (e.g., number of devices located) is effective in building skill, motivation, and self-regulation. Thus, the teacher uses this sequence with her students. For each device, she teaches them a set of steps to use as they self-regulate their performances to identify instances of the device in text. Initially, students are asked to follow the steps in locating the device. Once they are able to reliably identify examples, they are asked to switch to outcome goals. They have a target number of examples to find for each device, and as they read the text and identify examples they keep a running count.

Ms. Ming periodically asks students to assess their attributions for their successes and difficulties in finding each type of literary device. Although locating some examples for some devices can be difficult, students are able to locate examples successfully most of the time. Thus, if they are having difficulty it likely involves inadequate strategy use or insufficient effort. For example, if they are skimming text, then they are likely to miss examples; if they inadequately apply a strategy, then they might misidentify a device. She is trying to ensure that students attribute their difficulties to controllable factors (low effort, improper strategy use) and attribute their successes to effort, strategy use, and increased skill. The latter attributions will motivate students as they engage in self-regulated learning.

CONCLUSION

In this chapter, I have shown that attributions are key influences on students' motivation for self-regulated learning. Educators can facilitate effective self-regulation by providing attributional feedback to students that stresses factors that they can control—such as effort and strategy use—that will help improve students' self-regulated learning. Because much school learning involves students' self-regulating their academic work outside school (e.g., homework, assignments), it is important that teachers do what they can to ensure that students do not use debilitating attributions. The examples given show ways that teachers can make small changes in their instructional activities to incorporate an attributional component. By so doing, they help students build their academic skills, motivation, and self-regulated learning.

REFERENCES

Bandura, A. (1986). *Social foundations of thought and action: A social cognitive theory.* Englewood Cliffs, NJ: Prentice Hall.

Bandura, A. (1997). *Self-efficacy: The exercise of control.* New York: Freeman.

Butkowsky, I. S., & Willows, D. M. (1980). Cognitive-motivational characteristics of children varying in reading ability: Evidence for learned helplessness in poor readers. *Journal of Educational Psychology, 72,* 408–422.

Collins, J. (1982, March). *Self-efficacy and ability in achievement behavior.* Paper presented at the meeting of the American Educational Research Association, New York.

Heider, F. (1958). *The psychology of interpersonal relations.* New York: Wiley.

Kelley, H. H. (1967). Attribution theory in social psychology. In D. Levine (Ed.), *Nebraska Symposium on Motivation* (Vol. 15, pp. 192–238). Lincoln: University of Nebraska Press.

Kelley, H. H., & Michela, J. (1980). Attribution theory and research. *Annual Review of Psychology, 31,* 457–501.

Pintrich, P. R. (2000). The role of goal orientation in self-regulated learning. In M. Boekaerts, P. R. Pintrich, & M. Zeidner (Eds.), *Handbook of self-regulation* (pp. 451–502). San Diego, CA: Academic Press.

Relich, J. D., Debus, R. L., & Walker, R. (1986). The mediating role of attribution and self-efficacy variables for treatment effects on achievement outcomes. *Contemporary Educational Psychology, 11,* 195–216.

Schunk, D. H. (1982). Effects of effort attributional feedback on children's perceived self-efficacy and achievement. *Journal of Educational Psychology, 74,* 548–556.

Schunk, D. H. (1983). Ability versus effort attributional feedback: Differential effects on self-efficacy and achievement. *Journal of Educational Psychology, 75,* 848–856.

Schunk, D. H. (1984). Sequential attributional feedback and children's achievement behaviors. *Journal of Educational Psychology, 76,* 1159–1169.

Schunk, D. H. (1987). Peer models and children's behavioral change. *Review of Educational Research, 57,* 149–174.

Schunk, D. H. (1994). Self-regulation of self-efficacy and attributions in academic settings. In D. H. Schunk & B. J. Zimmerman (Eds.), *Self-regulation of learning and performance: Issues and educational applications* (pp. 75–99). Hillsdale, NJ: Erlbaum.

Schunk, D. H. (2001). Social cognitive theory and self-regulated learning. In B. J. Zimmerman & D. H. Schunk (Eds.), *Self-regulated learning and academic achievement: Theoretical perspectives* (2nd ed., pp. 125–151). Mahwah, NJ: Erlbaum.

Schunk, D. H., & Cox, P. D. (1986). Strategy training and attributional feedback with learning disabled students. *Journal of Educational Psychology, 78,* 201–209.

Schunk, D. H., & Gunn, T. P. (1986). Self-efficacy and skill development: Influence of task strategies and attributions. *Journal of Educational Research, 79,* 238–244.

Schunk, D. H., & Rice, J. M. (1986). Extended attributional feedback: Sequence effects during remedial reading instruction. *Journal of Early Adolescence, 6,* 55–66.

Shell, D. F., Murphy, C. C., & Bruning, R. H. (1989). Self-efficacy and outcome expectancy mechanisms in reading and writing achievement. *Journal of Educational Psychology, 81,* 91–100.

Weiner, B. (1979). A theory of motivation for some classroom experiences. *Journal of Educational Psychology, 71,* 3–25.

Weiner, B. (1992). *Human motivation: Metaphors, theories, and research.* Newbury Park, CA: Sage.

Weiner, B., Frieze, I. H., Kukla, A., Reed, L., Rest, S., & Rosenbaum, R. M. (1971). *Perceiving the causes of success and failure.* Morristown, NJ: General Learning Press.

Wigfield, A., & Eccles, J. S. (2002). The development of competence beliefs, expectancies for success, and achievement values from childhood through adolescence. In A. Wigfield & J. S. Eccles (Eds.), *Development of achievement motivation* (pp. 91–120). San Diego, CA: Academic Press.

Zimmerman, B. J. (1998). Developing self-fulfilling cycles of academic regulation: An analysis of exemplary instructional models. In D. H. Schunk & B. J. Zimmerman (Eds.), *Self-regulated learning: From teaching to self-reflective practice* (pp. 1–19). New York: Guilford Press.

Zimmerman, B. J. (2000). Attaining self-regulation: A social cognitive perspective. In M. Boekaerts, P. R. Pintrich, & M. Zeidner (Eds.), *Handbook of self-regulation* (pp. 13–39). San Diego, CA: Academic Press.

Zimmerman, B. J. (2006). Enhancing students' academic responsibility and achievement: A social-cognitive self-regulatory account. In R. J. Sternberg & R. Subotnik (Eds.), *Optimizing student success in school with the other three Rs: Reasoning, resilience, and responsibility* (pp. 179–197). Greenwich, CT: Information Age.

Zimmerman, B. J., & Kitsantas, A. (1999). Acquiring writing revision skill: Shifting from process to outcome goals. *Journal of Educational Psychology, 89,* 241–250.

11

Goal Setting:
A Key Proactive Source of Academic Self-Regulation*

Barry J. Zimmerman

INTRODUCTION

We are, in a very real sense, defined by the goals that we set for ourselves. Our goals commit us behaviorally to a particular standard or outcome: "A goal is the object or aim of an action, for example, to attain a specific standard of proficiency, usually within a specified time limit" (Locke & Latham, 2002, p. 705). This standard becomes a source of personal feedback about our effectiveness and self-regulatory control. The importance of goal setting to the attainment of one's aspirations was first studied by Lewin and his colleagues (Lewin, Dembo, Festinger, & Sears, 1944). Today, there is an extensive body of research, encompassing diverse areas of expertise, indicating the importance of goal setting to one's learning proficiency and performance attainments (e.g., Burton, Nayler, & Holliday, 2001; Locke & Latham, 1990; Schunk, 1989, 2001).

This chapter addresses the role of goals in students' efforts to self-regulate their learning, with particular attention to the issue of motivation. More specifically, I discuss first the motivational qualities of goals and the properties of goals that influence their effectiveness. Second, I address the relationship between goals and other self-regulatory processes and beliefs, and finally I describe how a self-regulation coach helped an at-risk student set goals and

* I would like to thank Dale H. Schunk for his helpful recommendations regarding an earlier draft of this chapter.

implement associated self-regulatory processes to enhance her academic achievement. Although research on academic functioning is
given priority in this chapter, research with employment and athletic
tasks is included when necessary to give the most complete picture
of the effectiveness of goal setting. However, this review does not
consider studies of students' goal orientation, which focus on reasons for engaging in academic tasks (Anderman, Austin, & Johnson,
2002) rather than the act of goal setting. The role of students' goal
orientations is discussed by other contributors to this volume (e.g.,
chapters 7 and 13).

SETTING EFFECTIVE GOALS

Motivational Influences of Goals

The goals that students set for themselves affect their motivation to
learn in four major ways (see Table 11.1). First, goals motivate students' *choice* of and *attention* to goal-relevant tasks and away from
goal-irrelevant tasks. There is evidence that students who set specific
learning goals for their reading chose and attended to goal-related
prose passages more often than goal-unrelated passages (Rothkopf

TABLE 11.1   Motivational Influences of Goals

Goal Effects on Motivationon	Examples of Goal Setting
Goals enhance one's *choice* of and *attention* toward goal-relevant tasks and away from goal-irrelevant tasks.	After setting the goal of becoming a police officer, Jenny, a high school senior, chose to read exclusively on the topic.
Goals increase one's *effort* to attain them.	As the date of the entrance exam for the police academy grew closer, Jenny redoubled her efforts to study.
Goals sustain one's *persistence* in pursuing them.	Jenny's application to the police academy was denied because of her poor physical condition, but she persisted toward her professional goal by undertaking physical fitness training.
Goals increase one's *affective reactions* to targeted outcomes.	Jenny found that her goal of becoming a police officer led her to feel increasing satisfaction and positive feelings about herself as she improved her physical fitness.

& Billington, 1979). These students also retained information better about goal-related passages than goal-unrelated passages. Second, goals also motivate learners to exert higher levels of *effort*. Students who set high goals for themselves expend greater effort than students who set low goals—whether effort is measured physiologically (Bandura & Cervone, 1983) or psychologically (Bryan & Locke, 1967). Third, goals also motivate greater *persistence* over time. For example, when students were allowed to self-regulate the time they spend on a prose learning task, those who set high goals persisted longer than those who set low goals for themselves (LaPorte & Locke, 1976).

Fourth, higher-quality goals influence students' learning indirectly by producing heightened arousal and other *affective reactions*, such as greater self-satisfaction or less defensiveness. For example, students' who set learning process goals (i.e., involving the use of strategies) for themselves reported significantly greater satisfaction with their learning outcomes than students who did not set any goals (Zimmerman & Kitsantas, 1997). These differences in satisfaction were in turn highly predictive of the students' level of learning ($r = .72$).

Advantageous Properties of Goals

Eight advantageous properties of goals are illustrated in Table 11.2. The first key property of goals is their *specificity*. General goals, such as "Do your best," do not enhance academic attainment reliably (Schunk, 1989). Specific goals are more effective than general or vague goals because progress toward specific goals is easier to gauge (Bandura, 1988). A second advantageous property of goals is their temporal *proximity*. Proximal goals, such as daily completion rates for pages of a term paper, are hypothesized to be more effective than distal goals, such as weekly page completion rates, because the proximal goals provide more immediate feedback about one's progress. When feedback is delayed for a week, learners cannot evaluate the effectiveness of their writing strategies promptly, and this can slow their rate of progress. Bandura and Schunk (1981) found that students who set daily (i.e., proximal) goals for their math class work displayed higher motivation (i.e., self-efficacy beliefs) and math achievement than students who set weekly (i.e., distal) goals.

TABLE 11.2 Examples of Advantageous Properties of Goals

Advantageous Goal Properties	Examples of Goal Setting
Specificity of goals	*Specific goal:* I will increase my test score to a B or higher. *General goal:* I will try to do better on my tests.
Proximity of goals	*Proximal goal:* I will complete one page of problems by the end class. *Distal goal:* I will finish the book by the end of the semester.
Hierarchical organization of short- and long-term goals	For my *short-term goal,* I will master the definitions of foreign language words assigned in class, and for my *long-term goal,* I will increase the size of my vocabulary during spontaneous conversations in the language.
Congruence or lack of conflict among one's goals	My goal of reaching the honors list is compatible with my parents' goals for me.
Difficult or challenging goals	My goal of learning all the verbs in the Spanish book is difficult but achievable for me.
Self-set or assigned *origins* of goals	*Self-set goals:* I will pass a course in algebra with at least a C in school. *Assigned goals:* My teacher expects me to pass algebra with at least a C.
Conscious quality of goals	I am aware of the need to monitor my essay writing metacognitively if I want to improve through practice.
Focus of goals on learning processes or performance outcomes	My first goal is to focus on *learning* writing revision *processes* (e.g., a strategy for correcting sentence fragments) before shifting to *performance outcomes,* such as improving my grade in a writing class.

This is not meant to imply that distal or long-term goals cannot be helpful. Long-term goals may prompt self-regulated learners to set short-term goals for themselves, but the former goals are unlikely to help poorly regulated learners. For example, when a highly self-regulated girl decides to qualify for the spelling team at her school, she would also set short-term goals to reach her long-term objective, such as setting daily practice goals until her spelling becomes competitive. When long-term goals are integrated with short-term goals in a *hierarchy,* there are self-regulatory benefits (Zimmerman, 2000). When combined hierarchically, short-term goals provide proximal feedback about learning progress, and long-term or distal goals stretch a person's self-regulatory vision further into the future. Learners with hierarchical goals can work productively over long periods of time without requiring outside sources of motivation or direction. Thus, hierarchical integration is a third advantageous property of goals.

A fourth desirable property of goals involves their degree of *congruence*. Students often find themselves caught between contradictory achievement goals, which reduces their effectiveness (Locke, Smith, Erez, Chah, & Schaffer, 1994). Most parents expect that their children will spend their time productively in school and earn acceptable grades, but peer groups can pressure students to set low achievement goals to avoid labels of intellectual "geek" or "nerd." For example, there is evidence (Steinberg, Brown, & Dornbusch, 1996) that fewer than 32% of high school students think it is important to get good grades in school. One of six students deliberately hides personal interest in doing well in class because of worry about what his or her friends might think. More than 50% of the students never discuss their schoolwork with their friends. Finally, by high school, students' friends become more influential than parents. These disturbing facts reveal the presence of high levels of conflict regarding students' goals. The act of goal setting and pursuit is nested within a social group context that can enhance or undermine students' effectiveness in school.

A fifth advantageous property of students' goals involves the level of *difficulty*. From a self-regulatory perspective, students who set ambitious goals for themselves should achieve better than students who set easily attainable goals (Locke & Latham, 1990). The latter goals fail to provide much satisfaction because the students' degree of progress is minimal, and this limits their motivational power. There is extensive evidence that setting difficult goals leads to higher levels of performance than easy goals. For example, Schunk (1983) studied the effects of goal difficulty in mathematical training, and he found that difficult goals (i.e., completing a higher number of problems) during study sessions led to greater math proficiency than easy goals (completing a lower number of problems). However, difficult goals are not theorized to be helpful in guiding students' self-regulation if these goals are not also attainable. A failure to attain overly ambitious goals can produce adverse self-reactions, such as attributions to insufficient ability, which in turn can be devastating to academic motivation.

In research on these issues, Schunk (1983) developed a procedure for ensuring that difficult goals would be perceived as attainable.

The teacher informed one half of the students in each goal condition directly that they could attain the goal (i.e., "You can work the designated number of problems."). The other half of the students were informed indirectly that students who were similar to them had been able to work the designated number of problems. Schunk found that direct encouragement led to higher perceptions of self-efficacy than indirect encouragement.

Schunk's (1983) study revealed that goal difficulty does not always motivate superior forms of self-regulation if difficult goals are not also attainable. A better descriptive label for this property of one's goals would be their *challenge* because this label involves both attainability and difficulty. Setting goals that are optimally challenging depends on other self-regulatory processes, such as one's self-evaluative proficiency, and there is evidence that higher-achieving students are better able to judge their current proficiency level better than poorly regulated learners (Chen, 2003).

A sixth advantageous property of one's goals involves their *origin*. It has been widely hypothesized that personally selected or constructed goals would be more effective in guiding self-regulation than goals assigned by others (McCombs, 2001; APA Task Force, 1993). Students who set goals for themselves are expected to be more committed to attaining them because such goals are based on self-perceptions of autonomy and self-determination (Deci & Ryan, 1991). There is evidence to support this hypothesis. Schunk (1985) studied goal setting with elementary students who were learning disabled. In a study involving mathematical problem solving, some students set performance goals each session (in terms of problems completed), other students had comparable goals assigned, and a third group of students did not set or receive learning goals. Self-set goals led to the highest level of math skill on a posttest and the highest perception of self-efficacy. Students in the two goal conditions displayed higher motivation in terms of the number of problems that were completed during each session than students in the no-goal condition. Students who set their own goals judged themselves as more confident of attaining their goals at the start of each session than students who were assigned goals.

Research on the issue of goal origins has proven more complex than expected because students in self-set goal conditions often set higher goals for themselves than those that were assigned by the instructor (Locke & Latham, 2002). To resolve this confounding, research was conducted on workers' performance in settings in which the difficulty of assigned goals was controlled, but contradictory findings were reported. Latham and colleagues (e.g., Latham & Saari, 1979) reported no differences between self-set goals and assigned goals on worker's performance, whereas Erez and colleagues (e.g., Erez & Kanfer, 1983) reached the opposite conclusion from their research. However, there were procedural differences in the way that goals were assigned between the two research groups. To explain their divergent findings, Latham and Erez joined forces to study this issue (Latham, Erez, & Locke, 1988). They tested the integrative hypothesis that assigned goals are equally effective to self-set goals when the purpose or rationale for the assigned goals is given. This new hypothesis shifts the causation from the origin of a goal to its manifest acceptance. The students' acceptance of a goal was not assessed as an intervening variable in this study but rather was inferred from their behavioral outcomes.[1] The study revealed that the origin of a learner's goal was less important than its personal acceptance. Schunk's (1985) findings of a goal origin effect with elementary students despite controlling for difficulty of the goals may be explained by the absence of a specific rationale for students in the assigned goals group. Together, these studies suggest that effective goals can be assigned by social mediators, such as parents and teachers, if they convey a plausible rationale for their goals.

A seventh advantageous property of one's goals involves their *conscious* quality. Because goals are intentional in nature, they implicitly require a high level of consciousness, but there are researchers (Fitzsimons & Bargh, 2004) who have hypothesized that learners are influenced by low conscious goals as well (i.e., subconscious, unconscious, or nonconscious goals). A key issue is the relation between high and low conscious goals. There is evidence that conscious goals are more reliably and directly tied to task performance than unconscious motives (Howard & Bray, 1988; Locke & Latham, 2002) and that conscious goals are not related to subconscious aspects of achievement motivation as assessed by the Thematic Apperception Test. It appears that the heightened awareness that goals induce is beneficial to learning.

Perhaps the most widely discussed issue related to goal-related consciousness involves the role of automatic responding or automaticity—when an act is performed without reflection or intent (English & English, 1958). Learning a skill to a high level of proficiency (which is sometimes called *overlearning*) can induce automaticity, which is theorized to free up one's mental capacity to focus on other aspects of functioning than the act itself. For example, skilled readers do not need to focus on the structure of typical sentences to understand their meaning. However, when these readers encounter an unusually complex sentence, they will shift their attention from the outcomes of reading (i.e., the meaning of the text) to the process of reading (i.e., the structure of the complex sentence). Carver and Scheier (1991) discussed the role of three levels of consciousness in self-regulation: (a) an unconscious or automaticity level, (b) a conscious set of processes involved in decision making about self-information (such as goal setting and self-monitoring), and (c) an advanced level of consciousness involving self-awareness and self-reflection about the outcomes of one's decisions. Carver and Scheier posited that people continuously process and evaluate data from all levels of functioning. Through goal setting, learners can shift their attention to a particular level of consciousness.

Fitzsimons and Bargh (2004) reviewed research on nonconscious forms of self-regulation (i.e., automaticity). They hypothesized that, through frequent practice or use, goals become associated with those performance situations and habitual behaviors, such as when the desk in one's room becomes associated with a strategy for productive writing. In this research on nonconscious goals, a "priming" procedure was used that activates goal-relevant stimuli in a subtle and unobtrusive manner, such as walking into the room where the desk is located. There is evidence that physical or social environmental cues can trigger nonconscious goal-related behavior in a number of studies (e.g., Bargh, 1990; Fitzsimons & Bargh, 2003). However, there are a number of important limitations to nonconscious goals (Fitzsimons & Bargh, 2004). For example, a goal cannot be nonconsciously activated if it does not already exist in the mind of the individual and if there is no preexisting need state, such as an aspiring writer's need for and method of daily practice. Furthermore, a nonconscious goal does not enable a person to pinpoint its causal effectiveness, whereas a conscious goal enhances a person's awareness of how it influences his or her self-evaluations and self-reactions. Although nonconscious goals do trigger routinized courses of action, these goals are clearly limited in their impact on students' self-reflection and adaptation. These are significant self-regulatory limitations for learners who are acquiring new academic skills.

An eighth advantageous property of goals involves their *focus*: to enhance learning processes versus performance outcomes or products. Burton (1979) labeled this distinction *performance versus outcomes* in the field of athletic functioning, but Locke and Latham (2002) labeled this distinction *learning versus performance* in employment settings. Schunk and Swartz (1993) labeled this distinction *learning process versus product* in the field of academic functioning. Although these differences in descriptors can be tricky (e.g., the meaning of the word *performance*), the underlying distinctions are largely isomorphic. However, Kingston and Hardy (1997) have drawn an additional distinction between performance goals and outcome goals in athletics, with the former involving self-comparative standards (e.g., improvements in daily running time) and the latter involving socially competitive standards (e.g., winning a race). The relative impact of self versus social evaluative standards in self-regulation is discussed in the next section of this chapter.

According to Locke and Latham (2002), learning tasks are more complex than performance tasks because the former depend on one's ability to discover appropriate task strategies. By contrast, performance tasks are less complex because they have become automatized. There is meta-analytic evidence (Wood, Mento, & Locke, 1987) that the effect size of goals is much smaller with more complex (i.e., learning tasks, $d = 0.44$) than with less-complex tasks (i.e., performance tasks, $d = 0.77$). There is also research confirming Locke and Latham's hypothesis regarding the importance of strategies to success on learning tasks: Students' use of strategies was more predictive of performance outcomes than their performance goals (Chesney & Locke, 1991). Not only are performance goals limited in their effectiveness on learning tasks, but also they can actually interfere with skill attainment on complex learning tasks. In an air traffic controller simulation study, Kanfer and Ackerman (1989) found that learners who were given a general goal of "Do your best" showed higher levels of skill attainment than performance goal instructions (i.e., to attain high scores). These unexpected findings pointed to the need for studies that directly contrasted learning and performance outcome goals on learning types of tasks.

A series of studies that addressed these issues was conducted by Schunk, Zimmerman, and their colleagues. In a study of elementary school students' acquisition of writing skill, Schunk and Swartz (1993) compared the effectiveness of learning process goals (i.e., executing the writing strategy), learning product goals (i.e., producing para-graphs as outcomes of writing practice), and general goals (i.e., doing your best) in acquiring writing skills. Although students who set process goals displayed more writing skill than students who set product goals, these differences did not attain statistical significance in this study. However, when adult feedback about adhering to their goals was given to some of the students in the process goal group, they exhibited significantly better writing than classmates who set product goals or general goals. Apparently, adhering to their goals was difficult for these young students, but when they were reminded, they displayed the expected effects on this learning task, and these effects remained evident after a delay of 6 weeks.

Zimmerman and Kitsantas (1996) conducted a study of athletic functioning with an older group of students, adolescent girls. These girls were randomly assigned to one of three conditions based on the type of goals (learning process, performance outcome, or a no-goal control). All participants received identical throwing instructions, but the process goal group was instructed to focus on a dart-throw-ing strategy while practicing. The performance outcome group focused on getting the highest scores (i.e., closest to the "bull's-eye") on the target as they practiced, and the control group students were informed about the dart-throwing task and the scoring system but were not given any goal-setting instructions and did not practice dart throwing. These researchers found that girls who set learning process goals had higher dart-throwing scores than did girls who set performance outcome goals or girls who set general goals. The dart-throwing performance of the outcome goal group signifi-cantly surpassed that of students who did not set goals. This study clearly demonstrated that learning goals (involving implementing a dart-throwing strategy) enhanced skill acquisition better than per-formance outcome goals even though the latter criterion (i.e., dart-throwing scores) served as the dependent measure in the study. But, this does not mean that outcome goals are unimportant in self-regu-lated learning.

In a subsequent study using the same dart-throwing task, Zim-merman and Kitsantas (1997) investigated a developmental hypoth-esis based on a social cognitive model of self-regulated learning with high school girls. These researchers theorized that learning process goals would be more effective at the outset of efforts to learn a new skill but that after the skill becomes automatized, outcome goals would be more effective. In addition to a learning process and performance outcome goal group, a shifting goal group was included in which the students initially set learning process goals (i.e., completing dart-throwing strategy steps), and after automaticity was attained (i.e., repeated throwing of the darts without missing any steps), they were shifted to performance outcome goals (i.e., optimizing their dart-throwing scores). Girls in the control group in this study practiced dart throwing without setting any goals. Half of the girls in each goal-setting group recorded their goal outcomes (strategy steps executed properly vs. points scored on target). It was found that girls who shifted their goals at the point of automaticity displayed the highest level of dart-throwing skill on a posttest. They significantly surpassed girls who adhered to learning process goals throughout the practice session as well as girls in the performance and no-goal groups. Girls who adhered to learning process goals throughout the practice session significantly surpassed girls who adhered to outcome performance goals throughout the session. Girls in the performance outcome goal condition showed higher levels of dart-throwing skill than girls in the no-goal setting practice condition. Self-recording significantly improved the girls' dart throwing regardless of their type of goal setting.

In an extension study involving an academic writing task, Zimmerman and Kitsantas (1999) compared the effectiveness of these same four goal-setting conditions with high school girls. The writing task involved sentence revision exercises (involving a lengthy list of clauses), and all of the girls were shown a strategy for reducing redundancy and integrating important information into grammatically correct revisions. Girls in the process goal group were told to focus on executing the strategy steps, whereas girls in the performance outcomes goal condition were asked to focus on reducing the number of words in each exercise to a minimal number. This was a key criterion of effectiveness in the scoring system for the sentence revisions. Girls in the shifting goal group focused first on the revision strategy until it could be executed without errors, and then these students shifted their goal to optimizing performance outcomes. Half of the girls in each goal-setting group recorded their goal outcomes (strategy steps executed properly vs. number of words in completed sentences). As in the prior study, the girls in the shifting goal group displayed superior writing revisions than girls who adhered to a process goal throughout the practice session. Girls in the learning process goal condition surpassed the writing revision skill of girls who adhered to performance outcome goals throughout the practice session. Although the performance outcome goal group surpassed the mean of the no-goal control group, that contrast did not reach statistical significance. Self-recording significantly improved the girls' writing revisions regardless of their method of goal setting.

Taken together, the last two studies provide support for the conclusion that both learning process goals and performance outcome goals contribute to students' learning, but their relative effectiveness depends on students' level of automaticity. These studies also indicated that when goal setting was linked to other self-regulatory processes, such as strategy implementation and self-recording, its effectiveness was significantly enhanced, and the reasons for this finding are addressed next.

INTEGRATING GOAL SETTING WITH OTHER SELF-REGULATORY PROCESSES AND BELIEFS

I now turn to the issue of how goals serve as a vital component in students' efforts to self-relate their learning and motivation. A model of self-regulation of learning that integrates goal setting with other self-regulatory processes and beliefs is presented in Figure 11.1 (Zimmerman, 2000). Note that students' self-regulatory processes and motivational beliefs fall into three cyclical phases: forethought, performance, and self-reflection. *Forethought processes* precede efforts to learn and are designed to enhance those efforts. *Performance phase processes* occur during learning efforts and are designed to improve action and self-monitoring. *Self-reflection processes* occur after learning efforts and are designed to optimize a person's reactions to his or her outcomes. These self-reflections in turn influence forethought processes and beliefs regarding subsequent learning efforts, which completes the self-regulatory cycle.

The length of each self-regulatory cycle can vary from minutes to years, depending on learners' goals and feedback as well as other self-regulatory processes. For example, a student who gives him- or herself a daily test of learning of a list of spelling words would represent a daily cycle, whereas a student who tested him- or herself weekly would represent a weekly cycle. Thus, the frequency and quality of one's feedback can be self-regulated to a significant degree.

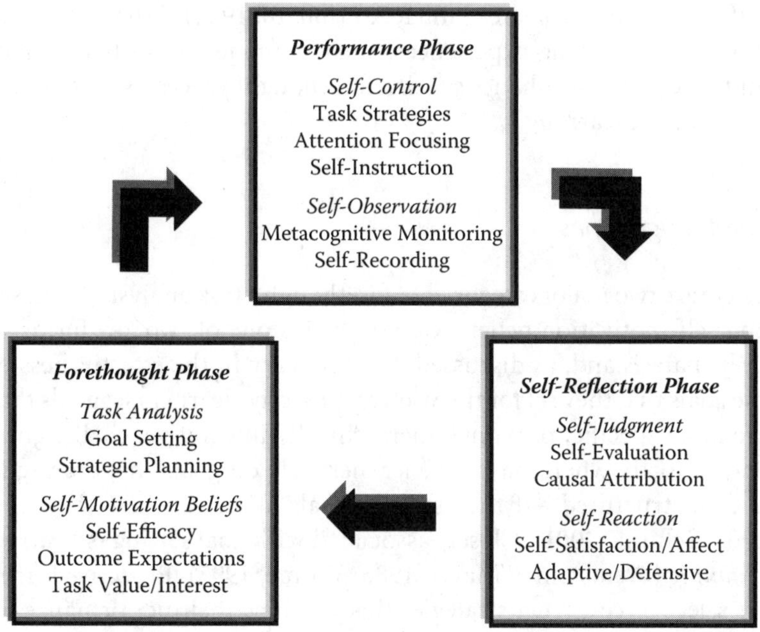

Figure 11.1   Self-regulatory phases and processes. (From "Motivating Self-Regulated Problem Solvers," by B. J Zimmerman & M. Campillo (2003), in *The Nature of Problem Solving*, J. E. Davidson & R. J. Sternberg (Eds.), Figure 8.1, p. 239, Cambridge University Press, New York. Copyright 2003 by Cambridge University Press. Reprinted with permission.)

The cyclical nature of this model also enables it to explain shifts in learning over protracted periods during which one's goal is a continuing process of growth.

Before discussing specific processes in the model, it is important to describe two key qualitative dimensions of self-regulation: proactive and reactive learning. It is widely assumed all learners attempt to self-regulate in some fashion (Winne, 1997), but they differ in their methods. From a cyclical phase perspective, *proactive* learners self-regulate more effectively because they engage in high-quality forethought, which in turn improves their self-regulatory functioning during subsequent phases. In contrast, *reactive* learners self-regulate less effectively because they rely mainly on self-reflective phase processes to improve their performance. Although reactive learners do display low-quality forethought processes, such as setting vague or general goals, their adaptive response to their personal feedback is limited. This adaptive feedback loop or cycle is a defining feature of self-regulation (Miller, Galanter, & Pribham, 1960). Later, I describe how social learning experiences, such as modeling, verbal tuition, and coaching can enhance specific forethought processes that underlie proactive learning.

Forethought Phase

There are two major categories of forethought: task analysis processes and self-motivation beliefs. *Goal setting* is one of two key forms of task analysis and, as discussed, learners vary in the effectiveness of the goals that they set for themselves. Proactive learners set goals that are more specific, proximal, hierarchically integrative, challenging, and so forth, whereas reactive learners rely on goals that are vague and unstructured—if they set any goals at all (Locke & Latham, 2002; Schunk, 2001). Closely associated with goal setting is *strategic planning* (Weinstein & Mayer, 1986; Winne, 1997). Proactive learners select or construct strategies that enhance their performance by aiding cognition, controlling affect, and directing motoric execution (Corno, 1993; Pressley, Woloshyn et al., 1995; Paris, Byrnes, & Paris, 2001). By contrast, reactive students begin studying with unfocused plans and instead rely on performance outcomes to improve their learning. It should be noted that students who set process goals for themselves join goal setting with strategy choice to optimize both forethought processes.

   Learners' commitment to setting and attaining high-quality goals depends on their self-motivational beliefs. Proactive learners are more committed to their goals, exert greater effort, and persist longer in attaining the goals than reactive learners. There are several motivational beliefs that have been found to influence students' goal commitment. One motivational belief involves the importance or *value* of the task or skill learned. When tasks are valued as important personally, they induce greater goal commitment (Wigfield, Tonks, & Eccles, 2004). For example, students who greatly value learning history will be more committed to ambitious practice goals than students who do not value this topic. A second motivational belief that affects learners' commitment to ambitious goals is their *outcome expectancies*. Proactive learners report high expectations regarding the outcomes of their learning, such as qualifying for a desired profession (e.g., becoming a historian). By contrast, reactive learners are less optimistic about the outcomes of their efforts to learn. Incentives have been used to enhance reactive learners' perceptions of goal outcomes. Schunk (1984) found that students who were given performance-contingent rewards in combination with setting specific goals displayed a higher level of mathematical learning than students who did not receive rewards. Another outcome expectancy linked to students' goal commitment involves social factors. Public commitment to a goal increases its importance because it raises the visibility of one's actions and credibility (Hollenbeck, Williams, & Klein, 1989).

A third motivational belief that can affect learners' goal commitment involves their perceptions of self-efficacy, the belief that one can attain a particular goal. *Self-efficacy* refers to beliefs about one's capabilities to attain a designated level of performance (Bandura, 1997). Proactive learners have reported higher self-efficacy regarding the attainment of their academic goals than reactive learners (e.g., Zimmerman, Bandura, & Martinez-Pons, 1992; Zimmerman & Bandura, 1994). Clearly, each of these three motivational beliefs can increase students' commitment to attaining their academic goals, but their goals can also affect their methods of learning as well.

Performance Phase

As noted in Figure 11.1, goal setting during the forethought phase influences two major classes of performance phase self-regulatory processes: self-control and self-observation. Self-control methods are designed to overtly and covertly enhance one's learning and performance. Proactive learners deploy strategies that are planned during the forethought phase, whereas reactive learners tend to plunge into learning tasks without formulating an explicit strategy to guide them. But, what types of goals do proactive learners use?

Learning process goals focus on implementing a particular method of learning, whereas performance outcome goals focus learners' self-observation on particular outcomes of their efforts to learn. Among the effective methods of self-control are *task strategies*, which are methods for reducing complex tasks to their essential parts and reorganizing them into a systematic performance sequence. For example, when students watch an English teacher revise the first draft of an essay, they might identify key steps, record them in their notes, and create an acronym to guide their writing. For example, the word *MESS* could be created to remind them to check an essay for *M*eaning, *E*nglish grammar (subject–verb agreement, sentence fragments), *S*tyle of sentences (active–passive, choice of words), and *S*pelling errors. A wide variety of task strategies have been identified, and their effectiveness has been documented (Pressley, Woloshyn et al., 1995; Weinstein & Mayer, 1986). These include study strategies, such as note taking, test preparation, and reading for comprehension, as well as performance strategies for optimizing writing, speaking, and problem solving.

A second method of self-control that has been influenced by goal setting involves *attention focusing*, which refers to methods designed to improve one's concentration and screen out other covert processes or external events, such as when a student uses earplugs to memorize a list of chemical symbols when studying in a noisy environment. As was reported (Rothkopf & Billington, 1979), students with specific learning goals paid attention to and learned goal-relevant prose passages better than goal-irrelevant passages. Kuhl (1985) studied dysfunctions in attention control, such as distraction and rumination about past mistakes. His research, along with that of others (Corno, 1993; Boekaerts & Niemivirta, 2000), demonstrated that strategies for focusing and screening out events can improve the quality of one's studying.

A third form of self-control that has been influenced by goal setting is *self-instruction* for guiding one's thoughts and actions. A wide range of self-verbalizations has been studied, ranging from mnemonic rehearsal to self-praise statements, and there is evidence that they can improve students' learning significantly (Schunk, 2001). For example, Schunk (1982) provided goal-setting training in mathematics to students who were low achievers. As their process goal during practice, some students were asked to verbalize their strategies and their problem-solving actions, whereas other students were asked just to verbalize their strategies or were not asked to verbalize their problem-solving actions. Students who verbalized both their strategies and problem-solving actions learned better than students who merely verbalized the strategies or did not verbalize at all.

In other goal-related research, Schunk and Cox (1986) asked some students to verbalize their problem-solving operations for the entire practice session and other students to verbalize only during the first half of the instructional session. This hypothesis tested Vygotsky's belief that verbalizations that are internalized are the most effective. It was found that the highest levels of problem solving and self-efficacy were manifested by students who verbalized continually during the session. Apparently, verbalization during only the initial practice period was insufficient to produce automaticity, which would have allowed the students to perform without overt verbal self-control. However, research by Meichenbaum (1977), which reduced self-instruction from overt forms to covert nonarticulated forms, has proven effective in helping learning disabled students overcome hyperactivity or impulsivity.

The second major class of performance phase functioning involves two key forms of self-observation: metacognitive monitoring and overt behavioral self-recording. Having set specific process and outcome goals for themselves, proactive learners can engage in more systematic forms of self-observation, such as metacognitive monitoring or self-recording in logs, charts, and portfolios. By contrast, reactive learners have trouble tracking personal outcomes metacognitively because they lack specific goals (Borkowski & Thorpe, 1994), and they fail to appreciate the potential advantages of behavioral self-recording, such as increasing the proximity, informativeness, accuracy, and valence of feedback regarding one's performance (Zimmerman & Kitsantas, 1996). There is evidence that goals influence the way that learners track their behavior metacognitively and behaviorally. For example, Locke and Bryan (1969) found that learners who were given feedback about multiple aspects of their performance on an automobile-driving task improved their performance only in areas associated with specific goals that they had set for themselves.

Self-Reflection Phase

Learners' goal setting during the forethought phase also affects their self-reflection phase processes. It is noted in Figure 11.1 that self-reflection phase processes fall into two major classes: self-judgments and self-reactions. Self-judgments involve self-evaluating one's learning performance and attributing causal significance to the outcomes. Proactive learners' *self-evaluate* by comparing their self-monitored outcomes to their forethought phase goals as a standard. By contrast, reactive learners lack these standards because they did not set specific goals during forethought, and as a result, they fail to evaluate or must fall back often on social comparisons with classmates to judge their effectiveness. Social comparisons can be counterproductive if the other students' start ahead of one and display similar increases in learning. Under such circumstances, students will self-evaluate their learning unfavorably despite having improved from earlier levels.

Schunk (1996) studied how goal-setting and self-evaluation processes influenced self-regulated learning. Elementary school students received instruction and then engaged in self-directed practice in mathematical subtraction. Schunk found that setting learning goals led to higher perceptions of self-efficacy and achievement than setting performance goals. He also discovered that the effectiveness of one's self-evaluation was influenced by its frequency. Students who were given frequent opportunities to self-evaluate their progress displayed higher achievement and greater self-efficacy regardless of whether learning or performance goals were adopted, but interestingly, students given infrequent opportunities to self-evaluate displayed higher achievement only if they set learning goals for themselves.

Schunk and Ertmer (1999) extended these findings in a study of computer skill learning with college students. When opportunities for self-evaluation were minimal, learning process goals led to higher strategy use, computer skill learning, and higher self-evaluations. In considering the last two studies together, it appears that students who focus on acquiring advantageous learning methods or strategies engage in more favorable self-evaluations than students who focus on optimizing performance outcomes when the opportunities for feedback were limited but not when they were generous. These outcomes are consistent with the shifting goal hypothesis based on students' degree of automaticity.

Self-evaluative judgments are linked closely to causal attributions about the results of learning efforts, such as whether students' failure is caused by their limited ability or insufficient effort. Reactive students attribute their errors to uncontrollable causes, such as fixed ability, whereas proactive students attribute errors to controllable causes, such as ineffective learning strategies. Attributions to uncontrollable variables discourage reactive students from further learning efforts (Weiner, 1979), whereas attributions of errors to controllable variables encourage proactive students to sustain efforts to learn. Zimmerman and Kitsantas (1999) found that setting either process or shifting goals led high school girls to attribute unfavorable outcomes on a writing revision task to ineffective strategy use. By contrast, setting outcome goals led these girls to attribute unfavorable outcomes to a lack of effort or low ability in revising written passages.

Students' forethought goal setting also influences their self-reactions to learning efforts (see Figure 11.1). Two key classes of self-reaction have been identified: self-satisfaction and adaptive inferences. The former self-reaction refers to perceptions of satisfaction or dissatisfaction and associated emotions regarding one's performance, such as elation or depression. There is extensive evidence that students will choose courses of action that result in self-satisfaction and positive affect and will avoid courses that produce dissatisfaction and negative affect (Bandura, 1991; Boekaerts & Niemivirta, 2000). Proactive learners make their self-satisfaction dependent on reaching their learning goals, which helps them to direct their actions and persist in their efforts (Schunk, 1983). By contrast, reactive learners do not link self-satisfaction to particular self-evaluative standards of success. In the Zimmerman and Kitsantas (1999) study, students who set shifting and learning process goals displayed significantly greater satisfaction with their acquisition of writing revision skill than students who set performance outcome goals or no goals, and the students' attributions to strategy use were highly predictive of their perceptions of self-satisfaction ($r = .57$).

The second form of self-reactions involves adaptive or defensive inferences, which are conclusions about whether one needs to alter personal approach during subsequent efforts to learn. Proactive learners make *adaptive inferences*, such as by modifying a strategy to make it more effective (Cleary & Zimmerman, 2001), whereas reactive students often resort to *defensive* reactions to protect them from future dissatisfaction and aversive affect, such as helplessness, procrastination, task avoidance, cognitive disengagement, and apathy (Garcia & Pintrich, 1994).

Finally, as noted in Figure 11.1, students' self-reactions to their learning efforts are hypothesized to influence their forethought processes regarding further efforts to learn, thus completing the self-regulatory cycle. In support of this model, there is evidence that positive self-satisfaction reactions of proactive students are highly predictive of their self-efficacy beliefs ($r = .71$) regarding further efforts to learn (Zimmerman & Kitsantas, 1997, 1999). There is also evidence that positive self-satisfaction reactions of proactive students are predictive of students' subsequent valuing of the learning task ($r = .66$). These enhanced self-motivational beliefs are a key source of proactive learners' greater sense of personal agency about continuing their cyclical self-regulatory efforts eventually to acquire a skill. In contrast, the self-dissatisfaction reactions of reactive students reduce their sense of efficacy and willingness to continue their learning efforts.

When proactive learners (such as experts) and reactive learners (such as uninformed novices) were compared regarding their forethought, performance, and self-reflection phase processes, significant differences were found in all three phases of the cyclical model (Cleary & Zimmerman, 2001).

EMPOWERING STUDENTS THROUGH SELF-REGULATORY TRAINING

There is extensive evidence that reactive students' inability to self-regulate their academic learning and performance is highly dependent on the poor goals that they set (Zimmerman & Martinez-Pons, 1986, 1988). But, how can reactive students learn to set and utilize forethought goals to guide self-regulation more effectively? From a social cognitive perspective (Zimmerman, 2000), students can acquire self-regulatory processes most easily from social sources, such as models or coaches. A Self-Regulation Empowerment Program (SREP) was developed, which is implemented by a self-regulation coach (SRC) who could be a teacher, counselor, or school psychologist (Cleary & Zimmerman, 2004). The SREP, which is based on the three-phase cyclical model of self-regulation, was field-tested in a case study of Anna, a 12-year-old student who was recommended by her classroom teachers because of her failing test grades in science and social studies. Previously, she was given a variety of school-based support services in an achievement center, such as remedial math and reading instruction, but she showed minimal improvement and was referred for participation in the SREP.

Diagnostic Assessment of Anna's
Self-Regulatory Strengths and Limitations

Regarding Anna's forethought phase processes, her progress notes and report cards revealed that she was performing most poorly in her science class (i.e., she received a grade of D). Although she completed most of her homework assignments, participated in class, and passed her lab reports, she failed the majority of her tests. Anna's repertoire of study strategies for her science tests were assessed by asking her to report retrospectively any organizational, rehearsal, and procedural strategies or methods that she used. She reported using two strategies to enhance recall: index cards and reading notes. Anna's motivational profile was assessed in part through questions about her forethought phase processes, such as those of goal setting, self-efficacy, and intrinsic interest. During the performance phase, the SRC asked Anna to think aloud as she used her index cards and reviewed her notes.

She was also asked about various self-control phase processes (e.g., self-recording and focusing attention). These questions sought to reveal whether Anna kept track of her studying behaviors as well as whether she used various self-control procedures to maintain her motivation and focus. During the self-reflection phase, the SRC asked Anna about her self-evaluations, causal attributions, and adaptive inferences.

Developing Anna's Self-Regulated Learning Skills

Empowerment   The diagnostic assessment revealed Anna's low sense of empowerment. She engaged in a negative motivational cycle involving low self-efficacy perceptions, displayed little self-awareness of the causes of her struggles, and felt that she could not improve her failing grades. To combat these unfortunate beliefs, Anna was asked to use a graphing procedure designed to increase her awareness of the effectiveness of her study strategies. The SRC asked Anna to plot her previous three test grades as well as the strategies that she used to prepare for the tests. These scores provided a baseline index of her class functioning before the SREP intervention began. The SRC then attempted to establish the link between her test grades and study strategies by stating, "You are using strategies, which is fantastic, ...

but it is possible that the strategies you are using are not working or helping you get good test grades. Your failing grades have more to do with the strategies that you used to prepare for the tests than how smart you are or how hard the teacher is." This social feedback conveyed to Anna that her failing test grades could be attributed to her ineffective learning strategies, which could be readily improved by learning new strategies or by changing existing ones.

Strategy Use   During a series of training sessions, the SRC and Anna discussed a variety of alternative strategies that she could use to study for her science tests (i.e., graphic organizers, tables, attending extra help sessions). These discussions were accompanied by the SRC's modeling of the use of graphic organizers for comparing and contrasting scientific information. The SRC demonstrated how to execute the steps for creating a graphic organizer while verbalizing his thoughts. Anna was encouraged to practice this strategy and develop her own graphic organizers. As she practiced, the SRC provided her with feedback and prompts to help her internalize the learning strategy.

Cyclical Feedback Loop   The self-regulation graph was designed to empower Anna to engage in positive cycles of motivation and learning. The graph enabled Anna to set learning process goals (i.e., create and use graphic organizers when preparing for each test), to self-record the use of this strategy, to set academic performance outcome goals (i.e., improved test grades), and to evaluate strategy effectiveness and goal progress. Anna recorded her three prior test grades as well as her strategies for each test. The SRC helped Anna attribute her poor grades to ineffective strategies rather than to uncontrollable factors, such as her mental ability, teacher difficulty, or test difficulty.

The SRC reviewed Anna's grades, and collaboratively, they set a challenging performance goal (i.e., a grade of 75 or better). After this goal was set and plotted on the graph, the SRC showed Anna how to track her study strategies for the tests. After Anna received a test score, the SRC instructed her to plot it on the graph and interpret it in terms of self-reflection phase processes (e.g., self-evaluating, making causal attributions, and making adaptive inferences). For example, after Anna earned a grade of 90 on her first intervention phase test, the SRC asked her to plot the score (which she was thrilled to do).

Then, she was shown how to evaluate her performance outcomes by using goal-based criteria, namely, by comparing her current grade with her performance goal of a grade of 75. The SRC highlighted the connection between her grades and her use of the graphic organizer strategy to prepare for the tests to help her make appropriate attributions and adaptive inferences. It was emphasized that her improved test score of 90 was the result of her newly acquired study strategies. The SRC then reinforced the premise that success in school was largely under her control and depended on her ability to use learning strategies effectively. As result of this SREP intervention, Anna's grades in both science and social studies improved substantially.

CONCLUSION

Students' attainment of their academic aspirations requires more than hope or good intentions: It depends on the specific qualities of the goals that they set for themselves. Reactive learners have not grasped this fundamental principle, and they rely on naturally occurring feedback and social comparisons to make progress, but this progress is limited. By contrast, proactive learners recognize the vital role that high-quality goals play in students' academic success, particularly when students are learning in self-directed settings, such as during homework. Goals that are specific and proximal provide focused and timely feedback for students. Academic goals that are not in conflict with peer group goals induce greater commitment, and hierarchically integrated goals provide long- as well as short-term guidance. Goals that challenge students in their level of difficulty and goals that are self-set or perceived as reasonable motivate students better than easy or arbitrary goals. Although goals function to some degree automatically below students' level of consciousness, conscious goals have additional benefits, such as producing greater self-awareness and superior self-reactions.

These important properties of students' goals depend on their relationship with other self-regulatory processes. Goals set during the forethought phase not only influence students' choice of learning method and motivational commitment but also influence performance phase goal implementation and self-observation. Forethought phase goals also affect self-reflection phase standards that students use to self-evaluate their performance efforts and the way that students attribute causation to their efforts to learn, especially when those efforts are unsuccessful. Students who are satisfied with their performance outcomes or are self-efficacious about adapting their learning strategies are more motivated to sustain cyclical efforts to learn. These enhanced self-motivational beliefs are a key source of proactive learners' greater sense of personal agency about continuing their cyclical self-regulatory efforts eventually to attain their goals.

This cyclical model has been used to guide educational interventions with at-risk students and involves training in goal-setting and related self-regulatory processes. The effectiveness of an SREP, which is implemented by an SRC, was discussed. A student who was poorly motivated and reactive in her goal setting displayed improvements in not only her goal setting and self-regulation, but also in her academic success. Clearly, learning to set effective goals is an important quality of a self-motivated learner.

NOTE

1. Goal acceptance is similar conceptually to goal commitment in goal-setting research except that the latter variable is assessed directly as an individual difference variable (Seijts & Latham, 2000).

References

Anderman, E. M., Austin, C. C., & Johnson, D. M. (2002). The development of goal orientation. In A. Wigfield & J. S. Eccles (Eds.), *Development of achievement motivation* (pp. 197–220). San Diego, CA: Academic Press.

APA Task Force on Psychology in Education. (1993, January). *Learner-centered principles: Guidelines for school redesign and reform.* Washington, DC: American Psychological Association and Mid-Continent Regional Educational Laboratory.

Bandura, A. (1988). Self-regulation of motivation and action through goal systems. In V. Hamilton, G. H. Bower, & N. H. Frijda (Eds.), *Cognitive perspectives on emotion and motivation* (pp. 37–61) Dordrecht, The Netherlands: Kluwer Academic.

Bandura, A. (1991). Self-regulation of motivation through anticipatory and self-reactive mechanisms. In R. A. Dienstbier (Ed.), *Perspectives on Motivation: Nebraska symposium on motivation* (Vol. 38, pp. 69–164). Lincoln: University of Nebraska Press.

Bandura, A. (1997). *Self-efficacy: The exercise of control.* New York: Freeman.

Bandura, A., & Cervone, D. (1983). Self-evaluative and self-efficacy mechanisms governing the motivational effects of goal systems. *Journal of Personality and Social Psychology, 45,* 1017–1028.

Bandura, A., & Schunk, D. H. (1981). Cultivating competence, self-efficacy, and intrinsic interest through proximal self-motivation. *Journal of Personality and Social Psychology, 41,* 586–598.

Bargh, J. A. (1990). Auto-motives: Preconscious determinants of social interaction. In E. T. Higgins & R. M. Sorrention (Eds.), *Handbook of motivation and cognition. Vol. 2: Foundations of social behavior* (pp. 93–130). New York: Guilford Press.

Boekaerts, M., & Niemivirta, M. (2000). Self-regulated learning: Finding a balance between learning goals and ego-protective goals. In M. Boekaerts, P. Pintich, & M. Zeidner (Eds.), *Handbook of self-regulation* (pp. 417–451). San Diego, CA: Academic Press.

Borkowski, J., & J. G., & Thorpe, P. K. (1994). Self-regulation and motivation: A life-span perspective on underachievement. In D. H. Schunk & B. J. Zimmerman (Eds.), *Self-regulation of learning and performance: Issues and educational applications* (pp. 45–73). Hillsdale, NJ: Erlbaum.

Burton, D. (1979). The impact of goal specificity and task complexity on basketball skill development. *The Sport Psychologist, 3,* 34–47.

Burton, D., Nayler, S., & Holliday, B. (2001). Goal setting in sport: Investigating the goal effectiveness paradox. In R. N. Singer, H. A. Hausenblas, & C. Janelle (Eds.), *Handbook of sports psychology* (2nd ed., pp. 497–528). New York: Wiley.

Bryan, J., & Locke, E. (1967). Goal setting as a means of increasing motivation. *Journal of Applied Psychology, 51,* 274–277.

Carver, C. S., & Scheier, M. F. (1991). Self-regulation and the self. In J. Strauss & D. R. Goethals (Eds.), *The self: Interdisciplinary approaches* (pp. 168–207). New York: Springer-Verlag.

Chen, P. P. (2003). Exploring the accuracy and predictability of the self-efficacy beliefs of seventh-grade mathematics students. *Learning and Individual Difference, 14,* 79–92.

Chesney, A., & Locke, E. (1991). An examination of the relationship among goal difficulty, business strategies, and performance on a complex management simulation task. *Academic of Management Journal, 34,* 400–424.

Cleary, T. J., & Zimmerman, B. J. (2001). Self-regulation differences during athletic practice by experts, non-experts, and novices. *Journal of Applied Sport Psychology, 13,* 185–206.

Cleary, T. J., & Zimmerman, B. J. (2004) Self-regulation empowerment program: A school-based program to enhance self-regulated and self-motivated cycles of student learning. *Psychology in the Schools, 41,* 537–550.

Corno, L. (1993). The best-laid plans: Modern conceptions of volition and educational research. *Educational Researcher, 22*(2), 14–22.

Deci, E. L., & Ryan, R. M. (1991). A motivational approach to self: Integration in personality. In R. Diensbier (Ed.), *Nebraska Symposium on Motivation. Vol. 38: Perspectives on motivation* (pp. 237–288). Lincoln: University of Nebraska Press.

English, H. B., & English, A. C. (1958). *Comprehensive dictionary of psychological and psychoanalytic terms.* New York: McKay.

Erez, M., & Kanfer, F. H. (1983). The role of goal congruence in goal setting and task performance. *Academy of Management Review, 8,* 454–463.

Fitzsimons, G. M., & Bargh, J. A. (2003). Thinking of you: Nonconscious pursuit of interpersonal goals associated with relationship partners. *Journal of Personality and Social Psychology, 84,* 148–164.

Fitzsimons, G. M., & Bargh, J. A. (2004). Automatic self-regulation. In R. F. Baumeister, & K. D. Vohs (Eds.), *Handbook of self-regulation: Research, theory, and applications* (pp. 151–170). New York: Guilford Press.

Garcia, T., & Pintrich, P. R. (1994). Regulating motivation and cognition in the classroom: The role of self-schemas and self-regulatory strategies. In D. H. Schunk & B. J. Zimmerman (Eds.), *Self-regulation of learning and performance: Issues and educational applications* (pp. 127–153). Hillsdale, NJ: Erlbaum.

Hollenbeck, J., Williams, C., & Klein, H. (1989). An empirical examination of the antecedents of commitment to difficult goals. *Journal of Applied Psychology, 74,* 18–23.

Howard, A., & Bray, D. (1988). *Managerial lives in transition.* New York: Guilford Press.

Kanfer, R., & Ackerman, P. L. (1989). Motivation and cognitive abilities: An integrative aptitude treatment interaction approach to skill acquisition. *Journal of Applied Psychology, 74,* 657–690.

Kingston, M. G., & Hardy, L. (1997). Effects of different types of goals on processes that support performance. *The Sport Psychologist, 11,* 277–293.

Kuhl, J. (1985). Volitional mediators of cognitive behavior consistency: Self-regulatory processes and action versus state orientation. In J. Kuhl & J. Beckman (Eds.), *Action control* (pp. 101–128). New York: Springer.

LaPorte, R., & Nath, R. (1976). Role of performance goals in prose leaning. *Journal of Educational Psychology, 68,* 260–264.

Latham, G. P., Erez, M., & Locke, E. (1988). Resolving scientific disputes by the joint design of crucial experiments by the antagonists: Applications to the Erez-Latham dispute regarding participation in goal setting. *Journal of Applied Psychology, 73*, 753–772.

Latham, G. P., & Saari, L. M. (1979). The effects of holding goal difficulty constant on assigned and participatively set goals. *Academic of Management Journal, 22*, 163–168.

Lewin, K., Dembo, T., Festinger, L., & Sears, R. (1944). Level of aspiration. In J. Hunt (Ed.), *Personality and the behavior disorders* (Vol. 1, pp. 333–378). New York: Ronald Press.

Locke, E. A., & Bryan, J. (1969). The directions function of goals in task performance. *Organizational Behavior and Human Performance, 4*, 35–42.

Locke, E. A., & Latham, G. P. (1990). *A theory of goal setting and task performance.* Englewood Cliffs, NJ: Prentice Hall.

Locke, E. A., & Latham, G. P. (2002). Building a practically useful theory of goal setting and task motivation: A 35-year odyssey. *American Psychology, 57*, 705–717.

Locke, E. A., Smith, K., Erez, M., Chah, D., & Schaffer, A. (1994). The effects of intra-individual goal conflict on performance. *Journal of Management, 20*, 67–91.

McCombs, B. L. (2001). Self-regulated learning and academic achievement: A phenomenological view. In B. J. Zimmerman & D. H. Schunk (Eds.), *Self-regulated learning and academic achievement: Theoretical perspectives* (2nd ed., pp. 67–123). Mahwah, NJ: Erlbaum.

Meichenbaum, D. (1977). *Cognitive-behavior modification: An integrative approach.* New York: Plenum.

Miller, G. A., Galanter, E., & Pribham, K. (1960). *Plans and the structure of behavior.* New York: Holt, Rinehart and Winston.

Paris, S. G., Byrnes, J. P., & Paris, A. H. (2001). Constructing theories, identities, and actions of self-regulated learners. In B. J. Zimmerman & D. H. Schunk (Eds.), *Self-regulated learning and academic achievement: Theoretical perspectives* (2nd ed., pp. 253–287). Mahwah, NJ: Erlbaum.

Pressley, M., Woloshyn, V., & Associates (Ed.). (1995). *Cognitive strategy instruction that really improves children's academic performance* (2nd ed.). Brookline, MA: Cambridge, MA.

Rothkopf, E., & Billington, M. (1979). Goal-guided learning from text: Inferring a descriptive processing model from inspection times and eye movements. *Journal of Educational Psychology, 1*, 310–327.

Schunk, D. H. (1982). Verbal self-regulation as a facilitator of children's achievement and self-efficacy. *Human Learning 1*, 265–277.

Schunk, D. H. (1983). Goal difficulty and attainment information: Effects on children's achievement. *Human Learning, 2,* 107–117.

Schunk, D. H. (1984). Enhancing self-efficacy and achievement through rewards and goals: Motivational and informational effects. *Journal of Educational Research, 78,* 29–34.

Schunk, D. H. (1985). Participation in goal setting: Effects on self-efficacy and skills of learning disabled children. *Journal of Special Education 19,* 307–317.

Schunk, D. H. (1989). Social cognitive theory and self-regulated learning. In B. J. Zimmerman & D. H. Schunk (Eds.), *Self-regulated learning and academic achievement: Theory, research, and practice* (pp. 83–110). New York: Springer-Verlag.

Schunk, D. H. (1996). Goal and self-evaluative influences during children's cognitive skill learning. *American Educational Research Journal, 33,* 359–382.

Schunk, D. H. (2001). Social cognitive theory and self-regulated learning. In B. J. Zimmerman & D. H. Schunk (Eds.), *Self-regulated learning and academic achievement: Theoretical perspectives* (2nd ed., pp. 125–151). Mahwah, NJ: Erlbaum.

Schunk, D. H., & Cox, P. D. (1986). Strategy training and attributional feedback with learning disabled students. *Journal of Educational Psychology, 78,* 201–209.

Schunk, D. H., & Ertmer, P. A. (1999). Self-regulatory processes during computer skill acquisition: Goal and self-evaluative influences. *Journal of Educational Psychology, 91,* 251–260.

Schunk, D. H., & Swartz, C.W. (1993). Goals and progressive feedback: Effects on self-efficacy and writing achievement. *Contemporary Educational Psychology, 18,* 337–354.

Seijts, G. H., & Latham, G. P. (2000). The construct of goal commitment: Measurement and relationships with task performance. In R. Goffin & E. Helmes (Eds.), *Problems and solutions in human assessment* (pp. 315–332). Dordrecht, The Netherlands: Kluwer Academic.

Steinberg, L., Brown, B. B., & Dornbusch, S. M. (1996). *Beyond the classroom.* New York: Simon-Schuster.

Weiner, B. (1979). A theory of motivation for some classroom experiences. *Journal of Educational Psychology, 71,* 3–25.

Weinstein, C. E., & Mayer, R. E. (1986). The teaching of learning strategies. In M. C. Wittrock (Ed.), *Handbook of research on teaching* (3rd ed., pp. 315–327). New York: Macmillan.

Wigfield, A., Tonks, S., & Eccles, J. S. (2004). Expectancy-value theory in cross-cultural perspective. In D. M. McInerney & S. Van Etten (Eds.), *Big theories revisited* (Vol. 4, pp. 165–198). Greenwich, CT: Information Age.

Winne, P. H. (1997). Experimenting to bootstrap self-regulated learning. *Journal of Educational Psychology, 89,* 397–410.

Wood, R., Mento, A., & Locke, E. (1987). Task complexity as a moderator of goal effects. *Journal of Applied Psychology, 17,* 416–425.

Zimmerman, B. J. (2000). Attainment of self-regulation: A social cognitive perspective. In M. Boekaerts, P. Pintrich, & M. Zeidner (Eds.), *Self-regulation: Theory, research, and applications* (pp. 13–39). Orlando, FL: Academic Press.

Zimmerman, B. J., & Bandura, A. (1994). Impact of self-regulatory influences on writing course attainment. *American Educational Research Journal, 31,* 845–862.

Zimmerman, B. J., Bandura, A., & Martinez-Pons, M. (1992). Self-motivation for academic attainment: The role of self-efficacy beliefs and personal goal setting. *American Educational Research Journal, 29,* 663–676.

Zimmerman, B. J., & Campillo, M. (2003). Motivating self-regulated problem solvers. In J. E. Davidson & R. J. Sternberg (Eds.), *The nature of problem solving* (pp. 233–262). New York: Cambridge University Press.

Zimmerman, B. J., & Kitsantas, A. (1996). Self-regulated learning of a motoric skill: The role of goal setting and self-monitoring. *Journal of Applied Sport Psychology, 8,* 69–84.

Zimmerman, B. J., & Kitsantas, A. (1997). Developmental phases in self-regulation: Shifting from process to outcome goals. *Journal of Educational Psychology, 89,* 29–36.

Zimmerman, B. J., & Kitsantas, A. (1999). Acquiring writing revision skill: Shifting from process to outcome self-regulatory goals. *Journal of Educational Psychology, 91,* 1–10.

Zimmerman, B. J., & Martinez-Pons, M. (1986). Development of a structured interview for assessing students' use of self-regulated learning strategies. *American Educational Research Journal, 23,* 614–628.

Zimmerman, B. J., & Martinez-Pons, M. (1988). Construct validation of a strategy model of student self-regulated learning. *Journal of Educational Psychology, 80,* 284–290.

12

The Weave of Motivation and Self-Regulated Learning

Philip H. Winne and Allyson F. Hadwin

INTRODUCTION

An analysis of self-regulated learning (SRL) and motivation is at once simple and intensely complicated. It is simple because everything a student does can be said to be motivated. Without motivation, except for reflexive behavior like the eye blink reflex, there is no behavior, including SRL. Beneath this simplicity, however, is a complex weave of students' knowledge, feedback they create and feedback they receive, and thoughts about whether they and the environment in which they learn might be different from the way it is now. To untangle this weave, we begin by describing our view of SRL. Next, we dissect what a task is and set a stage for then considering how to distinguish "just behaving" from self-regulating learning. With these three cornerstones in place, we can set out our view of motivation to create a foundation for discussing how SRL and motivation intersect. Standing on this foundation, we review representative research that speaks to how SRL and motivation interlink. Throughout, we track Isabelle as she navigates a mathematics problem. We conclude with observations about where research is lacking and what could be contributed by new research on this topic.

WHAT IS SELF-REGULATED LEARNING?

The construct of SRL emerges from an assumption that students exercise agency by consciously controlling and intervening in their learning. Within limits established by their current capabilities, as well as the constraints and affordances in their environment, students exercise agency by setting goals. Students also exercise agency by making choices about how they strive to reach those goals, including how intensely to engage in a task and how long to persist if the task cannot be completed almost instantly or effortlessly.

Importantly, self-regulation emerges when students judge there might be better ways to achieve their goals than whichever method they are currently using and then act on these judgments. More specifically, students exercise agency when they metacognitively monitor properties of their engagement in goal-directed tasks. If those properties stand in an unfavorable profile relative to goals they hold, then self-regulating students consider options about how to make strategic adjustments. The adjustments they make can address any and all of their behavior, motivational states, cognition, and metacognition itself. Students exercise agency by choosing an option they predict has the best chance to achieve their goals given the current conditions of their work. The implication that follows from this framework for learning is important: Self-regulating students strategically experiment with their learning, fine-tuning it over time and across tasks.

In a chapter we published nearly a decade ago, we described SRL as unfolding over four flexibly sequenced phases of recursive cognition (Winne & Hadwin, 1998) (see Figure 12.1). By recursive, we mean that the results of engagement in any particular phase can feed into metacognitive monitoring that occurs in any previous or subsequent phase. In the phase of task perception, students scan their environment, including tasks set by a teacher, exercises posed by a textbook's author, and knowledge they have about themselves. Using the information they perceive, students construct a personalized profile of the task at hand. This personalized profile inherently includes affective responses to the task (Pintrich, 2003). It also includes other information that can influence motivational states, such as judgments about self-efficacy. The result of this phase is a personalized perception of the task the student may be about to undertake.

After developing a sense of the task, students engage in setting goals and planning in the context of the task as it was framed in the first phase. Now, students consider what they are asked to achieve and construct a profile of what they want to achieve (Pintrich, 2003). As a result, students may set one or several goals for which they will strive. *Goals* can refer to overt behaviors, forms of cognitive

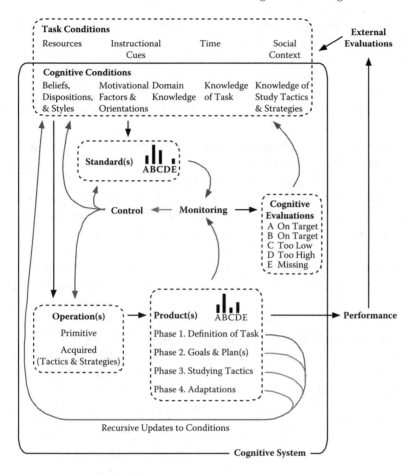

Figure 12.1   Winne and Hadwin's four-phase model of self-regulated learning.

engagement, changes in motivation, or all three. Goals always grow out of task perceptions. For example, if a student's perception of a task includes feelings of anxiety about the ability to complete it, a goal might be set to lower anxiety. This might be accompanied by a plan to realize this goal. For example, the student might plan to ally with a peer who is expert in this area or use self-talk to "get through" the task: "I can do this, just go one step at a time."

In the phase of enacting, students put their plan into action by activating study tactics and taking other steps to reach goals. In the case of the student who adopted self-talk as a method for lowering anxiety, work takes two forms. This student works on the task itself and keeps anxiety at tolerable levels by talking herself through the task step by step. Because students often hold multiple goals, successfully engaging in a task means choosing methods that reflect goals in all of the cognitive, behavioral, and motivational arenas simultaneously. For example, students may strive to find a balance between meeting performance standards and keeping anxiety at a tolerable level.

In the fourth phase of adaptation, students deliberate about how to change their methods for completing tasks like this one to close gaps they perceive between the results of their work and goals. They may attempt to increase effectiveness beyond the goal originally set. Or, they may abandon the task altogether. In the example of a student who elected to work with a peer to reduce anxiety about the task, it might be judged that the peer was not helpful. As a result, another peer or a different tack entirely might be sought next time.

In our four-phase model of SRL, each phase can be considered a kind of subtask, but we find it more helpful to treat academic tasks as spanning all four phases. It is also important to reiterate that most everyday academic assignments—solving a mathematics problem, searching for a resource on the Internet, or working to understand material in a history textbook—involve recursion. This highlights that intermediate products students generate as they work inside the start and end points of a task—a step, if you will—form the basis for what happens next in the overall task. In other words, students traverse multiple recursions of the four phases to complete each academic task. As a result, task perceptions may become more accurate and complete, goals may become more specific, and students may experiment with multiple strategies during the completion of one assignment or task.

HOW A STUDENT COPES WITH TASKS

Throughout this chapter, we refer to a fictional example of a student and an academic task to illustrate the weave of our model of SRL and motivation. Imagine Isabelle, our fictional student, is assigned this problem:

> During a recent census, a man told the census taker that he had three children. When asked their ages, he replied, "The product of their ages is 72. The sum of their ages is the same as my house number." The census

taker ran to the door and looked at the house number. "I still can't tell," she complained. The man replied, "Oh that's right, I forgot to tell you that the oldest one likes chocolate pudding." The census taker promptly wrote down the ages of the three children. How old are they? (Ask Dr. Math)

In each phase of SRL, we (as outsiders) model students' activities in terms of five features that provide a road map for considering how a student COPES with a task. COPES is an acronym of the first letters for conditions, operations, products, evaluations, and standards.

The first feature of tasks is their conditions. *Conditions* establish context for students' work. In Figure 12.1, we name several powerful types of conditions that research has shown to influence learning. Some are external to the student, such as resources, instructional cues, time, and social context. Other conditions are internal to the student, such as beliefs about the nature of knowledge and knowing, motivational factors, and knowledge per se.

Consider the math problem just introduced. Conditions for this task might include

- Prior knowledge about the problem-solving process (general knowledge).
- Prior knowledge about factoring algebraic expressions (cognitive domain knowledge).
- Prior knowledge about past failure with math problems like this one (self-knowledge about performance).
- Self-efficacy (self-beliefs) about this problem.
- Anxiety about doing math problems (self-knowledge about affect that arises in this context).

Each of these conditions contributes to the profile Isabelle constructs in the task definition phase of SRL to describe what this task is. These conditions also influence how she goes about constructing this profile. When Isabelle experiences intense anxiety on recognizing that this is an algebra word problem, this anxiety condition might interfere with reading the rest of the problem. Her sense of it may be inaccurate because she did not examine the problem in full. As a result, even though she might set goals and enact strategies for controlling anxiety, she will be handicapped by not having a complete perception of the problem information she needs to solve it.

Operations are the second feature of each phase of SRL. *Operations* are cognitive manipulations of information. They are what students do to work on tasks. Winne (2001) proposed a heuristic of five primitive (that is, not usefully decomposable) operations: searching, monitoring, assembling, rehearsing, and translating (SMART). Every day, students apply various combinations of operations to information in various formats, such as textual, symbolic, diagrammatic, pictorial, and so forth. As they do, these operations construct understanding, retrieve and apply strategies for solving problems, and power SRL itself. In our math problem-solving example, Isabelle initially retrieved and applied strategies for controlling her anxiety. Then, in later phases of the SRL cycle, she may retrieve strategies for systematically tackling the problem using her knowledge of factoring (a cognitive condition).

Products are the results of operations students carry out on information and knowledge. When, for example, searching is carried out, the product is what is found. When assembling is the operation applied to previously unconnected elements of information, the product is a synthesis of those elements. There are products generated in each phase of SRL. A representation of the task is the product of Phase 1. Goals and plans are products of Phase 2. Products are not limited to cognitive outcomes; affective features—feelings and emotions—are also products. These can be generated in any phase of SRL.

It is a matter of debate whether affect is inherently generated and intrinsically understood as students engage in a task or, whether students reflect on their engagements in a task and then evaluate what their affect is (Schacter & Singer, 1962). When Isabelle developed a perception about the math problem she was posed (Phase 1 of our model of SRL) and recalled past experiences about tasks similar to this one, associative memory automatically generated a forecast about what to expect if she tries to solve the problem. In this scenario, affect plays the role of a condition of a task that is contemplated and simultaneously affected what Isabelle understood about the problem.

Evaluations are information students obtain about products they create as they move in and out of the phases of SRL. A weak feeling of knowing about how to start working on the problem (e.g., evaluating a plan in Phase 2 of SRL as vague) and feedback in the form of an exasperated look from a teacher when a student is taking too long to complete a task (e.g., evaluating behavior as too slow in Phase 3 of SRL) are examples of evaluations of products. An internal feeling that understanding is just beyond the horizon is an evaluation about the inappropriateness of a study tactic or the inaccuracy of initial perceptions about a task. In our problem-solving example, Isabelle evaluated that she was unable to construct an accurate and complete understanding of the problem because her anxiety level was too high. That evaluation led to a plan to "talk herself through" the problem to lower her anxiety.

Standards are criteria that make evaluations possible. In each phase of SRL, standards provide the key ingredient for generating evaluations because standards are the criteria for monitoring products. Perfect spelling in an essay, time spent to apply a learning strategy, and a written record of having applied a checking routine in long division illustrate standards. Importantly, students have standards for affects they experience and that they forecast. That is, each student has a threshold for each affect. Simplistically, this standard divides a continuum into two regions: "good" and "not good." Relative to their standards, students may describe their experience of an activity or the prospect of that experience as interesting or boring, joyous or mournful, or "worth it" or worthless.

In our problem-solving example, Isabelle's standards for task perception might include the ability to identify key data in the problem, labeling the type of problem, activating and considering relevant prior knowledge, and the ability to control anxiety to the extent that she can read and comprehend the problem.

WHEN BEHAVIOR IS AND IS NOT SELF-REGULATED

To reiterate a key point, we propose the hallmark of SRL is adaptation or change. Regulation entails metacognitive control that emerges from metacognitive monitoring. Students may regulate or adapt behavior or cognition as well as motivational states. But, what distinguishes "mere" changes in these psychological features from genuine self-regulated adaptation? To make this distinction, we introduce a way to map events using a design represented as If–Then–Else.

If refers to conditions of the task.
Then refers to collections of operations judged to be appropriate.

Else refers to another collection of operations that might be tried if
the first set does not satisfy standards.

Consider a tactic for working on a task, such as Isabelle's self-talk.
In this If–Then–Else way of looking at tactics, Ifs are the conditions
of the task, such as Isabelle's intense anxiety when she began reading
the math problem. For particular conditions, one or a collection of
operations—Thens—might be appropriate. In response to Isabelle's
intense anxiety, she searched for tactics that might operate under
this condition. She chose self-talk.

The third part of this way of describing tactics, the Else, allows for
something to happen when the chosen operations are evaluated as
insufficient. In that case, the student does something Else.

In our example, Isabelle followed the following If–Then–Else
sequence:

If I experience intense anxiety when I am reading the math
problem.
Then I should use self-talk to reduce my anxiety.
Else when self-talk is evaluated as not reducing my anxiety, I will try
working with a peer.

When students switch from a Then to an Else—because evaluations of products created by the Then do not match standards—this
is self-regulation. When students choose which Then to apply based
on the conditions falling in the If part of this design, this is simple
discrimination learning. For example, it is discrimination learning
to behave like this: See a red traffic light, stop. See a yellow light,
make a judgment about whether it is safe to proceed through the
intersection.

What can be regulated? There are three possibilities that can be
described using the COPES description of tasks:

Change Conditions

The student might depart from a direct path to completing the task
and try to change the task's conditions. For example, judging that a
draft of an essay is weak for lack of content, the student may decide

to seek more raw materials by surfing the Internet. In the case of Isabelle and her math problem, in response to experiencing intense anxiety about this math problem, she might look for a different math question on the test, one that invokes less anxiety.

Change Operations

The student might judge that the operations that were default options for addressing this task are not sufficient or not necessary to generate products that pass evaluation. For example, a student trying to prove a proposition about angles and tangents to circles might judge it is not sufficient to add angles surrounding a vertex. Or, the student might judge it is not necessary to draw a diagram representing the elements of the proof. Isabelle might decide that positive self-talk is not sufficient for alleviating her anxiety with respect to the math problem, so she will seek help from a peer rather than rely on self-talk to get her through this problem.

Change Standards

The student might decide that the standard she originally adopted for this task is too high (or too low) or that a particular standard is not appropriate. For example, a reader might lower a standard from the ability to summarize an entire chapter to just listing two or three key ideas. Or, the reader might determine that it will not lead people to think she is stupid if she asks for the definition of a technical term the textbook uses repeatedly. Isabelle, for example, might alleviate her anxiety by increasing her standard for the amount of effort to invest in this problem-solving activity.

ASSEMBLING SELF-REGULATED LEARNING AND MOTIVATION

From our perspective, motivational states are products of a phase of SRL. As soon as a product is generated, it can become a condition contributing to SRL in future recursions or phases of SRL. For example, generating a negative affect about a particular type of task, as Isabelle did on presentation of the math problem, is an outcome of Phase 1 of SRL. This perception serves as a condition in subsequent phases in which Isabelle set a goal to reduce that feeling. This view acknowledges the roles that beliefs, affect, and other motivational constructs play in the SRL process.

As students move through the phases of SRL, they are constantly and inherently experiencing affect with every product they create. When a student's perceptions of the profile of affect differs from the student's profile of affective standards—when they *evaluate* affects— they experience motivation, an impetus to move into a different state.

Based on our analysis using the If–Then–Else framework about how students work on tasks, we noted there were just three ways a student could self-regulate learning: change conditions, change operations, and change standards. Any such change is the result of evaluations the student creates or receives about how well products satisfy standards for those products.

When students self-regulate, they temporarily stand back from direct engagement with their work. They metacognitively monitor products created in Phase 1 about what they perceive a task to be. In Phase 2, they monitor products in the form of goals and plans. In Phase 3, the products they evaluate can be perceptions of effort that arise inherently or their satisfaction with an answer to a problem. In Phase 4, they can evaluate alternatives they generate about how to change conditions, operations, or standards for a task to make it more satisfying.

When a student moves into the next round of a task and changes a previous approach or a planned approach, that change is a result of motivation. The student is motivated to fit the profile of affect experienced to the profile of affects the student prefers. The shorthand for being in a state that affords a change and then making a change is the label *motivation*.

Throughout this chapter, we refer to making such changes as regulating a motivational state. We posit that regulating a motivational state follows a similar process to regulating other aspects of learning. That is, students recognize a discrepancy between products and evaluations relative to standards and follow one of three possibilities to regulate motivational state: They change conditions, operations, or standards.

HOW DO STUDENTS STRATEGICALLY REGULATE MOTIVATIONAL STATES?

Research that can speak clearly to relations between motivation and SRL would have to meet several standards. First, a student's initial approach to one of the phases of SRL would need to be documented. Second, to distinguish changes in behavior from SRL requires data that can describe changes in conditions, operations, or standards over time or across tasks. Third, because students' self-reports about their behavior, such as how they study, can be inaccurate (Winne & Jamieson-Noel, 2002; see also Winne, Jamieson-Noel, & Muis, 2002), data are required about actual behavior to corroborate what students self-report (Pintrich, 2003). There is a large pool of studies that offers evidence students can describe strategies they *might* use to regulate motivational states and emotional states. But, in this research, key elements are missing that examine (a) students' metacognitive awareness of goals and standards they use to monitor motivational states or the effectiveness of strategies they use to regulate motivational states, (b) how students' actual use of specific strategies for regulating motivational state calibrate to their self-reported use of strategies, and (c) relations between strategic regulation of motivational state and performance.

Few research studies meet these standards. Most investigations have been correlational studies about what students say they would do about learning at one point in time. As a result, we examine select studies that address our question, How do students strategically regulate motivational states?

Strategies for Regulating Motivational State

Wolters's (1998) study provided evidence that students describe themselves as actively regulating affective aspects in their learning. He asked students to describe "what they would do to if they wanted to get themselves to continue working on the task" (p. 227) under three different task conditions that characterize the material to be studied as (a) irrelevant, (b) difficult, or (c) boring. In Table 12.1, we summarize Wolters's findings according to his classification of broad strategies and examples of strategies students reported in his study.

Importantly, Wolters found that college students reported different strategies depending on the task condition (irrelevant, difficult,

TABLE 12.1   Wolters's (1998) Identification of Strategies for Regulating Motivational State

Category of Strategies	Examples of Specific Strategies
Extrinsic regulation	Remind oneself of goals and desires to perform well
	Reward oneself for completing components of the task
	Reward oneself for specific performance
Intrinsic regulation	Make material more valuable
	Make material more relevant
	Make material more enjoyable
	Make material more interesting
	Attempt to influence feelings of competency (efficacy)
Information processing	Seek help
	Engage cognitive learning strategies[a]
Volition	Change the environment
	Change the timing of tasks
	Attempt to maintain or decrease attention
	Try harder
	Regulate emotional reactions to task

[a] Most frequently described strategies for regulating motivation.

or boring). This type of selective application of strategies to match task conditions characterizes students' reports of SRL in general (Hadwin, Winne, Stockley, Nesbit, & Woszczyna, 2001). The difference between these strategies and other more cognitive or information-processing strategies referred to as *study skills* is that the strategies students described in Wolters's study address goals associated with motivational states rather than goals associated with cognition.

That students report choosing and experimenting with strategies for maintaining motivational states under different task conditions implies that they regulate motivational states. It follows then that these students set goals and standards about motivational states and attempt to monitor and regulate their engagement relative to those standards. Although research shows that students monitor effort and ability (Rabinowitz, Freeman, & Cohen, 1992; Schunk, 1983), research needs to examine more thoroughly (a) the types of goals and standards students adopt with respect to motivational state, (b) strategies they actually employ to regulate motivational state, and (c) the degree to which they are metacognitively aware of the goals, standards, and strategies used to monitor and change motivational states during learning activities. New research on these topics may afford opportunities to understand better how students strategically regulate motivational states during learning tasks and across learning contexts. In such research, students should face complex learning tasks that involve simultaneously balancing multiple goal profiles that describe motivational state, cognition, and standards (goals).

Applying our model of SRL to Wolters's (1998) findings, Table 12.2 lists goals students may set. For each goal, we suggest a hypothetical

TABLE 12.2   Examples of Motivational Goals, Standards, and Regulating Strategies

Motivational Goal	Motivational Standard	Potential Operations
Persist with this task	If I start to procrastinate or stall in completing the task. Then …	… take a 5-minute break and return to the task refreshed
	If the effort I exert decreases, Then …	Else … study at a time when I am more focused
Maintain an optimal level of anxiety for maximum performance	If anxiety increases to the point that my efforts are disabled. Then …	… self-talk: "Don't stress about this, you know what you are doing." Else … get mad. "I know this stuff and no one is going to trick me into failing to demonstrate that on a
	If anxiety decreases to the point that I do not even care anymore, Then …	stupid test" … remind myself that I have a lot riding on this
Maintain my interest in this task	If interest begins to decrease, Then …	… make studying into a game Else … try to relate the material to something I know Else … make it more interesting Else
Maintain confidence that I can complete the task successfully	If my confidence is not strong or I feel I cannot be successful at this task, Then …	… break things into smaller pieces that seem more attainable Else … seek help from peers

standard and corresponding strategies for regulating motivational states. We know of no research that examined the degree to which students self-regulate motivational state by connecting types of goals with specific conditions, standards, and strategies in If-Then-Else scripts that are the mark of strategic SRL.

It would be naïve to think that one set of strategies for regulating motivational states will work for all or even most situations or tasks. Just as students need to learn strategies for regulating cognitive engagement, they also need to learn strategies for regulating their motivational states within tasks. However, strategies for regulating motivational state within a task are mostly absent from study skills texts (Hadwin, Tevaarwerk, & Ross, 2005).

Evidence of Regulating Motivational State

What evidence exists to support the idea that students self-regulate motivational state? We illustrate using research on emotion because emotion represents a well-recognized characteristic of motivational states (Pintrich, 2003). Research on regulating emotion primarily focuses on monitoring and regulating emotion responses during nonlearning tasks. For example, Dillon and LaBar (2005) found that when asked to adopt a goal of enhancing, maintaining, or decreasing physiological emotional responses to stimuli, people assign cognitive and attentional resources toward this task. Rather than engaging in a particular learning task, participants in Dillon and LaBar's study were shown images and merely asked to control their physiological emotional responses to those images. Human eye blink startle responses were measured because they have been shown to be affected by conscious regulation of negative emotion. Dillon and LaBar's results provide empirical evidence that people can learn to regulate motivational states by regulating their physiological reactions. Future research might explore the regulation of those same physiological emotional responses in the context of learning tasks that present students with specific cognitive and behavioral learning goals.

Regulating emotional state, an internal condition of learning tasks, has been found to mediate effects on task performance when students receive error management training that encourages them to make and learn from errors while studying computer programming (Keith & Frese, 2005). Training to manage errors (with and without accompanying metacognitive training) produced better performance than training to avoid errors. However, in think-aloud protocols collected during task engagement, these researchers also heard participants reporting that error management training led to emotion control that learners believed to enhance their performance on transfer tasks. "From a self-regulatory perspective, emotional self-regulation (emotion control) and cognitive self-regulation (metacognition) were equally important for adaptive transfer to occur" (p. 687). Studies that train emotion control in learning have great potential to advance understandings about how students regulate motivational states and how that regulation affects learning outcomes. This type of research is also rare at present.

In our math problem example, Isabelle's approach reflects emotion regulation. By planning to use self-talk as she works and by refocusing on features of problem solving rather than anxiety, Isabelle is attempting to regulate her emotional response (product) to this word problem. In general, we posit that regulating emotion as well as other motivational states requires students to set motivational standards for monitoring the products of strategies they use. Unfortunately, this type of strategic regulation of motivation during academic tasks is not yet empirically examined in the literature on SRL.

Do Students' Perceptions of Effort Influence Their Choices for Self-Regulating Learning?

We agree with Pintrich (2000, 2003; see also Schunk, 2005) that motivational factors interact with other behavioral, contextual, and cognitive variables to change the course of self-regulatory processes. Studies such as that of Rabinowitz et al. (1992), which we describe next, demonstrate this process.

Effort can be considered a standard that applies to operations. Rabinowitz et al. (1992) examined how standards motivated learners' choices about study tactics. In their study, undergraduates participated in two sessions. In the first session, they used a study tactic, clustering. For half the students, the tactic was easy to use because the materials were easy to categorize. The opposite was the case for the rest of the participants in this experiment. Then, in the second studying session, both groups of learners studied content for which using the same clustering tactic was moderately difficult. So, one group experienced a shift from low to moderate effort, and the other experienced a shift from high to moderate effort.

In the second study session, students who studied content that was to cluster in the first session continued to use clustering. Only one student abandoned this tactic. Having experienced a motivational state in which categorizing was easy to use and produced good results, they were motivated to continue using that tactic. In sharp contrast, about 46% of students who studied content that was hard to categorize in the first session abandoned clustering on what, for them, was an easier context for using clustering. This suggests these students had a negative affective reaction to a difficult-to-use tactic in the first session, and this motivational state depressed their choice to use it again. To generalize, operations that are more difficult to use are abandoned, even if they work well.

CONCLUSION

Using our COPES framework, we described self-regulation as involving two main features: (a) recognizing a discrepancy between a current state (product) and evaluations (feedback) relative to a desired state (standards) and (b) taking action (operating) within a context (conditions) to change that discrepancy. The first of these features defines being in a motivational state, and the second describes doing something to change that motivational state. In this sense, SRL is an instance of motivated behavior.

What our model illuminates is that SRL has three distinct targets for change: conditions that characterize tasks, operations that create products, and standards by which products are judged when students (and others) create evaluations of products. Because motivational states are conditions, the recursive property we ascribe to SRL allows that students may focus on changing motivation as much as they may change other elements. Self-regulated motivation is a relatively new view on how behavior changes and one that complicates attempts to understand how motivation relates to learning, including SRL. Notwithstanding, our account explicitly acknowledges that students can have multiple and separate goals simultaneously when they focus on changing conditions, operations, and standards.

A question that may naturally arise with respect to this description is, What is not self-regulated? We attempted to address this by answering that, definitionally, self-regulation is a phenomenon by which options are considered after a product has been created. It is in relation to this criterion that we find current research to be uninformative. Although there is a plethora of studies that relate students' perceptions of motivated states to intentions for future behavior, few validate whether intentions are realized and, when they are not, what students do to correct the situation. These are essential qualities to satisfy claims that SRL was engaged and which and how motivational states played roles in SRL.

An implication of our analysis is that cognitive and motivational learning strategies should be developed and should put three questions in focus for students: (a) What goals do you have for your motivational state (standards)? (b) How will you be able to know if your motivational state changes or wavers (evaluations and which standards)? (c) Which strategies (operations) are appropriate when motivational state shifts to a suboptimal level? We hypothesize that helping students to (a) develop metacognitive awareness of their motivational states within academic tasks and (b) increase metacognitive monitoring of their motivational states may afford more active and productive learning. In other words, motivation should not be viewed as elusive and uncontrollable, a trait that a student just has to endure. Instead, we suggest motivation be viewed as a collection of attributes about self and tasks that students can learn to regulate for their benefit.

REFERENCES

Ask Dr. Math. *Ages of three children*. Retrieved September 4, 2006, from http://mathforum.org/library/drmath/view/58492.html

Dillon, D. G., & LaBar, K. S. (2005). Startle modulation during conscious emotion regulation is arousal-dependent. *Behavioral Neuroscience, 119*, 1118–1124.

Hadwin, A. F., Tevaarwerk, K. L., & Ross, S. (2005, April). *Do study skills texts foster self-regulated learning: A content analysis*. Paper presented at the annual meeting of the American Educational Research Association, Montreal, Quebec, Canada.

Hadwin, A. F., Winne, P. H., Stockley, D. B., Nesbit, J., & Woszczyna, C. (2001). Context moderates students' self-reports about how they study. *Journal of Educational Psychology, 93*, 477–487.

Keith, N., & Frese, M. (2005). Self-regulation in error management training: Emotion control and metacognition as mediators of performance effects. *Journal of Applied Psychology, 90*, 677–691.

Pintrich, P. R. (2000). The role of goal orientation in self-regulated learning. In M. Boekaerts, P. R. Pintrich, & M. Zeidner (Eds.), *Handbook of self-regulation* (pp. 452–494). San Diego, CA: Academic Press.

Pintrich, P. R. (2003). A motivational science perspective on the role of student motivation in learning and teaching contexts. *Journal of Educational Psychology, 95*, 667–686.

Rabinowitz, M., Freeman, K., & Cohen, S. (1992). Use and maintenance of strategies: The influence of accessibility to knowledge. *Journal of Educational Psychology, 84*, 211–218.

Schacter, S., & Singer, J. E. (1962). Cognitive, social, and physiological determinants of emotional state. *Psychological Review, 69*, 379–399.

Schunk, D. H. (1983). Ability versus effort attribution feedback: Differential effects on self-efficacy and achievement. *Journal of Educational Psychology, 75*, 848–856.

Schunk, D. H. (2005). Self-regulated learning: The educational legacy of Paul R. Pintrich. *Educational Psychologist, 40*, 85–94.

Winne, P. H. (2001). Self-regulated learning viewed from models of information processing. In B. J. Zimmerman and D. H. Schunk (Eds.), *Self-regulated learning and academic achievement: Theoretical perspectives* (2nd ed., pp. 153–189). Mahwah, NJ: Erlbaum.

Winne, P. H., & Hadwin, A. F. (1998). Studying as self-regulated engagement in learning. In D. Hacker, J. Dunlosky, & A. Graesser (Eds.), *Metacognition in educational theory and practice* (pp. 277–304). Hillsdale, NJ: Erlbaum.

Winne, P. H., & Jamieson-Noel, D. (2002). Exploring students' calibration of self reports about study tactics and achievement. *Contemporary Educational Psychology, 27*, 551–572.

Winne, P. H., Jamieson-Noel, D. L., & Muis, K. (2002). Methodological issues and advances in researching tactics, strategies, and self-regulated learning. In M. L. Maehr & P. R. Pintrich (Eds.), *Advances in motivation and achievement* (Vol. 12, pp. 121–155). Greenwich, CT: JAI.

Wolters, C. A. (1998). Self-regulated learning and college students' regulation of motivation. *Journal of Educational Psychology, 90*, 224–235.

13

The Motivational Role of Adaptive Help Seeking in Self-Regulated Learning

Richard S. Newman

INTRODUCTION

An important aspect of the learning process is asking questions about material one does not understand. When students work independently, monitor task performance, and recognize difficulties they cannot overcome on their own, requesting assistance from a more knowledgeable individual can be an adaptive learning strategy. Unfortunately, students often fail to take the initiative to obtain needed help with schoolwork. Students often sit passively, waiting for the teacher to come to them. They may be afraid that if they ask for help, classmates will think they are incompetent. Or, if they do ask for help, students often do so in what might be considered a nonadaptive way. Sometimes, they ask for assistance when it is not necessary, for example, when they have not first attempted the work on their own. They may be more interested in just getting the answer than in understanding the assignment. And, sometimes students ask questions simply to get attention from either the teacher or classmates.

The chapter is organized in three sections. First, I briefly review the academic help-seeking literature, focusing on how researchers have theoretically conceptualized and empirically operationalized adaptive help seeking. Second, to better understand adaptive help seeking, I contrast it with several types of nonadaptive actions in which students often engage when they encounter academic difficulty. This discussion centers on students' assessment of whether help is necessary. The final section of the chapter addresses practical concerns of teachers, particularly how to support students' efforts at adaptive help seeking.

WHAT IS ADAPTIVE HELP SEEKING?

Theoretical Conceptualization

Adaptive help seeking is a strategy of self-regulated learning (see Boekaerts, Pintrich, & Zeidner, 2000; Karabenick, 1998; Schunk & Zimmerman, 1998; Zimmerman & Schunk, 1989). Why is adaptive help seeking considered a "strategy"? It is a strategy in the sense that it is a goal-directed and intentional action that mediates the relationship between academic difficulty and successful task completion (Newman, 1994). This conceptualization follows from the work of Nelson-Le Gall (1985). More generally, it can be considered an aspect of mature coping, by which an individual faced with adversity matches a particular action or strategy to a specific stressor (Boekaerts, 1999; Skinner, Edge, Altman, & Sherwood, 2003).

Different from other learning strategies (e.g., rehearsal, self-testing, use of reference books), adaptive help seeking is social; it involves other people (Newman, 2000). At first glance, the role of others contradicts the "self" part of self-regulation. According to Vygotsky (1978), a child's cognitive development is necessarily linked to social influences. The young child is an active participant in social interaction with an adult caregiver—usually a parent. Assistance, for example, in the context of assembling puzzles, is provided in the form of scaffolding, by which the adult carefully monitors how the child is doing and what the child needs so that just the right amount of help—not too little and not too much—can be given. The adult provides needed assistance and gradually weans the child from unneeded assistance. In time, the child takes over the adult's regulating role. This developmental process has been described as a transition from other-regulation to self-regulation. What often is overlooked in accounts of Vygotsky's theory is the benefit of returning at times to other-regulation. Faced with difficult tasks, learners may require assistance from someone more knowledgeable than they are. An important aspect of self-regulation is knowing when it is necessary to fall back to other-regulation. The self decides when it is time for input from the other; utilization of scaffolding is under the direction of the self. In other words, the learner is the "construction worker" as well as the object of the construction. This dual role is characteristic of many life activities that involve the development of expertise, for example, learning how to swim or learning a hobby. Individuals go back and forth between depending on others, gradually developing independence, pushing oneself toward self-sufficiency, asking an expert for further assistance, when necessary pushing oneself to new limits, and so on. Willingness to depend on others, over the life span, is a marker of cognitive, social, and emotional maturity (Ainsworth, 1989).

In this chapter, I distinguish adaptive from nonadaptive help seeking. Two specific aspects of self differentiate the two constructs. First, adaptive help seeking involves self-reflection. Utilizing social and cognitive competencies, adaptive help seekers carefully consider three sets of questions (i.e., decisions or criteria) when they encounter academic difficulties:

1. *Necessity of the request* (e.g., I'm confused. ... What exactly don't I understand? ... and, what *do* I understand? Have I tried my hardest, using *all* possible skills, strategies, and resources to do the assignment on my own? ... If so, and I am still confused, I guess I need to ask for help.).
2. *Content of the request* (e.g., What exactly should I ask for? Should I just say, "I don't understand?" ... Or ... should I be more specific? Is it OK for me to interrupt the teacher? ... Do I need to raise my hand? ... say, "please"? ... say "excuse me"?).
3. *Target of the request* (e.g., Whom should I ask? Who is most likely to know the answer? Who is least likely to make me feel "dumb"? ... I feel more comfortable asking my friend, but the teacher always knows more ... plus, the teacher might think I'm copying if I ask my friend.).

A second aspect of self that differentiates adaptive from nonadaptive help seeking is affect and motivation. In addition to decision making regarding the questions of necessity, content, and target, adaptive help seekers possess intrapersonal, self-system resources (Connell & Wellborn, 1991) that support their effort and interest and allow them to persist in the face of factors that can inhibit or undermine help seeking (e.g., social comparison among peers, teachers and classrooms emphasizing grades rather than learning). These affective-motivational resources include:

1. *Goals* (e.g., desire to learn, to get good grades, to work collabora- tively, to affiliate with classmates).
2. *Self-beliefs* (e.g., self-efficacy and perceived competence that allow one to tolerate difficult assignments while knowing that one can enlist help from an adult if one needs to).
3. *Emotions* (e.g., self-esteem that allows one to admit to others his or her limitations; a sense of enjoyment and pride regarding schoolwork).

Importantly, the help-seeking process is not sequential. Affective-motivational resources are not simply independent add-on compo- nents that follow the decision making in a temporal fashion. Yes, certain goals, beliefs about oneself, and feelings are needed to trans- form a decision to ask for help into action (i.e., actually raising one's hand in class). But, they also enter into the decision making (per- haps making requests for help more or less adaptive). Also, social- cognitive competencies involved in the decision making influence what students try to accomplish and how they feel about their efforts (perhaps bolstering or damping their sense of caring about whether they succeed). Indeed, a "fusing of skill and will" is characteristic of self-regulated action (Paris, 1988; see also Boekaerts, 2006).

Operationalizing Adaptive Help Seeking

Although this conceptualization involving self-reflection (i.e., regard- ing necessity, content, and target of request) and affective-motiva- tional resources (i.e., goals, self-beliefs, emotions) has strong intuitive appeal, only a few researchers have attempted to empirically opera- tionalize adaptive help seeking. In this section, I review these stud- ies. Focusing on developmental findings (i.e., adaptive help seeking in relation to students' age, grade level, and knowledge), I discuss, first, research that has taken into account necessity (i.e., independent of content of the request) and, second, research that has taken into account content matched to necessity. Little research has examined choice of target, and no research to my knowledge has examined choice of target in conjunction with content or necessity. The dis- cussion focuses on teachers (vs. peers) as helpers. Although help- seeking studies have involved various motivational constructs (e.g., achievement goals, social goals, self-efficacy, perceived competence), I focus the present discussion on achievement goals (for a more complete review of the literature, see Newman, 2000, 2002).

Necessity of Help   The criterion *necessity* can be considered the foundation on which the other criteria (i.e., content and target) rest. Adaptive help seeking is restricted to occasions when assistance is "truly" needed. Research on metacognition and self-regulated learning consistently has shown developmental and individual differences in children's ability to assess accurately when they need assistance. With age and knowledge, students increasingly are aware when their knowledge is lacking, comprehension is incomplete, or they are confused; and with increasing accuracy they callibrate subjective judgments of confidence to actual task performance (see Brown, Bransford, Ferrara, & Campione, 1983; Newman, 2000; Winne, 2001).

To incorporate *necessity* into research on help seeking, experimental procedures have been used to simulate one-to-one tutoring (e.g., giving the student a difficult task and an opportunity to request help from an adult), with initial failure considered an objective measure of need. Help seeking following initial failure can be interpreted as appropriate, or necessary, whereas help seeking following an initial solution that is correct is inappropriate, or unnecessary. Nelson-Le Gall (1987) asked third and fifth graders to define vocabulary words with the option of requesting help. Children gave a tentative, initial answer; were given the option of requesting help; and then were asked for a final answer. Third graders tended to make more unnecessary requests for help than did fifth graders. Using a similar procedure with fifth graders, van der Meij (1990) found that students with relatively poor vocabularies asked significantly more unnecessary questions than did classmates with good vocabularies.

Utilizing subjective judgments of confidence, several studies have considered lower confidence as an indicator of stronger perceived need for help. To examine third and fifth graders' help seeking, Nelson-Le Gall, Kratzer, Jones, and DeCooke (1990) followed the same experimental procedure used by Nelson-Le Gall (1987), although children also were asked to judge how confident they were that tentative, initial answers were correct. Nelson-Le Gall et al. (1990) found that subjective judgments of need matched objective standards (i.e., actual correctness of an initial answer) more often among fifth graders (and those with good verbal skills) than among third graders (and those with poor skills). Further, fifth graders (and those with good skills) sought help more often when they perceived an initial solution to be incorrect than when correct; third graders (and those with poor skills), on the other hand, were equally likely to seek help when a solution was perceived to be incorrect versus correct.

Content of Request Matched to Necessity   Of course, not all requests for help (even though they are in response to legitimate need) are adaptive. Given a particular task situation, certain types of requests are more appropriate than others. Help-seeking research has tended to focus on several types of informational questions: requests for explanations, hints, confirmations, and final answers (Good, Slavings, Harel, & Emerson, 1987).

How have researchers incorporated content along with necessity in their operationalization of adaptive help seeking? Recall that, following an initial answer, children in the studies of Nelson-Le Gall (1987) and Nelson-Le Gall et al. (1990) were given the option of requesting help and then were asked for a final answer. They could request one of two types of help: (a) hints (i.e., indirect help in the form of the target word used in a sentence) or (b) direct answers (i.e., the correct, final answer supposedly "left behind by another child who had done well on the task"). According to Nelson-Le Gall (1985), asking for a hint is indicative of "instrumental" help seeking (i.e., it indicates a desire to clarify or refine current knowledge), whereas asking for a direct answer is indicative of "executive" help seeking (i.e., it indicates either a lack of knowledge or desire for expedient task completion). Fifth graders (and children with good skills) asked the experimenter for more hints than direct answers, whereas third graders (and those with poor skills) showed no preference (see also Nelson-Le Gall & Jones, 1990). Importantly, when fifth graders (and children with good skills) did ask for direct answers, these requests were on trials for which the children felt especially unsure of themselves (i.e., their confidence was low), whereas third graders (and those with poor skills) did not show this relationship between type of request and confidence. In other words, among only the more experienced learners was there evidence of adaptiveness as operationalized according to matching specific type of request to perceived need.

In the work of Butler and Neuman (1995; see also Butler, 1998), second and sixth graders could ask for either hints or complete solutions while working on difficult puzzles. Necessity was incorporated into the computation of a proportional help-seeking score by dividing the number of puzzles for which the child requested help by the number of puzzles the child was not able to solve alone. Time elapsed before an initial request for help was also measured. Although the measure of necessary help seeking showed no grade effect, older children took more time before requesting help than did younger children, suggesting more perseverance in the face of difficulty.

Finally, in the study by Newman and Schwager (1995), third and sixth graders were asked to solve a series of math problems explicitly designed to be beyond the students' current level of proficiency. Sessions were individualized, simulating a one-to-one tutorial. For each problem, students could ask as many questions as they wanted, choosing among five types of help: (a) explanations, (b) hints, (c) confirmation (of an answer), (d) the final answer, and (e) other. All questions were completely answered by an experimenter. At the start, children were assigned to one of two goal conditions; they were told to work to achieve either a learning, or mastery, goal (i.e., to learn and understand how to do the problems) or a performance goal (i.e., to do better than other students and "look smart"; for discussion of these and other achievement goals, see Elliott, 1999; Midgley, 2002; Pintrich, 2000). Coding of spontaneously generated questions revealed a number of nonspecific, vague statements and questions indicating a lack of understanding (e.g., "My head is hollow!" or "30!?"). Adaptive help-seeking sequences were operationalized as an independent attempt to solve a problem, followed by an incorrect answer, which in turn was followed by a request for an explanation or hint; nonadaptive help-seeking sequences involved either an immediate request for the final answer following no independent work or independent work followed by an incorrect answer and then no additional work. Results showed that sixth graders were more likely than third graders to ask for hints and less likely simply to ask for the final answer or vaguely express a lack of understanding. Students with learning goals were more likely than those with performance goals to request feedback (i.e., confirmation of an answer), presumably to help them debug errors and resolve difficulties. Students rarely exhibited adaptive sequences. The two types of nonadaptive sequence were more frequent and were exhibited more often by students with performance goals than by those with learning goals.

In sum, adaptive help seeking requires an accurate assessment that assistance is necessary and not simply expedient. Based on this assessment, students thoughtfully tailor the content and target of a request to meet their specific needs and successfully carry out the request. Developmental findings indicate that, with age and knowledge, children are increasingly aware of when they need help, increasingly likely to request help when it is necessary, and increasingly able to match particular types of requests (e.g., hints vs. final answers) to particular task demands. Findings show that achievement goals are related to help seeking. Students with learning (vs. performance) goals are more interested in obtaining feedback about the correctness of their work, whereas students with performance (vs. learning) goals are more likely to seek help in seemingly nonadaptive ways (i.e., immediately asking for help when it may not be necessary or failing to ask for help when it is necessary).

NONADAPTIVE ACTIONS IN RESPONSE TO ACADEMIC DIFFICULTY

Conceptualizing Adaptive Help Seeking in Relation to Alternative Actions

In contrast to experimental studies, the majority of help-seeking research has not assessed either objectively or subjectively the necessity of help or measured actual help-seeking behavior (from which one might be able to infer necessity). Typically, students are given questionnaires and asked to report their likelihood or intentions of seeking help, for example, in math class. Wording of items as conditional statements takes into account perceived need for help (e.g., "If I get stuck on a math problem, I ask someone for help so I can keep working on it"). Whereas experimental studies allow more precise assessment of whether help is necessary for task completion, self-report studies allow an assessment of how students respond to academic difficulties in the classroom. This research consistently shows that adaptive help seeking in the "real world" of classroom learning is rare. Students typically would rather make mistakes than let the teacher or classmates know they are having difficulty (Newman, 2002; A. M. Ryan, Pintrich, & Midgley, 2001).

When students encounter difficulties and do *not* seek help adaptively, what exactly *do* they do? Clearly, many elementary, middle, and high school students are disengaged from the learning process (e.g., Covington, 1992; Steinberg, Dornbusch, & Brown, 1997). Disengagement can take many forms. Some students are passive, ignoring and avoiding opportunities to seek needed and available assistance. Others ask for assistance without first attempting work on their own, thereby precluding any possible challenge associated with genuine engagement. Of course, teachers and researchers must be careful in their assessments; when a student encounters difficulty and appears to be disengaged, he or she may be quietly involved in productive thought.

To more fully understand adaptive help seeking, it is useful to contrast it with several nonadaptive ways in which students often respond to academic difficulty. Because adaptive help seeking is contingent on an accurate assessment of whether help is necessary, analyzing students' "stumbling" at this particular point in the self-regulatory process can be informative. Table 13.1 illustrates four distinct ways in which students can calibrate their actions to assessments of need:

TABLE 13.1   Calibration of Action to Need

Is Help Necessary?	Action	
	Seek Help	Do *Not* Seek Help
	Quadrant I	*Quadrant III*
Yes	Adaptive help seeking	Nonadaptive avoidance of help seeking
	(Autonomous help seeking)[a]	(Avoidant-covert action)[a]
	(Appropriate help seeking)[b]	(Avoidance of help seeking)[b]
	Quadrant II	*Quadrant IV*
No	Nonadaptive dependent help seeking	Adaptive "other action"
	(Executive help seeking)[a]	
	(Dependent help seeking)[b]	

[a] Butler (1998).
[b] Ryan et al. (2005).

I. *Adaptive help seeking* (i.e., asking for help when it *is* necessary).

II. *Nonadaptive dependent help seeking* (i.e., asking for help when it *is not* necessary).

III. *Nonadaptive avoidance of help seeking* (i.e., *not* asking for help when it *is* necessary).

IV. *Adaptive "other action"* (i.e., *not* asking for help when it *is not* necessary).[1]

All theory and research on help seeking arguably are based on these four action-to-need approaches to task difficulty (for alternative terminologies, see Table 13.1). Researchers, either implicitly or explicitly, have conceptualized (a) adaptiveness according to Quadrants I and IV and (b) nonadaptiveness according to Quadrants II and III.

Research on Adaptive Help Seeking in Relation to Alternative Actions

Several researchers have attempted empirically to contrast adaptiveness and nonadaptiveness. Three studies, by Ruth Butler, Allison Ryan, and me, are of particular note.

Butler's (1998) research contrasted Quadrants I, II, and III. Butler theorized that students' reluctance to seek help can be explained by three distinct help-avoidance (HA) orientations (i.e., autonomous, expedient, ability focused). Each orientation, or belief system, "contains" reasons why an individual at times does not seek help as well as reasons why the individual at other times does seek help. In the questionnaire phase of the study, fifth and sixth graders who said they do not seek help when they want to be challenged also said there are times when they do seek help (e.g., if it is necessary in order to learn). Students who said they do not seek help when they want to avoid the time it would take to talk to the teacher also said there are times when they do seek help (e.g., if obtaining the answer will allow them to finish quickly). And, students who said they do not seek help when they want to conceal the fact they are having difficulty also said there are times when they do seek help (e.g., if they feel pressure to get a good grade). In a second phase of the study, students worked on difficult math problems. They were given the opportunity to request hints or final answers; the experimental set-ting was arranged so that they had another way of getting help—by cheating (i.e., covertly copying the correct answer). Findings showed that each HA orientation was associated with a distinct pattern of help seeking. Hints (i.e., autonomous help seeking) were requested most often by students with a predominant autonomous HA ori-entation (cf. Quadrant I); requests for final answers (i.e., executive help seeking) were most common and latency the quickest among students with an expedient HA orientation (cf. Quadrant II); and cheating (i.e., avoidant-covert action) was most common among students (boys only) with an ability-focused HA orientation (cf. Quadrant III).

A. M. Ryan, Patrick, and Shim (2005) also contrasted Quadrants I, II, and III. Fifth- and sixth-grade teachers classified their students into three groups according to their observed help-seeking tenden-cies: (a) appropriate help seeking (e.g., "The student asks for help when he truly needs it but is not overly dependent") (cf. Quadrant I); (b) dependent help seeking (e.g., "The student asks for help the min-ute he encounters difficulty") (cf. Quadrant II); and (c) avoidance of help seeking (e.g., "The student does not ask for help when he needs it") (cf. Quadrant III). Students' self-reports of help-seeking tenden-cies provided validity to teachers' classifications. On questionnaires, avoidant help seekers had the most maladaptive psychological self-profile, with relatively low learning goals, high performance-avoid-ance goals, low perceived competence, little perceived emotional and academic support from their teacher, and little positive affect in class. On most questionnaire measures, dependent help seekers were most similar to the appropriate help seekers. However, on three measures, dependent help seekers were similar to avoidant help seekers: Both groups of students had poor report card grades and achievement test scores, and both experienced high amounts of anxiety in class.

Finally, recall findings from the work of Newman and Schwager (1995). Students showed evidence of three distinct action-to-need sequences. There were adaptive help-seeking sequences, consist-ing of an independent attempt to solve a problem, followed by an incorrect answer, which in turn was followed by a request for help (cf. Quadrant I). Students also showed evidence of two nonadaptive sequences: (a) immediately requesting assistance when it may not be necessary (cf. Quadrant II); and (b) failing to request assistance when it is necessary (cf. Quadrant III).

Missing Link: Role of Affective-Motivational Factors

According to this conceptualization of adaptive help seeking, students may know that help is not needed but still go to their teacher for assistance; likewise, they may know that help is needed but still respond with passivity. Transforming a correct decision into a correct action requires affective-motivational resources. Goals, self-beliefs,

TABLE 13.2   Motives in Relation to Action-to-Need Patterns

Is Help Necessary?	Action	
	Seek Help	Do *Not* Seek Help
	Quadrant I	*Quadrant III*
	Goals	Goals
	Mastery (learning)	Performance-avoidance
	Autonomous HA orientation[a]	Ability-focused HA orientation[a]
Yes	Self-beliefs	Self-beliefs
	High self-efficacy and perceived competence	Low self-efficacy and perceived competence
	Emotions	Emotions
	High self-esteem, happiness, pride	Low self-esteem, anxiety, hopelessness, depressive symptoms
	Quadrant II	*Quadrant IV*
	Goals	Goals
	Performance-approach	Mastery (learning)
	Work-avoidance	Autonomous HA orientation [a]
	Expedient HA orientation[a]	
No	Self-Beliefs	Self-Beliefs
	Low self-efficacy and perceived competence	High self-efficacy and perceived competence
	Emotions	Emotions
	Low self-esteem, anxiety	High self-esteem, happiness, pride

Note: HA = help avoidance.
[a] Butler (1998).

and emotions are important motives that may help differentiate adaptive help seeking from nonadaptive alternative responses (see Table 13.2).

First, consider actions represented in Quadrants I and IV. The two quadrants presumably represent different actions taken at different times by the same self-regulated learner. Nonaction (i.e., not seeking help) cannot be observed, and therefore we can never be sure what the student is "really doing." But, the self-regulated learner in Quadrant IV may well engage in a host of alternative actions, which are observable. For example, the student might (a) realize a problem is incorrect but continue to work independently, with a "burst of new energy" or perhaps a new strategy; (b) take a break; or (c) correctly conclude that the task has been completed and then either move on to another task or reward him- or herself (e.g., by watching TV or going to bed). In both quadrants, it is likely that students' actions are motivated by learning goals and autonomous HA orientations and are related to positive self-efficacy, perceived competence, and self-esteem, as well as overall interest and enjoyment at school.

Next, consider actions represented in Quadrants II and III. Students who exhibit nonadaptive dependent help seeking (Quadrant II) may be motivated by performance goals, most likely performance-approach goals (i.e., desire to look competent). Working alone elicits anxiety. Self-efficacy and perceived competence required to do assignments independently are poor; they may also lack self-confidence needed to approach classmates for assistance. Perceived by peers and perhaps also by teachers as demanding and pestering, children who are overly dependent run the risk of developing a reputation as emotionally immature. Alternatively, students who seek assistance when it is not necessary may be motivated by work-avoidance goals and an expedient HA orientation. Wanting to finish their work quickly, without effort, and preferring to spend their time with friends, they may seek help without even stopping to consider whether they can accomplish the task on their own. Students who exhibit nonadaptive avoidance of help seeking (Quadrant III) may be motivated by performance-avoidance goals (i.e., desire not to look incompetent) and an ability-focused HA orientation. Public disclosure of academic difficulties makes these students feel especially vulnerable. Self-efficacy and perceived competence are poor. They lack self-confidence needed to approach either classmates or their teacher for assistance. Working with others elicits anxiety, so they disengage. Failure may seem so inevitable that they ask themselves, "Why should I even try to get help?" A sense of hopelessness, despair, and lack of purpose may be manifest in depressive symptoms. However, recall findings from the work of Butler (1998). Under pressure from parents or peers to get good grades (i.e., students' motivation is external rather than self-determined; R. M. Ryan & Deci, 2000), these students' concerns about performance may lead to risk-oriented help seeking (i.e., cheating; see Anderman, Griesinger, & Westerfield, 1998).

Quadrants II and III represent qualitatively different, non-self-regulated actions perhaps taken at different times by the same student. One also can envision the two actions as characteristic of two qualitatively different "types" of students. Individual differences (i.e., between Quadrants II and III) in student profiles raise intriguing developmental questions: Are the two types of students socialized differently? Can one expect for these students different academic and social outcomes? Is dependent help seeking perhaps a developmental precursor to avoidance of help seeking? The last question raises the issue of risk and resilience: Are dependent help seekers at risk, over time, of becoming avoidant help seekers? If so, how might educational interventions counteract that risk and provide overly-dependent children a healthier (i.e., self-regulated) developmental trajectory?

Speculation about nonadaptive dependent help seeking raises an important methodological issue. Although help with schoolwork may not be necessary according to an objective standard (e.g., one's capabilities or actual task performance), it may be necessary to fulfill a student's desire to reduce anxiety or desire for expedience. That is, necessity must be considered in the context of individual students' goals, self-beliefs, and emotions (cf. Boekaerts, 1999). To understand underlying causes of nonadaptive help seeking—and, more generally, to understand "self-aspects" of self-regulation—researchers must pay greater attention to the role of affective-motivational variables (see Nadler, 1998; Schutz & Davis, 2000; Weiner, 2000).

THE ROLE OF TEACHERS

It is important to remember that help seeking is a social transaction (Jackson, Mackenzie, & Hobfoll, 2000; Newman, 2000). Thus, adaptive help seeking, if it is to be successful, requires a teacher's presence and willingness to help. The last section of the chapter is organized according to self-system needs (i.e., relatedness, autonomy, and competence) that underlie students' self-regulated learning (Connell & Wellborn, 1991) and ways in which teachers can provide children with involvement, support for autonomy, and support for competence and thus facilitate adaptive help seeking (for teachers' influence on achievement motivation, see Stipek, 2002).

Involvement with Students

One mechanism by which teachers can promote adaptive help seeking in their classroom is teacher-student involvement. In classrooms where teachers share their time, energy, and nurturance, students tend to be attentive, effortful, self-expressive, and interested in learning. Teachers perceived as caring typically establish classrooms characterized by *intersubjectivity* (i.e., attunement of teacher's and child's purpose, focus, and affect). In such a classroom, teachers are able to take the child's perspective and understand his or her thinking (e.g., regarding a particular academic task) and, based on this understanding, appropriately guide the child's learning. Caring teachers tend to listen, ask questions, inquire if students need help, make sure students understand difficult material, and provide help in a nonthreatening way. When they experience this type of communication, students learn that teachers are trustworthy helpers; this may mitigate the power differential characteristic of many student-teacher relations (Patrick, Anderman, & Ryan, 2002).

With supportive teacher involvement, students come to recognize that the benefits of help seeking can outweigh the costs. What are the benefits? In early elementary years, children who approach their teacher for assistance generally do so because of global, affective traits of the teacher (e.g., niceness and kindness). With age, children become aware of additional ways in which the teacher can meet their needs. By the middle of elementary school, children judge a teacher as helpful when he or she is aware of their problems and gives them advice, time, and encouragement to ask questions in class, thereby helping them to learn. Elementary school students also see their teachers in a negative light. As early as Grade 2, students fear negative reactions (e.g., "I think she might think I'm dumb") if they ask for help (Newman & Goldin, 1990). Perceived costs are heightened when teachers are unwilling to help. Because of a need to protect their self-worth, older students especially are afraid of "looking dumb" in front of their teacher. Throughout the school years, students compare the benefits and costs of help seeking. In the early years, benefits generally win out; in later elementary and middle school years and beyond, students typically struggle in deciding what to do when they need assistance with schoolwork (Newman, 1990).

Support for Autonomy

Self-regulated learners generally feel autonomous. An important way in which teachers can support autonomy and facilitate adaptive help seeking involves the achievement goals teachers establish in their classroom (Ames, 1992). When they emphasize the importance of long-term mastery, autonomy, and intrinsic value of learning (e.g., by using criterion-referenced grading and collaborative activities), teachers foster classroom learning goals. On the other hand, when teachers stress the importance of grades, in particular, the social comparison of grades among students (e.g., by using norm-referenced grading and competitive activities), they foster classroom performance goals. Performance-avoidance goals (i.e., desire not to look dumb) versus performance-approach goals (i.e., desire to look smart) have an especially adverse effect on learning (Elliott, 1999).

In addition to establishing a particular goal for the whole classroom, teachers must adjust to children's personal goals, which presumably are established by parents and by teachers in previous grades. Some students are personally motivated by learning goals and tend to request feedback about whether their work is correct or not; other students are personally motivated by performance goals and tend not to be interested in this sort of information. When students who are concerned about grades are placed in a learning goal classroom, they tend to overcome, and perhaps compensate for, their personal tendencies to avoid help seeking (Newman, 1998). By being attuned to individual students' personal goals, teachers can potentially assist disengaged students who otherwise might avoid help and give up. For example, teachers can try to shape and modify personal performance goals to learning goals. In a setting in which learning and understanding are emphasized, teachers might illustrate to students the benefit of carefully monitoring their performance and requesting information and feedback that hone in on their exact needs. In this way, "smart help seekers" can potentially increase their skills and understanding, which in turn lead to good performance and good grades. In other words, perceived costs of help seeking (e.g., potential embarrassment) can be outweighed by the benefits.

Support for Competence

How can teachers help children be—and feel—competent regarding adaptive help seeking? Teachers establish, and students internalize, patterns of discourse in the classroom. Children learn the value, usefulness, and skills of questioning. It is important that students respect rather than criticize peers who ask for assistance. Questions and probes that teachers use to diagnose misconceptions may eventually help students ask intelligent questions, both of themselves and of others. Teacher feedback lets children know when they need help. Giving no more assistance than is necessary may help children distinguish between adaptive and overly dependent help seeking. Certain children (e.g., low achievers) often learn not to volunteer questions to avoid negative feedback and embarrassment (Eccles & Wigfield, 1985). Explicitly encouraging students to strategically use the help that is given to them (e.g., going back to an incorrect problem and trying to solve it again) may help children continue to monitor their understanding, determine if they need further assistance, and iteratively request help in increasingly explicit, precise, and direct ways (Webb & Palincsar, 1996). Through scaffolded experiences (e.g., teachers responding to requests for help with hints and contingent instruction rather than direct and controlling answers), the child has an opportunity to master difficult tasks and learn that questioning is a valuable means for solving problems. When teachers demonstrate that dilemmas and uncertainty can be tolerated—and perhaps shared and even transformed into intellectual challenge—students may realize that it is normal not to be able to solve all problems independently (Newman, 2000, 2002).

In addition to necessity and content of requests, my conceptualization of adaptive help seeking involves a third criterion, namely, the suitability of the child's choice of help giver. Teachers can support adaptive help seeking by helping students assess specific learning situations to determine the particular person who is most likely to meet their particular needs. For example, when stuck on a difficult math problem, perhaps the student is best served by not immediately going to a friend or neighbor for help. On reflection, the student may realize that he or she could ask Mary ("the class math whiz") rather than Mr. Smith ("who may be smart in math but explains things in too complicated a way") for help. Choice of target obviously is a relevant criterion only in classrooms where students have the option of seeking help from the teacher or peers, where they can choose among teachers and teachers' aides, or where they can choose among different peers. Teachers can establish their classroom to maximize and diversify potential sources for help. Although most research has focused on students seeking help from adults, other sources focus on peers as helpers (Webb, Ing, Kersting, & Nemer, 2006) and help seeking in the context of computer-based learning (Aleven, McLaren, & Koedinger, 2006).

CONCLUSION

Adaptive help seeking is a strategy of self-regulated learning. The process of adaptive help seeking involves self-reflection and self-related affective-motivational factors. What exactly is adaptive about adaptive help seeking? It is effective, in the short term, in helping students solve problems, maintain task engagement and interest, and learn; it is effective, in the long term, in providing skills and understanding needed for handling difficulties independently in the future and for lifelong intellectual development. In spite of clear benefits, students often do not utilize the strategy. This leads to the question, When students encounter difficulties and do *not* seek help adaptively, what exactly *do* they do? The chapter focused on differences between adaptive help seeking and alternative, nonadaptive actions (i.e., dependent help seeking and avoidance of help seeking) and the role of teachers in facilitating students' adaptive help seeking.

In addition to direct benefits for the student, adaptive help seeking provides indirect benefits because it benefits teachers and classmates. Adaptive help seeking can have a positive effect on teachers' sense of engagement; it indicates that the student is interested in their teaching. It thus can strengthen teacher–student involvement.

When a student asks questions, teachers are given feedback and diagnostic information about their teaching, about what is understood and what is not; this can be invaluable for the whole class. Adaptive help seeking can contribute to a classroom culture of inquisitiveness, collaboration, and intellectual discourse. It models for the rest of the class an ideal way of learning. Teachers facilitate the strategy by providing students involvement and support for their autonomy and development of competence. But, there can be a reciprocal effect on teachers. To take their role (as facilitator of adaptive help seeking) seriously, teachers must be patient, listen to students' questions, not rush to give a response, explain how to do problems rather than just supply answers, and value errors as diagnostic information. Teachers can be reminded by their students to pay attention to the individual needs of children—their goals, self-beliefs, and emotions. Adaptive help seeking and adaptive help giving are linked in important ways. Indeed, adaptive help seeking can be a motivator for students' as well as teachers' self-regulation.

NOTE

1. Quadrants II and III represent actions that are inaccurately calibrated to need. Whether an individual can accurately identify a "true" state of necessity is beyond the theoretical scope of this chapter. Thus, a student whose action is represented in Quadrant II (i.e., nonadaptive dependent help seeking) might seek help either because of an inaccurate assessment that help is necessary or in spite of an accurate assessment that help is not necessary. Similarly, a student whose action is represented in Quadrant III (i.e., nonadaptive avoidance of help seeking) might fail to seek help either because of an inaccurate assessment that help is not necessary or in spite of an accurate assessment that help is necessary.

REFERENCES

Ainsworth, M. D. S. (1989). Attachments beyond infancy. *American Psychologist, 44,* 709–716.

Aleven, V., McLaren, B. M., & Koedinger, K. R. (2006). Towards computer-based tutoring of help-seeking skills. In S. A. Karabenick & R. S. Newman (Eds.), *Help seeking in academic settings: Goals, groups, and contexts* (pp. 368–424). Mahwah, NJ: Erlbaum.

Ames, C. (1992). Classrooms: Goals, structures, and student motivation. *Journal of Educational Psychology, 84,* 261–271.

Anderman, E. M., Griesinger, T., & Westerfield, G. (1998). Motivation and cheating during early adolescence. *Journal of Educational Psychology, 90,* 84–93.

Boekaerts, M. (1999). Coping in context: Goal frustration and goal ambivalence in relation to academic and interpersonal goals. In E. Fydenberg (Ed.), *Learning to cope: Developing as a person in complex societies* (pp. 175–197). Oxford, U.K.: Oxford University Press.

Boekaerts, M. (2006). Self-regulation: With a focus on the self-regulation of motivation and effort. In W. Damon & R. Lerner (Series Eds.) & I. E. Sigel & K. A. Renninger (Vol. Eds.), *Handbook of child psychology. Vol. 4: Child psychology in practice* (6th ed., pp. 345–377). New York: Wiley.

Boekaerts, M., Pintrich, P. R., & Zeidner, M. (Eds.). (2000). *Handbook of self-regulation.* San Diego, CA: Academic Press.

Brown, A. L., Bransford, J. D., Ferrara, R. A., & Campione, J. C. (1983). Learning, remembering, and understanding. In J. H. Flavell & E. M. Markman (Eds.), *Carmichael's manual of child psychology* (Vol. 1, pp. 77–166). New York: Wiley.

Butler, R. (1998). Determinants of help seeking: Relations between perceived reasons for classroom help-avoidance and help-seeking behaviors in an experimental context. *Journal of Educational Psychology, 90,* 630–643.

Butler, R., & Neuman, O. (1995). Effects of task and ego achievement goals on help-seeking behaviors and attitudes. *Journal of Educational Psychology, 87,* 261–271.

Connell, J. P., & Wellborn, J. G. (1991). Competence, autonomy, and relatedness: A motivational analysis of self-system processes. In M. R. Gunnar & L. A. Sroufe (Eds.), *Self processes in development: Minnesota Symposium on Child Psychology* (Vol. 23, pp. 43–77). Hillsdale, NJ: Erlbaum.

Covington, M. V. (1992). *Making the grade: A self-worth perspective on motivation and school reform.* Cambridge, U.K.: Cambridge University Press.

Eccles, J. S., & Wigfield, A. (1985). Teacher expectations and student motivation. In J. B. Dusek (Ed.), *Teacher expectations* (pp. 185–226). Hillsdale, NJ: Erlbaum.

Elliott, A. J. (1999). Approach and avoidance motivation and achievement goals. *Educational Psychologist, 34,* 169–189.

Good, T., Slavings, R., Harel, K., & Emerson, H. (1987). Student passivity: A study of question asking in K–12 classrooms. *Sociology of Education, 60,* 181–199.

Jackson, T., Mackenzie, J., & Hobfoll, S. E. (2000). Communal aspects of self-regulation. In M. Boekaerts, P. Pintrich, & M. Zeidner (Eds.), *Handbook of self-regulation* (pp. 275–302). San Diego, CA: Academic Press.

Karabenick, S. A. (Ed.). (1998). *Strategic help seeking: Implications for learning and teaching.* Hillsdale, NJ: Erlbaum.

Midgley, C. (Ed.). (2002). *Goals, goal structures, and patterns of adaptive learning.* Mahwah, NJ: Erlbaum.

Nadler, A. (1998). Relationship, esteem, and achievement perspectives on autonomous and dependent help seeking. In S. A. Karabenick (Ed.), *Strategic help seeking: Implications for learning and teaching* (pp. 61–93). Hillsdale, NJ: Erlbaum.

Nelson-Le Gall, S. (1985). Help-seeking behavior in learning. In W. Gordon (Ed.), *Review of research in education* (Vol. 12, pp. 55–90). Washington, DC: American Educational Research Association.

Nelson-Le Gall, S. (1987). Necessary and unnecessary help-seeking in children. *Journal of Genetic Psychology, 148,* 53–62.

Nelson-Le Gall, S., & Jones, E. (1990). Cognitive-motivational influences on the task-related help-seeking behavior of black children. *Child Development, 61,* 581–589.

Nelson-Le Gall, S., Kratzer, L., Jones, E., & DeCooke, P. (1990). Children's self-assessment of performance and task-related help seeking. *Journal of Experimental Child Psychology, 49,* 245–263.

Newman, R. S. (1990). Children's help-seeking in the classroom: The role of motivational factors and attitudes. *Journal of Educational Psychology, 82,* 71–80.

Newman, R. S. (1994). Adaptive help seeking: A strategy of self-regulated learning. In D. H. Schunk & B. J. Zimmerman (Eds.), *Self-regulation of learning and performance: Issues and educational applications* (pp. 283–301). Hillsdale, NJ: Erlbaum.

Newman, R. S. (1998). Students' help seeking during problem solving: Influences of personal and contextual achievement goals. *Journal of Educational Psychology, 90,* 644–658.

Newman, R. S. (2000). Social influences on the development of children's adaptive help seeking: The role of parents, teachers, and peers. *Developmental Review, 20,* 350–404.

Newman, R. S. (2002). What do I need to do to succeed … when I don't understand what I'm doing!?: Developmental influences on students' adaptive help seeking. In A. Wigfield & J. Eccles (Eds.), *Development of achievement motivation* (pp. 285–306). San Diego, CA: Academic Press.

Newman, R. S., & Goldin, L. (1990). Children's reluctance to seek help with schoolwork. *Journal of Educational Psychology, 82,* 92–100.

Newman, R. S., & Schwager, M. T. (1995). Students' help seeking during problem solving: Effects of grade, goal, and prior achievement. *American Educational Research Journal, 32*, 352–376.

Paris, S. G. (1988). Motivated remembering. In F. E. Weinert & M. Perlmutter (Eds.), *Memory development: Universal changes and individual differences* (pp. 188–205). Hillsdale, NJ: Erlbaum.

Patrick, H., Anderman, L. H., & Ryan, A. M. (2002). Social motivation and the classroom social environment. In C. Midgley (Ed.), *Goals, goal structures, and patterns of adaptive learning* (pp. 85–108). Mahwah, NJ: Erlbaum.

Pintrich, P. R. (2000). The role of goal orientation in self-regulated learning. In M. Boekaerts, P. Pintrich, & M. Zeidner (Eds.), *Handbook of self-regulation* (pp. 451–502). San Diego, CA: Academic Press.

Ryan, A. M., Patrick, H., & Shim, S. O. (2005). Differential profiles of students identified by their teacher as having avoidant, appropriate, or dependent help-seeking tendencies in the classroom. *Journal of Educational Psychology, 97*, 275–285.

Ryan, A. M., Pintrich, P. R., & Midgley, C. (2001). Avoiding seeking help in the classroom: Who and why? *Educational Psychology Review, 13*, 93–114.

Ryan, R. M., & Deci, E. L. (2000). Self-determination theory and the facilitation of intrinsic motivation, social development, and well-being. *American Psychologist, 55*, 68–78.

Schunk D. H., & Zimmerman, B. J. (1998). *Self-regulated learning: From teaching to self-reflective practice.* New York: Guilford.

Schutz, P., & Davis, H. (2000). Emotions and self-regulation during test taking. *Educational Psychologist, 35*, 243–256.

Skinner, E. A., Edge, K., Altman, J., & Sherwood, H. (2003). Searching for the structure of coping: A review and critique of category systems for classifying ways of coping. *Psychological Bulletin, 129*, 216–269.

Steinberg, L., Dornbusch, S. M., & Brown, B. B. (1997). *Beyond the classroom.* New York: Simon and Schuster.

Stipek, D. (2002). *Motivation to learn: Integrating theory and practice.* Boston: Allyn and Bacon.

van der Meij, H. (1990). Question asking: To know that you do not know is not enough. *Journal of Educational Psychology, 82*, 505–512.

Vygotsky, L. S. (1978). *Mind in society: The development of higher psychological processes* (M. Cole, V. John-Steiner, S. Scribner, & E. Souberman, Eds.). Cambridge, MA: Harvard University Press.

Webb, N. M., Ing, M., Kersting, N., & Nemer, K. M. (2006). Help seeking in cooperative learning groups. In S. A. Karabenick & R. S. Newman (Eds.), *Help seeking in academic settings: Goals, groups, and contexts* (pp. 65–121). Mahwah, NJ: Erlbaum.

Webb, N. M., & Palincsar, A. S. (1996). Group processes in the classroom. In D. C. Berliner & R. C. Calfee (Eds.), *Handbook of educational psychology* (pp. 841–873). New York: Simon and Schuster Macmillan.

Weiner, B. (2000). Intrapersonal and interpersonal theories of motivation from an attributional perspective. *Educational Psychology Review, 12,* 1–14.

Winne, P. H. (2001). Self-regulated learning viewed from models of information processing. In B. J. Zimmerman & D. H. Schunk (Eds.), *Self-regulated learning and academic achievement: Theoretical perspectives* (pp. 153–189). Mahwah, NJ: Erlbaum.

Zimmerman, B. J., & Schunk, D. H. (1989). *Self-regulated learning and academic achievement: Theory, research, and practice.* New York: Springer-Verlag.

14

Gender, Self-Regulation, and Motivation

Judith L. Meece and Jason Painter

INTRODUCTION

Current data, reports, studies, and assessments demonstrate that achievement and educational attainment gaps once present between males and females in the United States have been eliminated in most cases and significantly decreased in other cases (Wirt et al., 2004). In fact, females are doing as well as or better than males on many achievement and educational achievement indicators. Male-female differences in many important subject categories, including study skills, verbal-reading, math-computation, abstract reasoning, spatial skills, and natural sciences, are small (Willingham & Cole, 1997).

Despite the findings that suggest that gender differences in academic capabilities are for the most part insignificant, evidence suggests that gender differences in attitudes, expectancies, motivation, self-beliefs, goals, and self-regulation do exist in specific academic domains. These differences not only influence their students' academic performance, but also determine choices students make regarding academic tasks, future courses, and careers they pursue. Albert Bandura realized this in 1986 when he wrote, "Educational practices should be gauged not only by the skills and knowledge they impart for present use but also by what they do to [students'] beliefs about their capabilities, which affects how they approach the future" (p. 417).

This review examines gender differences in self-regulatory processes. It begins with a look at research examining gender differences in self-regulated learning (SRL). For the purposes of this review, SRL includes cognitive or metacognitive processes that activate or sustain behaviors toward the attainment of a goal (Zimmerman, 1989). The research reviewed examines gender differences in elementary and secondary students' use of SRL strategies across a number of different academic domains, including mathematics and science, in which boys have outperformed girls until recently. We next examine gender differences in goals and self-efficacy beliefs, which play a critical role in self-regulatory processes. Gender differences in self-efficacy and other competency-related beliefs tend to be larger than what is found in terms of SRL and achievement. This research also indicates that gender differences in self-beliefs are most pronounced for sex-typed achievement domains, such as mathematics, reading, science, and athletics. Such findings suggest that gender-related differences in self-efficacy beliefs may arise from cultural stereotypes of male and female abilities. The review ends with a brief discussion of sociocultural influences on self-efficacy beliefs and achievement striving.

GENDER DIFFERENCES
IN SELF-REGULATED LEARNING

Self-regulated learning is an important construct on academic learning in current research efforts for psychological and educational researchers. Research on *self-regulation* has focused on the individual's capacity to monitor and modify behavior, cognition, and affect (and sometimes the individual's environment) to achieve a goal (Zimmerman, 1989). Self-regulation has been seen in the research literature as relevant to various lines of research, including metacognition, achievement goals, intrinsic motivation, action control, appraisal processes, autonomy and self-determination in goal setting, and cognitive or metacognitive strategy use in the implementation of goals. Paul Karoly (1993) offered the following definition as a conceptual roadmap and organizational aid for self regulation:

> Self-regulation refers to those processes, internal and/or transactional, that enable an individual to guide his/her goal-directed activities over time and across changing circumstances (contexts). Regulation implies modulation of thought, affect, behavior, or attention via deliberate or automated use of specific mechanisms and supportive metaskills. The processes of self regulation are initiated when routinized activity is impeded or when goal-directedness is otherwise made salient (e.g., the appearance of a challenge, the failure of habitual action patterns, etc). (p. 25)

Self-regulated learning is linked to increases in learning, higher academic performance, and enhanced academic motivation and engagement (Ablard & Lipschultz, 1998; Alexander & Judy, 1988; Bouffard-Bouchard, Parent, & Larivee, 1991; Pintrich, 2000a; Pintrich & De Groot, 1990; Zimmerman, 1989, 2000; Zimmerman & Bandura, 1994; Zimmerman & Martinez-Pons, 1986, 1990). Pintrich and De Groot (1990), for example, found that students who reported greater self-regulatory strategy use also reported higher levels of intrinsic motivation, self-efficacy, and achievement. Similarly, Zimmerman and Martinez-Pons (1986) found that high-achieving students were more likely than low-achieving students to report using 13 of the 14 self-regulatory behaviors identified by these researchers. More generally, Schunk and Zimmerman (1994), in a review of several studies, concluded that self-regulated learners are likely to have more adaptive cognitive, motivational, and achievement outcomes than their classmates who fail to self-regulate.

A number of different SRL models derived from various theoretical perspectives exist in the current educational psychology literature, including Boekaerts (Boekaerts & Niemivirta, 2000), Borkowski (1996), Pintrich (2000b), Winne (Winne & Hadwin, 1998), and Zimmerman (2000). Puustinen and Pulkkinen (2001) carried out a critical review and comparison of these models. Boekaert's model originated out of Kuhl's (1985) action control theory and Lazarus and Folkman's (1984) transactional stress theory. Borkowski's model was derived from the information-processing and metacognitive research traditions (Brown, 1978; Flavell & Wellman, 1977; Sternberg, 1985). Pintrich and Zimmerman's models drew on the same background theory, social cognitive theory (Bandura, 1986). Winne's model was more broadly rooted in various theoretical backgrounds, including the work of Bandura and Zimmerman, Carver and Scheier (1990), Kuhl (Kuhl & Goschke, 1994), and Paris and Byrnes (1989). Puustinen and Pulkkinen (2001) concluded that all the models assume SRL proceeds from some type of preparatory or preliminary phase (forethought, task analysis, planning, goal setting), through the actual performance or task completion phase (strategy use and monitoring), to an appraisal or adaptation phase (performance feedback and reflection).

Empirical research in gender differences related to SRL has mainly focused on the models drawn from social cognitive theory (Ablard & Lipschultz, 1998; Patrick, Ryan, & Pintrich, 1999; Zimmerman

& Martinez-Pons, 1990). Models developed from social cognitive theory stress that learners set, pursue, and attain goals by self-organizing, becoming proactive, and using cognitive and self-regulatory strategies that are directed and restricted by perceptions of efficacy, interest, value, goal orientations, and affective components (Pintrich & De Groot, 1990; Pintrich & Schrauben, 1992; Zimmerman, 2002).

Research on gender differences in students' use of self-regulation learning strategies generally shows that girls are more likely to use these strategies than boys. For example, Zimmerman and Martinez-Pons (1990) interviewed students in Grades 5, 8, and 11 to determine whether differences could be detected by sex in the use of 14 SRL strategies. The study included a range of different learning contexts, including completing homework, writing a short paper, preparing for an important test, and taking a test. Across these various learning situations, girls reported higher use than boys of goal-setting, planning, record-keeping, monitoring, and environmental-structuring strategies. No significant gender differences were reported for SRL strategies involving behavioral functioning.

Ablard and Lipschultz (1998) also examined gender differences in SRL by specific learning context with self-report data from 222 seventh-grade students who had scored in the top 3% on a standardized achievement test. The researchers found that girls had a significantly higher total SRL score than boys, even after controlling for differences in achievement and motivation. They also found that girls reported greater use of SRL strategies than boys in certain types of learning contexts. For example, when writing a short paper and when preparing for tests in reading and writing, girls reported that they used more SRL strategies than boys.

Other studies revealed that gender differences in students' use of SRL strategies are dependent on the academic domain. In mathematics, for example, studies showed greater use of SRL strategies by girls than boys in mathematics. Pokay and Blumenfeld (1990) investigated the use of SRL strategies by high school students in geometry. Compared to boys, girls reported greater use of metacognitive, general cognitive, and specific geometry strategies than did boys. Girls also reported stronger effort management patterns than boys. In a study of seventh- and eighth-grade students, Patrick et al. (1999) also found that girls reported higher levels of cognitive strategy use than boys in mathematics. These differences appeared even though boys reported stronger efficacy for mathematics than girls.

A few studies have examined gender differences in students' SRL for science. Three studies (Anderman & Young, 1994; Neber & Schommer-Aikins, 2002; Pintrich & De Groot, 1990) reported no gender differences in strategy use among elementary, middle, or high school students. In contrast, Meece and Jones (1996) reported gender differences in science-related strategy use for a sample of fifth- and sixth-grade students. The gender difference was moderated by ability. Average-ability girls reported greater use than boys of active learning strategies, which included monitoring understanding of material or reviewing answers. No gender differences were found among high- and low-achieving students.

Given gender differences in reading abilities, it is surprising that few studies have focused on students' use of SRL strategies in this area. Research focused on writing suggests that girls express greater confidence for self-regulation in elementary school (Pajares, Miller, & Johnson, 1999) and in middle school (Pajares, Britner, & Valiante, 2000; Pajares & Valiante, 2001). Specifically, girls expressed greater confidence than boys in their capability to use strategies such as finishing homework assignments on time, studying when there are other things to do, remembering information presented in class and textbooks, and participating in class discussions. Pajares and Valiante (2002) extended these findings to elementary and high school students.

Summary

Both self-report and survey methods have been used to examine gender differences in SRL based on social cognitive theory. Gender differences have also been examined across various domains of academic functioning. Overall, with a few exceptions, the data indicate greater use of SRL strategies by girls than boys across the different domains examined. These findings are noteworthy for several reasons.

First, the results are consistent with other research indicating that girls tend to be more self-disciplined and self-controlled than boys (Duckworth & Seligman, 2006). Self-discipline involves the ability to exert conscious control over responses and thinking to achieve a higher goal (e.g., thinking about an answer before responding, controlling emotions when frustrated, etc.). Measures of self-discipline, like SRL, are positively linked to achievement test scores and academic ability. As such, the ability to regulate and to exert control over behavior may serve as one of the many mediating processes by which gender influences academic performance (Duckworth & Seligman, 2006).

In addition, earlier studies suggested that girls were less likely than boys to engage in meaningful learning (Ridley & Novak, 1983) or autonomous learning (Fenemma & Peterson, 1985). Specifically, it was proposed that boys were more likely than girls to exercise control over their learning, to relate learning to previous knowledge, and to evaluate and use complex problem solutions. It was further proposed that greater use of these strategies facilitated achievement in mathematics and sciences, especially at the advanced levels. Research on self-reports of SRL and self-discipline provides little support for this view of female and male achievement (Duckworth & Seligman, 2006; Meece & Jones, 1996).

GENDER DIFFERENCES IN ACHIEVEMENT ORIENTATION GOALS

Social cognitive theory maintains that goals play an important role in self-regulation processes (Bandura, 1986). Symbolically represented as a desired outcome, goals help to organize, direct, and guide behavior. In school settings, goals can take a number of different forms, including gaining teacher or peer approval, obtaining a good grade, gaining knowledge, making friends, becoming popular, gaining admission to college, and so on. Goals differ in specificity, content, and proximity (Pintrich & Schunk, 2002). Goals that are attainable within a short period of time (proximal) and framed in terms of discrete actions (specific) have the most positive effect on self-regulation processes (Schunk, 1989).

Achievement goal theory has dominated research on motivation since the early 1980s. In this theory, goals are defined by whether the anticipated or desired outcome involves increasing or demonstrating competence. A *learning* or *mastery* goal orientation is defined as a desire to develop one's competencies, to master a task, or to improve intellectually, whereas a *performance* goal orientation is concerned with demonstrating high ability relative to others, competing for grades, or gaining recognition for ability (Ames, 1992; Dweck & Elliot, 1983; Nicholls, 1984). Performance goals have been further differentiated into *performance-approach* goals, which focus on the attainment of favorable judgments of competence, and *performance-avoidance* goals, which focus on avoiding unfavorable judgments of ability (A. J. Elliot & Church, 1997; A. J. Elliot & Harackiewicz, 1996).

Consistent with social cognitive theory, the goals individuals adopt in learning settings have important implications for a wide range of academic behaviors. In general, a mastery focus is positively related to a preference for challenging activities (Ames & Archer, 1988); to high levels of interest, task involvement, and persistence (E. Elliot & Dweck, 1988; Harackiewicz, Barron, Pintrich, Elliot, & Thrash, 2002; Stipek & Kowalski, 1989); and to reported use of learning strategies that enhance conceptual understanding and recall of information (Ames & Archer, 1988; Meece, Blumenfeld, & Hoyle, 1988; Meece & Miller, 2001; Nolen, 1988). In contrast, performance-oriented goals tend to be associated with surface-level learning strategies (Graham & Golan, 1991; Meece et al., 1988; Nolen, 1988; Stipek & Gralinski, 1996) and self-handicapping strategies (Urdan, Midgley, & Anderman, 1998). However, some evidence suggests that performance-approach goals may be positively related with achievement outcomes, especially for college students (Harackiewicz et al., 2002).

Comparatively few studies have examined gender differences in achievement goal orientation in elementary and secondary school populations. In a study of motivation and strategy use in elementary science, Anderman and Young (1994) reported that girls were more learning focused and less ability focused in science than were boys, even though girls reported lower levels of self-efficacy in science. In another study, Meece and Jones (1996) reported gender differences, favoring boys, in elementary school students' science-related efficacy beliefs; however, no main effects for gender were reported for mastery and performance goal scales. Gender effects were also moderated by the students' ability level. In the low-ability group only, boys reported a stronger mastery goal orientation than did girls. In a third study based on a sample of ethnically and economically mixed sixth-grade students, Middleton and Midgley (1997) found that African American girls reported a stronger learning goal orientation than African American boys. No differences in goal orientations were found for

European American students. In contrast to these findings, Greene and her colleagues (Greene, DeBacker, Ravindran, & Knows, 1999) reported no gender differences in high school students' learning and performance goals in mathematics. Taken together, these studies reveal no clear pattern of gender differences in students' achievement goal orientations. Gender differences are moderated by ability, race, and classroom context.

GENDER DIFFERENCES IN EFFICACY AND COMPETENCY-RELATED BELIEFS

A key motivational belief underlying self-regulatory processes is self-efficacy (Bandura, 1986; Schunk, 1994; Zimmerman & Kitsantas, 2005). *Self-efficacy* refers to a person's judgment of personal confidence to learn, to perform certain tasks successfully, or to succeed in academic endeavors (Bandura, 1986). Although involving judgments of personal capabilities, self-efficacy beliefs are distinct from objective measures of ability. According to Bandura (1986), performance on complex or challenging tasks involves both skills and a strong sense of efficacy to use those skills effectively. More specifically, task engagement is enhanced when students enter learning situations with positive perceptions of their skills and abilities to perform the task at hand. While engaged in the task, students need to make positive judgments of their progress and to attribute their progress to ability, effort, and effective use of strategies that enhance self-efficacy and motivation (Schunk, 1994). For these reasons, self-evaluation and attribution process play a central role in self-regulatory processes.

Numerous studies reported gender differences in self-efficacy and other competency-related beliefs. Gender differences in competency beliefs are found early in school and tend to be more gender differentiated than objective measures of ability. In the following sections, we review research on gender differences in self-efficacy judgments and causal attribution patterns. We also include research based on Eccles and colleagues' (1983) expectancy-value model of academic choice. In this model, competency beliefs take two forms. Self-concepts of ability involve domain-specific evaluations of competence, whereas expectancies involve judgments concerning the probability of success within a specific academic domain. Like self-efficacy, both constructs function as cognitive motivators of academic behaviors (Schunk & Zimmerman, 2006).

Self-Efficacy Beliefs

Self-efficacy theory has been widely used to understand gender differences in motivation and achievement patterns (Bussey & Bandura, 1999). As described next, sex role socialization processes may bias children's perceptions of personal efficacy in an achievement domain. Much of this research on gender differences in self-efficacy has indeed focused on academic areas that are traditionally viewed as male or female domains of achievement. For example, numerous studies documented that boys tend to report higher self-efficacy beliefs than girls about their performance in math and science (Anderman & Young, 1994; Pajares, 1996, Pintrich & De Groot, 1990; Zimmerman & Martinez-Pons, 1990). The results of Whitley's (1997) meta-analysis of studies of gender differences in computer-related attitudes and behavior also revealed a similar pattern as men and boys exhibited higher computer self-efficacy than did their female counterparts. When the context is language arts, gender differences are reversed. For example, Pajares and Valiante (1997, 2001) reported that middle school girls had higher writing self-efficacy than boys even though there were no gender differences in actual writing performance.

Research also suggests that gender differences in self-efficacy are linked to age or grade level (Schunk & Pajares, 2002), with differences beginning to emerge in the middle school years (Bandura, Barbaranelli, Caprara, & Pastorelli, 2001; Wigfield, Eccles, & Pintrich, 1996). In Whitley's (1997) meta-analysis of computer self-efficacy, mean effect sizes for gender differences varied depending on the age of the sample: 0.09 for grammar school (elementary and middle school/junior high), 0.66 for high school, 0.32 for college, and 0.49 for adult samples. Age-related gender differences in self-efficacy beliefs are generally attributed to increased concerns about conforming to gender-role stereotypes, which typically coincide with the entry into adolescence (Wigfield et al., 1996). However, research on gender differences in self-efficacy beliefs have not found a consistent pattern of gender differences among young adolescents (Pajares & Graham, 1999; Roeser, Midgley, & Urdan, 1996).

Other Competency-Related Beliefs

Research based on the Eccles et al. (1983) model of academic choice has also documented important differences in boys' and girls' competency-related beliefs. This research focused on domain-specific self-concepts of ability and achievement expectations. Studies using an expectancy-value framework indicated that small gender differences in children's self-perceptions of ability begin to emerge in early elementary school (Eccles, Wigfield, Harold, & Blumenfeld, 1993). As with self-efficacy beliefs, the results tend to follow gender norms and expectations. Boys report more positive competence beliefs for sports and mathematics than girls, and girls report more positive competence beliefs for instrumental music than boys (Eccles et al., 1993). These gender differences emerge even though boys and girls perform equally well in these domains (Eccles et al., 1993).

In addition, cross-sectional and longitudinal research indicated that all children experience declines in their competency beliefs over the course of schooling (Wigfield & Eccles, 2000; Wigfield et al., 1997). However, the rate of change differs by gender and by achievement domain. Girls' perceptions of their math abilities decline at a slower rate than boys, such that gender gaps in mathematic competence decrease over time (Fredricks & Eccles, 2002; Jacobs, Lanza, Osgood, Eccles, & Wigfield, 2002). For language arts, boys and girls begin elementary school with similar ability perceptions, but boys' perceptions rapidly decline in elementary school. By middle school, there are significant differences in boys' and girls' competency ratings for language arts. Like mathematics, gender gaps in language arts are somewhat smaller by high school (Jacobs et al., 2002). By contrast, gender differences in the sports domain, favoring boys, remain stable across all grades of school (Fredricks & Eccles, 2002; Jacobs et al., 2002).

Causal Attribution Patterns

Research using an attribution framework has also identified gender differences in the ways that children and adults interpret or explain their successes and failures. Specifically, this research has examined the extent to which boys and girls attribute their successes and failures to different factors, such as ability, effort, task difficulty, and luck. Studies suggested that boys are more likely than girls to attribute their successes to internal causes (e.g., ability or effort) that would enable them to maintain high efficacy beliefs and expectations for future performances. Girls, on the other hand, are less likely than boys to attribute their successes to their talents and abilities, even when they outperform boys (Eccles-Parsons, Adler, & Meece, 1984; Stetsenko, Little, Gordeeva, Grasshof, & Oettingen, 2000). However, these patterns are not consistently found across all studies, and findings appear to be more marked for achievement areas that are sex typed as masculine or feminine domains (Frieze, Whitley, Hanusa, & McHugh, 1982). In mathematics, for example, girls are less likely than boys to attribute their successes to ability. Instead, girls attribute their successes to effort and hard work, which may undermine their expectations for success as mathematics increases in difficulty (Eccles et al., 1983; Parsons, Meece, Adler, & Kaczala, 1982; Wolleat, Pedro, Becker, & Fennema, 1980). Similar differences in causal attribution patterns have also been noted for successes and failures in science courses (Kahle & Meece, 1994; A. K. F. Li & Adamson, 1995). By contrast, few studies reported gender differences for achievement tasks involving verbal and language abilities (Parsons et al., 1984). Thus, gender differences in causal attribution patterns are evident but depend on the achievement domain. Studies also suggested that results vary depending on student ability level and research methodology, such as open-ended versus rank-order questions (Parsons, Meece et al., 1982).

Causal Attributions and Learned Helplessness

Because of differences in attribution patterns, researchers have argued that girls may be more prone than boys to learned helplessness (Dweck, 1986). Learned helplessness occurs when someone attributes failure to a lack of ability and gives up easily or shows a steady regression in problem-solving strategies when confronted with failure. Early studies of children's attribution patterns in laboratory settings identified gender differences in causal attribution and behavior patterns that are consistent with learned helplessness (Dweck & Reppucci, 1973). However, as with studies of causal attributions, findings were not consistent across studies. For example, Parsons, Meece et al. (1982) used school-related learning tasks (number sequences and anagrams) to examine gender differences in learned helplessness patterns within a sample of adolescents (Grades 8 through 10). Although male and female students reported differential attributions to ability for successes and failures on the math problems, these causal attribution patterns did not translate into gender differences in behavioral responses (see also Kloosterman, 1990). That is, no differences were noted in persistence, expectancy judgments, or error rates for either math or anagram problems. In fact, girls persisted longer than boys on the math tasks when they experienced failure. Thus, attribution measures tend to provide the strongest support for gender differences in learned helplessness. As discussed, responses on attribution measures are influenced by many situational factors, including sex role stereotypes (McHugh, Frieze, & Hanusa, 1982; Parsons, Meece, et al., 1982; Parsons et al., 1984).

Summary

Numerous studies have examined gender differences in competency-related perceptions. Compared with research on SRL, gender differences in self-perceptions depend on the academic domain examined. Gender differences in self-efficacy and competency beliefs favor girls in writing and reading and favor boys for mathematics, science, computer technology, and sports. Most studies find gender differences in self-beliefs, even when actual ability differences are taken into account. Given the positive influence of self-efficacy beliefs on academic achievement and participation (Schunk & Pajares, 2002), it is important to understand what contributes to these gender patterns. In the next section, we consider gender role conceptions and beliefs.

SOURCES OF EFFICACY: GENDER ROLE CONCEPTIONS AND BELIEFS

Identity processes play a critical role in the development of motivation. According to Erikson (1963), a key aspect of identity development is to integrate self-conceptions with societal expectations. In many Western societies, mathematics and science are traditionally viewed as male domains of achievement, whereas reading and language arts are stereotyped as areas in which women typically excel

(Eccles, 1994). For example, studies revealed that parents and teachers stereotype mathematics as a male domain of achievement (Eccles et al., 1983; Jacobs & Eccles, 1992; Jussim & Eccles, 1992; Keller, 2001; Tiedemann, 2000). Adults also perceive traits relevant to learning mathematics (e.g., competitiveness, logic, self-reliance) as more descriptive of male than female students (Fenemma & Peterson, 1985). When parents and teachers hold these traditional stereotypes, they perceive boys to be more competent than girls in mathematics, whereas the opposite pattern holds for reading or language arts (Eccles, 1994). Gender-differentiated views of children's academic abilities are found quite early in school, even when there are no differences in actual abilities (Yee & Eccles, 1988). For example, even in kindergarten, mothers expect their sons to do well in mathematics and their daughters to do well in reading (Lummis & Stevenson, 1990). In addition, parents' and teachers' gendered beliefs are modestly linked to children's stereotyping of mathematics (Eccles, 1994; Jacobs & Eccles, 1992; Keller, 2001; Tiedemann, 2000). Thus, if endorsed, cultural stereotypes regarding which sex is more talented in a particular area can lead children to rate their own abilities in a gender-stereotypic direction (Eccles, 1994). As described, gender differences in children's self-efficacy and competency beliefs are most pronounced in sex-typed domains such as mathematics, science, language arts, sports, and music. For this reason, several researchers have argued that cultural stereotypes play an important role in how children assess their abilities within different academic domains [Bussey & Bandura, 1999; Eccles et al., 1993; Meece, Eccles (Parsons), Kaczala, Goff, & Futterman, 1982; Pajares & Valiante, 2001, 2002].

Several studies supported this view. Studies conducted in the United States, Australia, and Japan indicated that both male and female students stereotype mathematics as male domains of achievement (Eccles et al., 1983; Hyde, Fennema, Ryan, Frost, & Hopp, 1990; Tartre & Fennema, 1995). Across studies, male students tend to stereotype mathematics as a male domain more than females. Male students also believe that members of their own sex are better at math than are girls. This pattern has been reported for elementary and secondary students (Forgasz, 1995; Jacobs, 1991; Tiedemann, 2000). However, contrary to expectations, a link between children's domain stereotypes and self-perceptions of ability has not been firmly established. In a study of mathematics, for example, Eccles and colleagues (1983) found that adolescents' perceptions of mathematics as more useful for men than women were unrelated to their self-perceptions of math ability and expectations. In contrast, Eccles and Harold (1991) found a strong association between adolescents' stereotyping of sports and self-perceptions of athletic abilities.

Cultural stereotypes of academic domains may have a greater impact when children's self-conceptions also conform to gender role expectations (Eccles et al., 1983). If, for example, mathematics or science is sex typed as a male domain, then students' self-perceptions of their feminine and masculine traits may affect their ability assessments within a particular achievement area. By middle childhood, children's self-conceptions are differentiated along gender lines. For example, most studies showed that girls use "feminine" characteristics (e.g., gentle, warm, sympathetic) to describe themselves, and boys use "masculine" characteristics (e.g., dominant, competitive, assertive) to describe themselves (Ruble & Martin, 1998). A few studies have tested the influence of gender role orientations on children's self-perceptions in gender stereotypic areas of achievement. Eccles et al. (1983) used the Personality Attributes Questionnaire (PAQ) to measure adolescents' femininity/expressivity and masculinity/instrumentality. For both boys and girls, instrumentality positively predicted ability and expectations self-perceptions in mathematics. The expressivity scale was unrelated to these self-perception measures. Among college students, Hackett (1985) found that a masculine orientation was positively associated with mathematics self-efficacy. In a more recent study, Pajares and Valiante (2001) used the Children's Sex Role Inventory (CSRI) to examine the influence of masculine and feminine gender role orientations on middle school students' self-perceptions in writing, a domain traditionally viewed as female. For this achievement domain, students' self-ratings of femininity/expressivity exerted the strongest influence on self-efficacy and self-concept ratings. With gender role orientations included in prediction equations, the students' gender was no longer a significant predictor of competency beliefs in writing. Accordingly, these studies suggest that measures of gender role identity may be more predictive of efficacy and competency ratings than gender alone. Both boys and girls who view themselves as possessing masculine traits report greater efficacy for mathematics. Similarly, both boys and girls who view themselves as expressive report greater efficacy for reading and writing activities.

In summary, research has identified some important ways cultural stereotypes and gender role conceptions influence children's competency-related perceptions. Effects depend on two conditions: (a) students endorse cultural stereotypes regarding gendered domains of achievement and (b) students view their own traits and abilities in a gender stereotypic manner. Existing evidence provides support for both conditions. It is worth noting that in most studies measures of prior achievement were more predictive of competency beliefs than were sex role stereotypes and beliefs (Eccles et al., 1983). It is also important to point out that most studies in this section were conducted prior to 1990. Some evidence suggests that gender stereotyping of some academic domains, such as mathematics, has declined in recent years. For example, a study of Australian adolescents reported no gender stereotyping of mathematics; students perceived girls and boys as equally capable in mathematics (Forgasz, Leder, & Kloosterman, 2001). In addition, children's gender conceptions have begun to show more flexibility concerning male and female roles over the last 15 years (Ruble, Martin, & Berenbaum, 2006). Additional research is needed to determine whether relations predicted and established by prior research still hold today.

CONCLUSION

Educational research concerning gender has focused on differences in standardized tests, school grades, cognitive abilities, attitudes, motivation, self-beliefs, and course participation. Efforts to close gender gaps in some school subjects, particularly mathematics and science, have been relatively successful. Evidence suggests that gender inequities in mathematics and science present in the 1970s have narrowed substantially or perhaps closed altogether. However, current research indicates that girls are performing consistently better than boys on standardized tests of reading and writing. Despite data suggesting some improvement in gender inequities, gender differences continue to appear in young people's self-regulation and self-efficacy beliefs in specific academic domains.

Regarding research on SRL, much of the data favor girls. Compared to male students, girls report more goal setting, planning, monitoring of performance, environmental structuring, seeking assistance, and so forth. On the whole, the data indicate a deeper level of cognitive investment in learning activities. These differences are noteworthy because several of the studies reviewed were conducted in male sex-typed subject areas such as mathematics (Pokay & Blumenfeld, 1990) or science (Anderman & Young, 1994; Meece & Jones, 1996), in which gender differences in self-efficacy and competency beliefs tend to favor boys more than girls. Zimmerman and Martinez-Pons (1990) have also reported that girls display greater self-regulation of learning but express lower confidence in their academic capabilities than do boys.

Goals and self-efficacy beliefs play an important role in self-regulation processes. As with self-regulation, evidence suggests that girls are approaching learning tasks with a stronger mastery orientation than are boys. Similarly, girls express more efficacy than boys for self-regulation. These types of motivational beliefs are most directly linked to the types of SRL strategies needed to enhance conceptual understanding and achievement (Meece, Anderman, & Anderman, 2006).

Research on competency-related beliefs presents a more mixed pattern of results. In general, gender differences are larger when students are asked to make general assessments of their abilities, especially in sex-typed subject areas such as mathematics or writing (e.g., "How good are you at math?"). These gender differences appear even when previous achievement is equated. One explanation for this discrepancy is the task specificity of efficacy beliefs. Gender differences may be more prevalent in measures that elicit group comparisons or evaluations. In making these assessments, cultural stereotypes or gender expectations may lead to more biased assessments (Schunk & Meece, 2006). Evidence suggests that certain academic domains (e.g., reading, mathematics, or science) are stereotyped as more relevant for one gender than the other. In sex-typed domains, boys may be more "self-congratulatory" in their responses, whereas girls may be more modest about their abilities (Wigfield et al., 1996) or even discount their own talent as a cause for their success (Stetsenko et al., 2000). Whatever the explanation, it appears that girls are investing more cognitive effort despite their lower assessments of self-efficacy or competence.

IMPLICATIONS FOR EDUCATION

The research discussed in this chapter has important implications for school professionals. With the exception of reading and writing, gender gaps in student achievement have been declining over the last decades. In some areas of achievement, such as mathematics, gender differences in ability perceptions are greater than what is found for achievement scores. Research reviewed in this chapter indicates that stereotypes of academic domains can lead to biased self-perceptions of ability. Furthermore, research on stereotype threat suggests that simply invoking gender stereotypes can undermine task performance by negatively affecting self-efficacy beliefs (Bussey & Bandura, 1999). Over time, these self-perceptions can lead students to place less value on achievement areas for which they report less confidence in their abilities (Jacobs et al., 2002). Both competency and value beliefs have a strong impact on activity choices, engagement, and performance, especially in the adolescent years when young people exercise greater control over their use of time (Eccles, Wigfield, & Schiefele, 1998; Schunk & Meece, 2006). Research suggests that self-efficacy beliefs formed in middle and high school are strong predictors of young people's future educational and occupational aspirations (Bussey & Bandura, 1999), and recent labor force participation statistics indicate that women continue to be underrepresented in math- or science-related careers (Meece, 2006). Other evidence indicates that the messages young people receive about their self-efficacy can help them to persist and persevere as they choose challenging careers in mathematics, science, or technology (Zeldin & Pajares, 2000).

For students with low self-efficacy beliefs, it is important for teachers to recognize that students derive a sense of competence or self-efficacy from role models, feedback about performance, and their direct experience with activities (Bandura, 1986; Bussey & Bandura, 1999). Teachers can help enhance their students' ability perceptions and SRL through strategy instruction and feedback practices. Table 14.1 shows a number of ways teachers can create a classroom environment that cultivates SRL. All curriculum areas provide opportunities to allow student autonomy, varied instructional strategies, and SRL. Educators must emphasize students' role in their own learning and shift some of the responsibility for learning from themselves to the learner. Educators can facilitate learning by focusing on those features over which students can exert control: amount of effort, setting goals, monitoring understanding and progress, persistence, seeking assistance, managing time effectively, and so forth. Educators need to provide opportunities for students to self-monitor, revise work, receive frequent feedback, and reflect on their own thinking and learning processes. When providing feedback, teachers

TABLE 14.1   Changing Instructional Approaches for Self-Regulated Learning

Less Emphasis On	More Emphasis On
Competing for grades	Improving and understanding subject matter content
Teaching curriculum	Teaching students
Teacher control	Supporting students as independent learners
Teacher lectures	Student discourse
End of unit/chapter exams	Frequent assessments and feedback
Passive learning	Active, cooperative, and inquiry learning
Teachers as dispenser of knowledge	Facilitating and encouraging student-directed learning
One instructional strategy	Various instructional strategies
Memorization and rote learning	Goal-setting, self-monitoring, reflection, and other metacognitive strategies
Correct answers	Effort, persistence, and thinking processes related to the correct answers

need to focus on the effort, persistence, and the thinking processes involved in their academic work. Students of all ages need forums for student discourse, critical questioning, and debate. It is important for teachers to understand that their goal is not only to dispense knowledge but also to help equip students with self-regulated strategies that will provide them with the tools necessary for becoming independent thinkers and learners for life. Many reform efforts in mathematics, reading, and science are focused on helping students to become strategic learners and problem solvers.

Schunk (1984) has shown that as students improve their SRL skills, they develop a greater sense of competence, which leads to increased persistence, higher levels of performance, and more intrinsic interest in learning. Teachers also need to convey the functional value of learning strategies for different types of tasks because less-skilled students often lack knowledge concerning when and why to apply certain learning strategies. In addition, research demonstrated that teacher feedback that links skill improvement to the use of specific strategies ("You are getting these problems correct because you are using the distributive property.") or to increased competency ("You're getting really good at solving these types of equations.") can result in a higher sense of efficacy (Schunk & Gunn, 1986). Overall, studies suggest that young people will develop strong self-efficacy beliefs and engage in more self-regulatory strategies when teachers stress the value of learning strategies for improving their abilities and for overcoming learning difficulties.

Much more attention needs to be focused on changing the masculine image of science and mathematics and the feminine image of reading and writing. School instructional activities may play a role in reinforcing these patterns (Meece & Scantlebury, 2006). For example, some researchers have speculated that curriculum activities and materials in literacy tend to be more aligned with the learning interests and preferences of girls than those of boys (Brozo, 2002; Connell, 1996). Other researchers suggested that whole-class lessons at the middle and high school levels tend to be dominated by boys (Parsons, Kaczala, & Meece et al., 1982; Tobin & Garnett, 1987). Girls tend to respond more negatively than boys to competitive learning conditions (Eccles, 1994). In contrast, girls have more positive perceptions of their abilities and expectations for success in mathematics classrooms where individualized or cooperative learning is the primary mode of instruction (Parsons, Kaczala et al., 1982). Thus, it is important for teachers to use a mix of curriculum materials and teaching approaches to avoid biasing the learning environment of the classroom in favor of one gender over the other.

Finally, it is critical to avoid gender stereotypes when making judgments of students' interests and competencies. Some evidence suggests that teachers overestimate girls' effort in mathematics, which may lead girls to attribute their successes more to effort than to ability (Madon et al., 1998). Research suggests that students of all ages are quite skilled at interpreting messages they receive from teachers about their abilities (Weinstein, 1989). Teachers' expectations function as self-fulfilling prophecies, affecting students' self-concepts of ability, motivation, and academic performance (Weinstein & McKown, 1998). For these reasons, it is important for teachers to form accurate perceptions of their students' abilities based on the students' behavior and performance in the classroom rather than preconceived ideas about male and female abilities.

Significant reforms have taken place in mathematics and science teaching over the last decade. These efforts involve increasing the use of inquiry, problem solving, group learning, and authentic tasks in the classroom. It is anticipated that reform efforts will have positive benefits for both boys and girls. At present, it is not clear how these reform efforts are helping both boys and girls to develop confidence in their mathematics and science abilities. Teachers need to be strong advocates for program evaluations that examine gender differences in a range of different educational outcomes, including self-efficacy beliefs and motivation.

Finally, this review documented important gender differences in students' reported use of self-regulation that has not received much attention in previous research. Given gender differences in efficacy and competency beliefs, it is not clear why boys and girls are reporting differential use of SRL strategies. These findings are inconsistent with research showing positive links between self-efficacy and SRL (Schunk & Pajares, 2002). Perhaps boys are reporting less cognitive effort than girls to maintain high perceptions of ability or to disguise low ability in subject areas traditionally viewed as a masculine domain (Meece & Jones, 1996). On the other hand, girls may report more cognitive effort than boys on some learning tasks to compensate for lower levels of efficacy and confidence. For both boys and girls, gendered patterns of self-regulation have important consequences. Boys may not be working up to their fullest potential, whereas girls' efforts can lead them to experience disappointment and distress when they do not do well (Pomerantz, Altermatt, & Saxon, 2002). Also, as mentioned, research indicated that teachers are more likely to attribute girls' successes to effort and hard work rather than ability (Q. Li, 1999; Maddon et al., 1998). These attributions help to maintain engagement but are likely to undermine expectations for success as learning tasks become more challenging (Eccles et al., 1983; Parsons et al., 1984). Gender differences in how students approach and respond to achievement activities need further attention and examination.

REFERENCES

Ablard, K. E., & Lipschultz, R. E. (1998). Self-regulated learning in high-achieving students: Relations to advanced reasoning, achievement goals, and gender. *Journal of Educational Psychology, 90*, 94–101.

Alexander, P. A., & Judy, J. E. (1988). The interaction of domain-specific and strategic knowledge in academic performance. *Review of Educational Research, 58*, 375–404.

Ames, C. (1992). Classrooms: Goals, structures, and student motivation. *Journal of Educational Psychology, 84*, 261–271.

Ames, C., & Archer, J. (1988). Achievement goals in the classroom: Student learning strategies and motivation processes. *Journal of Educational Psychology, 80,* 260–267.

Anderman, E. M., & Young, A. J. (1994). Motivation and strategy use in science: Individual differences and classroom effects. *Journal of Research in Science Teaching, 31,* 811–831.

Bandura, A. (1986). *Social foundations of thought and action: A social cognitive theory.* Englewood Cliffs, NJ: Prentice Hall.

Bandura, A., Barbaranelli, C., Caprara, V. G., & Pastorelli, C. (2001). Self-efficacy beliefs as shapers of children's aspirations and career trajectories. *Child Development, 72,* 187–206.

Boekaerts, M., & Niemivirta, M. (2000). Self-regulated learning: Finding a balance between learning goals and ego-protective goals. In M. Boekaerts, P. R. Pintrich, & M. Zeidner (Eds.), *Handbook of self-regulation* (pp. 417–450). San Diego, CA: Academic Press.

Borkowski, J. G. (1996). Metacognition: theory or chapter heading? *Learning and Individual Differences, 8,* 391–402.

Bouffard-Bouchard, T., Parent, S., & Larivee, S. (1991). Influence of self-efficacy on self-regulation and performance among junior and senior high school age children. *International Journal of Behavioral Development, 14,* 153–164.

Brown, A. L. (1978). Knowing when, where, and how to remember: A problem of metacognition. In R. Glaser (Ed.), *Advances in Instructional Psychology* (Vol. 1). Hillsdale, NJ: Erlbaum.

Brozo, W. G. (2002). *To be a boy, to be a reader: Engaging teen and preteen boys in active literacy.* Newark, DE: International Reading Association.

Bussey, K., & Bandura, A. (1999). Social cognitive theory of gender development and differentiation. *Psychology Review, 106,* 676–713.

Carver, C. S., & Scheier, M. F. (1990). Origins and functions of positive and negative affects: A control-process view. *Psychological Review, 97,* 19–35.

Connell, R. W. (1996). Teaching the boys: New research on masculinity, and gender strategies for schools. *Teachers College Record, 98,* 206.

Duckworth, A. L., & Seligman, M. (2006). Self-discipline gives girls the edge: Gender in self-discipline, grades, and achievement test scores. *Journal of Educational Psychology, 98,* 198–208.

Dweck, C. S. (1986). Motivational processes affecting learning. *American Psychologist, 41,* 1040–1048.

Dweck, C. S., & Elliot, E. S. (1983). Achievement motivation. In E. M. Hetherington (Ed.), *Handbook of child psychology. Volume 4: Socialization, personality, and social development* (pp. 643–691). New York: Wiley.

Dweck, C. S., & Reppucci, N. D. (1973). Learned helplessness and reinforcement responsibility in children. *Journal of Personality and Social Psychology, 25,* 109–116.

Eccles, J. S. (1994). Understanding women's educational and occupational choices: Applying the Eccles et al. model of achievement-related choices. *Psychology of Women Quarterly, 18,* 585–609.

Eccles, J. S., Adler, T. F., Futterman, R., Goff, S. B., Kaczala, C. M., & Meece, J. L. (1983). Expectancies, values and academic behaviors. In J. T. Spence (Ed.), *Achievement and achievement motives* (pp. 75–146). San Francisco: Freeman.

Eccles, J. S., & Harold, R. D. (1991). Gender differences in sport involvement: Applying the Eccles' expectancy-value model. *Journal of Applied Sport Psychology, 3,* 7–35.

Eccles, J. S., Wigfield, A., Harold, R. D., & Blumenfeld, P. (1993). Age and gender differences in children's self- and task perceptions during elementary school. *Child Development, 64,* 830–847.

Eccles, J. S., Wigfield, A., & Schiefele, U. (1998). Motivation to succeed. In W. Damon (Series Ed.) & N. Eisenberg (Volume Ed.), *Handbook of child psychology* (5th ed.). *Vol. 3: Social, emotional, and personality development* (pp. 1017–1095). New York: Wiley.

Eccles-Parsons, J., Adler, T. F., & Meece, J. L. (1984). Sex differences in achievement: A test of alternative theories. *Journal of Personality and Social Psychology, 46,* 26–43.

Elliot, A. J., & Church, M. A. (1997). A hierarchical model of approach and avoidance achievement motivation. *Journal of Personality and Social Psychology, 72,* 218–232.

Elliot, A. J., & Harackiewicz, J. M. (1996). Approach and avoidance achievement goals and intrinsic motivation: A mediational analysis. *Journal of Personality and Social Psychology, 70,* 461–475.

Elliot, E., & Dweck, C. (1988). Goals: An approach to motivation and achievement. *Journal of Personality and Social Psychology, 54,* 5–12.

Erikson, E. H. (1963). *Childhood and society.* New York: Norton.

Fenemma, E., & Peterson, P. (1985). Autonomous learning behavior: A possible explanation of gender-related differences in mathematics. In L. C. Wilkinson & C. B. Marrett (Eds.), *Gender-related differences in instruction* (pp. 17–35). New York: Academic Press.

Forgaz, H. J. (1995). Gender and the relationship between affective beliefs and perceptions of Grade 7 mathematics classroom learning environments. *Educational Studies in Mathematics, 28,* 153–173.

Forgaz, H., Leder, G., & Kloostersman, P. (2001). New perspectives on the gender stereotyping of mathematics. *Mathematics Thinking and Learning, 6,* 389–420.

Fredricks, J. A., & Eccles, J. S. (2002). Children's competence and value beliefs from childhood through adolescence: Growth trajectories in two male-sex-typed domains. *Developmental Psychology, 38,* 519–533.

Frieze, I. H., Whitley, B. E., Hanusa, B. H., & McHugh, M. C. (1982). Assessing the theoretical models for sex differences in causal attributions for success and failure. *Sex Roles, 8,* 333–343.

Graham, S., & Golan, S. (1991). Motivational influences on cognition: Task involvement, ego involvement, and depth of information processing. *Journal of Educational Psychology, 83,* 187–196.

Greene, B. A., DeBacker, T. K., Ravindran, B., & Krows, A. J. (1999). Goals, values, and beliefs as predictors of achievement and effort in high school mathematics classes. *Sex roles: A Journal of Research, 40,* 421–458.

Hackett, G. (1985). The role of mathematics self-efficacy in the choice of math-related majors of college women and men: A path analysis. *Journal of Counseling Psychology, 32,* 47–56.

Harackiewicz, J. M., Barron, K. E., Pintrich, P. R., Elliot, A. J., & Thrash, T. (2002). Revision of achievement goal theory: Necessary and illuminating. *Journal of Educational Psychology, 94,* 638–645.

Hyde, S., Fenemma, E., Ryan, M., Frost, L. A., & Hopp, C. (1990). Gender comparisons of mathematics attitudes and affect: A meta-analysis. *Psychology of Women Quarterly, 14,* 299–324.

Jacobs, J. E. (1991). Influence of gender stereotypes on parent and child mathematics attitudes. *Journal of Educational Psychology, 83,* 518–527.

Jacobs, J. E., & Eccles, J. S. (1992). The impact of mothers' gender-role stereotypic beliefs on mothers' and children's ability perceptions. *Journal of Personality and Social Psychology, 63,* 932–944.

Jacobs, J. E., Lanza, S., Osgood, D. W., Eccles, J. S., & Wigfield, A. (2002). Changes in children's self-competence and values: Gender and domain differences across Grades 1 though 12. *Child Development, 73,* 509–527.

Jussim, L., & Eccles, J. S. (1992). Teacher expectations II. Construction and reflection of student achievement. *Journal of Personality and Social Psychology, 63,* 947–961.

Kahle, J. B., & Meece, J. (1994). Research on gender issues in the classroom. In D. L. Gabel (Ed.), *Handbook of research on science teaching and learning* (pp. 1559–1610). New York: Macmillan.

Karoly, P. (1993). Mechanisms of self-regulation: A systems view. *Annual Review of Psychology, 44,* 23–52.

Keller, C. (2001). Effect of teachers' stereotyping on students' stereotyping of mathematics as a male domain. *The Journal of Social Psychology, 14*, 165–173.

Kloosterman, P. (1990). Attributions, performance following failure, and motivation in mathematics. In E. Fennema & G. C. Leder (Eds.), *Mathematics and gender* (pp. 96–127). New York: Teachers College Press.

Kuhl, J. (1985). From cognition to behavior: Perspectives for future research on action control. In J. Kuhl & J. Beckmann (Eds.), *Action control: From cognition to behavior.* Berlin: Springer-Verlag.

Kuhl, J., & Goschke, T. (1994). A theory of action control: mental subsystems, modes of control, and volitional conflict-resolution strategies. In J. Kuhl & J. Beckmann (Eds.), *Volition and personality: Action versus state orientation* (pp. 93–124). Seattle, WA: Hogrefe & Huber.

Lazarus, R. S., & Folkman, S. (1984). *Stress, appraisal, and coping.* New York: Springer.

Li, A. K. F., & Adamson, G. (1995). Motivational patterns related to gifted students' learning of mathematics, science and English: An examination of gender differences. *Journal for the Education of the Gifted, 18*, 284–297.

Li, Q. (1999). Teachers' beliefs and gender differences in mathematics: A review. *Educational Researcher, 41*, 63–76.

Lummis, M., & Stevenson, H. W. (1990). Gender differences in beliefs and achievement: A cross-cultural study. *Developmental Psychology, 26*, 254–263.

Madon, S., Jussim. L., Keiper, S., Eccles, J., Smith, A., & Palumbo, P. (1998). The accuracy and power of sex, social class, and ethnic stereotypes: A naturalistic study in person perception. *Personality and Social Psychology Bulletin, 24*, 1304–1318.

McHugh, M. C., Frieze, I. H., & Hanusa, B. H. (1982). Attributions and sex differences in achievement: Problems and new perspectives. *Sex Roles, 8*, 467–479.

Meece, J. L. (2006). Introduction to special issue. Explaining women's math and science related career choices at the end of the 20th century: Large scale and longitudinal studies from four nations. In H. M. G. Watt & J. S. Eccles (Eds.), *Educational research and evaluation, 12*, 297–304 .

Meece, J., Anderman, E., & Anderman, L. (2006). Classroom goal structure, student motivation, and academic achievement. *Annual Review of Psychology* (Vol. 57, pp. 487–503). Chippewa Falls, WI: Annual Reviews.

Meece, J., Blumenfeld, P. C., & Hoyle, R. (1988). Students' goal orientations and cognitive engagement in classroom activities. *Journal of Educational Psychology, 80,* 514–523.

Meece, J. L., Eccles (Parsons), J. S., Kaczala, C., Goff, S. B., & Futterman, R. (1982). Sex differences in math achievement: Toward a model of academic choice. *Psychology Bulletin, 91,* 324–348.

Meece, J. L., & Jones, M. G. (1996). Gender differences in motivation and strategy use in science: Are girls rote learners? *Journal of Research in Science Teaching, 33,* 393–404.

Meece, J. L., & Miller, S. D. (2001). A longitudinal analysis of elementary school students' achievement goals in literacy activities. *Contemporary Educational Psychology, 26,* 454–480.

Meece, J. L., & Scantlebury, K. S. (2006). Gender and schooling: Progress and persistent barriers. In J. Worrell & C. Goodheart (Eds.), *Handbook of girls' and women's psychological health* (pp. 283–291). New York: Oxford University Press.

Middleton, M. J., & Midgley, C. (1997). Avoiding the demonstration of lack of ability: An underexplored aspect of goal theory. *Journal of Educational Psychology, 89,* 710–718.

Neber, H., & Schommer-Aikins, M. (2002). Self-regulated learning with highly gifted students: The role of cognitive, motivational, epistemological, and environmental variables. *High Abilities Studies, 13,* 59–74.

Nicholls, J. G. (1984). Achievement motivation: Conception of ability, subjective experience, task choice, and performance. *Psychological Review, 91,* 328–346.

Nolen, S. B. (1988). Reasons for studying: Motivational orientations and study strategies. *Cognition and Instruction, 5,* 269–287.

Pajares, F. (1996). Self-efficacy beliefs in academic settings. *Review of Educational Research, 66,* 543–578.

Pajares, F., Britner, S. L., & Valiante, G. (2000). Relation between achievement goals and self-beliefs of middle school students in writing and science. *Contemporary Educational Psychology, 25,* 406–422.

Pajares, F., & Graham, L. (1999). Self-efficacy, motivation constructs, and mathematics performance of entering middle school students. *Contemporary Educational Psychology, 24,* 124–139.

Pajares, F., Miller, M. D., & Johnson, M. J. (1999). Gender differences in writing self-beliefs of elementary school students. *Journal of Educational Psychology, 91,* 50–61.

Pajares, F., & Valiante, G. (1997). Influence of self-efficacy on elementary students' writing. *Journal of Educational Research, 90,* 353–360.

Pajares, F., & Valiante, G. (2001). Gender differences in writing motivation and achievement of middle school students: A function of gender orientation? *Contemporary Educational Psychology, 26*, 366–381.

Pajares, F., & Valiante, G. (2002). Students' self-efficacy in their self-regulated learning stages: A developmental perspective. *Psychologia, 45*, 211–221.

Paris, S. G., & Byrnes, J. P. (1989). The constructivist approach to self-regulation and learning in the classroom. In B. J. Zimmerman & D. H. Schunk (Eds.), *Self-regulated learning and academic achievement: Theory, research, and practice* (pp. 169–200). New York: Springer-Verlag.

Parsons, J., Adler, T. F., & Kaczala, C. M. (1982). Socialization of achievement attitudes and beliefs: Parental influences. *Child Development, 53*, 322–339.

Parsons, J. E., Adler, T., & Meece, J. L. (1984). Sex differences in achievement: A test of alternate theories. *Journal of Personality and Social Psychology, 46*, 26–43.

Parsons, J. E., Kaczala, C., & Meece, J. L. (1982). Socialization of achievement attitudes and beliefs: Classroom influences. *Child Development, 53*, 322–339.

Parsons, J. E., Meece, J. L., Adler, T. F., & Kaczala, C. M. (1982). Sex differences in attributions and learned helplessness. *Sex Roles, 8*, 421–432.

Patrick, H., Ryan, A. M., & Pintrich, P. R. (1999). The differential impact of extrinsic and mastery goal orientations on males' and females' self-regulated learning. *Learning and Individual Differences, 11*, 153–172.

Pintrich, P. R. (2000a). Multiple goals, multiple pathways: The role of goal orientation in learning and achievement. *Journal of Educational Psychology, 92*, 544–555.

Pintrich, P. R. (2000b). The role of goal orientation in self-regulated learning. In M. Boekaerts, P. R. Pintrich, & M. Zeidner (Eds.), *Handbook of self-regulation* (pp. 451–502). San Diego, CA: Academic Press.

Pintrich, P. R., & De Groot, E. V. (1990). Motivational and self-regulated learning components of classroom academic performance. *Journal of Educational Psychology, 82*, 33–40.

Pintrich, P. R., & Schrauben, B. (1992). Students' motivational beliefs and their cognitive engagement in classroom academic tasks. In D. H. Schunk & J. L. Meece (Eds.), *Student perceptions in the classroom* (pp. 149–183). Hillsdale, NJ: Erlbaum.

Pintrich, P. R., & Schunk, D. H. (2002). *Motivation in education. Theory, research, and applications* (2nd ed.). Columbus, OH: Merrill Prentice Hall.

Pokay, P., & Blumenfeld, P. C. (1990). Predicting achievement early and late in the semester: The role of motivation and use of learning strategies. *Journal of Educational Psychology, 82*, 41–50.

Pomerantz, E., Altermatt, E. R., & Saxon, J. L. (2002). Making the grade but feeling distressed: Gender differences in academic performance and internal distress. *Journal of Educational Psychology, 94,* 396–404.

Puustinen, M., & Pulkkinen, L. (2001). Models of self-regulated learning: A review. *Scandinavian Journal of Educational Research, 45,* 269–286.

Ridley, D., & Novak, J. (1983). Sex-related differences in high school science and mathematics enrollments: Do they give males a critical headstart toward science- and math-related careers? *Alberta Journal of Educational Research, 29,* 308–318.

Roeser, R. W., Midgley, C., & Urdan, T. C. (1996). Perceptions of the school psychological environment and early adolescents' psychological and behavioral functioning in school: The mediating role of goals and belonging. *Journal of Educational Psychology, 88,* 408–422.

Ruble, D. N., & Martin, C. L. (1998). Gender development. In W. Damon (Series Ed.) & N. Eisenberg (Vol. Ed.), *Handbook of child psychology: Vol 3. Social, emotional, and personality development* (pp. 993–1016). New York: Wiley.

Ruble, D. N., Martin, C. L., & Berenbaum, S. A. (2006). Gender development. In N. Eisenberg (Ed.), *Handbook of child psychology. Vol. 3: Social, emotional, and personality development* (6th ed., pp. 858–932). New York: Wiley.

Schunk, D. (1984). Self-efficacy perspective on achievement behavior. *Educational Psychologist, 19,* 45–58

Schunk, D. H. (1989). Self-efficacy and achievement behaviors. *Educational Psychology Review, 57,* 149–174.

Schunk, D. H. (1994). Self-regulation of self-efficacy and attributions in academic settings. In D. H. Schunk & B. J. Zimmerman (Eds.), *Self-regulation of learning and performance: Issues and educational applications* (pp. 75–99). Hillsdale, NJ: Erlbaum.

Schunk, D. H., & Gunn, T. P. (1986). Self-efficacy and skill development: Influences on task strategies and attributions. *Journal of Educational Research, 79,* 238–244.

Schunk, D. H., & Meece, J. L. (2006). Self-efficacy development in adolescents. In F. Pajares & T. Urdan (Eds.), *Self-efficacy beliefs in adolescents* (pp. 71–96). New York: Information Age Publishing.

Schunk, D. H., & Pajares, F. (2002). The development of academic self-efficacy. In A. Wigfield & J. S. Eccles (Eds.), *Development of achievement motivation* (pp. 16–31). New York: Academic Press.

Schunk, D. H., & Zimmerman, B. J. (1994). *Self-regulation of learning and performance: Issues and educational applications.* Hillsdale, NJ: Erlbaum.

Schunk, D. H., & Zimmerman, B. J. (2006). Competence and control beliefs: Distinguishing the means and ends. In P. A. Alexander & P. H. Winne (Eds.), *Handbook of Educational Psychology* (2nd ed., pp. 349–368). Mahwah, NJ: Erlbaum.

Sternberg, R. J. (1985). *Beyond IQ. A triarchic theory of human intelligence.* Cambridge, U.K.: Cambridge University Press.

Stetsenko, A., Little, T. D., Gordeeva, T., Grasshof, M., & Oettingen, G. (2000). Gender effects in children's beliefs about school performance: A cross cultural study. *Child Development, 71,* 517–527.

Stipek, D., & Gralinski, J. H. (1996). Children's beliefs about intelligence and school performance. *Journal of Educational Psychology, 88,* 397–407.

Stipek, D. J., & Kowalski, P. (1989). Learned helplessness in task-orienting versus performance-orienting testing conditions. *Journal of Educational psychology, 81,* 384–391.

Tartre, L. A., & Fenemma, E. (1995). Mathematics achievement and gender: A longitudinal study of selected cognitive and affective variables [Grades 6–12]. *Educational Studies in Mathematics, 28,* 199–217.

Tiedemann, J. (2000). Parents' gender stereotypes and teachers' beliefs are predictors of children's concept of their mathematical ability in elementary school. *Journal of Educational Psychology, 92,* 144–151.

Tobin, K., & Garnett, P. (1987). Gender related differences in science activities. *Science Education, 71,* 91.

Urdan, T., Midgley, C., & Anderman, E. M. (1998). The role of classroom goal structure in students' use of self-handicapping strategies. *American Educational Research Journal, 35,* 101–135.

Weinstein, R. (1989). Perception of classroom processes and student motivation: Children's view of self-fulfilling prophecies. In C. Ames & R. Ames (Eds.), *Research on motivation in education: Vol 3. Goals and cognitions* (pp. 187–221). New York: Academic Press.

Weinstein, R. S., & McKown, C. (1998). Expectancy effects in "context": Listening to the voices of students and teachers. In J. Brophy (Ed.), *Advances in research on teaching. Vol. 7: Expectations in the classroom.* Greenwich, CT: JAI Press.

Whitley, B. E. J. (1997). Gender differences in computer-related attitudes and behavior: A meta-analysis. *Computers in Human Behavior, 13,* 1–22.

Wigfield, A., & Eccles, J. S. (2000). Expectancy-value theory of achievement motivation. *Contemporary Educational Psychology, 25,* 68–81.

Wigfield, A., Eccles, J. S., & Pintrich, P. R. (1996). Development between the ages of 11 and 25. In R. C. Calfee, & D. C. Berliner (Eds.), *Handbook of educational psychology* (pp. 148–185). New York: Prentice Hall International.

Wigfield, A., Eccles, J. S., Suk Yoon, K., Harold, R. D., Arbreton, A. J. A., Freedman-Doan, C., et al. (1997). Change in children's competence beliefs and subjective task values across the elementary school years: A 3-year study. *Journal of Educational Psychology, 89,* 451–469.

Willingham, W. W., & Cole, N. S. (1997). *Gender and fair assessment.* Mahwah, NJ: Erlbaum.

Winne, P. H., & Hadwin, A. F. (1998). Studying as self-regulated learning. In D. J. Hacker & J. Dunlosky (Eds.), *Metacognition in educational theory and practice* (pp. 277–304). Mahwah, NJ: Erlbaum.

Wirt, J., Choy, S., Rooney, P., Provasnik, S., Sen, A., & Tobin, R. (2004). *The condition of education 2004.* Washington, DC: U.S. Department of Education.

Wolleat, P. L., Pedro, J. D., Becker, A. D., & Fennema, E. (1980). *Sex differences in cognitive functioning: Developmental issue.* New York: Academic Press.

Yee, D. K., & Eccles, J. S. (1988). Parent perceptions and attributions for children's math achievement. *Sex Roles, 19,* 317–333.

Zeldin, A. L., & Pajares, F. (2000). Against the odds: Self-efficacy beliefs of women in mathematical, scientific, and technological careers. *American Educational Research Journal, 37,* 215–246.

Zimmerman, B. J. (1989). A social cognitive view of self-regulated learning. *Journal of Educational Psychology, 81,* 329–339.

Zimmerman, B. J. (2000). Attaining self-regulation: a social cognitive perspective. In M. Boekaerts, P. R. Pintrich, & M. Zeidner (Eds.), *Handbook of self-regulation* (pp. 13–39). San Diego, CA: Academic Press.

Zimmerman, B. J. (2002). Becoming a self-regulated learner: An overview. *Theory Into Practice, 41,* 64–72.

Zimmerman, B. J., & Bandura, A. (1994). Impact of self-regulatory influences on writing course attainment. *American Educational Research Journal, 31,* 845–862.

Zimmerman, B. J., & Kitsantas, A. (2005). The hidden dimension of personal competence: Self-regulated learning and practice. In A. Elliot & C. S. Dweck (Eds.), *Handbook of competence and motivation* (pp. 509–526). New York: Guilford Press.

Zimmerman, B. J., & Martinez-Pons, M. (1986). Development of a structured interview for assessing student use of self-regulated learning strategies. *American Educational Research Journal, 23,* 614–628.

Zimmerman, B. J., & Martinez-Pons, M. (1990). Student differences in self-regulated learning: Relating grade, sex, and giftedness to self-efficacy and strategy use. *Journal of Educational Psychology, 82,* 51–59.

15

The Motivational Roles of Cultural Differences and Cultural Identity in Self-Regulated Learning

Dennis M. McInerney

INTRODUCTION

Theories of motivation and learning are developed to understand and manage individual and group engagement in activities specifically related to work, social, and educational domains. Historically, most theories of motivation and learning were developed in Westernized developed nations, particularly the United States and Europe (Heckhausen, 1991). Theories of learning and motivation house within them core values reflective of the societies and cultures in which the theories are developed. This is natural as the essential elements of human learning and motivation in specific contexts reflect deeply embedded cultural values, and the theoreticians are themselves a product of these contexts. When motivational and learning theories are transported to new cultural and social settings to understand and manage individual and group behavior, there might be a mismatch. In other words, core values in diverse groups, as well as the meaning of the situations and contexts in which core values are salient, might vary to such an extent that they make the application, analysis, and practical outcomes of the theories problematic (see, e.g., Boykin et al., in press; Boykin & Bailey, 2000; Boykin, Tyler, & Miller, 2005; Delgado-Gaitan, 1994; Deyhle & LeCompte, 1994; Hollins, 1996; Rubie, Townsend, & Moore, 2004; Trueba, 1993). As Tyler, Anderman, and Haines (2006) put it, "What can be currently gleaned from

the research literature on culturally relevant pedagogy and achievement is when classroom instruction and activities do not incorporate
or reflect the value-laden, culture-based behavioral preferences and
tendencies of ethnic minority students, school difficulties emerge"
(p. 66). Ferrari and Mahalingam (1998) believed that the manner in
which learners meaningfully engage in school and other educational
settings and benefit from the experiences presented reflects the cultural environment in which they are socialized. Personal, social, and
cultural histories shape student engagement. These histories include
gender, class, race, religion, and family.

Curricula, learning activities, and the means used to stimulate
student engagement are therefore set in social, political, religious,
and cultural contexts that define what is acceptable and valued.
Within these social, cultural, religious, and political contexts individuals and groups seek success by participating in activities that
develop the skills and dispositions needed to excel in their cultural
and social milieu. Therefore, what defines academic engagement and
success in one cultural and social milieu may not be the same as what
defines engagement and success in another. Engagement in learning
is therefore complex when viewed through sociocultural lenses, and
any attempt to describe this complexity in diverse cultural and social
settings without reference to sociocultural influences must necessarily be an oversimplification.

To evaluate the role culture plays in learning and motivation in
the context of theory, it is essential first to understand what culture
and cultural identity are. It is also essential to articulate clearly the
components of any theory such as self-regulated learning in the context of culture and cultural identity. In other words, what meanings do the elements of a theory such as self-regulated learning have
within a particular cultural framework? Finally, it is essential to
understand the potential impacts of culture and cultural differences
on learning, motivation, and self-regulation.

WHAT IS CULTURE?

Culture is one of those constructs that is defined in a multitude of
ways depending on theoretical perspectives. Often, it is ill defined
or not defined at all, even when used as an independent variable in
research. Culture may refer to material culture or subjective culture

(Triandis, 2002). *Culture,* from a subjective perspective, has been defined as the values, traditions, and beliefs that mediate the behaviors of a particular social group (Parsons, 2003). Subjective culture has also been defined as a society's characteristic way of perceiving its social environment (Triandis, 2002). Another definition of subjective culture is the "how and why we behave in certain ways, how we perceive reality, what we believe to be true, what we build and create, and what we accept as good and desirable" (Westby, 1993, p. 9). Embedded in these definitions of culture are values and belief systems that potentially influence academic task engagement and performance and can be used to benchmark the relevance of constructs (reflecting values) that are embedded within particular theoretical perspectives on motivation and learning. For example, subjective culture addresses issues such as beliefs, attitudes, norms, roles, and values, each of which would have implications for learning and motivation. Indeed, Schwartz (1992) listed 10 sets of values (self-direction, stimulation, hedonism, achievement, power, security, conformity, tradition, benevolence, and universalism), each of which potentially has an impact on academic behavior (Brickman, Miller, & McInerney, 2005; Liem, 2006).

Culture has increasingly been related to how individuals approach tasks and activities carried out in home, school, and work contexts (see, e.g., Cole, 1999; Tyler et al., 2006). Culture is often classified as individualistic/collectivist, modern/traditional, vertical/horizontal, Western, Confucian, and so on. Each of these classifications provides a template for comparing one group to another. The templates can also be used to evaluate the likely match between a theoretical perspective on learning or motivation and the cultural complexities of a particular society. Among values and cultural characteristics that may be considered in the context of motivation and learning theories are individualism, collectivism/interconnectedness, competition, time perspective, group orientation, help seeking, the nature of knowledge and who shares various levels of knowledge, spirituality, harmony, affect, responsibility, communal ownership vs. individual ownership, respect for elders, and active learning versus passive learning through observation. Questions that might be asked from a cultural perspective are as follows: What personal characteristics are to be developed as individuals are schooled? Is there an emphasis on children being obedient, quiet, and cordial or adventurous and active? What emphasis is placed on group versus individual responsibility or a person as responsible to self or to others? What emphasis is placed on valuing cognitive expertise over social expertise? Clearly, in some groups self-regulated behavior may include actively seeking new experiences, being adventurous, trying new skills, demonstrating individual expertise and responsibility, help seeking, and monitoring progress in these behaviors. Alternatively, self-regulation in other groups may include group orientation, doing things to support others, and showing deference to others. In other words, the interpersonal functioning knowledge to be acquired through self-regulatory processes might be different from one group to another.

By its nature, culture has embedded within it notions of self-regulation and self-regulated behavior for individuals to conform to the norms of their group to preserve and develop the culture. Therefore, cultural values and beliefs may have an impact on the nature of motivation and learning processes adopted generally and on self-regulatory processes specifically in particular groups (see, e.g., Eaton & Dembo, 1996; Liem, 2006; Park, 2000; Salili, Fu, Tong, & Tabatabai 2001). For example, Chinese society is characterized by social orientation and collectivism, and under the influence of Confucian philosophy, the Chinese place great importance on piety, hard work, and education. The Chinese believe that the best way to learn a subject is through repeated practice and memorization (Salili et al., 2001). Classrooms in China are highly structured and teacher centered, with students taking notes and listening carefully. Learning is assessed through numerous assignments and tests. Many other aspects of a Confucian-based approach to education would have an impact on the way in which self-regulation and other learning and motivational behaviors are constructed. A Western context for learning and motivation might be characterized by less concern for academic excellence as for overall education and less concern with testing. However, in the United States, for example, in light of the No Child Left Behind Act and state mandates for competency testing at different grades, this may be changing.

Religion and Culture

Religion and culture are closely allied (Siu, 1996). Among religions that potentially have an impact on learning, motivation, and self-regulation are Buddhism, Christianity, Hinduism, Sikkism, Islam, and animism. Although there is little available literature examining the relationship between religion and self-regulation in educational settings, more broadly based literature on Buddhism and Hinduism, for example, emphasizes self-management and self-control (de Silva, 2000). The importance of managing one's own behavior, including self-control, is emphasized in numerous places in Buddhist texts (de Silva, 2000). Within Buddhism, a number of self-control strategies are emphasized, such as anger control, stimulus control, and control of unwanted and intrusive cognitions, each of which could reasonably be argued to influence one's approach to learning (de Silva, 2000). Perhaps the clearest example of the relationship among religion, motivation, and self-regulation stems from the Protestant ethic. Max Weber (Weber, 1904, 1905) coined the term *Protestant ethic*, the key elements of which were diligence, punctuality, deferment of gratification, and primacy of the work domain (Rose, 1985). The close connection of Protestantism and economic progress under capitalism in comparison to societies that were predominantly Catholic suggests that the Protestant work ethic permeated the economic and labor systems of particular countries, and the notion of self-regulation and motivation to work was imbued in the citizens. Again, it is not a stretch to posit that there may still be today differences in the self-regulatory styles of students from predominantly strong and traditional Protestant backgrounds and those from predominantly strong and traditional Catholic backgrounds, although as Hill (1996) noted, the Protestant ethic diffused to much of the Western world generally, so differences between Christian groups have perhaps become blurred.

Confucianism, as indicated, although not a religion, also has a potential impact and is a predominant consideration in any examination of cross-cultural differences between Asian and Western groups. Min (1995), in a discussion of Asian Americans, illustrated how several cultural values emanating from Confucianism, intersecting with religious values, are common threads that tie all Asian American groups together: emphasis on educational achievement; shame as a behavioral influence; respect for authority; high regard for the elderly; the centrality of family relationships and responsibilities; self-control and restraint in emotional expression; group orientation; middle position virtue; and filial piety. Each of these values has a potential impact on motivation and self-regulated behavior in diverse cultural settings, and many have been implicated in the achievement of Asian students at school.

Cultural Identity

We are all familiar with the notion of self-identity, and there is a vast body of literature on this. There is also a growing body of literature on cultural identity. *Cultural identity* refers to one's incorporation of the cultural values, beliefs, and practices of one's ethnic group (Kronqvist, 1996; Phinney, 1990, 1991). In most instances, this is a relatively unconscious process; however, if individuals are part of one or more ethnic groups through mixed marriages or a minority ethnic group members within a larger dominant society, then the concept of cultural identity becomes more salient (Der-Karabetian & Ruiz, 1993; Pak, 2001; Phinney, 1990, 1991). It seems that one's cultural identity should have an impact on the way people are motivated and learn and any self-regulatory learning behaviors they might adopt. In the case of learners in diverse settings, there could be tensions among what is expected of them educationally, socially, and culturally. Research has been directed at examining the relationship between strength of cultural or ethnic identity and school achievement if the individual is part of an ethnic minority and if the individual is part of a majority indigenous group that is subjected to change agents through globalization, as with people in Papua and New Guinea. Clearly, one's cultural identity will moderate the nature of motivational and learning behavior in which one engages and, as I illustrate in this chapter, is implicated in the adoption or otherwise of self-regulatory learning behaviors.

SELF-REGULATED LEARNING

Self-regulated learning has been defined as self-generated thoughts, feelings, and actions for attaining educational goals that include such processes as planning and managing time; attending to and concentrating on instruction; organizing, rehearsing, and coding information; establishing a productive work environment; and using social resources effectively (see, e.g., Schunk, 2001). Self-regulation views learning as an activity that students do for themselves in a proactive way rather than as a covert event that happens to them reactively as a result of teaching experiences; they are self-starters (Corno, 1987; Schunk, 2001; Zimmerman, 2000, 2004). Students are self-regulated to the degree that they are metacognitively, motivationally, and behaviorally active participants in their own learning process (Zimmerman, 2000). Self-regulated students also monitor the effectiveness of their learning methods or strategies and respond to this feedback in a variety of adaptive ways. Because self-regulation is self-initiated, it also involves important motivational beliefs, such as self-efficacy, outcome expectations, task interest or valuing, a learning goal orientation, and self-satisfaction with one's learning and performance (Zimmerman, 2000, 2004).

The elements of self-regulation have been grouped into the *forethought phase* (including task analysis such as goal setting and strategic planning and self-motivation beliefs such as self-efficacy, outcome expectations, task interest and valuing, and goal orientation); the *performance phase* (including self-control and self-observation strategies); and the *self-reflection phase* (including self-judgment such as self-evaluation and causal attribution and self-reaction, including self-satisfaction and affect, and adaptive defensive mechanisms) (Zimmerman, 2004). Self-regulatory skills are acquired through social modeling, social guidance and feedback, and social collaboration. There are four key subprocesses: (a) attending to a model, (b) encoding the information for retention, (c) enacting the demonstrated responses motorically, and (d) motivating oneself to perform the modeled behaviors (Zimmerman, 2004). It is apparent from this brief overview of the theory that social factors reflected in the culture and the context of learning are important in learning self-regulatory skills, and that there is a close link between self-regulation and motivation (Zimmerman, 2004; see also Salili et al., 2001).

From a subjective culture perspective, we should be able to scrutinize self-regulated learning (Gutierrez & Rogoff, 2003). It should be a simple step to consider the social modeling elements of particular cultures and how these might have an impact on the nature and acquisition of self-regulatory skills. What is explicit and implicit in the self-regulatory model of motivation and learning? What are the core elements of self-regulated learning, and are these core elements universal? Zimmerman (2001) stated that, "The key issue defining learning as self-regulated is not whether it is socially isolated, but rather whether the learner displays personal initiative, perseverance, and adaptive skill pursuing it" (p. 1). It is in contrast to theories of learning that viewed the learner as reactive, that is, approaches to learning in which students were theorized not to initiate or substantially supplement experiences designed to educate themselves. Self-regulated learning theories assume that students can (a) personally improve their ability to learn through selective use of metacognitive and motivational strategies; (b) proactively select, structure, and even create advantageous learning environments; and (c) play a significant role in choosing the form and amount of instruction they need (Zimmerman, 2001). How well would this paradigm fit across cultures? Zimmerman and others (Zimmerman & Martinez-Pons, 1986, 1988; Zimmerman & Risemberg, 1997) outlined 14 self-regulated learning strategies that are used to guide cross-cultural research on self-regulation (see, e.g., Purdie, Hattie, & Douglas, 1996). These strategies are

1. Self-evaluation
2. Organizing and transforming (rearranging and restructuring instructional materials)
3. Goal setting and planning
4. Seeking information (from nonsocial sources such as a book)
5. Keeping records and monitoring
6. Environmental restructuring (rearranging the physical setting to make learning easier)
7. Self-consequating (arranging for rewards or punishment for success or failure)
8. Rehearsing and memorizing
9–11. Seeking assistance from peers, teachers, and adults
12–14. Reviewing tests, notes, and texts

Are there differences between cultural groups on these related to the values of the culture? What is emphasized? What is deemphasized? It would seem that there should be differences.

The Paradox of Self-Regulation across Cultures

The predominant paradigm of self-regulation is based on Western theorizing and research. This paradigm is frequently applied to other cultural groups to ascertain whether they are more or less self-regulating and how the level and nature of self-regulation relates to motivation and achievement outcomes. However, is it not possible that there are other paradigms of self-regulation that are reflective of diverse cultural values and beliefs? Within a particular cultural framework, self-regulation might involve behavior such as conformity, working toward preset goals determined by others, diligence, respect for information transferred through didactic teaching, memorization, and rote learning. Behavior outside this framework, such as challenging accepted wisdom, seeking alternative answers, seeking choice, setting personal goals, and utilizing diverse modes of learning, might be construed by teachers and parents as poorly regulated and cause problems for students within the classroom and beyond. Western research clearly demonstrates that when students are self-regulating (i.e., metacognitively, motivationally, and behaviorally active) participants in their own learning processes, they are more likely to achieve well. If these self-regulating characteristics are absent, then students are thought to be more likely to be poorly motivated and underachieving. However, if students from a Confucian-derived educational background engage in learning behavior that seems antithetical to the Western model, yet appear motivated and achievement oriented, are they not self-regulated? The issue is whether students working within alternative paradigms of self-regulation are indeed motivated and achieve effectively. The research literature on this seems to suggest that both possibilities exist. Some authors argued that students from cultures that are embedded in traditional values such as collectivism or Confucianism do very well provided the educational environment matches their learning approaches. There is, indeed, compelling evidence of the superior academic achievement for Asian students as compared with Western students, particularly in mathematics and science (see Stevenson & Lee, 1996, for a review).

However, some authors argued strenuously that when cultures externally control and compel students to engage in particular learning experiences, compulsion leaves little room for self-regulation, and that students are shortchanged in development of effective cognitive skills that lead them to be productive, creative, and independent learners (see Ho, Peng, & Chan, 2001a, 2001b; Liu & Littlewood, 1997; Siu, 1996). In investigative research on Confucian eritage education, Ho et al. (2001a, 2001b) reported a series of characteristics of students from Confucian heritage-based educational institutions; these characteristics are, in their view, the antithesis of self-regulated characteristics. Among these are lack of autonomy in making decisions, emphasis on ranking and testing, and passivity in learning. In their description of Chinese students (Ho et al., 2001b), nothing could be further from the description of a self-regulated learner from a Western perspective:

> They expect their teachers to instruct, and expect themselves to be instructed—"spoon fed." They rely heavily on handouts and notes taken in lectures. ... Independence and initiative are lacking. Looking for direction and structure, students expect their teachers to give them explicit directions on what to study, what materials they should read and when to read them, and what tasks or assignments they should complete and how to do them. They feel uneasy about unstructured situations or freedom of choice. ... They are hesitant to ask questions and do not participate actively in class. (pp. 226–227)

However, apart from self-regulation or lack of self-regulation, there are other forces that contribute to the academic achievement of Asian background students. The Chinese and Japanese cultures, for example, place exceptional importance on education and effort, parents set stringent achievement standards, and the continuing filial piety of children motivates them to fulfill their parents' ambitions for them. Such a set of features may contribute to an attitude of self-criticism, in contrast to the Western attitude of education as self-enhancement (see, e.g., Kitayama, Markus, Matsumoto, & Norasakkunkit, 1997; see also Eaton & Dembo, 1996). So, in structured situations and with the social/cultural forces outlined playing a part, students achieve well. These students may not reveal high levels of self-regulated behavior as reflected in Western models of self-regulation. It is also possible that when these students are placed in less-structured situations (such as in an alternative educational environment emphasizing choice, problem solving, or individual goal setting or in an overseas university system), they may not achieve highly (see, e.g., Kurman, 2001).

Relationship among Culture, Motivation, and Self-Regulation

I have described elements of culture and cultural identity and of self-regulated learning. What might be the relationships among culture, motivation, and self-regulation? Is the nature of self-regulation for learning the same across cultures? What are the cultural determinants of self-regulatory behavior, such as family, religion, and sense of the future? Does one self-regulate to preserve the past, understand and operate in the present, or to set a future? Self-regulated learning is also goal directed. If the theory is correct, then appropriate goal setting is essential to effective learning in all cultures. What is the nature of goal setting in different cultures? Self-regulated learning is also associated with mastery goals. Which goals are most salient for individuals from different cultural groups? It is necessary to unpack the essential elements of the theory that might have cultural meaning, taking each of the elements of the theory listed and relating them to cultural values salient in particular cultural communities (Ladson-Billings, 2001). In this regard, a brief examination of emics and etics in cross-cultural research is required and useful.

Emics and Etics and Self-Regulation

The emic-etic distinction relates to two goals of cross-cultural research (Headland, Pike, & Harris, 1990). The first goal is to document valid principles that describe behavior in any one culture based on constructs that the people themselves perceive as meaningful and important. This is referred to as an *emic analysis.* The second goal of cross-cultural psychology is to abstract from sets of data from diverse cultures those features of behavior that appear to be universal. This is referred to as an *etic analysis* (see, e.g., Brislin, 1980; Headland et al., 1990). The concept of self-regulation appears to have appeal and usefulness as an etic construct. Use of this construct potentially allows for linking studies across cultures to examine the ways in which students self-regulate in learning situations and how self-regulation relates to effective achievement. However, a danger in this is that original theory and research developing the self-regulatory paradigm from one cultural perspective may be used as a template for self-regulation research in outside cultures or situations without exploration of the cultural specifics of self-regulation. When such an imposition of a theoretical and research template occurs, potentially valuable information on self-regulation is lost. Therefore, although the concept of self-regulation is a useful and important etic, to understand fully its workings in various cultures the emic dimension must be taken into account. As I examine, the emics of self-regulation have often been ignored in self-regulation research carried out in diverse cultures. Figure 15.1 illustrates the

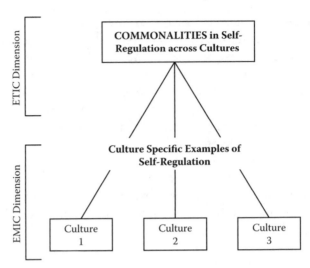

Figure 15.1 A search for common elements by examining the subjective meaning of self-regulation cross culturally.

combined emic-etic approach that should be used in any investigation of self-regulation.

REVIEW OF RESEARCH

I have considered some issues that I think are important in our analysis of the potential relationships among culture, cultural identity, motivation, and self-regulation. In this section, I review empirical literature dealing with cultural differences, cultural identity, motivation, and self-regulation to tease out what are the salient issues that cross-cultural researchers address; how they operationalize culture and cultural differences, cultural identity, motivation, and self-regulation; and what has been found regarding the interrelationships of these across cultures.

Studies

Olaussen and Bråten (1999) suggested that cross-cultural research on self-regulated learning still lacks a well-developed conceptual framework for understanding cultural differences in the use of self-regulated learning strategies. They believed that the uncritical use of American-made principles of strategy instruction to help students become more self-regulated learners may not necessarily meet with success in other countries because diverse countries differ in learning contexts, as well as in values and beliefs about education. Olaussen and Bråten illustrated how cultural differences influence the value placed on education (by this they mean schooling), the relative importance of ability and effort in achievement, and the importance of social support, most particularly that of parents and peers. Each of these three factors has been implicated in effective self-regulated learning. Aspects of self-regulated learning, such as strategy use, are therefore, according to Olaussen and Bråten, likely to be related to students' cultural membership. To examine this, Olaussen and Bråten studied strategic learning among Norwegian college students using the Learning and Study Strategies Inventory (LASSI). Although on most scales there was considerable similarity between the Norwegian sample and the U.S. norming sample, they found a difference on the motivation and attitude subscales that reflected potential cultural differences. They suggested that Norwegian students tend to value education somewhat more than American students; American students may have a stronger belief in the value of effort than the Norwegian students. However, the authors concluded that their research confirmed American theory and research and indicated that principles of self-regulated learning, specifically study strategies covered by LASSI, generalized to their Norwegian sample.

Purdie and Hattie (1996) investigated whether differences in self-regulated learning exist among groups of students from Australian and Japanese backgrounds and the applicability of a Western model of learning to students from different cultures. The authors utilized a modified version of the 14 categories of self-regulated learning strategies originally developed by Zimmerman and Martinez-Pons (1986), which was expanded to 24 categories on the basis of the analysis of the responses to the Student Learning Survey. Purdie and Hatties's analysis indicated two self-regulation strategies that appear to be salient for each of the groups in the study: self-checking and environmental structuring. However, there were many differences between the groups, with, for example, the Australian group reporting more other-checking, self-testing, outlining and drafting, organizing notes and files, goal setting and planning, keeping records, using self-consequences, seeking teacher assistance, reviewing notes, and reviewing tests and other completed work. The Japanese students reported more memorizing and reviewing textbooks.

Purdie et al. (1996), in a further comparative study of self-regulation, found that although Japanese students utilized memorization and rehearsal strategies more often than their Australian counterparts, they were far less likely than the Australian students to view learning as memorizing and reproducing but rather as a process of understanding, and their use of memorization and rehearsal was related to this. There is therefore a need for researchers to consider carefully the ramifications of what is meant by particular learning styles across cultures. Rote memorization is often considered a low-level learning strategy in Western contexts, and Asian students have often been criticized as surface learners because they seem to utilize this strategy more frequently than Western students. In this example, memorization was a high-level self-regulatory technique used to *enhance* understanding. Purdie et al. argued that this nexus between memorization and understanding flows from Confucian conceptions of teaching and learning. Following from this, the notion of learning also appears to be broader for the Japanese students than the Australian students in this study. Specifically, Australian students saw learning in relation to studying or performing academic tasks in classrooms. Japanese students considered learning more than classroom based and including notions of personal fulfillment, reflecting thereby a greater concurrence between the culture of the school and that of the society in general.

The issue of memorization and the role it plays in self-regulatory behavior seems to be a recurring theme in a number of research articles. For example, Salili et al. (2001) compared the effect of culture and context of learning on student motivation and self-regulation by examining whether particular components from the Patterns of Adaptive Learning Study (PALS) showed differences among three groups (Hong Kong [HK] Chinese, Chinese Canadians, and Canadian students of European origin) based on hypotheses related to Confucian versus Canadian backgrounds. They found that HK students scored lower on self-regulation, cognitive strategies, and learning goal orientation and higher on memorization than both groups of Canadian students. HK Chinese also spent significantly more time studying, were more anxious, and felt less competent than the other two groups. Self-regulation and cognitive strategies correlated positively with effort, self-efficacy, and learning goal for the three groups of students. The Canadian Chinese group fell between the HK Chinese and Canadian students on many of the measures, indicating a transitional effect as they become acculturated to Western values within school settings. The study, along with that of Urdan and Giancarlo (2000), discussed next, illustrates the impact of culture and levels of acculturation on motivation and self-regulation and the changing face of self-regulation as individuals become more acculturated in Western educational settings.

In a study by Urdan and Giancarlo (2000) of the relationship among generational status (recently arrived migrant, first-generation migrant, and third- or more generation migrant), family obligation and relatedness, personal goals, and goal structures on self-regulation and achievement, the primary interest was whether personal goal orientations (mastery, performance approach, and performance avoidance) and perceived classroom goal structures were associated with self-regulation and achievement in high school English classrooms differently depending on the generational status of the student and the degree to which students felt a sense of obligation to their family. Urdan and Giancarlo speculated that a student's generational status and sense of family obligation and relatedness would moderate the effects of personal goals and goal structures on self-regulation and achievement in English. The authors found that high achievers were more self-regulating than lower achievers, and students with strong mastery goal orientations, a strong perception of a mastery goal structure, and strong family obligation were more self-regulating than those low in these three variables. The important point to emerge from this study from the point of view of this chapter is the importance of considering family and cultural values in hypothesizing about self-regulated behavior.

Throughout a number of the studies reviewed in this chapter, the salience of family to self-regulation varied across cultural groups. For example, Gorrell, Hwang, and Chung (1996) examined the similarities and differences between Korean and American students in their reported use of self-regulated learning strategies (self-evaluation, goal setting, planning, seeking information, self-monitoring, environmental restructuring, rehearsing and memorizing, seeking peer assistance, and seeking teacher or adult assistance) when presented with school and outside-school scenarios. Their results showed that although both American and Korean students exhibited relatively high levels of self-regulation, Korean children had higher self-regulation scores on non-school-based problems than American children, but that American children had higher self-regulation scores for school-based problems. The authors speculated that the reason for the Korean students showing higher self-regulation for non-school-based problems was caused by cultural differences in the homes and the schools. They suggested that Korean parents expected their children to achieve in a wide variety of activities even before going to school, which may lead them to having more experiences in planning and organizing problem-solving activities out of school. Conversely, American children, they suggested, tended to experience more independent activity in the classroom than their Korean counterparts, thus gaining greater opportunities to engage in self-regulated problem solving in school. The Korean students also indicated that in out-of-school activities they applied more direct effort or active participation, such as studying at home, whereas the American students indicated more often that they would seek help from others. Gorrell et al. (1996) suggested Korean students appeared more focused on individual accomplishments and task-oriented behavior than the American students, who appeared to rely more heavily on family support. However, as the authors noted, the differences were a matter of degree rather than kind, and more detailed investigation is necessary to examine these apparent differences.

In terms of personal self-regulation (Gorrell et al., 1996), there were considerable similarities in the reported use of strategies by cultural group. There were two differences noted. Regarding self-regulated strategies for completing homework, Korean students more frequently mentioned direct effort than American children; American children more frequently mentioned help seeking than Korean children. Regarding having special ways to improve study at home, Korean students mentioned active participation in learning more than American students; the American students again mentioned help seeking more frequently than Korean students.

In the context of a specific self-regulatory behavior (i.e., choosing between high or low levels of difficulty), Kurman (2001) found that there are cultural differences in self-regulation in achievement settings between Singaporeans and Israelis. This finding was hypothesized on the basis of the categorization of both countries on an individualist/collectivist dimension, specifically power distance, otherwise referred to as level of hierarchy or vertical collectivism within a culture. Low power distance cultures believe in a basic equality between people, whereas cultures with high power distance have a great deal of respect for different types of formal and social hierarchies. Low power distance cultures value and encourage initiative much more than do high power distance cultures. Kurman argued that it is reasonable to predict that in cultures with low power distance, people will be willing to take more chances and will try to cope with more risky, difficult assignments. Singapore was high in power distance; Israel was low. On the basis of this, Kurman assumed that Singaporeans would be conservative and choose lower levels of difficulty as compared to Israelis, and that this lower level may further restrict their self-regulation efficiency. This was indeed what the study demonstrated. Kurman concluded that self-regulation processes of Singaporeans in achievement settings, in comparison to Israelis, do not maximize their level of achievement. Specifically, in the context of this chapter, the author stated that, "A safe conclusion of the study is that self-regulation processes are highly affected by cultural norms that must be considered in any general discussion of self-regulation processes" (p. 501).

Self-Regulation and Self-Efficacy

Within the self-regulation paradigm, self-efficacy is considered a major factor related to achievement. Eaton and Dembo (1996, 1997) sought to investigate whether culturally influenced beliefs or self-efficacy beliefs better explained achievement motivation for Asian American and non-Asian students. Their study found that Asian American students reported significantly lower levels of situational self-efficacy beliefs than did their non-Asian counterparts. However, Asian students outperformed non-Asian students on the achievement task. The cultural belief fear of academic failure better explained achievement motivation for Asian Americans than did self-efficacy beliefs. In explaining the higher achievement of the Asian American students, Eaton and Dembo offered the view that their higher scores might not involve a difference in motivational behavior but in their willingness to comply to adult authority (teacher or researcher) or to school demands because of the authoritarian parenting styles of Asian parents. They suggested that the fear of academic failure stems from Asian American parental stress on academic success for their children, and that low performance elicits family criticism and shame. Therefore, parental pressure serves as one of the primary catalysts behind Asian American students' motivational behavior. Again, this would fit within the suggestion that these students are self-regulating through different dynamics that cause them to complete more of their homework, listen more to class instruction, and receive more positive feedback from instructors, all of which are self-regulatory in nature, and each relates positively to school performance. Within the self-regulation model, the motivational beliefs of outcome expectations would subsume fear of failure as well as personal benefits during the forethought phase. However, there has been little attention to fear of failure in self-regulation research, yet it may be salient to self-regulatory strategies for Asian students.

As indicated, self-efficacy is an important component of self-regulated learning. Klassen (2004) asked whether efficacy beliefs operate in the same way across cultures. In line with what I suggested, Klassen, quoting Fiske et al. (1998), stated that "many of the findings currently regarded as 'basic to ... psychology are a function of particular cultural frameworks.'" He stated that although extensive research has been devoted to the study of efficacy beliefs in education, most of the work has involved Western, typically American, participants, and that cross-cultural research can begin to clarify how different cultural beliefs and practices shape efficacy beliefs and help explain how efficacy beliefs might operate as a function of culture. Basing his study on the hypothesized differences in cultures on the individualist/collectivist typology, he investigated whether the appraisal of self-efficacy and self-efficacy sources (i.e., the source from which people derive their efficacy beliefs) are related to cultural dimensions, specifically those of Indo Canadian and Anglo Canadian students. He suggested that: "The self-oriented sources—past performance and emotional arousal—may be more highly valued among individualistic cultural groups, whereas the other—oriented dimensions of social persuasion and vicarious experience may be stronger influences among persons with collectivist leanings" (p. 732).

Among the findings of importance is that there were significant differences among the motivation variables of interest (self-efficacy, fear of failure, and perceived parental value of academics), with the Indo Canadian group significantly higher on each of these variables. For the four sources of self-efficacy, Anglo Canadians were higher on vicarious experience, and Indo Canadians were higher on social persuasion. There were no differences between the two groups for past performance or emotional arousal. The correlations between each of these four sources of efficacy and self-efficacy followed the same pattern for the two groups, with past performance most strongly correlated for each group. Self-efficacy was a relevant factor influencing performance for both cultural groups. But, and more importantly for purposes of this chapter, Klassen found that the South Asian Indo Canadian students viewed the world through a different cultural lens, with a stronger emphasis on social comparison and social hierarchy, and that this unique cultural perspective influenced the ways in which they were motivated to achieve and the ways in which their motivation beliefs were formed (p. 739). The Indo Canadian students displayed a more vertically oriented self in which hierarchy and status were emphasized and in which one's self was compared with other selves. For the Indo Canadians, the hierarchy-oriented group perceived parental value of academics was significantly higher than for the Anglo Canadian group, suggesting, as has been the case in the other reviewed research, that the salience of parents is more important in self-regulation-related areas for Asian groups than for Western background groups. Anglo Canadian students were less vertical or comparison oriented in outlook and more self-oriented in terms of both predictors of performance and predictors of self-efficacy.

Klassen (2004) argued that the Indo Canadian brand of self-efficacy is shaped much more strongly by others, with Punjabi Sikh students forming their confidence from their perceptions of how others are doing and what others tell them about their own abilities to achieve. In a comparison of self-beliefs the other-oriented or comparative variable of self-concept was needed in addition to self-efficacy to explain performance for the Indo Canadians, whereas self-efficacy and previous performance were sufficient to explain current performance for the Anglo Canadian students. Klassen (p. 739) concluded that, "The findings from the present investigation strongly suggest that cultural practices and beliefs may influence the types of information people attend to and use as indicators of personal efficacy," and the "combination rules or heuristics that people use to weight and integrate efficacy information from different sources in constructing beliefs about their personal efficacy." A cross-cultural, universal understanding of self-efficacy needs to take into account that, in some cultures, "Others will be assigned much more importance, will carry more weight, and will be relatively focal in one's own behavior."

Yamauchi and Greene (1997) investigated the extent to which ethnicity, gender, grade level, and length of residence in a community were associated with students' perceived academic self-efficacy among a sample comprised largely of secondary school students in a rural, predominantly Native Hawaiian community in Hawaii. Students completed two scales from the Children's Multidimensional Self-Efficacy Scales (Bandura, 1989): the Self-Efficacy for Self-Regulated Learning and Self-Efficacy for Academic Achievement scales. The reported levels of self-efficacy were compared with data from a similar study elsewhere in the United States (Zimmerman, Bandura, & Martinez-Pons, 1992). The Hawaiian students had lower perceived self-efficacy for academic achievement in all academic domains except biology. Yamauchi and Green suggested that the lower scores of the Hawaiian students on academic self-efficacy may reflect their cultural proclivity to understate and not to brag about their positive beliefs about themselves. They stated, "Previous research indicates that those from more collectivist cultural communities tend to downplay their personal accomplishments and abilities, when interacting with member of their own community" (p. 9).

Yamauchi and Greene (1997) conducted a multiple regression analysis to examine the relationship between gender, ethnicity, years of residence on the island, and grade level and the outcome variables perceived academic self-efficacy and self-efficacy for self-regulated learning. These analyses showed a significant effect for these variables predicting students' perceived self-efficacy for self-regulated learning tasks, but not for self-efficacy for academic achievement. Gender and ethnicity contributed the most to predicting perceived self-efficacy for self-regulated learning with males and Native Hawaiians associated with lower self-efficacy for self-regulated learning. In an attempt to explain why Hawaiian boys are lower in self-efficacy for self-regulated learning than Hawaiian girls and other groups, Yamauchi and Green suggested that the sociocultural context provides different information to Native Hawaiian boys and girls regarding their performances at home and school and about their roles in the community. They believe that school-related tasks, especially those regarding self-regulated learning, are more similar to the tasks asked of girls at home (i.e., to organize themselves and siblings to get work done and to interact with adults in ways that promote group cohesion). In contrast, they suggested that Hawaiian boys may be acting in ways at school that resist authority and reinforce peer group solidarity. For purposes of this chapter, it is clear that findings from this study emphasize that cultural and sociocultural factors have an impact on self-efficacy for self-regulation.

What Do We Take from the Reported Studies?

In the work of Chiu, Salili, and Hong (2001), the editors of the series *Multiple Competencies and Self-Regulated Learning: Implications for Multicultural Education* stated the following;

> Many contributors of this volume believe that current research and conceptualizations on the universal principles of self-regulated learning may provide a useful framework to guide transformation of school culture. As noted, the contributors themselves are from diverse cultural backgrounds. Despite the heterogeneity of their cultural experiences, they seem to agree that teachers could apply universal principles of self-regulated learning to create an optimal learning environment that values student diversity and focuses on the basic purposes of learning. (pp. 9–10)

I do not think that it is this simple. It appears, as Weiner argued in the context of attribution theory (2004; see also McInerney & Van Etten, 2004a), that the theoretical template for self-regulated learning has relevance across cultures, but the specifics of what comprises the construct and how the construct is related to other variables, such as achievement outcomes, vary across groups. It seems that self-regulation, including time management, metacognitive and learning strategies, effective and strategic practice, goal directedness, and a sense of self-efficacy, are related to motivation and high achievement regardless of the cultural background of the learner. It is also apparent, however, that there are differences in the way these qualities may be manifest across cultures specifically regarding the nature and valuing of education, the relative salience of effort and ability, the role played by fear of failure, the salience of different learning strategies such as memorization and help seeking, the salience of self-efficacy, and the role played by parents and other social agents. It is also apparent that certain cultural and educational settings may make it more difficult for self-regulatory processes considered to be optimal in Western settings to be developed and utilized by students.

APPLICATION

In the beginning of this chapter, I briefly described the importance of emics and etics. I now relate this more specifically to the self-regulation research overviewed. The construct self-regulation appears to be universal (an etic construct), but the way in which it is operationalized across cultures (the emic dimension) needs to be considered more carefully. In the beginning of this chapter, I stated that from a subjective culture perspective we should be able to scrutinize self-regulated learning. It should be a simple step to consider the social modeling elements of particular cultures and how these might have an impact on the nature and acquisition of self-regulatory skills. What is explicit and implicit in the self-regulatory model of motivation and learning? What are the core elements of self-regulated learning, and are these core elements universal? Each of the core elements of self-regulated learning theory reflecting a Western perspective should and can be critiqued from a cultural perspective. For example, the 14 key elements (self-evaluation, organizing and transforming, goal setting and planning, seeking information, keeping records and monitoring, environmental structuring, self-consequences, rehearsing and memorizing, seeking social assistance, and reviewing records) and the phases (forethought, performance, self-reflection) and mechanisms (modeling through four key subprocesses) must be critically examined in any cross-cultural research. However, little of the reviewed research critiqued these core elements from a cultural perspective.

I also asked, What might the relationships between culture, motivation and self-regulation be? Is the nature of self-regulation for learning the same across cultures? What are the cultural determinants of self-regulatory behavior, such as family, religion, and sense of the future? Does one self-regulate to preserve the past, to understand and operate in the present, or to set a future? What is the relationship of self-regulated learning to appropriate goals across cultures? Again, none of the cited research addressed these issues directly, and these are significant issues in any attempt to portray a theoretical perspective such as self-regulation as universal. Self-regulation should not be coupled with an exclusive set of characteristics such as the 14 characteristics as this becomes an imposed etic or, as sometimes referred to, a pseudoetic construct. For example, self-regulation in one culture might mean emphasis on group allegiance and conformity to group norms for achieving valued goals and appropriate outcomes; in another, self-regulation might mean emphasis on individual determination and choice of goals and appropriate outcomes. In other words, one has to regulate oneself to fit in with the predominant view of appropriate behavior, which includes learning, within a particular cultural framework. The first interpretation of self-regulation might lead individuals to utilize rote learning, rehearsal, and memorization, while the latter might lead individuals to utilize independent problem solving, choice, and decision making. In this way, the paradox of the Asian learner (i.e., that although Asian students appear not to be self-regulated, they appear motivated and achieve well) might be addressed. If one reinterprets self-regulation as conforming effectively to the learning norms of one's society, then successful Asian students could be construed as self-regulated. It is also important to distinguish what are adaptive self-regulatory strategies and those that are maladaptive and to distinguish those that might be maladaptive in one cultural setting but adaptive in another.

Cultures also change, and it is apparent from some of the literature cited relating to acculturation levels that there are changing norms of what is appropriate learning-relevant behavior, and that new paradigms of appropriate self-regulation are emerging. It is moot at the moment the degree to which these emerging paradigms of self-regulation will converge with those dominant in the West. Stereotypes of Asian cultural values influencing school achievement might also need to be updated. For example, Trueba, Cheng, and Ima (1993) found evidence that some Asian American students do not accept the traditional values of obedience, moderation, humility, and harmony, viewing them as dysfunctional in a modern society.

What emerges from many of the studies is that use of self-regulated strategies, however variably defined, is related to enhanced academic performance. The more students use self-regulation in their learning directly relates to their enhanced achievement. However, the nature of the learning and self-regulatory strategies varies somewhat by cultural group. There are strategies that seem to be primary across most groups. There are also strategies that seem to be more salient in particular groups, such as memorization. It is also apparent from the research that moderator variables, such as the influence of others (parents and peers), the perceived importance of education (some groups value education/schooling differently from others), has an impact on self-regulation differentially across cultural groups.

All of the cited studies approached self-regulated learning from a Western perspective and to varying degrees attempted to validate the self-regulation theoretical framework and measures for the diverse cultural groups investigated. Comparisons were generally drawn with Western samples, in particular with samples from the United States and Australia. This approach is "top down," and although there is nothing wrong with this approach provided researchers validate their instruments in the various cultural settings, it is a pseudoetic approach. In other words, there is an explicit belief that the values and constructs enshrined in the Western models of self-regulated learning have universality (that is, are etic) without really demonstrating this through independent studies in which truly etic qualities of self-regulation can be derived. There was no attempt in any of the cited studies to grow a theory of self-regulated learning from the bottom up by carefully designing studies that looked at the emic nature of self-regulation in diverse cultures. Such an approach may end by discovering that what is construed as self-regulation in a Western context has great similarity with indigenous notions of self-regulation and self-regulated learning. Alternatively, the indigenous conception, particularly in divergent cultures, might be unique and idiosyncratic. Such an approach would also allow researchers to extract true etic dimensions of self-regulated behavior. The current approach to cross-cultural research on self-regulated learning simply allows the testing of preexisting assumptions of self-regulation. It allows little (but by no means none) opportunity to discover new and important self-regulation characteristics from non-Western perspectives that might nevertheless shed important light on self-regulation generally.

It seems from this analysis that researchers and practitioners need to be careful to distinguish between the theoretical elements of the theory and its specific content in cultural context. In other words, the theory can act as a template for guiding investigation and practice, but the content of how self-regulation is defined, measured, and applied needs to be sensitive to context. It might be, however, that some contexts are less suited to enhancing educational achievement, and contexts may need to be changed to allow for a range of adaptive self-regulatory practices to enhance the achievement of children at

TABLE 15.1 Self-Regulatory Influences That Need to Be Considered in Cultural Context

Social Influences	Approaches to Learning	Definitions of Learning and Knowledge	Incentives	Consequences
Class and social hierarchy	Ability/ Effort	Changing/ Immutable	Ability beliefs/ Effort beliefs	Employment
	Collective initiative/ Individual initiative			Individual attainment/ Group attainment
Family	Deep learning/ Surface learning	Cognitive/ Behavioral	Deferment of gratification/ Immediate gratification	
Gender	Didactic/teacher controlled/ Exploratory/ problem solving	Constructed/ Received	Fear of failure	Knowledge
Peer group	Environmental Restructuring		Future orientation	Pride
Politics	Goal orientation	Self-enhancement/Social	Goal setting	Ranking
Religion	Help-seeking	Studying and performing tasks	Individual progression	Selection
Respect for authority	Memorizing	Deep/surface	Outcome expectations	Shame
	Persistence		Prestige	
	Planning		Previous performance	
	Record keeping		Self-efficacy	
	Self-checking		Shame	
	Self-control		Social solidarity	
	Time management		Success	
	Willpower			

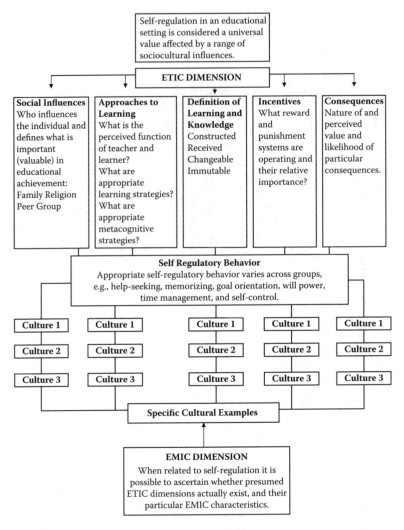

Figure 15.2   The relationship between etics and emics in self-regulation.

school and beyond. Table 15.1 explores some of the dimensions of self-regulation theory that might be etic and the emic content that might define these in particular cultures. Figure 15.2 reviews key elements of self-regulatory behavior highlighted in the various studies reviewed.

It is obvious from this review that each of these elements must be considered in cultural context; each has nuances of meaning; and theoreticians, researchers, and educators must be sensitive to this. There is no one-size-fits-all template of self-regulation. There is no one set of 10 principles that can be applied in each and every classroom. Further research needs to tease out when particular self-regulatory practices, such as fear of failure and rote memorization, are adaptive in specific learning environments and when they might be maladaptive. An assumption cannot be made that particular self-regulatory behaviors are necessarily adaptive or maladaptive. This issue is of crucial importance in educational environments characterized by diversity, particularly when a newly arrived "out group" is educated in Western educational environments.

REFERENCES

Bandura, A. (1989). *Multidimensional scales of perceived self-efficacy.* Unpublished test, Stanford University, Stanford, CA.

Boykin, A. W., Albury, A., Tyler, K. M., Hurley, E. A., Bailey, C. T., & Miller, O. A. (in press). The influence of culture on the perceptions of academic achievement among low-income African and Anglo American elementary students. *Cultural Diversity and Ethnic Minority Psychology.*

Boykin, A. W., & Bailey, C. T. (2000). *The role of cultural factors in school relevant cognitive functioning: Synthesis of findings on cultural contexts, cultural orientations, and individual differences* (Tech. Rep. No. 42). Washington, DC: Center for Research on the Education of Students Placed at Risk (CRESPAR)/Howard University.

Boykin, A. W., Tyler, K. M., & Miller, O. A. (2005). In search of cultural themes and their expressions in the dynamics of classroom life. *Urban Education, 40,* 521–549.

Brickman, S. J., Miller, R. B., & McInerney, D. M. (2005, November). *Values, interests and environmental preferences for the school context.* Paper presented at the annual meeting of the Australian Association for Research in Education, Sydney, NSW, Australia.

Brislin, R. W. (1980). Translation and content analysis of oral and written materials. In H. C. Triandis & J. W. Berry (Eds.), *Handbook of cross-cultural psychology. Methodology* (Vol. 2, pp. 389–444). Boston: Allyn and Bacon.

Buddhism and psychotherapy Web site. Retrieved April 4, 2006, from http://ccbs.ntu.edu.tw/FULLTEXT/JR-JHB/jhb94220.htm

Chiu, C-Y., Salili, F., & Hong, Y-Y. (2001). The role of multiple competencies and self-regulated learning in multicultural education. In C-Y. Chiu, F. Salili, & Y.-Y. Hong (Eds.), *Multiple competencies and self-*

regulated learning: Implications for multicultural education. Research in multicultural education and international perspectives (Vol. 2, pp. 3–13). Greenwich, CT: Information Age.

Cole, M. (1999). Cultural psychology: Some general principles and a concrete example. In Y. Engeström & R. L. Punamaki (Eds.), *Perspective on activity theory.* Cambridge, U.K.: Cambridge University Press.

Corno, L. (1987). Teaching and self-regulated learning. In D. C. Berliner & B. V. Rosenshine (Eds.), *Talks to teachers* (pp. 249–266). New York: Random House.

Delgado-Gaitan, C. (1994). Socializing young children in Mexican-American families: An inter-generational perspective. In P. M. Greenfield & R. R. Cocking (Eds.), *Cross cultural roots of minority child development* (pp. 55–86). Hillsdale, NJ: Erlbaum.

Der-Karabetian, A., & Ruiz, Y. (1993). Affective bicultural and global-human identity scales for Mexican-American Adolescents. ERIC Document Reproduction Service No. ED 376 394.

De Silva, P. (2000). Buddhism and psychotherapy: The role of self-control strategies. *His Lai Journal of Humanistic Buddhism, 1*, 169–182. Retrieved April 4, 2006, from http://ccbs.ntu.edu.tw/FULLTEXT/JR-JHB/jhb94220.htm

Deyhle, D., & LeCompte, M. (1994). Cultural differences in child development: Navajo adolescents in middle schools. *Theory Into Practice, 33*, 156–167.

Eaton, M. J., & Dembo, M. H. (1996, April). *Difference in the motivational beliefs of Asian American and non-Asian students.* Paper presented at the annual meeting of the American Educational Research Association, New York.

Eaton, M. J., & Dembo, M. H. (1997). Differences in the motivational beliefs of Asian American and non-Asian students. *Journal of Educational Psychology, 89*, 433–440.

Headland, T. N., Pike, K. L., & Harris, M. (1990). Emics and etics: The insider/outsider debate. Retrieved 4/4/2006 from http://www.sil.org/~headlandt/ee-intro.htm

Ferrari, M., & Mahalingam, R. (1998). Personal cognitive development and its implications for teaching and learning. *Educational Psychologist, 33*, 35–44.

Fiske, A. P., Kitayama, S., Marjus, H. R., & Nisbett, R. E. (1998). The cultural matrix of social psychology. In D. T., Gilbert, S. T. Fiske, & G. Lindzey (Eds.), *The handbook of social psychology* (4th ed., Vol. 2, pp. 915–981). New York: McGraw-Hill.

Gorrell, J., Hwang, Y. S., & Chung, K. S. (1996, April). *A comparison of self-regulated problem-solving awareness of American and Korean children.* Paper presented at the annual meeting of the American Educational Research Association, New York.

Gutierrez, K. D., & Rogoff, B. (2003). Cultural ways of learning: Individual traits or repertoires of practices. *Educational Researcher, 32,* 19–25.

Heckhausen, H. (1991). *Motivation and action.* Berlin: Springer-Verlag.

Hill, R. B. (1996). *History of work ethic.* Retrieved April 4, 2006, from http://www.coe.uga.edu/~rhill/workethic/index.html

Ho, D. Y.-F., Peng, S.-Q., & Chan, F. S.-F. (2001a). Authority and learning in Confucian-heritage education: A relational methodological analysis. In C.-Y. Chiu, F. Salili, & Y.-Y. Hong (Eds.), *Multiple competencies and self-regulated learning: Implications for multicultural education. Research in multicultural education and international perspectives* (Vol. 2, pp. 29–47). Greenwich, CT: Information Age.

Ho, D. Y.-F., Peng, S.-Q., & Chan, F. S.-F. (2001b). An investigative research in teaching and learning in Chinese society. In C.-Y. Chiu, F. Salili, & Y.-Y. Hong (Eds.), *Multiple competencies and self-regulated learning: Implications for multicultural education. Research in multicultural education and international perspectives* (Vol. 2, pp. 215–244). Greenwich, CT: Information Age.

Hollins, E. R. (1996). *Culture in school learning: Revealing the deep meaning.* Mahwah, NJ: Erlbaum.

Kitayama, S., Markus, H. R., Matsumoto, H., & Norasakkunkit, V. (1997). Individual and collective processes in the construction of the self: Self-enhancement in the United States and self-criticism in Japan. *Journal of Personality and Social Psychology, 69,* 925–937.

Klassen, R. M. (2004). A cross-cultural investigation of the efficacy beliefs of South Asian immigrant and Anglo Canadian non-immigrant early adolescents. *Journal of Educational Psychology, 96,* 731–742.

Kronqvist, E.-L. (1996). The development of the identity in the cultural context. ERIC Document Reproduction Service No. ED 403 049.

Kurman, J. (2001). Self-regulation strategies in achievement settings. Culture and gender differences. *Journal of Cross-Cultural Psychology, 32,* 491–503.

Ladson-Billings, G. (2001). *Cross-over to Canaan: The journey of the new teachers in diverse classrooms.* San Francisco: Jossey-Bass.

Liem, A. D. (2006). *The influences of sociocultural and educational contexts on approaches to learning.* Unpublished doctoral dissertation, National University of Singapore.

Liu, N. F., & Littlewood, W. (1997). Why do students appear reluctant to participate in classroom learning discourse? *System, 25,* 371–384.

McInerney, D. M., & Van Etten, S. (2004a). Big theories revisited: The challenge. In D. M. McInerney & S. Van Etten (Eds.), *Research on sociocultural influences on motivation and learning. Big theories revisited* (Vol. 4. pp. 1–11). Greenwich, CT: Information Age.

McInerney, D. M., & Van Etten, S. (2004b). *Research on sociocultural influences on motivation and learning. Vol. 4: Big theories revisited.* Greenwich, CT: Information Age.

Min, P. G. (1995). An overview of Asian Americans. In P. G. Min (Ed.), *Asian Americans: Contemporary trends and issues* (pp. 10–37). Thousand Oaks, CA: Sage.

Olaussen, B. S., & Bråten, I. (1999). Students' use of strategies for self-regulated learning: Cross-cultural perspectives. *Scandinavian Journal of Educational Research, 43,* 409–432.

Pak, J. H. (2001, August). *Acculturation and identity of Korean women.* Paper presented at the 109th APA Convention, San Francisco, August. ERIC Document Reproduction Service No. ED 471, 438.

Park, C. C. (2000). Learning style preferences of Southeast Asian students. *Urban Education, 35,* 245–268.

Parsons, E. C. (2003). Culturalizing instruction: Creating a more inclusive context for learning for African American Students. *High School Journal, 86*(4), 23–30.

Phinney, J. (1990). Ethnic identity in adolescents and adults: A review of research. *Psychological Bulletin, 108,* 499–514.

Phinney, J. (1991). Ethnic identity and self-esteem: A review and integration. *Hispanic Journal of Behavioral Sciences, 13,* 193–208.

Purdie, N., & Hattie, J. (1996). Cultural differences in the use of strategies for self-regulated learning. *American Educational Research Journal, 33,* 845–871.

Purdie, N., Hattie, J., & Douglas, G. (1996). Student conceptions of learning and their use of self-regulated learning strategies: A cross-cultural comparison. *Journal of Educational Psychology, 88,* 87–100.

Rose, M. (1985). *Reworking the work ethic: Economic values and socio-cultural politics.* London: Schocken.

Rubie, C. M., Townsend, M. A. R., & Moore, D. W. (2004). Motivational and academic effects of cultural experiences for indigenous minority students in New Zealand. *Educational Psychology, 24,* 143–160.

Salili, F., Fu, H.-Y., Tong, Y.-Y., & Tabatabai, D. (2001). A cross-cultural comparison of the effect of culture and context of learning on student motivation and self-regulation. In C.-Y. Chiu, F. Salili, & Y.-Y. Hong (Eds.), *Multiple competencies and self-regulated learning: Implications for multicultural education research in multicultural education and international perspectives* (Vol. 2, pp. 123–140). Greenwich, CT: Information Age.

Schunk, D. (2001). Social cognitive theory and self-regulated learning. In B. J. Zimmerman & D. Schunk (Eds.), *Self-regulated learning and academic achievement. Theoretical perspectives* (pp. 125–151). Mahwah, NJ: Erlbaum.

Schwartz, S. H. (1992). Universals in the content and structure of values: Theoretical advances and empirical tests in 20 countries. In M. Zaqnna (Ed.), *Advances in experimental social psychology* (Vol. 25, pp. 1–65). New York: Academic Press.

Siu, S.-F. (1996). *Asian American students at risk. A literature review*. Report No. 8, Baltimore, MD: Johns Hopkins University, Center for Research on the Education of Students.

Stevenson, H. W., & Lee, S. Y. (1996). The academic achievement of Chinese students. In M. H. Bond (Ed.), *The handbook of Chinese psychology* (pp. 124–142). Hong Kong: Oxford University Press.

Triandis, H. (2002). Subjective culture. In W. J. Lonner, D. L. Dinnel, S. A. Hayes, & D. N. Sattler (Eds.), *Online readings in psychology and culture* (unit 15, chap. 1). Bellingham, WA: Center for Cross-Cultural Research, Western Washington University. Retrieved 4/4/2006 from http://www.wwu.edu/~culture

Trueba, H. T. (1993). From failure to success: The roles of culture and cultural conflict in the academic achievement of Chicano students. ERIC Document Reproduction Service No. ED 387285.

Trueba, H. T., Cheng, L. R. L., & Ima, K. (1993). *Myth or reality: Adaptive strategies of Asian Americans in California*. Washington, DC: Falmer Press.

Tyler, K., Anderman, M., & Haines, R. T. (2006). Identifying the connection between culturally relevant pedagogy, motivation and academic performance among ethnic minority youth. In D. M. McInerney, M. Dowson, & S. Van Etten (Eds.), *Research on sociocultural influences on motivation and learning: Effective schools* (Vol. 6). Greenwich CT: Information Age.

Urdan, T., & Giancarlo, C. (2000). Differences between students in the consequences of goals and goal structures: The role of culture and family obligation. ED ERIC Document Reproduction Service No. 454 331.

Weber, M. (1904, 1905). *Die protestantische ethik und der geist des kapitalismus. Archiv fur sozialwissenschaft, 20–21*. Translated by T. Parsons. *The protestant ethic and the spirit of capitalism*. New York: Charles Scribner's Sons.

Weiner, B. (2004). Attribution theory revisited: Transforming cultural plurality into theoretical unity. In D. M. McInerney & S. Van Etten (Eds.), *Research on sociocultural influences on motivation and learning* (Vol. 4, pp. 12–30). Greenwich, CT: Information Age.

Westby, C. (1993). Developing cultural competence: Working with culturally/linguistically diverse families. In teams in early intervention introductory module. Albuquerque, NM: Training and Technical Assistance Unity, University of New Mexico School of Medicine.

Yamauchi, L. A., & Greene, W. L. (1997, March). *Culture, gender, and the development of perceived academic self-efficacy among Hawaiian adolescents.* Paper presented at the annual meeting of the American Educational Research Association, Chicago.

Zimmerman, B. J. (2000). Attaining self-regulation: A social cognitive perspective. In M. Boekaerts, P. R. Pintrich, & M. Zeidner (Eds.), *Handbook of self-regulation* (pp. 13–39). San Diego, CA: Academic Press.

Zimmerman, B. J. (2001). Theories of self-regulated learning and academic achievement: An overview and analysis. In B. J. Zimmerman & D. H. Schunk (Eds.), *Self-regulated learning and academic achievement. Theoretical perspectives* (pp. 1–37). Mahwah, NJ: Erlbaum.

Zimmerman, B. J. (2004). Sociocultural influence and students' development of academic self-regulation: A social-congnitive perspective. In D. M. McInerney & S. Van Etten (Eds.), *Research on sociocultural influences on motivation and learning. Big theories revisited* (Vol. 4, pp. 139–164). Greenwich, CT: Information Age.

Zimmerman, B. J., Bandura, A., & Martinez-Pons, M. (1992). Self-motivation for academic attainment: The role of self-efficacy beliefs and personal goal setting. *American Educational Research Journal, 29,* 663–676.

Zimmerman, B. J., & Martinez-Pons, M. (1986). Development of a structured interview for assessing student use of self-regulated learning strategies. *American Educational Research Journal, 23,* 614–628.

Zimmerman, B. J., & Martinez-Pons, M. (1988). Construct validation of a strategy model of student self-regulated learning. *Journal of Educational Psychology, 80,* 284–290.

Zimmerman, B. J., & Risemberg, R. (1997). Self-regulatory dimensions of academic learning and motivation. In G. Phye (Ed.), *Handbook of academic learning. Construction of knowledge* (pp 106–125). New York: Academic Press.

Contributors

Carol S. Dweck
Stanford University
Stanford, California

Allison Master
Stanford University
Stanford, California

Suzanne Hidi
University of Toronto
Toronto, Ontario, Canada

Mary Ainley
University of Melbourne
Melbourne, Victoria, Australia

Frank Pajares
Emory University
Atlanta, Georgia

Judith L. Meece
The University of North Carolina
at Chapel Hill
Chapel Hill, North Carolina

Jason Painter
The University of North Carolina
at Chapel Hill
Chapel Hill, North Carolina

Richard S. Newman
University of California at Riverside
Riverside, California

Willy Lens
University of Leuven
Leuven, Belgium

Maarten Vansteenkiste
University of Leuven
Leuven, Belgium

Allan Wigfield
University of Maryland
at College Park
College Park, Maryland

Laurel W. Hoa
University of Maryland
at College Park
College Park, Maryland

Susan Lutz Klauda
University of Maryland
at College Park
College Park, Maryland

Johnmarshall Reeve
University of Iowa
Iowa City, Iowa

Richard M. Ryan
University of Rochester
Rochester, New York

Edward L. Deci
University of Rochester
Rochester, New York

Hyungshim Jang
University of Wisconsin–Milwaukee
Milwaukee, Wisconsin

Dennis M. McInerney
National Institute of Education
Nanyang Technological University
Singapore

James W. Fryer
University of Rochester
Rochester, New York

Andrew J. Elliot
University of Rochester
Rochester, New York

Lyn Corno
Teachers College,
Columbia University
New York, New York

Philip H. Winne
Simon Fraser University
Burnaby, British Columbia, Canada

Allyson Hadwin
University of Victoria
Victoria, British Columbia, Canada

Dale H. Schunk
The University of North Carolina
at Greensboro
Greensboro, North Carolina

Barry J. Zimmerman
Graduate Center, City University
of New York
New York, New York

Author Index

A

Ablard, K. E., 341, 342
Ackerman, B. P., 91
Ackerman, P. L., 275
Adamson, G., 349
Adler, T. F., 117, 349
Ainley, M., 79, 82, 85–86, 91–93, 101
Aleven, V., 332
Alexander, P. A., 86–87, 91, 341
Altermatt, E. R., 358
Altman, J., 316
Ames, C., 53, 55, 64, 181, 330, 345
Anderman, E. M., 21, 60–61, 66, 122, 268,
　　　　328–329, 343, 345, 347, 354
Anderman, L. H., 60–61, 66, 354
Anderman, M., 369
Anderson, J. R., 197
Anderson, R. C., 198
Anderson, V., 87
APA Task Force on Psychology in
　　　　Education, 272
Archer, J., 53, 55, 64, 345
Aronson, J., 32
Ashby, F. G., 95
Ask Dr. Math, 301
Atkinson, J. W., 54, 144, 148–149, 172
Au, K. H., 185
Austin, C. C., 268

B

Bailey, C. T., 369
Baird, W., 86–87
Bandura, A., 10–11, 19, 32, 78–82, 91–93,
　　　　96, 111–116, 119–121, 125–127,
　　　　170, 199, 249–251, 254, 269, 281,
　　　　285, 339, 341, 344, 346–347, 351,
　　　　355, 388

Barbaranelli, C., 347
Barbosa, P., 187, 189
Barch, J., 230
Bargh, J. A., 134, 201, 273–274
Baron, R. M., 93
Barron, K. E., 8, 56, 59, 62, 66, 79, 345
Bartmess, E. N., 32
Battle, A., 13, 171, 176
Battle, E., 171–172
Baumeister, R. F., 142, 161, 223
Becker, A. D., 349
Beckman, J., 147
Beer, J. S., 35
Belfiore, P. J., 238
Bellack, A., 204
Bembenutty, H., 152
Benware, C., 17, 232
Berenbaum, S. A., 353
Berndorff, D., 78, 85, 91–92, 98
Bernieri, F., 234
Betz, N. E., 124
Biddle, S., 34
Billington, M., 269, 282
Binet, A., 33
Birch, D., 144, 148–149
Birney, R., 54, 67
Black, A. E., 159
Blackwell, L. S., 7, 32, 34, 38, 44–45
Blumenfeld, P. C., 4, 98, 123, 342, 345, 354
Boekaerts, M., 1, 5, 19, 68, 78, 81, 83, 100,
　　　　141, 172, 199, 224, 282, 285, 316,
　　　　318, 328, 341, 348
Bong, M., 60–61
Bonner, S., 2, 119
Borkowski, J. G., 283, 341
Boscolo, P., 79
Bouas Henry, K., 57
Bouffard-Bouchard, T., 3, 120, 341
Bourg, T., 82
Bower, G. H., 197

403

Subject Index